Understanding Expertise
in Teaching

THE CAMBRIDGE APPLIED LINGUISTICS SERIES
Series editors: Michael H. Long and Jack C. Richards

This series presents the findings of work in applied linguistics which are of direct relevance to language teaching and learning and of particular interest to applied linguists, researchers, language teachers, and teacher trainers.

Recent publications in this series:
Cognition and Second Language Instruction *edited by Peter Robinson*
Computer Applications in Second Language Acquisition *by Carol A. Chapelle*
Contrastive Rhetoric – Cross-cultural Aspects of Second Language Writing *by Ulla Connor*
Corpora in Applied Linguistics *by Susan Hunston*
Criterion-Referenced Language Testing *by James Dean Brown and Thom Hudson*
Culture in Second Language Teaching and Learning *edited by Eli Hinkel*
Exploring the Second Language Mental Lexicon *by David Singleton*
Focus on Form in Classroom Second Language Acquisition *edited by Catherine Doughty and Jessica Williams*
Immersion Education: International Perspectives *edited by Robert Keith Johnson and Merrill Swain*
Interfaces Between Second Language Acquisition and Language Testing Research *edited by Lyle F. Bachman and Andrew D. Cohen*
Learning Vocabulary in Another Language *by I.S.P. Nation*
Network-based Language Teaching – Concepts and Practice *edited by Mark Warschauer and Richard Kern*
Pragmatics in Language Teaching *edited by Kenneth R. Rose and Gabriele Kasper*
Research Perspectives on English for Academic Purposes *edited by John Flowerdew and Matthew Peacock*
Researching and Applying Metaphor *edited by Lynne Cameron and Graham Low*
Second Language Vocabulary Acquisition *edited by James Coady and Thomas Huckin*
Sociolinguistics and Language Teaching *edited by Sandra Lee McKay and Nancy H. Hornberger*
Text, Role, and Context – Developing Academic Literacies *by Ann M. Johns*

Understanding Expertise in Teaching

Case Studies of Second Language Teachers

Amy B. M. Tsui
The University of Hong Kong

PUBLISHED BY THE PRESS SYNDICATE OF THE UNIVERSITY OF CAMBRIDGE
The Pitt Building, Trumpington Street, Cambridge, United Kingdom

CAMBRIDGE UNIVERSITY PRESS
The Edinburgh Building, Cambridge CB2 2RU, UK
40 West 20th Street, New York, NY 10011-4211, USA
477 Williamstown Road, Port Melbourne, VIC 3207, Australia
Ruiz de Alarcón 13, 28014 Madrid, Spain
Dock House, The Waterfront, Cape Town 8001, South Africa

http://www.cambridge.org

© Amy B. M. Tsui 2003

This book is in copyright. Subject to statutory exception
and to the provisions of relevant collective licensing agreements,
no reproduction of any part may take place without
the written permission of Cambridge University Press.

First published 2003

Printed in the United States of America

Typeface Sabon 10½ / 12 pt.   *System* LATEX 2_ε [TB]

A catalog record for this book is available from the British Library.

Library of Congress Cataloging in Publication Data
Tsui, Amy B. M.
Understanding expertise in teaching : case studies of second language
teachers / Amy B. M. Tsui.
    p.   cm. – (Cambridge applied linguistics)
Includes bibliographical references and index.
ISBN 0-521-63207-2 – ISBN 0-521-63569-1 (pbk.)
1. Language and languages – Study and teaching – Teacher education – Case studies.
2. English language – Study and teaching – Foreign speakers – Case studies.   I. Title.
II. Cambridge applied linguistics series
P51 .T78 2002
418'.0071–dc21   2002066519

ISBN 0 521 63207 2 hardback
ISBN 0 521 63569 1 paperback

Contents

Series Editors' Preface		*page* ix
Acknowledgments		xi
Chapter 1	Introduction	1
Chapter 2	Conceptions of Expertise	9
Chapter 3	Characteristics of Expert and Novice Teachers	22
Chapter 4	Teacher Knowledge	42
Chapter 5	The Case Studies	67
Chapter 6	The Professional Development of the ESL Teachers	79
Chapter 7	Teacher Knowledge and Managing the Classroom for ESL Learning	136
Chapter 8	Teacher Knowledge and the Enactment of the ESL Curriculum	177
Chapter 9	Taking on the Challenge: Exploring Process Writing	225
Chapter 10	Understanding Expertise in Teaching	245
Appendix 1	Reader's Comment Form on First Draft for the Second Writing Task (Angel's First Draft)	283
Appendix 2	Learner Training in Making Revisions	285
References		287
Index		303

Series Editors' Preface

While the nature of expertise has long attracted the attention of researchers in the field of cognitive psychology, until recently it has been relatively less explored in relation to classroom teaching and even less so in the field of second and foreign language teaching. Yet an understanding of how skilled and expert practitioners carry out their work is crucial to many aspects of teacher education. For example, it provides a benchmark against which less successful teaching can be compared. It provides information relevant to the design of teacher education programs. It provides a model of successful teaching that can be used to help understand the difficulties faced by novice teachers. It helps us understand the route novice teachers pass through as they acquire new knowledge and skills, and it helps us better understand the complexity of teaching.

While it is relatively easy to arrive at a common sense understanding of what we mean by expertise, it has proved a somewhat elusive concept for researchers to pin down and investigate. The author of this book has therefore provided a major service to the field of applied linguistics in this first detailed study of what expertise in language teaching consists of and how it develops in language teachers.

Through exploring the classroom practices and knowledge of her subjects in four fascinating and illuminating case studies, Tsui succeeds in clarifying the nature of expertise in ESL teaching, the factors that shape and influence its development, and how teachers employ their expertise in teaching. In the process, Tsui critically examines an extensive literature on teacher cognition and shows how teachers' theories, knowledge, experience, and goals shape their classroom practices and their transitions from novices to experts. But as the author emphasizes, the book does not set out to generalize about ESL teachers as a profession: rather it seeks to explore the concept of expertise in teaching using ESL teachers as its subject matter.

This book thus provides a valuable addition to the literature on teacher cognition in second language teaching and will be of considerable interest to teachers, and teacher educators in TESOL, as well as others interested in better understanding the nature of expertise. It provides an excellent example of how theory and research can illuminate our understanding of a familiar process such as teaching, and prompt us to rethink some of the assumptions we often hold about the nature of teaching and how teaching skills are acquired.

Michael H. Long
Jack C. Richards

Acknowledgments

As a teacher educator, I have always been fascinated by excellent teachers and have always wondered how they have gotten to where they are now. Some of these teachers are my former students, I am pleased to say. A year's sabbatical from the University of Hong Kong allowed me to embark on a study of Marina, a teacher whom I have always admired, and three of her colleagues, one of whom was my student when the study was conducted, and two who became my students after the study.

A study of this kind depends very much on whether the teachers are willing to give me time amid their very busy teaching schedules. I am immensely grateful to the four teachers, Marina, Eva, Ching, and Genie (pseudonyms), for allowing me to intrude not only into their professional lives at work but also into their private lives. In particular, I owe a great debt to Marina, who was always very willing and ready to spend time with me even when she had had only an hour's sleep the night before. I also wish to thank the school's principal, whose name shall remain unknown, for her kind support.

Since the idea of writing this book was first conceived, I have benefited from discussions with a number of people. James Calderhead, whose work I admire, gave me invaluable advice on narrowing the scope of my study at a very early stage. Brian Cooke and Graham Lock read the book proposal and the sample chapters. Their insightful comments helped me to obtain very positive feedback from the reviewers. The reviewers of the sample chapters, one of whom is Devon Woods, gave me very detailed feedback, which helped me to shape the rest of the book. I thank all of them for helping me to get the writing off the ground.

When I emerged from heaps and heaps of drafts, I wondered if anybody would be interested in reading this book at all. Ference Marton generously offered to read it on the plane on his way to a conference. His constructive criticism was immensely encouraging and his comments helped me to see my work from a new perspective. Peter Falvey, amid writing his own book and getting six research students through their Ph.D.s, went through every single chapter meticulously within two weeks, picking out inconsistencies, unclear concepts, and stylistic problems. I am very grateful to both of them for their generosity and friendship.

This book draws heavily on the work of Carl Bereiter and Marlene Scardamalia. I was lucky enough to discuss my work with them when they were visiting my department. I would like to thank both of them. In particular I must thank Marlene for reading several chapters and revisiting the notion of expertise with me amid her impossible schedule of managing her department and setting up projects in different parts of the world.

I also want to thank my research assistants who have meticulously transcribed the data and translated them from Cantonese to English: Michelle Woo, Grace Wong, Maria Chan, Ken Ho, and Sonia Cheung. Especially, I want to thank Maria for helping me to analyze the data with NUD*IST and Sonia for complying with my numerous requests. My technical colleagues, Samsom, Carven, and Benz helped me to videotape the lessons, and Dave made sure that my hard drive and zip drive were working properly. Winky Mok helped me with the final touches of the manuscript. I am grateful to all of them.

I am indebted to Jack Richards, the series editor, for encouraging me to put in a proposal when I shared my initial thoughts with him and for his positive and prompt responses to it. Mary Carson and Mary Vaughn have been most supportive and patient in answering my endless queries.

A number of colleagues kindly took over the running of the department when I locked myself up at home to finish the manuscript. They are Steve Andrews, Fran Lopez-Real, Flora Kan, Ida Mok, Nancy Law, and S. K. Tse, who have all served as Acting Head of Department. I thank them for their collegiality and friendship.

Finally, I must thank my husband, Chi Kin, for being most understanding and supportive, especially when I was working under pressure to meet the deadline. He asked me at one stage when he could have his wife back. As I am typing this line, I am pleased to tell him that he can now have his wife back.

1 Introduction

In all professions there are people who perform exceptionally well and whose performance is regarded as exemplary, to be emulated by fellow members in the profession, particularly novices. These people are often referred to as experts. When we say people are experts in their profession, we expect them to possess certain qualities, such as being very knowledgeable in their field; being able to engage in skillful practice; and being able to make accurate diagnoses, insightful analyses, and the right decisions, often within a very short period of time. However, what exactly constitutes their expertise is something that is not yet fully understood. Researchers in artificial intelligence have been trying for several decades to approximate the way the expert human mind works, but so far they have not been able to fully capture human expertise. In the past twenty years or so, expertise has become a topic that has drawn increasing attention from researchers in professional education.

Just as there are experts in other professions, there are experts in the teaching profession. As teachers or teacher educators, we have all come across teachers who are able to command students' respect, to motivate them to learn, to maintain their interest, to get them involved in tasks, and to sustain their attention, even on a hot Friday afternoon. The lessons seem to flow smoothly from one stage to another stage, integrating new information with what was covered in the previous lesson, the previous week, and even the previous year. These teachers seem to be able to get into the minds of their students and anticipate the questions that they will ask, the difficulties that they will have, and even the pranks that they will play – and these teachers will have effective means to counter them. The apparent effortlessness and fluidity with which these teachers accomplish the task of teaching in an environment as complex as the classroom had, for a long time, been taken as something that comes automatically with experience, until the last fifteen years or so when educational researchers began to study expertise in teaching.

1.1 Studies of Expertise in Teaching

Drawing on insights from the studies of expertise in other professions, and the studies of student-teachers, beginning teachers, and experienced teachers, investigations of teaching expertise have examined the characteristics of expert teachers and how they differ from novice teachers (see Berliner, 1994, for a detailed summary). These studies were heavily influenced by the information-processing model of the mind adopted by most of the expertise studies in other professions. The studies compared the cognitive processes in which expert and novice teachers engage when they plan and conduct lessons, and the quality of their reflections on their teaching. These studies show that expert teachers bear characteristics that have been identified in experts in other professions. According to Berliner (1992; 1995), expert teachers provide models of successful teaching that could serve as the scaffolding for novice teachers to attain a greater degree of competence (see Berliner, 1992; 1995). However, how far do these characteristics capture the nature of expert teachers' work and their teaching act in the classroom? Do expert teachers actually engage in the kinds of cognitive processes delineated as they conduct their everyday lives in their classrooms and their schools? How far do these characteristics highlight the *critical* differences between novice and expert teachers?

1.2 Neglected Aspects in Expertise Studies

As mentioned above, most of the expert-novice studies were based on information-processing theory in cognitive psychology, which assumes that the cognitive processes in which teachers engage take place in their minds and are independent of the context. However, ethnographic case studies of teachers' work and teachers' lives show that the knowledge and skills teachers develop are closely bound up with the specific contexts in which they work and in their own personal histories. This distinctive knowledge held by teachers has been characterized as personal, practical, and situated. The relationship between the knowledge that they develop and the context in which they work is dialectical. That is to say, teachers' knowledge must be understood in terms of the way they respond to their contexts of work, and this in turn shapes the contexts in which their knowledge is developed. Seen in this light, the way expert teachers relate to their contexts of work would be an important feature of expertise. This aspect, however, has not been fully addressed by existing studies in teaching expertise.

In addition to the above aspect, there seem to be two further areas that have not been given the attention that they deserve. First, as Bereiter and Scardamalia (1993) point out, like expert-novice studies in other domains, the focus of these studies has been on what experts can do that novices cannot. Few studies have investigated how and why expert teachers become what they are while their peers simply remain experienced nonexperts (see, however, Bullough, 1989; Bullough and Baughman, 1993; 1995). Second, most of the studies of novice and expert teachers have focused on the management of the classroom or on the generic aspects of teaching. Not many have investigated the subject-content aspect of teacher knowledge and the way novice and expert teachers deal with it in the classroom (for exceptions, see the work of Leinhardt and her colleagues at the University of Pittsburgh and the collection of studies in Brophy, 1991; Elbaz, 1983; Grossman, 1990). This is partly because many of these studies investigated teachers across a number of subject disciplines. Shulman (1987) points out that the management of the classroom and the "management of ideas" are equally important aspects of teacher knowledge (p. 1). Bereiter and Scardamalia (1993) further point out that understanding the knowledge base of expert teachers is a very important part of understanding expertise in teaching. In other words, to understand the knowledge base of expert teachers, it is necessary to include an investigation of their subject-specific knowledge, how it differs from that of novice teachers, and how expert teachers develop this knowledge.

Research on second-language teacher education has had a relatively late start. Although there is a body of practice in second-language teacher education, little has been done on second-language teachers that could provide a theoretical basis for second-language teacher education. The first substantial piece of work on second-language teacher education was a volume edited by Richards and Nunan (1990). Since then, there have been a number of studies in this area, notably those by Richards and Lockhart (1994) on reflective teaching in second language classrooms and an edited volume by Freeman and Richards (1996) on teacher learning in language teaching. Relatively little work has been done on expertise in ESL (English as a Second Language) teaching (see however, Richards, Li, and Tang, 1995) and still less on the *development* of expertise in ESL teaching.

This book is an attempt to further our understanding of teaching expertise through case studies of ESL teachers. It addresses the following questions:

- What are the *critical* differences between expert and novice teachers?
- How does a teacher become an expert teacher? What are the phases that he or she goes through in the process of acquiring expertise?
- What are the factors that shape the development of expertise?

After addressing these three questions, the concept of expertise will be revisited to see if we have come to a new understanding of expertise.

1.3 Case Studies of ESL Teachers

The case studies, which took a year and a half to complete, consist of four ESL teachers; Marina, Ching, Eva, and Genie. These four teachers have different academic backgrounds and professional training, are at different phases of their professional development, and have attained different levels of teaching competence. When the study began, Marina, the expert teacher, was in her eighth year of teaching. Genie was in her second year of teaching and was still very much a novice teacher. Eva and Ching, the experienced teachers, were both in their fifth year of teaching. The classroom practices and knowledge of these four teachers, specifically in ESL teaching, were investigated in order to gain a more comprehensive understanding of what constitutes expertise in ESL teaching. Investigations were also conducted on the professional developments of these four teachers, and the factors and sources of influence that shaped their development, in order to gain a better understanding of teaching expertise as a process rather than a state that is reached after a number of years of experience. The investigation of the professional development of Marina, in particular, will illuminate the process of acquiring and maintaining expertise.

1.4 Identifying Novice and Expert Teachers

Studying novice and expert teachers necessarily raises the question of how one identifies them. Identifying novice teachers is relatively straightforward. The term *novice teacher* is commonly used in the literature to describe teachers with little or no teaching experience. They are either student-teachers or teachers in their first year of teaching. Occasionally, the term *novice* is used for people who are in business and industry, but have an interest in teaching. These people have subject matter knowledge, but no teaching experience at all and no formal pedagogical training (see, for example, Sabers, Cushing, and Berliner, 1991). In some studies the term *postulant* has been used instead to distinguish them from novice teachers (see for example Berliner and Carter, 1989).

The identification of expert teachers is more problematic. As Bereiter and Scardamalia (1993) point out, it is much harder to identify an expert teacher than, say, an expert brain surgeon, who can remove brain tumors. This is because unravelling what distinguishes an expert from a nonexpert teacher is very difficult. There is as yet no reliable way of identifying expert teachers (see also Leinhardt, 1990). In all studies of novice and expert teachers, teaching experience (usually more than five years of teaching) is one of the criteria for selecting expert teachers.

In some studies it is the only criterion (see, for example, Peterson and Comeaux, 1987). In most studies, in addition to teaching experience, expert teachers were identified by nominations or recommendations from school administrators, usually the principal, or the school district board as outstanding teachers. In some cases the nominated teachers were further screened by the research team (see for example Sabers et al., 1991). In other cases there were further criteria such as being selected as a cooperating teacher by university faculties or a mentor-teacher by the school district boards (see, for example, Westerman, 1991; Swanson, O'Connor, and Cooney, 1990), being awarded teacher of the year by the state, and having attained a master's degree (see, for example, Swanson et al., 1990; Copeland, Birmingham, DeMeulle, D'Emidio-Caston, and Natal, 1994). In Leinhardt and Greeno's study (1986), expertise was linked to the academic achievement of students. Expert mathematics teachers were identified by the scores of their students being in the top 15 percent of the school for at least three years in the past five years. In Leinhardt, Putnam, Stein, and Baxter (1991), the criteria were extended to include supervisor and peer nomination.

Among the criteria cited in the research studies so far, the more frequently used criteria are years of teaching experience and recommendation by school administrators. Neither criterion is without problems. First, experience and expertise are not synonymous, as Bereiter and Scardamalia have so convincingly argued (see 1.3). Second, it is often unclear what criteria school principals used when recommending outstanding teachers, as pointed out by Olson (1992). Apart from individual variations in principals' recommendations, there are also cultural or societal variations. In different cultures or societies, the criteria for judging teaching expertise may vary. For example, a very examination-oriented education system may use student scores in public examinations as an important criterion for identifying expert teachers. The additional external and objective criteria used in the studies such as awards, academic qualifications, and student achievement are equally problematic. The use of student achievement as a criterion for determining excellence in teaching is questionable for a number of reasons, one of which is that it represents a narrow view of what effective teaching embraces (see Shulman, 1992, for a critique of the process-product research paradigm). The use of academic qualifications is problematic because an academic degree, be it a master's or even a doctoral degree, is no indication of teaching competence. There are professors who are very distinguished in their own fields but who are very poor teachers. The use of outside awards, such as the teacher of the year award as outlined by Berliner (1986) is also problematic in that, according to Berliner, the judges are often untrained, inexperienced, and from professions other than teaching.

So far, there have been no commonly accepted criteria or methods for identifying expert teachers. In fact, for the reasons outlined above, it is highly doubtful whether it is possible to formulate commonly accepted criteria, and how meaningful it is to do so. Very often, the terms *expert teacher* and *experienced teacher* are used interchangeably (see, for example, Peterson and Comeaux, 1987). There is also a tendency to equate expertise with technical specialization (see, for example, Welker, 1991). This reflects not so much a lack of clarity in thinking, or methodological weakness, as our limited understanding of expertise in teaching. While we are still trying to grapple with what constitutes expertise in teaching, we have no choice but to rely on a combination of criteria such as experience, reputation, and recommendation, as well as classroom observation to identify expert teachers. In the case studies of the four ESL teachers, the expert teacher, Marina, was identified in such a way. As we shall see in the concluding chapter, the investigation of Marina's expertise leads to a reconceptualization of the notion of expertise.

1.5 Overview of the Book

This book is written for teachers, teacher-educators, and researchers who are interested in teaching expertise, teachers' professional development, and teacher knowledge in general. The first part of the book (Chapters 2 through 4) provides reviews of important studies in expertise and expertise in teaching and teacher knowledge. In Chapter 4, a reconceptualization of teacher knowledge as integrated and situated is proposed. These chapters provide the background knowledge and the theoretical framework for understanding the discussion of the case studies, and especially the theoretical arguments in the concluding chapter, Chapter 10. The second part of the book (Chapters 5 through 9) provides detailed descriptions of the professional development of these four teachers, the thinking and knowledge of ESL teachers at different levels of teaching competence, and how they deal with specific aspects of ESL teaching. This part will be of special interest and relevance to ESL teachers and ESL teacher educators. Chapter 10 addresses unanswered questions and revisits the concept of expertise.

Chapter 2 examines three prominent theories of expertise which have been frequently cited in studies of expertise in teaching, and the critical features of expertise outlined by these theories: Dreyfus and Dreyfus (1986); Chi, Glaser, and Farr (1988); and Bereiter and Scardamalia (1993). Chapter 3 discusses studies on teaching expertise that have drawn on insights from the theories of expertise outlined in Chapter 2. These studies examined the cognitive processes in the preactive and interactive phases of teaching of expert and novice teachers, and found that many of the characteristics of experts in other domains were also found in expert teachers. This chapter raises questions with regard to how far these studies illuminate the nature of the novice and expert teachers' work in the classroom. It further points out the areas of expertise that have been neglected in these studies, namely, the acquisition of expertise in teaching and the nature of the knowledge of expert teachers.

To provide an interpretive framework for investigating the knowledge base of expert teachers, Chapter 4 outlines the conceptions of knowledge (notably Ryle, 1949 and Polanyi, 1966), which have influenced the characterizations of teacher knowledge as "knowing-in-action" and "reflection-in-action" (Schon, 1983), as "practical knowledge" (Elbaz, 1983), as "personal knowledge" (Clandinin and Connelly, 1987, 1991; Connelly and Clandinin, 1985, 1988, 1990, 1995; Clandinin, 1992), as "situated knowledge" (Leinhardt, 1988), and as content knowledge (Shulman, 1987). Drawing on insights from these characterizations, this chapter reconceptualizes teacher knowledge as an amalgamation of what has been conceived as distinctively identifiable knowledge domains, including knowledge of the subject matter, the learner, the curriculum, the context, pedagogy, and other curricular content. This amalgamation is influenced by the teacher's personal conceptions of teaching and learning, which is formed over the years as he or she comes under a number of sources of influence. Teacher knowledge and teachers' specific contexts of work are dialectically related and are constantly being construed and reconstrued as teachers engage in reflection and reframing. Chapter 5 outlines the research methodology and the ethical issues involved in case studies of this nature.

Chapter 6 reports on the professional development of the four ESL teachers. In particular, the professional development of Marina is discussed in detail. The professional developments of Marina, Ching, Eva, and Genie suggest that the development of expertise in teaching is a continuous and dynamic process in which knowledge and competence develop in previous stages and form the basis for further development. It is also a process in which highly competent teachers constantly set new goals for themselves and accept new challenges. In the process of achieving those goals and meeting these challenges, they gain new insights. It is in the process of constantly gaining new competence that expertise is developed.

Chapters 7 and 8 examine the classroom practices of these four teachers and the development of knowledge embedded in these practices. Chapter 7 deals with the management of ESL learning whereas Chapter 8 deals with enactment of the ESL curriculum. Chapter 7 compares how these four teachers respond to the classroom context and exploit it for ESL teaching and learning, how they shape an environment that is conducive to the communicative use of the English language in the classroom, and how they exploit the bigger context of work and manage resources for ESL teaching and learning. Chapter 8 examines the different ways in which these four teachers plan the curriculum and lessons and the way they deal with the teaching of grammar, which is considered by all of them as the most important area in the ESL curriculum – an area that they feel least or most confident teaching. The knowledge embedded in the enactment of the ESL curriculum is discussed.

Chapter 9 discusses the nature of the challenges that teachers come across in different stages of development. It points out that teachers are constantly confronted with challenges, no matter at which stage of professional development they are. The nature of the challenge, however, is different. While novice teachers are faced with challenges that are very basic to classroom teaching, such as maintaining order and discipline, the challenges that expert teachers are faced with, or rather, that they choose to face, often have to do with heightening their impact not only in their own classrooms but also in the wider educational community. Moreover, the challenges that they choose to meet and the way they meet them are often those that extend their level of competence. The rest of this chapter focuses on a major challenge that Marina took on in her eighth year of teaching to bring about change in the teaching of writing by adopting process writing for the entire school year at junior levels, that is, secondary one through three (Grades 7 through 9). It shows how, in the process of taking on this challenge, Marina extended the upper edge of her competence, came to a new understanding of process writing and developed her ability to play her role as a change agent. A detailed account is given of her rationale for trying out process writing, her own understanding of what process writing is, how it was implemented in her own classroom, how she guided and monitored the implementation by her colleagues, how the latter evaluated the implementation, and how she re-conceptualized process-writing. A comparison with Marina is made with the conceptualization of process writing, the classroom implementations, the reflections on and evaluations of the implementations by the three nonexpert teachers. Data from classroom observation, interviews, student work, questionnaire results, and panel meetings is used.

The final chapter, Chapter 10, addresses the neglected aspects of expertise studies at the beginning of this book and discusses the *critical* differences among the expert, experienced nonexpert, and novice teachers in the four case studies, and the development of expertise. On the basis of this discussion, the concept of expertise is revisited. The book closes with a brief reference to its relevance for teacher education. Readers who are interested to know the theoretical significance of the detailed accounts of the case study teachers can read this final chapter before reading Chapters 6 through 9.

2 Conceptions of Expertise

The systematic study of expertise began with the work of deGroot (1965), who investigated the differences between chess masters and less competent chess players. He found, for example, that chess masters are able to recognize and reproduce chess patterns very quickly and accurately whereas less competent players cannot. At about the same time, research had already begun on getting computers to simulate practical human intelligence in problem solving. Note the work of Herbert Simon and Allen Newall, which used an information-processing approach in getting computers to simulate master chess players (see Newall, 1963; Newall, Shaw, and Simon, 1963). Subsequently, there were further studies not only on experts in chess playing (see, for example, Newell and Simon, 1972; Simon and Chase, 1973), but on experts in other fields such as medicine, law, radiology, and aeronautics (Dreyfus and Dreyfus, 1986; Chi et al., 1988), nursing (Benner, 1984; Benner, Tanner, and Chesla, 1996), and physics problem solving (see, for example, Chi, Feltovich, and Glaser, 1981). More recent studies of expertise have covered experts in skills like dance (Solso and Dallop, 1995), music appreciation and performance (Sloboda, 1991), professional acting (Noice and Noice, 1997), and naturalistic decision-making of experts in a wide range of areas from nuclear power plant emergencies to the military (see, for example, the volume of collected papers in Zsambok and Klein, 1997). Some of these studies adopted an information processing approach, but some adopted fundamentally different approaches that are philosophical and phenomenological in orientation. In these studies various theories of expertise have been put forward to characterize experts and the ways in which they differ from novices.

In this chapter we shall examine some of the prominent theories of human expertise that have been most frequently cited in the study of teaching expertise and the critical features of expertise expounded in these theories. The insights provided by these theories will serve as the basis for discussing existing studies on expertise in teaching in Chapter 3.

2.1 Expertise as Intuition and Tacit Knowledge

One of the most frequently cited studies on expertise is Dreyfus and Dreyfus (1986), whose theory was first developed in reaction against claims by researchers working the cognitive psychology tradition, particularly in artificial intelligence, that the machine can simulate the human mind by means of analytic reasoning and rule formulation. They argued against the rationalist approach which perceives intelligent practice as the mere application of knowledge and rules to instrumental decision-making. For example, they observed that master chess players did not actually go through all the possible alternatives before coming to the best move, in the way that the computer had been programmed to do (Newall, Shaw, and Simon, 1963); they simply zeroed in on the most promising situation and then started testing out what they can do from there (see Dreyfus, 1972, p. 14). The interesting question is how human beings can immediately identify the most promising few possibilities, something computers cannot do. Dreyfus and Dreyfus (1980; 1986) studied the skill acquisition process of airplane pilots, drivers, and adult second-language learners, and put forward the following statement:

> Human understanding was a skill akin to knowing how to find one's way about the world, rather than knowing a lot of facts and rules for relating them. Our basic understanding was thus a *knowing how* rather than a *knowing that*. (1986, p. 4; original emphasis)

Their proposition echoes Gilbert Ryle's observation that the distinction between "knowing how" and "knowing that" is a false dichotomy and that knowing and action are one and the same thing (see Ryle, 1949, p. 32). Dreyfus and Dreyfus argued that "knowing how," not "knowing that," is at the very core of human expertise. For example, in flying or driving, the expertise of pilots or drivers lies in their hunches and intuitions gained through their experience rather than in their knowledge of a set of rules regarding how to operate the plane or the car. Dreyfus and Dreyfus observed that once pilots or drivers started consciously to apply rules to their behavior, their performance deteriorated, and they behaved like novices. Dreyfus and Dreyfus proposed a five-stage model of skill acquisition from novice to expert, which is briefly summarized below.

Stage 1: Novice

The novices' actions are guided by rules and a set of objective facts and features related to the skill. There is little consideration for the context of the actions. For example, the novice driver learning how to drive a stick-shift car is told at what speed to change gears and at what distance to follow the preceding car. These rules are given without the context of the traffic conditions. Novices are usually not taught the circumstances under which the rules should be violated, and they often judge their own performance by how well they follow the rules.

Stage 2: Advanced Beginners

After novices have had experience applying the rules in real situations, they begin to recognize situational elements that they need to consider for their actions. For example, an advanced-beginner driver will use engine sounds as well as context-free rules of gear-shifting to decide whether to change gears or not.

Stage 3: Competent

With more experience, competent performers learn how to cope with an overwhelming amount of information, by using both context-free rules and situational elements. They are now able to assess the situation and distinguish important from unimportant information. Their actions are goal-directed, and they make conscious planning decisions to achieve their goals. Because they make conscious decisions, they feel responsible for their actions and are emotionally involved with the outcome in a way that novices and advanced beginners seldom are.

Stage 4: Proficient

This stage is marked by the emergence of intuition, or know-how. Proficient performers are now able to act without conscious deliberation because, as a result of their experience, they can recall similar situations in the past and the courses of actions taken that were effective. They have "holistic similarity recognition" ability, which is the intuitive ability to recognize patterns without decomposing them into their component features (Dreyfus and Dreyfus, 1986, p. 28). At this stage, proficient performers still engage in analytical thinking and conscious decisions when they encounter information that they assess to be important on the basis of their experience. For example, on a rainy day the proficient driver may intuitively realize that he is driving too fast when he approaches a curve. He then decides consciously whether he should apply the brakes or remove his foot from the accelerator.

Stage 5: Expert

This stage is marked by effortless and fluid performance guided by intuition. Experts are now totally engaged in skilled performance so that their skills become part of themselves. There is no need for conscious decision-making or problem solving. They just do what normally works on the basis of their experience. It is only when the outcomes are critical, when the situation is novel, and when time allows that experts engage in conscious deliberation before acting.

Dreyfus and Dreyfus summarize their description of the five stages as follows:

> Thus according to our description of skill acquisition, the novice and advanced beginner exercise no judgment, the competent performer judges by means of conscious deliberation, and those who are proficient or expert make judgments based upon their prior concrete experiences in a manner that defies explanation (p. 36).

There are several critical features in Dreyfus and Dreyfus' model. First, expertise is characterized by "knowing how" rather than "knowing that." Expert knowledge is embedded in the expert's action rather than in a body of propositional knowledge that can be separated from action. Second, expertise is intuitive. According to Dreyfus and Dreyfus, "Hunches and intuitions, ..., are the very core of expert decision-making" (p. 10). Third, experience is a crucial factor in the development of expertise; for it is the only way through which intuition is acquired. They maintain that "a high level of skill in any *unstructured* problem area seems to require considerable concrete experience with real situations..." (original emphasis, p. 20). Fourth, most expert performance is automatic and nonreflective. It is only when the situation is novel, when there is time, and when the decisions are important that experts engage in deliberation before acting. This kind of deliberation requires reflecting critically on one's intuition. Dreyfus and Dreyfus referred to this kind of deliberation as "deliberative rationality" (p. 36), which was elaborated by Dreyfus (1997) as "detached, reasoned observation of one's intuitive behavior with an eye to challenging and perhaps improving intuition without replacing it by the purely theory-based action of the novice, advanced beginner, or competent performer" (p. 28). Finally, the intuition, or know-how, of experts is experiential and tacit; it cannot be articulated (Polanyi, 1966).

Benner (1984) applied the Dreyfus model of skill acquisition (see Dreyfus and Dreyfus, 1980, cited in Benner, 1984) to the analysis of expert nursing practice and found that much of the expert performance in nursing does not involve conscious deliberation and analytic judgment at all. Benner et al. (1996), working in the phenomenological paradigm, further adapted and enriched the Dreyfus model to the analysis of clinical judgment of expert nurses and illustrated how the technical rationality models of clinical judgment misrepresented the significant aspects of expert clinical judgment. Expert practice, according to them, is being able to "see" and "read" the "salient issues in the situation" without imposing a set of preconceived expectations and to respond to these salient issues with increased intuition (Benner et al., p. 142).

The Dreyfus model was found to capture powerfully the complexity of professional expertise that is acquired only after much experience in a specific domain when an intuitive, deep, and more holistic understanding of the situation enables the expert to identify very quickly the salient information and attend to the abnormal. It also highlights the fact that much of the knowledge that experts have is tacit and is embedded in their action. In Schon's words, it is "tacit knowing-in-action" (1983, p. 49).

Dreyfus' conception of expertise is a much more convincing way of looking at how experts operate than the conception of expertise based on an information-processing model. This is especially so in its emphasis on the tacit "knowing-how," gained as a result of years of experience. There are, however, certain features of expertise delineated in the Dreyfus model that can be questioned. First, what Dreyfus and Dreyfus refer to as "conscious deliberation" and "analytical thinking" in decision-making and problem-solving have been relegated to something that rarely occurs except when there are deviations from the normal pattern. This is true only if we are thinking about tasks that are repetitive and need to be completed in a very short period of time. For example, an expert teacher who has been conducting group work in class for a number of years may not need to make conscious decisions with regard to how to get students to work in groups since it is highly likely that they have already set up routines with which students are familiar. However, there are other tasks that are very much part of the professional lives of teachers which require conscious deliberation. For example, when teachers plan a lesson, evaluate curriculum materials, and decide on their scheme of work for the whole year, they are very much involved in conscious decision-making. In other words, whether conscious deliberation is involved depends on the nature of the task. For tasks that are routine and repetitive, and where rapid interpretation and decisions are needed, the automatic intuitive performance of experts is what distinguishes them from novices. However, for tasks that are not routine, and sometimes even problematic, it is often the kind of analytical thinking that experts engage in and the deliberative decisions that they make that distinguish them from novices.

Second, the model suggests that the acquisition of "knowing-how" through experience enables experts to act nonreflectively. Experience is undoubtedly a crucial factor. However, it does not necessarily result in the development of expertise. Some people never seem to improve although they have been at the job for a number of years. There is a familiar saying that states, for some people, eighteen years of experience is one year's experience repeated seventeen times. Experience will only contribute to expertise if practitioners are capable of learning from it. To learn from experience requires that practitioners constantly reflect on their practices. It is this combination of highly motivated learning and the ability to reflect on experience that distinguishes the novice from the expert (Berliner, 1994).

Third, the reason experts are able to make rapid interpretations and decisions, according to Dreyfus and Dreyfus, is that they have accumulated memories of numerous distinguishable situations as a result of their experience. Therefore, when they are faced with a situation or a problem, they can recall similar situations or problems as well as their associated interpretations or solutions. "At this point not only is a situation, when seen as similar to a prior one, understood, but the associated decision, action, or tactic simultaneously comes to mind" (Dreyfus and Dreyfus, 1986, p. 32). It is questionable whether the rapid interpretations and decisions that experts are able to make is because they simply recall similar situations and adopt the associated interpretations or solutions, or because they are able to learn from experience and hence identify salient features and perceive the situation in a way that differentiates them from novices.

2.2 Expertise as Conscious Deliberation and Organized Knowledge Base

Unlike Dreyfus and Dreyfus (1986) who see expertise as very much the "knowing how" in expert performance, Glaser and Chi (1988) adopt a cognitive psychological approach and see expertise as very much related to the cognitive processes of the mind. They summarize the findings of studies of expertise in a wide range of skills, including practical skills such as taking restaurant orders, mental calculation; and professional skills such as computer programming, judicial decision-making, and medical diagnosis (see Chi et al., 1988). They delineate the characteristics of experts that they believe are generalizable across domains (see also Glaser, 1990). The following is a brief summary:

1. Experts have developed a specialized domain of knowledge as a result of thousands of hours of practice. In domains of knowledge in which they do not specialize, they behave as novices.
2. Experts are able to recognize meaningful patterns in their specialized domain very quickly. This superior perceptual ability reflects the better organization and retrieval structures of their knowledge base. For example, chess masters are able to recognize clusters of the chess pieces they see, and radiologists are able to see patterns in numerous X-ray plates because they are able to retrieve the information stored in their minds much more quickly.
3. Experts are fast in their performance and problem-solving. Through extensive practice, they have developed automaticity in performing certain aspects of a task, and this frees up their conscious processing capacity for other aspects of the task. They are also able to arrive at a solution to a problem without an extensive search because of

their experience. For example, chess masters are able to play "lightning chess" because, as a result of their experience, they are able to recognize very quickly patterns and the sequence of moves that these patterns trigger.
4. Experts have skilled memory, both short-term and long-term. They are better able to recall more details than novices, again because the automaticity of their skills frees up resources for greater memory storage.
5. Experts see and represent a problem at a deeper and more principled level, whereas novices tend to do so at a superficial level. For example, when asked to organize categories in physics problems, expert physicists used principles of mechanics, whereas novices did not.
6. When problem-solving, experts try to understand a problem first, whereas novices tend to plunge immediately into finding the solution. A well-known example provided by Paige and Simon (1966) involved asking students to solve a simple algebra problem of finding out the length of the board before it was sawed into two pieces where one piece is two-thirds of the length of the board, and the other piece was longer than the first piece by four feet. While some students immediately applied equations and came up with a negative length, other students analyzed the problem and remarked that there was something wrong with the problem because one cannot have a board with negative length.
7. Experts have strong self-monitoring, or meta-cognitive, skills. They are more aware than novices of their mistakes, their failures to comprehend, and the difficulties that they will have in solving a problem. This reflects experts' greater domain knowledge as well as their different representation of that knowledge.

Though there are similarities between the features that they identified and those delineated in the Dreyfus and Dreyfus model, for example, the importance of experience in the development of expertise, and the speed and automaticity of their performance, there are two important differences.

The first difference is that while Dreyfus and Dreyfus (1986) argue that expertise is embedded in the skilled performance in which experts are engaged, and that this "knowing how defies explanation" (p. 36), Glaser and Chi (1988) see expertise as having very much to do with the highly organized and sophisticated knowledge base that experts possess. This knowledge base enables experts to see and represent problems in a deeper and more principled manner, and to solve problems more skillfully. This echoes Chase and Simon's (1973) observation that the ability of chess masters to select the best possible moves in a very short time is due to their direct access to knowledge of chess configurations, which served as cues for retrieval of best move possibilities. They conclude that the differences between experts and novices in a wide range of domains are very much related to their immediate access to relevant knowledge (see also Ericsson and Smith, 1991). Furthermore, Glaser and Chi (1988) maintain that experts are able to access an organized body of conceptual and procedural knowledge with "superior monitoring and self-regulation skills" (p. xxi).

This leads us to the second difference. According to Glaser and Chi, experts do not just rely on their intuition. They engage in monitoring and self-regulation. In other words, they engage in conscious deliberation in their performance. This view is shared by Eraut (1994), who perceives deliberation as a critical feature of expertise, which lies at the heart of professional work. He argues that conscious deliberation is not rare in the lives of experts. For example, architects or engineers who work on a project for two years will have plenty of scope for reflection and deliberation. Experts will often be involved in teamwork or consultation, which necessarily involves deliberation. Eraut further points out that while the work of many professionals are routine cases and well-defined problems that can be handled automatically without deliberation, there are others that are ill-defined problems. These problems require conscious deliberation, and "it is the ability to cope with difficult, ill-defined problems rather than only routine matters which is often adjudged to be the essence of professional expertise" (Eraut, 1994, p. 152).

Dreyfus and Dreyfus' characterization of expert performance as largely automatic and nonreflective has also been questioned. Eraut (1994) points out that there are two reasons why experts need to be reflective: one is that the intuition and routinized behavior of experts may not be correct all the time (see also Leinhardt, 1990); the other is that their skills may get out-of-date. Hence, to engage in reflection and self-evaluation is very important for experts to maintain their expertise.

> Too many theories of professional expertise tend to treat experts as infallible, in spite of much evidence to the contrary. Not only do professionals succumb to many of the common weaknesses which psychologists have shown to be regular features of human judgment; but some allow aspects of their expertise to decay and become a little less relevant or even out of date. Thus there is a need for professionals to retain critical control over the more intuitive parts of their expertise by regular reflection, self-evaluation, and a disposition to learn from colleagues. This implies from time to time treating apparently routine cases as problematic and making time to deliberate and consult. (Eraut, 1994, p. 155)

The importance of reflection is central to Schon's (1983) influential theory of professional knowledge. He observes that professional practitioners often engage in "reflection-on-action" and "reflection-in-action." The former takes place after the action when they think back on what they have done or what they have experienced, often in order to prepare themselves for the future. The latter takes place during the action, especially when they encounter situations that are unanticipated, problematic, or unique, and they may arrive at a new way of looking at a problem or a phenomenon, hence generating a new understanding. He explains:

> ... professional practitioners often think about what they are doing, sometimes even while doing it. Stimulated by surprise, they turn thought back on action and on the knowing which is implicit in action.... There is some puzzling, or troubling, or interesting phenomenon with which the individual is trying to deal. As he tries to make sense of it, he also reflects on the understandings which have been implicit in his action, understandings which he surfaces, criticizes, restructures, and embodies in further action. (p. 50)

In other words, there seems to be an alternative conception of expertise, in which experts are characterized as possessing a body of highly organized and sophisticated knowledge, being able to engage in conscious deliberation, self-monitoring and self-evaluating as well as engaging in reflective practice. The questions that need to be addressed are first, how far the knowledge that experts develop can be separated from their expert performance and how far this knowledge can be articulated. Second, what is the place of conscious deliberation and reflection in expert performance and in the development of expertise?

2.3 Expertise as a Continuous Process

In much of the explications of expertise reported above, expertise is perceived as a *state* of superior performance reached as a result of years of experience and practice. Bereiter and Scardamalia (1993) propose that expertise should be seen as a *process* rather than a state. Most of the studies of expertise compare the performances of experts with those of novices on the same tasks. Bereiter and Scardamalia point out that this kind of comparison is not likely to help us understand expertise and how it is acquired. Experts, with plenty of practice and experience, inevitably perform better and faster than novices. What researchers need to do, they argue, is to study experts and experienced nonexperts, and investigate how experts develop their expertise over time.

Bereiter and Scardamalia's theory of expertise was developed from their study of writing, where they observed phenomena that contradicted findings commonly reported in expert-novice comparisons. First, expert-novice comparisons maintain that expertise is acquired through thousands of hours of practice. However, Bereiter and Scardamalia found that not many people become good writers, no matter how much practice they have had. Many people just become fluent bad writers. They also found that, contrary to Dreyfus and Dreyfus's theory, some drivers go through the stages of skill development from conscious rule learning to automatic operation of the car but do not end up being good drivers. This view is shared by Ericsson and Smith (1991), who point out that "one should be particularly careful about accepting one's number of years of experience as an accurate measure of one's level of expertise" (p. 27). They maintain that the learning mechanisms that mediate the improvements from experience have a crucial role to play in the acquisition of expertise.

Second, expert-novice comparisons assert that expert performance is characterized by automaticity, effortlessness, and fluidity. Bereiter and Scardamalia point out that this "on-top-of-it" image of experts does not seem to fit all experts. Many experts work very hard and long hours, and they often set standards for themselves and others that are slightly beyond reach. They argue that this image of effortless performance of experts could well be derived from the fact that the same task is given to the experts and the novices in expert-novice studies. The task is usually well below the competence level of experts so that novices can handle them as well, resulting in the experts being able to handle it without much effort. In order to test their hypothesis, they gave expert and less-competent writers a writing task on a topic like "describe your own job" where knowledge of the topic can be assumed, and where the task can be approached at any level they like. They found that the former, apart from producing much better writing with richer ideas, worked harder and took much longer time to complete the task than less-competent writers. They laboriously searched for ideas, evaluated and reconsidered them before arriving at a main point. By contrast, less-competent writers did much less thinking and arrived at the main point very quickly. The same results were obtained when they looked at learners of music and medicine. The fact that expert writers agonized over the writing task, argue Bereiter and Scardamalia, is because they took it as a challenging task of producing an original essay. Less-competent writers took it as a simple task of putting down all they knew about the job. In other words, it is the way expert writers *chose* to treat the task that distinguishes them from nonexperts.

Bereiter and Scardamalia make a similar observation about expert and nonexpert problem solving. They point out that the critical difference does not lie in the efficiency in problem-solving, but rather, in the kinds of problems that experts and nonexperts solve. They maintain that experts "tackle problems that increase their expertise, whereas nonexperts tend to tackle problems for which they do not have to extend themselves" (p. 78). Hence, it is when people work "at the edge of their competence" (p. 34) that they develop expertise. These observations lead to one of the core concepts in their theory of expertise – that experts approach a task in a way that maximizes their opportunities for growth, whereas nonexperts approach it in a way that minimizes these opportunities.

Another core concept in Bereiter and Scardamalia's theory of expertise is what they call "the *process* of expertise" (p. 82). They point out that with experience, conscious efforts to solve problems are replaced by well-developed routines.[1] For experts, the mental resources freed up by the use of routines will be "reinvested" in the pursuit of new goals and problem-solving at a higher level, which they did not have the capacity to deal with earlier. Nonexperts, however, will simply have a diminishing number of problems to solve as they develop routines to handle them. Bereiter and Scardamalia remark that "Given enough experience, everybody acquires the repertoire (of learned patterns and procedures). What gets people into ruts is reducing problems to levels that can be handled by those learned patterns and procedures" (p. 111). Hence, the critical distinction between experts and experienced nonexperts is not that the former do things well and the latter do things badly, but rather that experts *problematize* what seem to be routine practices and address them, whereas experienced nonexperts simply carry out practiced routines. "Reinvestment" and "progressive problem solving," according to them, are two aspects of the same process. It is a continuous process, and it is in this process of continually reinvesting their resources to take on further challenges that experts extend the growing edge of their expertise.

Bereiter and Scardamalia's theory brought two new perspectives to our understanding of expertise. First, most of the expertise studies compare expert and novice performances. One is never sure whether the characteristics of experts identified are critical features of experienced performance or expert performance. For example, the automaticity and effortlessness in routinized performance often associated with expertise could well be a consequence of experience. The majority of experienced teachers have a number of classroom management routines that novice teachers do not have. Yet, only a small percentage of them are expert teachers. By comparing experts with experienced nonexperts, Bereiter and Scardamalia helped to disentangle experience from expertise. Second, expert-novice comparisons give a static picture; they show what experts are like, but they do not show how experts acquire and maintain expertise. By looking at the process of acquisition of expertise, Bereiter and Scardamalia revealed characteristics of experts that were masked by expert-novice comparisons.

In the above discussion, we examined the characteristics of expertise proposed by different theories of expertise, which can be generalized across disciplines. This discussion is necessary because most studies

---

1 According to Bereiter and Scardamalia, a problem exists whenever there is a goal to which one does not have a known way to achieve (see 1993, p. 83).

of teaching expertise have drawn on the insights from these theories, especially the theories put forward by Dreyfus and Dreyfus (1986) and Glaser and Chi (1988). As we shall see in Chapter 3, many of the characteristics of experts and novices reported above have also been found in expert and novice teachers.

2.4 Summary

In this chapter some of the theories of expertise and prominent studies frequently cited in the study of teaching expertise have been examined. There are three aspects of expertise that have been discussed: First, the characteristics of expert performance; second, the critical features that distinguish experts from novices or experienced nonexperts; third, how expertise is acquired and maintained. There seems to be a large degree of convergence on the first aspect. All theories agree that experience and practice have an important role in the acquisition of expertise and that experts are able to attain a high standard of performance which is marked by automaticity, effortlessness, and fluidity. There are divergent views, however, with regard to the second aspect. In particular, there are debates about whether expert knowledge is intuitive and tacit knowledge embedded in expert performance or sophisticated and well-organized propositional knowledge external to expert performance that can be retrieved or accessed. There are also debates regarding whether conscious deliberation and reflection are features of expertise. Dreyfus and Dreyfus (1986) consider that it is the intuitive and routinized performance of experts brought about by experience that distinguish them from novices. Glaser and Chi (1988), however, see expertise as involving automatic performance as well as conscious deliberations and reflections. Eraut (1994) argues that it is not routinized performance but conscious deliberation in dealing with ill-defined problems that sets experts apart from novices. Furthermore, it is because of their ability to reflect and self-monitor that experts are able to maintain their superior performance. Most studies have addressed the first two aspects, but very few have addressed the third aspect. Bereiter and Scardamalia's theory of expertise as a continuous process is one of the few. Bereiter and Scardamalia (1993) assert that comparing novice and experts is not very helpful in understanding expertise because experience is often mistaken as expertise. They propose comparing experts with experienced nonexperts to disentangle experience from expertise. They further observe that the abundant comparative studies merely show what experts are like, but do not show how they get to where they are. They propose looking at how experts acquire and maintain expertise. Expertise, according to them, is a process, rather than a state, in which experts keep extending the upper edge of their competence by setting for themselves very high standards and working very hard to reach these standards. Bereiter and Scardamalia see the development and maintenance of expertise as a process in which experts continuously reinvest their mental resources, freed up by the acquisition of relevant knowledge through experience, in problematizing what is taken as routine, in reformulating problems and in solving them. Their conceptualization of expertise as a process rather than a state provides a new perspective for understanding expertise that departs from the way it has been understood in expert-novice comparisons. Most of the studies of expertise in teaching draw on the first two conceptions of expertise, particularly studies that have taken the form of expert-novice comparisons, which we shall review in the following chapter.

3 Characteristics of Expert and Novice Teachers

In the previous chapter, I reviewed three major theories of expertise and their delineation of the characteristics of experts across skills and disciplines. In this chapter, I shall examine the characteristics of novice and expert teachers that have been identified in the literature on teaching expertise and see to what extent they share the characteristics of novices and experts in other professions.

Studies of expertise in teaching mostly took the form of novice-expert comparisons. They drew on studies of teachers' mental processes in planning and decision-making, which were seen as a link between thought and action, and were heavily influenced by an information processing model of the mind in cognitive psychology (see Calderhead, 1996). In some studies, laboratory tasks were designed, and elicitations of teachers' thought processes were conducted. In other cases direct observations of classroom teaching and stimulated-recall interviews were used. Most studies comparing expert and novice teachers focused on their cognitive processes in different phases of teaching, taking on board the distinction made by Jackson (1968) between 'preactive' and 'interactive' phases of teaching. The former refers to the period before teaching, when teachers are planning the lesson and evaluating and selecting teaching methods and materials. The latter refers to the time when teachers are interacting with students in the classroom. Jackson pointed out that there are qualitative differences in what teachers do in these two phases. Clark and Peterson (1986) proposed a third phase, the "postactive" phase, to describe the period when teachers reflect on their teaching after a lesson and make decisions about subsequent teaching. However, as they themselves pointed out, the distinction in teacher thinking between the preactive and the postactive phases is not as marked as that between the preactive and interactive phases because of the cyclical nature of the teaching process. Reflections on teaching in the postactive phase often serve as input for planning in the preactive phases.

In the rest of this chapter, I shall discuss the findings of expert-novice studies in the preactive and the interactive phases of teaching. It should be noted, however, that decision-making in these two phases are intertwined and it is sometimes not easy to distinguish between the two.[1]

3.1 Preactive Phase

In the preactive phase, planning is considered the most important thinking process in which teachers engage (Kounin, 1970; Doyle, 1977; Yinger, 1979; Calderhead, 1984). Calderhead (1984) points out that "it is in planning that teachers translate syllabus guidelines, institutional expectations, and their own beliefs and ideologies of education into guides for action in the classroom. This aspect of teaching provides the structure and purpose for what teachers and pupils do in the classroom" (p. 69).

A model of planning, which consists of a linear sequence of decisions, which is widely adopted in teacher education programs, is that proposed by Tyler (1950). First of all, decisions are made about aims and objectives. Aims are the more general statement of purpose, and objectives are the specific realizations of aims. Decisions are then made about the content of the lesson, that is, the kind of materials or activities that would help to achieve the objectives. Following this, the organization of activities, or the presentation of materials, is decided upon. Finally, evaluations are made about the lesson. These evaluations serve as input for future lessons.

Research on the actual planning process of experienced teachers has found, however, that teachers seldom plan in the manner suggested by Tyler. Instead, they consider first aspects such as materials and resources, students' interests and abilities. Aims and purposes are considered last (see Taylor, 1970). The decisions that teachers make when planning have to do with mostly activities, teaching strategies, and content. Only a small proportion has to do with objectives (see Zahorik, 1975; Peterson, Marx, and Clark, 1978). For many teachers, activities or content are the basic structural units of planning and action in the classroom (Clark and Yinger, 1979; Kagan and Tippins, 1992; McCutcheon, 1980; Morine-Dershimer, 1979; Yinger, 1980). However, this does not mean that experienced teachers do not consider aims and objectives when they are planning. In Morine-Dershimer's (1979) study of the mental plan of teachers, it was found that when teachers were probed about objectives and teaching strategies, they had ready answers. This suggests that they did consider such aspects of instruction although these aspects may not have figured explicitly in stated plans. Nunan (1992) observes that though the plans and instructional objectives may be transformed in the teaching act, they provide a framework for the interactive decisions

---

1 I am grateful to Devon Woods for pointing this out to me.

during the lesson and the evaluation afterwards. In McCutcheon's study (1980), teachers reported that the objectives were implicit in the activities and that it was not necessary to write them down (see also Clark and Yinger, 1987). The question is therefore not *whether* teachers consider objectives, but *when* they do so. Mcleod (1981, cited in Clark and Peterson, 1986) found that teachers thought about intended learning outcomes more in the interactive phase than in the preactive phase. Sadro-Brown (1990) found that decisions about objectives and content were made at the yearly level, while decisions at the daily level typically concerned activities, instructional methods and materials, and individual student needs.

Calderhead (1984) proposed an alternative conception of teacher planning as a problem-solving process. He wrote:

Research on teachers' planning suggests that teachers engage in a process that contrasts sharply with the prescribed rational planning model.... the process of planning seems to be more appropriately conceptualized as a problem-solving process. Teachers, faced with a variety of factors such as pupils with certain knowledge, abilities and interests, the availability of particular textbooks and materials, the syllabus, the timetable, the expectations of head-teachers and others, and their knowledge of previous teaching encounters, *have to solve the problem of how to structure the time and experiences of pupils in the classroom*. Teachers, it seems, adopt a more pragmatic approach than that prescribed for curriculum design. Rather than start with a conception of what is to be achieved and deduce which classroom activities would therefore be ideal, teachers start with a conception of their working context and from that decide what is possible." (p. 74, original emphasis)

This problem-solving process is not linear, but cyclic and recursive. Teachers may begin with a vague conception of an activity that will take shape in the implementation process. It will then be refined and elaborated in subsequent implementations until it becomes a set of routines that is incorporated in their weekly or yearly planning (Clark and Yinger, 1987; Kagan and Tippins, 1992). In this process teachers will draw on their knowledge of a wide range of domains, such as knowledge of the students, the materials, teaching strategies, context (including the context of the classroom), the school, and the expectations of parents and students themselves. They will also plan in a way that suits their own personal style. One of the teachers in Sadro-Brown's study (1990) said, "I'm comfortable with the Frankenstein model that I've created" (p. 66; see also Sardo, 1982, cited in Clark and Peterson, 1986). Calderhead sums up planning as a "creative, interactive, problem-finding and problem-solving process" (1993, p. 15).

In the ensuing discussion, I shall examine the characteristics of expert and novice teachers' planning identified in the expert-novice comparative studies.

3.1.1 Lesson planning

When the planning processes of expert or experienced teachers were compared to those of novice teachers, it was found that some novices planned each lesson by following the Tyler model closely, whereas experienced or expert teachers never did. The latter were more concerned about the flow of the activities over a period of time, or how to get the classroom to "work" (Carter, Sabers, Cushing, Pinnegar, and Berliner, 1987). The reason novice teachers followed the model closely was because they were required to do so in their professional training courses. In fact, in a study on teacher planning, student teachers reported that they would not have done so in their practicum otherwise. (Neale, Pace, and Case, 1983; cited in Clark and Peterson, 1986). Brown and McIntyre (1992) observe the following:

> Not infrequently the students return to the college or university after a spell in a school bewailing the fact that teaching is not so straightforward, and their best laid plans have gone awry because of unexpected events, constraints, disruptions and so on. The model they have been given, they often claim, is unrealistic and takes inadequate account of the practicalities of schools and classrooms. (p. 69)

When the experienced teachers in their study were asked to comment on the current practices in the preparation of teachers, most of them remarked that "A formal 'aims and objectives' approach may have a place in planning the work of a class but it is divorced from the reality of how teachers think about their actual teaching" (ibid., p. 88).

Novice teachers were also found to adhere closely to the stated objectives in the prescribed curriculum guide. In Westerman's study (1991) the novice teachers explained their planning by making remarks such as, "The main topic is graphs, and the curriculum guide gives you an instructional objective," and "I just had to make sure that they met all the objectives" (p. 296). The expert teachers demonstrated more autonomy in their planning. While they used the curriculum guidelines for building their lessons, they made modifications according to the needs of their students and their own goals. One of the expert teachers commented, "I always do what I am supposed to do (i.e., teach the curriculum objectives), but then how I implement it comes from my own self" (ibid.). Novice teachers, on the other hand, lacked confidence to depart from what was prescribed or to try out alternative teaching methods even though they believed the alternatives might be better than what they were currently using (see Borko and Livingston, 1989).

In other words, novice teachers tend to act according to rules and guidelines laid down by people with authority, whereas expert teachers rely on their own judgment and exercise autonomy when planning.

3.1.2 Long-term and short-term planning

Besides the differences outlined above, most expert teachers were found to engage in longer-term planning (cf. McCutcheon, 1980).[2] Besides lesson planning, they also engaged in unit planning, daily planning, weekly planning, term planning, and yearly planning. When they engaged in yearly planning, they established the content to be covered, a sequence for the curriculum components for the whole year, and a timeline for content coverage. When they planned at the unit or chapter level, they determined a timeline for each topic. Their decisions were often made on the basis of how things went in the previous year (Yinger, 1980; Borko and Livingston, 1989).

Novice teachers, on the other hand, were found to engage in short-term planning, usually not going beyond the next couple of sections or pages. One reason was that they had to spend so much time and energy preparing for teaching the following day that they did not have the spare capacity to think too far ahead. A novice teacher in Borko and Livingston's study (1989) remarked that her lack of experience and professional knowledge had an impact on her planning. She commented:

> This is all so new to me that thinking up, I have to do a lot of thinking ahead of time. I really do. I have to think out what kind of questions to ask. I have to think out the answers to the questions...so that my answers are theoretically correct and yet simple enough to make sense... I can't ad-lib it too well. (see also Westerman, 1991)

Expert teachers, by contrast, were described as much more efficient in lesson planning. They had various plans in their memory because of their previous experience, and they rarely had to design classroom activities from scratch. They usually had well-mastered routines for these activities. For these teachers, planning often involved recalling how the lesson went the last time it was taught, and deciding whether amendments were needed. Unlike experts, novices had little or no previous experience to fall back on and less knowledge of their students and the teaching materials. They had to devote plenty of time and energy to design activities and to think of techniques to set up and maintain them. Calderhead (1984) points out that what is "routine" to experienced teachers are "conscious decisions" to novice teachers (p. 15).

3.1.3 Written and mental lesson plans

Differences were also identified between the forms of the lesson plans that expert and novice teachers make. Most studies reported that expert

---

2 McCutcheon's study (1980, p. 11) found that experienced teachers did not engage in long-range planning. For some of them it was because long-range planning was handled by the textbooks. Others reported that planning too far ahead would lead to inflexibility; they could not incorporate children's interests.

teachers planned their lessons mentally, sometimes with brief notes resembling a list for grocery shopping as a reminder. McCutcheon observes that the richest form of planning is the mental dialogs that teachers engage in before writing the plans or before the lesson. These mental dialogs include rehearsing a lesson and recalling what happened when a similar lesson was taught. These dialogs often take place continuously, even through the summer months. The teachers in his study said that they "take school home" (p. 8). He also found that expert teachers planned at odd moments like taking a shower, watching football, or driving home (see also Morine-Dershimer, 1979; McCutcheon, 1980; Calderhead, 1984; Livingston and Borko, 1989).

Novice teachers' plans were found to be much more detailed. Some of them wrote down what they were going to say and the actions that they intended to carry out, even noting down what they would write on the blackboard. Sometimes they just read their notes out. (Calderhead, 1984; Borko and Livingston, 1989). In Kagan and Tippin's study (1992), when secondary teachers were not confident about their knowledge of subject matter and their ability to maintain discipline in disruptive classes, they scripted their lessons into minilectures to make sure that the content they delivered was correct and to show the disruptive students that they "mean business."

It was argued that one reason why expert teachers seldom need to write detailed lesson plans is that they have a rich memory of previous lessons that they can call on when they are planning. They also have repertoires of well-mastered routines for a variety of situations that they can call upon easily when planning lessons. Another possible reason is their belief that it is impossible to determine in great detail how a lesson should proceed. There are many contingencies in the classroom that will affect the development of the lesson. Brown and McIntyre (1992) found that the experienced teachers had basic, consistent, planned patterns for their teaching, but the patterns were "almost infinitely flexible and implementation was crucially influenced by the conditions which impinged upon their teaching" (p. 44). These conditions included students' behavior and performance, availability of resources, time of the day, and time of the year. Expert teachers are able to anticipate possible situations in lessons and have contingency plans to deal with these situations (Housner and Griffey, 1985; Borko and Livingston, 1989). They are also able to anticipate the difficulties that students are likely to have, and they have in store a number of routines that they can immediately call upon in response to student cues (Carter et al., 1987). Novice teachers often have difficulties anticipating problems in the classroom and the difficulties that students have with the curriculum, and novice teachers are reluctant to depart from their plans in response to student cues (Borko and Livingston, 1989; Kagan and Tippins, 1992).

In other words, while expert teachers incorporate an element of flexibility in their plans, they plan for what they want to achieve in the lesson and the general direction that the lesson should take. They are always prepared to respond to cues in the classroom and change their plans. Novice teachers, on the other hand, being less able to anticipate problems, are much less flexible in their planning.

3.1.4 Planning thoughts

Although the written lesson plans of expert teachers are very brief, their mental plans are very rich. Expert teachers in Westerman's study (1991) thought in terms of how their individual lessons fit into the entire curriculum, how the lessons related to the curriculum content already covered earlier in the year, and how they were related to other subjects in the curriculum. Novice teachers had difficulties making sense of the sequence of topics in textbooks and consequently they planned each lesson as discrete units on the basis of the prescribed objectives without understanding how the units fit together (Schram, Feiman-Nemser, and Ball, 1989).

Expert teachers take into consideration students' prior learning, academic performances, and abilities when planning lessons. They also pay attention to competencies and difficulties of individual students and make strategic decisions accordingly (Calderhead, 1984; Housner and Griffey, 1985). In Carter et al.'s study (1987), when expert teachers were asked to take over a new class, they were more concerned about finding out the students' knowledge of the subject matter for the teacher's benefit. Novice teachers, on the other hand, focused more on reviewing the content with students for the latter's benefit rather than for their own benefit. In studying teachers' statements about planning, Leinhardt (1989) found that the expert teachers in her study always began their planning by stating what their students had learned the day before, whereas none of the novice teachers did (see also Paine, 1989; Carter, Cushing, Sabers, Stein, and Berliner, 1988; Fogarty, Wang, and Creek, 1983). Their planning thoughts contained more details and included student actions, not just teacher action, and planning for test point(s) within the lesson, which were checkpoints to evaluate student understanding or lesson progress. Most of their plans demonstrated that the flow of the lesson was driven by instructional logic, whereas most of the novice teachers did not show any guiding logic to their instructional actions.

The above findings show that expert teachers draw upon a wide range of knowledge when they are planning, including knowledge of the pupils, both as a group and as individuals, the curriculum, classroom organization, student learning, and the subject matter. Novice teachers have a much less sophisticated knowledge base, and therefore, they have much less to draw upon.

3.1.5 Characteristics of expert and novice teachers in preactive teaching

To summarize the above discussion, we may say that there are four main characteristics of preactive thinking identified in the research literature, on which novice and expert teachers differ. The first characteristic is that in the planning process, expert teachers exercise more *autonomy*. Novice teachers' planning is guided by rules and models. As Dreyfus and Dreyfus (1986) point out, these rules are often devoid of context. This is why novice teachers often have problems implementing their plans in the classroom when there are many contextual elements affecting the general direction of the lesson. Expert teachers, on the other hand, are fully aware of the contextual variables that they need to consider when planning. From their experience, they know what works in the classroom and what does not. Hence they are much more ready to depart from rules and take responsibility for their own actions.

The second characteristic is that expert teachers are much more *efficient* in lesson planning. They spend much less time planning, and yet their planning is often much more effective. According to the research literature, this is because expert teachers have in store well-established routines that they can call upon when planning. They can also recall their experience in teaching similar lessons and make whatever amendments necessary. It appears that there is a certain degree of "automaticity" and "effortlessness" in their planning, because they can rely on routinized behavior and "what normally works," especially if they are planning for something that they have taught before. In this respect, expert teachers seem to be similar to experts in other fields. However, the research literature also found that expert teachers' mental plans are much richer and that they do engage in detailed planning. Since this is the case, how far can we say that their planning is "effortless"? Furthermore, we can see that expert teachers also engage in conscious deliberation and reflection when they are doing long-term planning, when they consider whether they need to make any amendments to what they did the year before, and when they make mental plans. Teachers who have high professional standards often reflect on how their lessons went in previous years and how they could improve on them. As Bereiter and Scardamalia (1993) point out, teachers who always go by routinized behavior and "what normally works" are those who get into a rut and wallow in mediocrity. Therefore, how far is their planning "automatic"?

The third characteristic of preactive thinking is that expert teachers are much more *flexible* in planning; they are much more responsive to contextual cues, and much more ready to make changes to their plans accordingly. In other words, it is the way teachers relate to their specific context of work that differentiate the expert from the novice. For expert teachers, the context is very much an integral part of their teaching act, whereas for novice teachers, context is very often taken as something external and ignored.

The fourth characteristic is that the planning thoughts of expert teachers reflect a *rich and integrated knowledge base*. When they plan, they integrate their knowledge of the curriculum, the students, teaching methods and strategies, the context including expectations of the principal, teachers and parents, the classroom setting, the time of the day, the time of the year, and so on.

The discussion in this section shows that teacher thinking and decision-making in the preactive phase are inextricably linked to those in the interactive phase. Decisions made in the preactive phase are subject to modification as teachers implement them in the classroom. As pointed out above, one of the characteristics of expertise in teaching is teachers' ability to respond to the contingencies in the classroom. We shall therefore turn to the interactive phase of teaching and examine the differences between novice and expert teachers that have been identified.

3.2 Interactive Phase

The classroom is a complex and relatively unpredictable environment where many things happen very quickly at the same time. Doyle, drawing on the work of Jackson (1968) and Smith and Geoffrey (1968), depicts the classroom as follows:

> A classroom is *multidimensional* in that many events occur over time, many purposes are served, and many people with different styles and desires participate. The sheer quantity of elements, in other words, is large. In addition, many events in a classroom occur *simultaneously*. While phrasing a question, a teacher must monitor different levels of involvement in work, search for an appropriate student to answer, anticipate interruptions, and judge whether particular students are violating classroom rules.... The simultaneous occurrence of multiple elements shortens the time frame and confers *immediacy* to the flow of classroom experience. Decisions must be made rapidly with little time for reflection. At the same time, these qualities of classroom life together with a high frequency of interruptions make the course of events at a given moment *unpredictable*." (1979, p. 44; my emphasis)

Because of the multidimensionality, simultaneity, immediacy, and unpredictability of the classroom, teachers need to be able to process simultaneously transmitted information very quickly, to attend to multiple events simultaneously, to detect signs of disruptive behavior and to act on them before they become problems (Kounin, 1970). This is a very demanding task. Copeland (1987) describes teachers who are successful classroom managers as having "eyes in the back of the head" (p. 220).

Various attempts have been made to capture teachers' cognitive processes in the interactive phase. For example, Peterson and Clark (1978), based on a model of teacher thinking proposed by Snow (1972, cited in Peterson and Clark, 1978), put forward a model of decision-making in the interactive phase. The model represents a cyclical process in which teachers observe cues from students and decide whether student behavior is within tolerable limits. If it is, then they continue with the lesson. If not, they decide whether there are alternative teaching behaviors that can bring student behavior back to tolerable limits. If they do not have an alternative, they will continue with the lesson as before. If they do, then they may make the decision to behave differently, or they may still decide to continue as before.

Calderhead (1984) points out that not all decisions made by teachers follow the same model. He suggests that there are three types of decisions that we make in everyday life. The first type are decisions that involve a great deal of thinking, identifying the alternatives, and evaluating the possible outcomes. These decisions for example, making career choices, usually take time. He refers to them as "reflective decisions." The second type are those which have to be made instantaneously; there is very little time for considering alternatives and evaluating the outcome, as in when you are crossing the road and a bus is speeding toward you. He refers to them as "immediate decisions." The last type are decisions that are made so often that they become automatic and routine. For example, decisions to change gears when driving. He refers to them as "routine decisions." In different contexts, different types of decisions will be made. In the teaching situation, he points out, there are some decisions that are reflective, such as planning the curriculum and selecting teaching methods and materials. There are other decisions, however, which are, and must be, made immediately. For example, decisions regarding disciplinary problems cannot wait until the teacher has weighed several alternatives. If the disciplinary problems are unanticipated, then "immediate decisions" will be made; but if they are recurrent, then "routine decisions" will be made.

The term *routine* refers to a set of procedures which has been established over time to control and coordinate specific sequences of behavior (Yinger 1979). Researchers have proposed that by setting up routines, teachers make the timing, sequencing, and students' behavior predictable, hence reducing their information processing load and freeing up their capacity to monitor deviations from the original plan (Clark and Yinger, 1979; Joyce, 1979; Morine-Dershimer, 1979; Peterson and Clark, 1978; Shavelson and Stern, 1981). The use of routine is therefore a very important part of interactive teaching. In fact, it is considered to be an essential element in classroom survival (Brophy and Good, 1986; Calderhead, 1984; Doyle, 1986).

It has been pointed out that teacher decision-making usually takes place when the routine is not going ahead as planned. When that happens, contrary to Peterson and Clark's description in their model, teachers do not consider a number of alternatives. They are more likely to see if there is a routine available that they can use to deal with the anomaly. If there is no available routine, they will improvise. If the anomaly does not require immediate action, then they will respond to it either after the lesson or in a subsequent lesson (see Shavelson and Stern, 1981).

The studies reviewed above suggest that teachers' decision-making is triggered by student behavior that is not within the teacher's tolerance limit. However, investigations in the antecedents for teachers' interactive decisions showed that most of the time, the decisions were not made in response to students' intolerable behavior, but rather in response to a student's question, a choice of appropriate techniques, transition from one activity to another, insufficient time left in the lesson, shortage of materials, the teacher's own emotional state, and so on (Marland, 1977, Wodlinger, 1980, cited in Clark and Peterson, 1986; Forgarty et al., 1983). Clark and Peterson (1986) call for more descriptive research on how teachers make interactive decisions.

Studies of expert-novice teaching have drawn on the findings in teacher decision-making processes to compare the cognitive processes that expert and novice teachers are engaged in interactive teaching, which we shall discuss below.

3.2.1 Making sense of and attending to classroom events

As mentioned above, in interactive teaching, multiple events take place simultaneously at a very fast pace. To operate successfully in the classroom, teachers need to be able to make sense of the events and to respond to them. To investigate how expert and beginning teachers perceive and monitor the simultaneous occurrence of events in the classroom, Sabers et al. (1991) showed them a videotape of one classroom period that was edited into three tapes, each showing a different view of the classroom. These three tapes were played simultaneously and teachers were asked to monitor all three screens. They were asked to describe the instructional and management techniques used by the teacher, to think aloud about what they were seeing, to respond to questions about content, student and teacher attitudes, the environment, and to recall specific details afterwards. Sabers et al. found that expert teachers were able to make sense of the events that "puzzled" the beginning teachers (whom they called "advanced beginners") and "baffled" those without any classroom experience (whom they called "novices"). Beginning teachers, on the other hand, were overwhelmed by the complex incoming information. When asked to comment on the classroom events and the teacher's instructional practices, expert teachers frequently assigned meaning to the classroom events that they saw and made evaluative judgments about them. Beginning teachers' comments were often detailed but descriptive, "reminiscent of radio announcers reporting an athletic event" (p. 73). For example, one of the beginning teachers commented: "In the right monitor, we have the teacher lecturing, students taking notes," whereas one of the expert teachers commented: "on the left monitor, the students' note taking indicates that they have seen sheets like this and have had presentations like this before; it is fairly efficient at this point because they're used to the format they are using" (p. 72).

Similar to master chess players who can recognize thousands of chess patterns, expert teachers can readily recognize patterns in classroom events and hence make sense of them because of their hundreds and thousands of hours of experience in the classroom. In a study that Berliner and his colleagues conducted, novice and expert teachers were shown briefly a photographic slide of a science laboratory session three times. After each viewing, teachers were asked to write down what they saw and to update the information in the second and third viewing. After the second viewing, one of the expert teachers said, "It's not necessarily a lab class. There just seemed to be more writing activity. There were people filling out forms. It could have been the end of a lab class after they started putting the equipment away...." After the third viewing, the expert teacher said, "Yeah – there was... very little equipment out, and it almost appeared to be towards the end of the hour. The books appeared to be closed. Almost looked like it was a clean-up type situation" (Berliner, 1986, p. 11). The expert teacher's perception was correct; it was a cleaning-up activity at the end of a laboratory session. It is likely that because classroom events were perceived in a meaningful way, expert teachers were able to recall them much better than novices who could not make sense of them (Peterson and Comeaux, 1987).

Besides being able to make sense of classroom events, expert teachers' perceptions of classroom events were also more analytical and interpretive. In Saber et al.'s study (1991), when asked to comment on the teacher's instructional practices, expert teachers gave more elaborate comments, which were analytical and interpretive, whereas beginning teachers merely described what they saw with little evidence of analytical thinking. The following are extracts of the comments from an expert and a beginning teacher.

Expert teacher: There was some formal lecture, and there was a formal activity. I think the technique that she used was very low key, perhaps a process type approach to teaching science rather than a very structured approach.

Beginning teacher: It looks... well, mostly lecture. She had some activities for the kids to do. Some use of media. She used the overhead a little bit. (p. 74)

Similar findings have been obtained in Berliner and his colleague's study reported above. Expert teachers were found to draw upon their rich store of classroom knowledge to interpret what they saw on the slide. For example, after viewing a slide of a mathematics lesson, one of the expert teachers said, "there aren't a whole lot of humorous math problems so I *assumed* a couple of the students must have been talking – from their facial expressions – about something other than the assignment" (Berliner and Carter, 1989, p. 60). Novice teachers' descriptions, according to Berliner and Carter, were detailed but "flat" (ibid.), with no explanations for what they described and showed little relationship between events. It is interesting to note that the expert teachers in this study were cautious in interpretation and demonstrated an awareness of the possible variables not presented in the slides that could affect their interpretation of the classroom events.

A further dimension on which expert and novice teachers were found to differ is selectivity. The term *selectivity*, as proposed by Corno (1981, p. 364), refers to "an ability to separate important from salient incidental information." One possible reason why, in Sabers et al.'s study (1991) reported above, the "advanced beginners" and "novices" experienced information overload when they were watching the videotapes is that they were not selective when they processed the information. As Doyle (1977) points out, the demand created by the complex environment of the classroom is very great and one of the strategies by which teachers deal with it is to simplify the complexity by being selective about the events to which they attend. His study of "successful" and "unsuccessful" student teachers[3] found that the former were better able to differentiate the immediate and long-term significance of classroom events. Morine and Vallance's study of more and less "effective" teachers[4] found that less "effective" teachers took into consideration more items of information on almost all aspects of their interactive decision-making compared to more "effective" teachers (Morine and Vallance, 1975, cited in Clark and Peterson, 1986, p. 279).

Similar findings have been reported in comparisons of expert and novice teachers. Sabers et al. (1991, p. 64) observe that expert teachers "assess only certain classroom behaviors and events, namely, those needing immediate teacher attention. Other perceived behaviors and events are rapidly assessed as being less critical, resulting in a decision by the teacher to delay action or to take no action at all." In many studies

---

3 "Successful" teachers were defined as those who maintained high levels of student involvement and low levels of disruption (see Doyle, 1977, p. 53fn).

4 'Effective' teachers were those whose students had higher gain scores on achievement tests, and less 'effective' teachers were those whose students had lower gain scores. This definition of *effectiveness* is typically used in the process-product paradigm (see Shulman, 1992).

it was found that what expert teachers attended to were things related to instructional objectives. Carter et al. (1987) gave expert and novice teachers detailed information about the students of a new class that they were going to take over, including grades, demographic data, and teacher comments. When they were asked to recall the information about these students, expert teachers could only remember the number of students in this class, but not the number of female and male students, the ethnicity of the students, and the number of students in a specified grade. However, they remembered that one of the students was visually impaired because they thought this information was important. Carter et al. point out that this could be because the number of students and the presence of a visually impaired student in the class have important implications for instructional and managerial decisions, but not the specific details about individual students. Novice teachers, on the other hand, remembered many more details about the students, but they did not differentiate the importance of the various pieces of information given to them.

Selectivity is also observed in the interactive teaching of expert teachers. Just as chess masters do not consider a large number of possibilities for the next move but only the good moves, expert teachers do not consider a large number of alternative routines when the lesson does not go according to what has been planned. In most cases they consider only one alternative routine (Shavelson and Stern, 1981).

In terms of the kind of events to which expert and novice teachers attend, novice teachers were found to attend more to student behavior, especially behavior that they consider to be unruly, and consequently, events related to the achievement of instructional objectives were given less attention (Veenman, 1984; Copeland, 1987; Sabers et al., 1991). By contrast, expert teachers were more concerned about instructional objectives. They were keen to maximize time on-task, to make sure that students were engaged in meaningful activities, and to minimize off-task time. Hence, they tended to ignore minor interruptions and inattention, and to attend to only major disruptions (Reynolds, 1992). Nunan's study (1992) showed that compared to inexperienced ESL teachers, experienced ones made twice as many decisions relating to language and focused significantly more on content than on classroom processes. Fogarty et al. (1983) found that in expert teachers' reports of the cues that led them to make interactive decisions, few pertained to students' disruptive behavior. This was partly because they ignored disruptive behavior and partly because they were able to prevent disruptive behaviors by picking up behavioral cues and taking action accordingly (Westerman, 1991; see also Reynolds, 1992). This suggests that the selectivity demonstrated by teachers is a reflection of their perception of what a classroom should be like (Peterson and Clark, 1978).

From the above findings, we can see that expert teachers are not only more *efficient* in recognizing meaningful patterns and making sense of multiple events, they are also more *selective* in attending to classroom events. In fact, the latter could be a reason for the former. They are better able to differentiate important from unimportant information and events through their experience. This frees their capacity to attend to the more important ones. Their criteria for selection are often governed by the instructional goals of the lesson and better student learning. As Berliner (1994, p. 182) points out, "Expertise, apparently, lets us process less, rather than more, of the information available from the environment, thus allowing more efficient use of the very limited working memory system that all of us possess."

3.2.2 Improvisational skills

The characteristics of expert teachers that we have discussed so far, efficiency and selectivity in making sense of and attending to classroom events, are very much related to the demands made on teachers as a result of the simultaneity and the multidimensionality of classroom events. The immediacy and unpredictability of classroom events require that teachers be able to respond to them very quickly, to improvise when the events are unpredicted, and to be flexible and ready to change their plans when need arises. Borko and Livingston (1989), using the metaphor of improvisational performance, propose that teaching not only involves cognitive skills but also improvisational skills.

Expert and novice teachers were found to differ in their ability to improvise. Borko and Livingston (1989) reported that in their study of mathematics teachers, expert teachers were able to use student responses and questions as springboards for further discussion and keep the lesson on track at the same time. They were able to maintain a balance between student-centeredness and content-centeredness. They were also able to generate on-the-spot examples and mathematical problems for illustration and clarification of concepts. By contrast, novice teachers had difficulties maintaining the direction of the lesson when responding to student questions. They also had problems with questions that were unplanned. Consequently, they decided to curtail questions so that they could get through what they had planned, despite the fact that they valued responsiveness to students. In other words, instead of modifying their plans to suit students' needs, novice teachers suited their own needs by ignoring the students (see also Westerman, 1991; cf. Nunan, 1992). Doyle's study (1977) of "successful" and "unsuccessful" teachers found that one strategy that the latter developed to simplify the complexity of the classroom environment was to localize attention to one region of the classroom and to engross students in one activity at a time. It seems that the novice teachers in Livingston and Borko's study, by not responding to students, were trying to reduce the complexity of the classroom by just focusing on their own delivery of content to students.

Many studies have pointed out that the reason why expert and experienced teachers are able to respond very quickly to classroom events and to improvise is because they have developed repertoires of routines for handling a variety of situations. As mentioned before, the use of routines is a very important part in interactive teaching; it creates and manages the learning environment (Doyle, 1986; Brophy and Good, 1986). Hence, like experts in other professions, the use of routines frees up mental resources of expert teachers so that they can deal with other nonroutinized aspects of teaching. Routines have often been taken as procedures that teachers pick up as they gather experience and in which there is very little thinking involved. This is probably because teachers are often unable to give a well articulated account of what is embedded in the routines that they use and why they use them. However, as Olson (1992) argues, "Teachers may not be able to give a well articulated, propositional account of their practice. But complex ideas about how to teach are embedded in the familiar routines of the classroom" (p. 55). Routines are realizations of teachers' conceptions of how life in the classroom should be structured to facilitate student learning. They are by no means thoughtless.

3.2.3 Problem representation and problem-solving

Just as experts in fields like physics and social science can represent and solve problems that are guided by principles (Chi, Feltovich, and Glaser, 1981; Chi et al., 1988), expert teachers are able to analyze and interpret classroom events and problems in a principled way and provide justifications for their suggestions for alternative practices. Peterson and Comeaux (1987) presented ten pairs of experienced[5] and novice teachers with three classroom scenes and asked them to describe the scenes, to analyze the problems that the teacher faced during interactive teaching, and to suggest alternatives. The findings showed that experienced teachers' analyses of classroom events reflected a knowledge of classroom procedures and principles of effective classroom teaching. They also provided justifications for their comments. For example, one of the experienced teachers commented on a teacher returning an essay test by pointing out that the teacher could read the essay aloud if it was a good one, or make some comments on errors made, or clear some misconceptions.

---

5 The term *experienced teacher* is used interchangeably with *expert teachers* in Peterson and Comeaux's paper.

This teacher said, "You can use the test as a learning experience rather than just hand it back, to put away, or throw away probably" (p. 328).

Novice teachers, by contrast, gave simple comments with little justification (see also Kagan and Tippins, 1992). As Berliner (1994) points out, the teacher's comment reflected the teacher's understanding of the pedagogical principle that tests can be used for teaching and learning and not just for evaluation purposes. He reported that in one of his expert-novice studies, when teachers were asked to respond to scenarios about educational problems associated with gifted children, they found that the responses from expert teachers' representations of the problem were much more sophisticated and principled. For example, one of scenarios described Mark, an eight-year-old Asian boy who had hearing problems but liked mathematics, science, and who had a strong interest in computers. In response to this scenario, novice teachers gave superficial responses like "Mark seems like a very talented individual with many diverse interests" and "Mark should be encouraged by his teacher to continue his science experiments and work on the computer." By contrast, one of the expert teachers wrote, "Mark's needs can be broken into three broad areas: academic enrichment, emotional adjustment, and training to cope with his handicap" (p. 175). Berliner pointed out that the sophisticated problem representation by the expert teacher was necessary for effective problem solving.

3.2.4 *Characteristics of expert and novice teachers in the interactive phase*

From the studies reported in the above discussion, we can see that the characteristics, identified in the expert-novice comparative studies, which differentiate expert teachers from novice teachers are quite similar to the characteristics which differentiate experts and novices in other domains. The first characteristic is *efficiency* in processing information in the classroom. Like experts in other fields, expert teachers are able to make sense of and recognize patterns in a large quantity of simultaneously transmitted information within a short period of time. The second characteristic is *selectivity* in processing information. Similar to expert chess players who are selective in processing only the good moves, expert teachers are more selective in information processing, and they often consider student learning the most important criterion for selection. The third characteristic is the ability of expert teachers to *improvise*. Expert teachers are better able to respond to student needs and classroom events that require decisions and actions because they have well-established routines, which they can call upon to respond to a variety of unanticipated events. Like experts in other domains, expert teachers attend to a larger number of important events in the classroom because of automaticity resulting from the use of routines. The fourth characteristic is that expert teachers' representation and analysis of problems are deeper and principled. Like experts in physics who used principles of mechanics to organize categories, expert teachers are able to offer interpretations and solutions that are guided by principles.

While these characteristics seem to be a convincing description of what expert teachers are capable of doing, how far do the cognitive processes identified capture the teaching act and the nature of teachers' work in the classroom? How far do these characteristics highlight *critical* differences between expert and novice teachers?

3.3 Knowledge Schemata

In the review of studies on teachers' cognitive processes in the preactive and interactive phases teaching, references have frequently been made to the knowledge base of expert and novice teachers. Teacher knowledge is very much understood from the perspective of cognitive psychologists who used the term *schema* to describe the way knowledge is stored in memory (see, for example, Anderson, 1977; Rumelhart, 1980). For example, Livingston and Borko (1989, p. 37) observe:

...the cognitive schemata of experts typically are more elaborate, more complex, more interconnected, and more easily accessible than those of novices.... Therefore, expert teachers have larger, better-integrated stores of facts, principles, and experiences to draw upon as they engage in planning, interactive teaching and reflection (see also Peterson and Comeaux, 1987; Borko and Livingston, 1989; Westerman, 1991; Leinhardt et al., 1991).

The characteristics of expert and novice teachers that have been identified in the research literature are believed to be related to their "knowledge schemata."

Expert teachers' ability to interpret, recognize meaningful patterns in, and make sense of multiple classroom events is attributed to their better-developed schemata for classroom events than novice teachers (see Peterson and Clark, 1978). Expert teachers' better recall of classroom events and their more principled ways of analyzing and solving problems are considered to be caused by their more-complex knowledge schemata (see Peterson and Comeaux, 1987). Peterson and Comeaux further argue that it is this knowledge schemata that affect teachers' perception and understanding of classroom events, the students, and their problem-solving, as well as decision-making in interactive teaching.

The rich and elaborate schemata of expert teachers are also considered to be crucial in helping them determine the relative importance and the relevance of information to their planning and teaching (see Carter et al., 1987). This is why they are able to attend selectively to information that is crucial to teaching. By contrast, novice teachers' schemata are still being developed in the process of decision-making. Therefore, they are less able to determine whether the information is relevant, and they consider much more information before they make decisions in both planning and teaching. Consequently, they are less efficient in both processes (see Livingston and Borko, 1989, p. 39).

The more sophisticated knowledge schemata of expert teachers are also used to account for improvisational skills. According to Livingston and Borko (1989), to improvise successfully, teachers need to have an extensive network of interconnected, easily accessible schemata from which they can select particular strategies, routines, and information in interactive teaching. Novice teachers have difficulties improvising when the lesson deviates from their plan. This, Livingstone and Borko explain, is because they do not have as many "appropriate schemata for instructional strategies to draw upon," nor do they have "sufficiently well-developed schemata for pedagogical content knowledge to enable the construction of explanations or examples on the spot" (ibid.). The extensive network of strategies and routines that expert teachers possess also enables them to plan more efficiently than novice teachers.

It is indisputable that expert teachers have much richer knowledge of all aspects of their work as a teacher than novice teachers. As Bereiter and Scardamalia (1993) point out, there are no experts who lack expert knowledge of their fields. However, does teacher knowledge consist of structured facts that are stored in individual teachers' memory and can be retrieved and accessed as necessary? Or is teacher knowledge embedded in the very act of teaching, which is highly context specific? How far does the concept of "knowledge schemata" accurately capture the nature of teacher knowledge, and how it is developed?

Many of the expert-novice studies focused on the management of the classroom or the more generic aspects of teacher behavior, such as pacing, questioning, explanation, or qualities like clarity and enthusiasm (see Ball, 1991; Brophy, 1991). They were relatively less focused on the "management of ideas" in the classroom (Shulman, 1987, p. 1) until Shulman's call for attention to teachers' subject matter knowledge in 1986 (see 4.1.4). As Shulman points out, both emphases are necessary.

The lack of attention to the knowledge of expert teachers until recently is partly because much of their knowledge is tacit. Very often, experts themselves are unaware of the knowledge that they have. Even if they are aware of it, they are unable to articulate it, as pointed out above. Unlike performance in the classroom, the knowledge that is embedded in it is not observable and often very difficult to tease out. The lack of attention is also partly because teachers have never been seen as possessing a body of professional knowledge (see Chapter 4 for a detailed discussion). Yet, as Bereiter and Scardamalia (1993) point out, understanding teachers' knowledge and how it is developed as they live through their experiences is crucial to the understanding of expertise.

3.4 Summary

In this chapter I have summarized the characteristics of novice and expert teachers as reported in studies of teaching expertise. Most of these studies compare the cognitive processes of expert and novice teachers, looking mainly at teacher planning in the preactive phase and teacher thinking and decision making in the interactive phase. The findings replicate to a large extent the common features identified in expertise studies in other domains, particularly those that adopted the information processing approach. Expert teachers are more efficient in planning and more selective in information processing. They are also able to recognize meaningful patterns quickly. They demonstrate more autonomy and flexibility in both planning and teaching. Because they have a large repertoire of routines on which to rely, they are able to improvise and respond to the needs of the students and the situation very quickly. The automaticity that is made possible by the availability of these routines allows them to direct their attention to more important information. Similar to experts in other domains, these characteristics of their cognitive processes are very much related to their sophisticated knowledge schemata and knowledge base. (See Berliner, 1994, for a discussion of the similarities between expert teachers and experts in other domains.)

A review of these studies shows that like expert-novice studies in other domains, the focus has been very much on what experts can do that novices cannot. The findings provide valuable insight into the complexities of teaching and the tacit knowledge that teachers gain through experience. However, like many expertise studies, there are relatively few studies that address the question of how expertise is developed and the ways in which their knowledge development differs from less experienced and novice teachers.

4 *Teacher Knowledge*

In Chapter 3, I outlined findings of studies on novice-expert teacher comparisons. I pointed out that these studies were heavily influenced by the information-processing model in cognitive psychology, and that though the features of expertise in teaching identified were commonly found in expertise studies in other domains, I questioned whether these studies accurately captured the way teacher knowledge is held and developed. I also pointed out the lack of attention being paid to the subject content aspects of teacher knowledge. In this chapter, I shall focus on approaches to investigating teacher knowledge, which are fundamentally different from the information processing model, and discuss the insights that they provide for investigating teachers' lives, teachers' knowledge and how it is acquired.

One of these approaches focuses on teacher knowledge as personal, practical, and tacit knowledge developed in the course of engaging in the teaching act and responding to the context of situation. It is very much influenced by the work of philosophers. Studies adopting this approach focus on teachers' personal understanding of the practical situations in which they work and how their professional knowledge is embedded in and developed through their daily practices. Another approach takes an anthropological perspective on teacher knowledge. It sees teacher knowledge as situated in the specific context in which teachers operate. It focuses on the characteristic features of the environment in which teachers work and the knowledge so developed. These studies are mostly interpretive case studies involving close analyses of teachers' own interpretation of their work and classroom events. A third approach examines the domains of teacher knowledge and focuses in particular on teachers' subject matter knowledge and the effective representation of this knowledge to students, referred to as pedagogical content knowledge. It adopts an analytical approach and sees teacher knowledge as more formal and propositional than personal and practical. Studies of teachers' pedagogical content knowledge focus on the relationship between teachers' subject matter knowledge, the quality of their instruction and the curricular decisions that they make. They include empirical studies as well as case studies involving interviews and intensive classroom observations. In the last section of this chapter, I shall present a reconceptualization of teacher knowledge and a framework for interpreting and understanding teachers' everyday practices and the knowledge embedded in these practices.

4.1 Teacher Knowledge as Reflective Practice and Personal Practical Knowledge

4.1.1 "Knowing how" and "tacit knowing"

The study of the knowledge held by teachers as a distinctive kind of knowledge which is fundamentally different from scientific or technological knowledge (considered systematic, rigorous, and objective), is very much influenced by the work of philosophers like Gilbert Ryle and Michael Polanyi. Ryle (1949) was the first one to point out that the distinction made between "knowing how" and "knowing that" is a misconstrual of the nature of knowledge (p. 29) and that to say that the former is an application of the latter is a misrepresentation of what happens in practice.

Polanyi, a scientist-turned-philosopher, explored human knowledge from the starting point that "we can know more than we can tell" (1966, p. 4) An example that he gave was knowing a person's face and being able to recognize it among thousands of people, and yet not being able to tell how one can recognize this face. He argues that this kind of *tacit* knowledge is an indispensable part of all knowledge, and that the declared aim of modern science to establish a strictly detached, objective, and formalized knowledge is misleading. Knowledge of theory, he observes, cannot be established until it has been interiorized and extensively used to interpret experience, and true knowledge lies in our ability to use it. Echoing Ryle (1949), Polanyi asserts that the more intellectual and the more practical kinds of knowledge do not exist independent of each other. Moreover, the explicit formalization of knowledge cannot replace its tacit counterpart. For example, he maintains:

> The skill of a driver cannot be replaced by a thorough schooling in the theory of the motorcar; the knowledge I have of my own body differs altogether from the knowledge of its physiology; and the rules of rhyming and prosody do not tell me what a poem told me, without any knowledge of its rules. (p. 20)

He used the term *knowing* to cover both theoretical and practical knowledge (p. 7).

4.1.2 "Knowing-in-action" and "reflection-in action"

One of the most influential works on studies of teacher knowledge and teachers' work is that of Schon (1983). Schon's conception of professional knowledge was very much influenced by the work of Polanyi (1966). In his work, *The Reflective Practitioner* (1983), Schon heavily criticized the view of professional knowledge expounded in the Technical Rationality model, which perceives professional knowledge as having four essential properties: specialized, firmly bounded, scientific, and standardized (p. 23). Hence, professions like medicine and law are considered "major" professions because they are grounded in systematic, rigorous, scientific knowledge or technological knowledge based on science. Professions like social work, librarianship, and education are considered "minor" professions because they lack such a knowledge base (Glazer, 1974). Professional knowledge is seen as consisting of a hierarchy of three components: the highest level is the underlying principle or basic science component, followed by an applied science component, from which diagnostic procedures and problem-solutions are derived. The lowest level is a skills component, which is the application of the underlying basic and applied science to actual performance (Schein, 1973). Hence, the more basic and general the knowledge, the higher the status of people who possess that knowledge. This hierarchical separation is reflected in the curricular pattern of professional education, which usually starts with a common science core, with the skills component, often called practicum or clinical work, occurring later.

Schon argues that this is a misconception of what professionals do. He points out that while it is true that there is a "high, hard ground" where practitioners can apply rigorous, research-based theory, there is also "a swampy lowland where situations are confusing 'messes' incapable of technical solution." (Schon, 1983, p. 42). In the world of practice, according to Schon, problems of great human concern are often not in the former but in the latter. Practitioners often find themselves in situations that are highly complex and fraught with uncertainty, instability, uniqueness, and value conflict (ibid., p. 39). They cannot simply apply research-based theory to problem-solving because problems do not present themselves as given. They have to identify the problem by making sense of situations that are ill-defined, messy, and full of uncertainties. Even when the problem has been identified, they may find that the problem is unique, so that they cannot solve it by applying established theory or technique. According to Schon, those who involve themselves in messy but important problems of great human concern often describe their methods of inquiry as "experience, trial and error, intuition, and muddling through" (ibid, p. 43). Following Polanyi, he proposes that what professionals do in their workaday life is "knowing-in-action," that is, their skillful practice reveals a kind of knowing that does not stem from a prior intellectual operation (ibid., p. 51). Echoing Ryle's (1949) conception of "knowing how," Schon points out that knowing and action are not two separate things but one; that is, the knowing is in the action itself. This kind of "knowing-in-action" is tacit.

Schon's conception of professional knowledge focuses on how professionals develop this kind of knowledge. He points out that although "knowing-in-action" is intuitive and automatic, practitioners do engage in reflection in two ways: they reflect-on-action and reflect-in-action. The former takes place when they reflect on what they have done or what they have experienced, often in order to prepare themselves for future actions. The latter takes place during the action, especially when they encounter situations which are unanticipated, problematic, or unique, and they arrive at a new way of looking at a phenomenon or a problem, hence generating a new understanding which leads to immediate action. The process of generating new understanding is called "reframing." Schon argues that when a practitioner is engaged in this kind of reflective process, he or she becomes a researcher in the practice context, and the knowledge acquired in this process is a legitimate form of professional knowing, which is rigorous in its own right (ibid., p. 69). The distinction that Schon makes between reflection-in-action and reflection-on-action, as Eraut (1994) points out, is more theoretical than real. When real examples are examined, it is difficult to draw the line between the two and the distinction disappears.

To the extent that professional knowledge is tacit and intuitive, and that professionals engage in reflection when they encounter unanticipated, problematic situations, Schon's conception of professional knowledge is similar to the position that Dreyfus and Dreyfus take with regard to expertise. However, insofar as Schon's conception of reflection as playing a central role in professionals' development of knowledge, he parts company with Dreyfus and Dreyfus.

4.1.3 Personal Practical Knowledge

One of the earliest systematic studies of teachers' knowledge is Elbaz's (1983) study of a very experienced high school teacher, Sarah. The study was motivated by the basic assumption that practical knowledge exists and that the nature and defining characteristics of this knowledge can be understood by examining teachers' everyday practices and the thinking behind these practices, and by getting teachers to tell stories about their teaching. Elbaz is not interested in whether Sarah is instructionally effective or whether her actions are predicted by theory. Rather, she is interested in what Sarah knows about her work, how she understands it, and how she uses her knowledge in carrying out her tasks as a teacher.

The study of Sarah led Elbaz to conclude that teachers hold a special kind of knowledge in distinctive ways. She refers to this kind of knowledge as *practical knowledge* because, according to her, the term "focuses attention on the action and decision-oriented nature of the teacher's situation, and construes her knowledge as a function, in part, of her response to that situation" (p. 5). This kind of knowledge is oriented to a particular practical context and social context, and is highly experiential and personal. Elbaz summarizes her conception of teacher's practical knowledge as follows:

> This knowledge encompasses first hand experience of students' learning styles, interests, needs, strengths and difficulties, and a repertoire of instructional techniques and classroom management skills. The teacher knows the social structure of the school and what it requires, of teacher and student, for survival and for success; she knows the community of which the school is a part, and has a sense of what it will and will not accept. This experiential knowledge is informed by the teacher's theoretical knowledge of subject matter, and of areas such as child development, learning and social theory. All of these kinds of knowledge, as integrated by the individual teacher in terms of personal values and beliefs and as oriented to her practical situation, will be referred to as 'practical knowledge' (1983, p. 5).

According to Elbaz, the above description includes five categories of knowledge, which reflect differences that are relevant to teachers: knowledge of subject matter, which includes not only knowledge of the subject discipline that the teacher is teaching, but also theories related to learning; knowledge of the curriculum, which refers to the structuring of learning experience and the curriculum content; knowledge of instruction, which includes classroom routines, classroom management, and student needs; knowledge of self, which includes knowledge of individual's characteristics such as one's own personality, age, attitudes, values and beliefs, as well as personal goals; and knowledge of the milieu of schooling, which refers to the social structure of the school and its surrounding community. These five categories of knowledge, according to Elbaz, are static. However, their relationship with the world of practice is dynamic. They shape practice, but they are also shaped by practice. They constitute "knowledge *of* practice" and "knowledge mediated *by* practice" (p. 47).

While Elbaz sees teacher's knowledge as intuitive and tacit, and less accessible in formally articulated and codified form, nevertheless, she sees deliberative process and intuitive and reflective processes as equally important. She argues that "deliberative process is the main way in which practical knowledge is examined in terms of its adequacy of particular problems, but intuitive and reflective processes that focus on general issues, goals, and beliefs are likely to be equally important for some teachers" (p. 15). Influenced by the work of Dewey (1938) and phenomenologists (for example, the work of Alfred Schutz, 1962–73; Schutz and Luckman, 1974), Elbaz sees a close interrelation between theory and practice. However, instead of taking knowing and action as one and the same thing, and theory as embedded in action, Elbaz considers teacher knowledge as not just knowledge of how to do things, but also knowledge that has propositional content. In other words, for her, there is a distinction between procedural knowledge, the "knowing how," and declarative knowledge, the "knowing that." She sees Schwab's (1969) call for the conceptualization of teacher's work in practical terms inadequate as a characterization of teachers' practice because teachers' actions are *informed by theory* rather than divorced from it. The "theoretical orientation" of the teacher's knowledge, however, is an implicit theory of knowledge which informs his or her practical knowledge (p. 21).

From the above discussion, we can see that Elbaz's approach to teacher knowledge was to bring together two opposing perspectives of knowledge, the empiric-analytical perspective, which sees knowledge as declarative; and the phenomenological perspective, which sees knowledge as procedural. What she tried to do, according to her, was to develop a way of studying teacher knowledge that "acknowledges the importance of theory while firmly situated in practice" (p. 23).

While Elbaz's work emphasizes the *practical* aspect of teacher knowledge in the sense of knowledge as a function of a teacher's response to the situation, the work of Clandinin and Connelly emphasizes the *personal* aspect of teacher knowledge, and refers to it as "personal practical knowledge." They argue that this kind of knowledge is "personal" because it is derived from a person's narrative, and it is "practical" because it is aimed at meeting the demands of a particular situation (see p. 185).

Adopting an experiential philosophical approach, Clandinin and Connelly see teacher knowledge as experiential and embodied in the narratives of a teacher's life (see Clandinin and Connelly, 1987). Therefore, they seek to understand the personal practical knowledge of teachers through teachers' narratives.

Our best understanding of teacher knowledge is a narrative one.... In this view of teachers' knowledge, teachers know their lives in terms of stories. They live stories, tell stories of those lives, retell stories with changed possibilities, and relive the changed stories. In this narrative view of teachers' knowledge, we mean more than teachers' telling stories of specific children and events. We mean that their way of being in the classroom is storied: As teachers they are characters in their own stories of teaching, which they author. (Connelly and Clandinin, 1995, p. 12)

Different from Elbaz, Connelly and Clandinin perceive teaching not as the application of theory; but as the *unification of theory and practice* through what they referred to as the "narrative unities" of experience of the teacher.

Narrative unity is a continuum within a person's experience which renders life experiences meaningful through the unity they achieve for the person. What we mean by unity is a union in a particular person in a particular time and place of all that has been and undergone in the past and in the past of the tradition which helps to shape him. (Connelly and Clandinin, 1985, p. 198)

According to Clandinin, in the stories that teachers tell and retell, live and relive, the "images" that they use are a powerful means by which their perception of work can be understood. An image embodies "a person's experience, finds expression in practice, and is the perspective from which new experience is taken" (1986, p. 166). For example, one of the images that was used by their teacher, Stephanie, was "classroom as home," and it was expressed in the way she tried to enhance a homelike environment of the classroom by making and displaying cookies in the way that she would at home. This image emerged from her early learning and teaching experience in which there was a lack of closeness. It also emerged from her home, school, and professional experience, which contributed to her perception of the classroom as a place to "live" and where her pupils felt comfortable and cared for.

The characterization of teachers' knowledge as "personal practical knowledge" is best summarized by Clandinin as follows:

It is knowledge that reflects the individual's prior knowledge and acknowledges the contextual nature of that teacher's knowledge. It is a kind of knowledge carved out of, and shaped by, situations; knowledge that is constructed and reconstructed as we live out our stories and retell and relive them through processes of reflection (1992, p.125).

4.2 Teacher Knowledge as Situated Knowledge

In the discussion of the conception of teacher knowledge as personal practical knowledge in the preceding section, frequent references have been made by researchers to the situated nature of teacher knowledge. The conception of teacher knowledge as "situated knowledge" is influenced by an anthropological and psychological approach to knowledge, notably in the works of Lave (1988) and Lave and Wenger (1991), which see knowledge as contextually developed as practitioners respond to the specific context in which they operate. It is diametrically opposed to conventional theories of action, knowledge, and learning in which context is seen as the container in which other things are placed, knowledge is a collection of real entities that reside in the head, and learning is a process of acquiring existing knowledge. For Lave, learning and participation in social practice is one and the same thing, and learning and knowing is an "engagement in changing processes of human activities" (1993, p. 12).

Lave's (1988) conception of knowledge as "situated knowledge" emanated from her study of everyday social practices. For example, in studying the practice of mathematics in a variety of common settings, such as in grocery shopping in the supermarket and in test situations, she observed that the same people responded differently in different settings: the problem was defined differently and the answers so developed were different.

The relationship between the problem and the answer is a dialectical one in that "the problem was defined at the same time as an answer developed during the problem." Problem and answer both "took form *in action* in a particular, culturally structured setting, the supermarket" (p. 2) (see also Lave et al., 1984; Scribner, 1984). Hence, she argued against taking cognition as something constant and stable held by the individual whereas the contexts in which they operate are specific and variable. Instead, she maintains that "persons-acting, arenas, activity appear to be implicated together in the very constitution of activity" (p. 170). In other words, the conventional division between the mind and body no longer exists, and setting, activity, and mind are connected through their constitutive relations with "the person-acting" (ibid., p. 181). A more appropriate unit of analysis should, therefore, be "the whole person in action, acting with the settings of that activity" (ibid., p. 17).

The notion of "situated knowledge" has been adopted by a number of researchers as a way of understanding teachers' work and their professional knowledge. Leinhardt (1988) investigated expert teachers' use of situated knowledge in selecting and using examples to explain elementary mathematical concepts. She found that just as in other forms of situated knowledge that is contextually developed, teacher knowledge is developed in the specific context of the school and classroom setting. And just as the former tends to make use of the characteristic features of the context when coming up with solutions, the knowledge that is embedded in the teaching act makes use of the features of the teaching situation, such as who the students are, what the classroom is like, the physical environment of the school, the time of the year and even the time of the day. In other words, this kind of knowledge is "embedded in the artifacts of a context" (p. 148). She observes that in dealing with the teaching task and in solving problems, teachers often use situated knowledge rather than "generative knowledge" which is context-free, principled, and can be generalized across situations because the former seems to be more accurately and flexibly used and more effective in helping learners learn and in solving problems than the latter. Yet, this kind of knowledge has been seen as rather low level, limited, and inelegant. Leinhardt points out that "we can learn much about the art of teaching if we seriously consider the nature of the environment in which teachers work and reason" (ibid., p. 147).

In this section I have discussed conceptions of teacher knowledge that have been influential in the teacher education literature. I have also discussed the different theoretical antecedents of these conceptions. I have shown that though they have different emphases, they share some common views about the nature of teacher knowledge. All of them see teachers as possessing a specialized kind of knowledge that is distinctly different from scientific or technological knowledge. It is knowledge that is very much embedded in teachers' daily teaching practices, oriented to the particular situation in which it arises and is often not articulated. While Elbaz and Connelly and Clandinin are interested in the kind of teacher knowledge that is embedded in teachers' narratives, stories, and images, Schon and his followers are interested in how teacher knowledge is developed through reflection and reframing. Leinhardt and researchers working with the notion of situated knowledge are interested in understanding the teaching act as a joint constitution of the context and the teacher-acting. The emphasis of practical knowledge is very much on the personal experiential knowledge of teachers as manifested in teachers' practical rules and principles, routines, rhythms, and images. The emphasis of knowing-in-action and reflective practice is on understanding teacher knowledge developed not only through experience but also on reflection, particularly when they come across problematic situations. The emphasis of situated knowledge is on the dialectical relationship between context and knowledge. These researchers provide perspectives for understanding teachers, teacher knowledge, and teaching in ways that are fundamentally different from studies of teacher expertise conducted so far. In the following section, we shall discuss yet another approach to teacher knowledge that is largely conceptual and analytical but which has been no less influential.

4.3 Teacher Knowledge as Content Knowledge[1]

Different from the conceptions outlined above, which emphasize the situated and experiential nature of teacher knowledge, Shulman's theory of teacher knowledge is conceptual and analytical (see Shulman, 1986; Wilson, Shulman, and Richert, 1987). Shulman points out that questions regarding how teachers' understanding of the subject matter affects the quality of their instructions, how teachers transform their knowledge of subject discipline into a form that is comprehensible to students, how teachers deal with faulty curriculum materials, and how they use their subject knowledge to generate explanations and representations, are central to teaching and that these questions have been neglected by researchers of practical knowledge. Wilson, Shulman, and Richert (1987) maintain:

---

1 The term *content knowledge* is used in the sense of Shulman (1986), which includes subject matter knowledge and pedagogical content knowledge, as opposed to pedagogical knowledge. In the teacher knowledge literature, the term *subject matter knowledge* sometimes encompasses pedagogical content knowledge, and sometimes refers strictly to knowledge of the discipline. In this book the term *subject matter knowledge* is used in the latter sense. Subject matter knowledge for teaching will be referred to as pedagogical content knowledge.

...by emphasizing the practical and to some extent, idiosyncratic knowledge that teachers use, these researchers present a truncated conceptualization of teacher knowledge. Teachers have theoretical, as well as practical, knowledge of the subject matter that informs and is informed by their teaching; any portrait of teacher knowledge should include both aspects." (p. 108)

Shulman (1986) refers to the neglect of subject matter in the various research paradigms for the study of teaching as the "missing paradigm."

In their necessary simplification of the complexities of classroom teaching, investigators ignored one central aspect of classroom life: the content of instruction, the subject matter. This omission also characterized most other research paradigms in the study of teaching. Occasionally subject matter entered into the research as a context variable – a control characteristic for subdividing data set by content categories.... But no one focused on the subject matter content itself. No one asked how subject matter was transformed from the knowledge of the teacher into the content of instruction. Nor did they ask how particular formulations of that content related to what students came to know or misconstrue. My colleagues and I refer to the absence of focus on subject matter among the various research paradigms for the study of teaching as the "missing paradigm" problem. (1986, p. 6)

To address questions relating to the "missing paradigm," Shulman and his colleagues at Stanford University launched a research program on "Knowledge Growth in Teaching," in which they studied the knowledge development of novice secondary teachers in English, science, mathematics, and social studies in the year of teacher preparation and the first year of their teaching. (For some of their studies, see the collection of papers in Brophy, 1991.) Shulman proposed for investigation a theoretical framework that distinguished among three categories of content knowledge: subject matter content knowledge, pedagogical content knowledge, and curricular knowledge. Subject matter knowledge includes the knowledge of the content of a subject discipline, that is, the major facts and concepts in that discipline and their relationships (see Grossman, 1990). It also includes its substantive and syntactic structures (Schwab, 1964). The substantive structures of a discipline refer to "the explanatory frameworks or paradigms that are used to guide inquiry in the field and to make sense of data" and the syntactic structures are "the canons of evidence that are used by members of the disciplinary community to guide inquiry in the field. They are the means by which new knowledge is introduced and accepted into that community" (Grossman, Wilson, and Shulman, 1989, p. 29). According to Shulman, teachers' knowledge of the explanatory or interpretive frameworks used in a discipline and how to conduct inquiry in that discipline has an important influence on their curricular decisions and how they represent the content and the nature of the discipline to the students. Pedagogical content knowledge refers to the representation of a subject by the use of analogies, examples, illustrations, explanations, and demonstrations in order to make it comprehensible to students. In order for a representation to be effective, teachers need to understand what makes a particular topic easy or difficult for students, what their preconceptions and misconceptions are, and what strategies are effective in dealing with their misconceptions. Curricular knowledge refers to knowledge of the programs and available materials designed for the teaching of particular topics at a given level. Subsequently, Shulman and his colleagues added four more categories of teacher knowledge: general pedagogical knowledge, which is knowledge of principles and skills of teaching and learning that are generally applicable across subjects; knowledge of educational aims, goals, and purposes; knowledge of learners, including knowledge of learners' characteristics and cognition, their learning development and motivation; and knowledge of other content, that is, content that is outside the scope of the subject that they are teaching. They suggest that teachers draw upon all these seven categories of teacher knowledge when they make decisions about their content teaching (see Wilson, Shulman, and Richert, 1987).

Shulman's conception of teacher knowledge has been very influential, and a number of studies have been conducted based on this conception, emphasizing especially the role of subject matter knowledge and its relation to pedagogical content knowledge. It is interesting to note, however, that Shulman was not the first one to propose that subject matter knowledge is an important component of teacher knowledge (see Carlsen, 1991), nor is he the first one to make a distinction between subject matter knowledge and pedagogical content knowledge, although the latter is his coinage (see Grossman, 1990). In expounding her conception of "practical knowledge," Elbaz (1983) specifically points out that "the teacher's subject matter knowledge, no less than other areas of her knowledge, is practical knowledge, shaped by and for the practical situation" (p. 55). Elbaz illustrates this point with data from her teacher, Sarah, to show how her knowledge of learning skills affected the way she organized the Learning Course that she directed, and how her knowledge was modified in the process of teaching (see also Buchmann, 1984). The distinction between subject matter knowledge and the specialized knowledge of subject matter for teaching dates back to Dewey (1902), who points out that a scientist's knowledge of the subject matter is different from the specialized understanding of the same subject matter by the teacher who is concerned with "how his own knowledge of the subject matter may assist in interpreting the child's needs and doings, and determining the medium in which the child should be properly directed" (p. 286).

Despite the fact that Shulman's conception is not revolutionary, it has made a strong impact on the study of teacher knowledge. This is probably because it was proposed at a time when most of the empirical research on teaching focused on generic aspects of teaching and neglected specific subject matter content (see Ball and McDiarmid, 1990). The lack of attention to subject matter content was partly due to the fact that earlier empirical studies, referred to by some as the "presage-product" research, failed to show significant correlation between teachers' subject matter knowledge and students' achievement (see Dunkin and Biddle, 1974). One reason for the lack of correlation is the way subject matter knowledge and student achievement were inadequately understood and assessed in these studies. Teachers' subject matter knowledge was assessed by the number of hours that they had taken in a subject, their grade point averages, and their scores in standardized achievement tests. Student achievement was assessed by standardized tests, all of which were inadequate indicators. Another reason for the lack of correlation is the erroneous assumption that the relationship between teacher knowledge and student achievement is linear; that there is a one-to-one correspondence between what teachers know and how much students learn (see Grossman, Wilson, and Shulman, 1989). By making a distinction between subject matter knowledge and pedagogical content knowledge, and by pointing out that successful teaching requires not just subject matter knowledge, but also pedagogical content knowledge, Shulman has offered a convincing explanation for the lack of correlation between teacher knowledge and student achievement in the earlier studies, and has reinstated the role of subject matter knowledge in teachers' professional knowledge base. He has persuasively argued that it is inadequate to discuss pedagogical skills without looking at the content of what is being taught, just as it is inadequate to discuss subject matter without looking at how it is being taught. The interrelationship between the two has been expounded by Wilson, Shulman, and Richert (1987) as follows:

Successful teachers cannot simply have an intuitive or personal understanding of a particular concept, principle, or theory. Rather, in order to foster understanding, they must themselves understand ways of *representing* the concept for students. They must have knowledge of the ways of transforming the content for the purposes of teaching. In Dewey's terms, they must 'psychologize' the subject matter. In order to transform or psychologize the subject matter, teachers must have a knowledge of the subject matter that includes a personal understanding of the content as well as knowledge of ways to communicate that understanding, to foster the development of subject matter knowledge in the minds of students. (p.110)

Subsequent to Shulman's call to search for the "missing paradigm," there have been a number of studies on how subject matter knowledge affects the process and quality of teaching. Studies have been conducted on mathematics teaching (see, for example, Ball, 1991), science teaching (see, for example, Hashweh, 1987; Smith and Neale, 1989; Carlsen,

1991; Munby and Russell, 1991), English teaching (see, for example, Grossman, Wilson, and Shulman, 1989; Grossman, 1990), and history teaching (see, for example Wilson, and Wineburg, 1988). However, the number of studies of the knowledge base of expert and novice teachers is relatively small (see, for example, Leinhardt and Smith, 1985; Leinhardt and Greeno, 1986; Leinhardt, 1989; Leinhardt et al., 1991; Gudmunsdottir and Shulman, 1989; Wineburg and Wilson, 1991).

Studies of the subject matter knowledge of teachers found that in preactive planning, teachers with less subject matter knowledge followed the textbook's structure closely, whereas those with more subject matter knowledge not only rejected the textbook's structure but were able to offer alternative organizations. They were better able than the former to detect ill-articulated themes and unimportant concepts, more ready to discard activities not essential to the development of the theme and to enrich and expand activities that develop the theme (see Hashweh, 1987; Lantz and Kass, 1987; Reynolds, Haymore, Ringstaff, and Grossman, 1988; Wilson and Wineburg, 1988).

In interactive teaching, teachers who had better subject knowledge were observed to be able to help students make conceptual connections, provide appropriate and varied representations, and construct active and meaningful dialogs with students. Teachers with limited knowledge were found to present the subject as a collection of static facts. Their subject representations consisted of impoverished or inappropriate examples and analogies. They also tended to emphasize seat work assignments and routinized student input as opposed to meaningful dialog. They might even overutilize rules, which can lead to misunderstandings (see Stein, Baxter, and Leinhardt, 1990). More knowledgeable teachers were also observed to be more likely to detect students' preconceptions and correct them, to deal with students' difficulties, and to exploit opportunities for useful digressions. By contrast, less knowledgeable teachers might reinforce misconceptions, incorrectly criticize students' correct answers, and accept erroneous results. The examination questions of more knowledgeable teachers required synthesis of ideas and higher intellectual processes, whereas those of less knowledgeable teachers were mainly recall questions (see Hashweh, 1985).

Less-knowledgeable teachers were also found to use a variety of strategies such as avoidance strategy. For example, in Grossman, Wilson, and Shulman's study (1989), the English teachers avoided teaching grammar whenever possible because they lacked knowledge of grammar. Their lack of knowledge also affected the style of their instruction. They resorted to straight lecturing to avoid student questions. For example, one English teacher in Grossman's study, because of her lack of confidence in grammar, went over the grammar homework review very quickly and avoided eye contact with her students so that they would not have the opportunity to ask what she perceived to be difficult questions (see Grossman, 1987, cited in Grossman et al., 1989).

The above studies show that teachers' disciplinary knowledge often has a decisive influence on the process, content, and quality of their instruction. Wilson and Wineburg (1988) further observe that the lack of knowledge in a particular discipline not only compromises the quality of teachers' instruction, but also limits their ability to learn and understand that particular discipline. In these studies, the discussions of subject matter knowledge were inextricably linked with teachers' representation of subject matter. Some studies have shown that although subject matter knowledge is necessary for successful teaching, it is not sufficient. For example, Munby and Russell's (1991) case study of a secondary chemistry teacher who had worked for eleven years as a research technician in chemistry showed that while the teacher's knowledge of chemistry enabled her to give clear, precise and accurate instructions, she was unable to show how each part of her instructions was related to the unit being taught and how forthcoming material was conceptually related to the material just taught. Nor was she able to provide opportunities for students to pursue the steps to solve problems independently. By contrast, her experience with laboratory work generated practical knowledge about managing laboratory work with her students. Her classroom teaching was in stark contrast to her laboratory sessions.

Indeed, in studies of the knowledge of expert and novice teachers, it is the different ways in which they represent subject matter knowledge to students that distinguish experts from novices. Leinhardt and her colleagues at the University of Pittsburgh investigated the following aspects of the teaching of novice and expert teachers: their activity structures and routines, their organization and content of subject matter knowledge, their lesson plans, goals and actions for teaching a particular topic, explanations, and representations (see Leinhardt and Smith, 1985; Leinhardt and Greeno, 1986; Leinhardt, 1989; Leinhardt et al., 1991). These studies show that expert teachers' reported mental lesson plans were detailed, rich, and demonstrated an awareness of critical points in content learning. Their lessons were characterized by fluid movement from one type of activity to another, with transparent goals and cohesive structures. Their explanations were clear and well-connected, and their lessons worked as an integrated whole. Their subject matter presentations were characterized by multiple-representation systems which were carefully selected, taking students from the familiar to the unfamiliar. They were able to introduce the total topic gradually by manageable bits and by careful judgment of the amount of repetition and practice that were needed. Novice teachers' lessons, by contrast, were characterized by fragmented lesson structures with ambiguous goals that were often abandoned. Their lessons did not fit together within or across topic boundaries. No steps were taken to ensure that students had the necessary procedural skills to handle the steps of a new procedure, and hence students were often taken from the unfamiliar to the unfamiliar. Novice teachers' explanations were not well connected, and they made mistakes that confused students conceptually. They also lacked the analytic skills to understand where failure occurred and when implicit goals were not achieved. Leinhardt (1989) suggested that the differences could be due to novice teachers' lack of a cohesive schema for a lesson and their lack of sufficient subject matter knowledge to be flexible when teaching. However, she also observed that although the novice math teachers in the study showed significant subject matter knowledge, they did not seem to be able to access it when teaching. Her summarizing statement on expertise, made on the basis of her data, shows the centrality of not only a sound knowledge base in subject matter but, more importantly, its effective representation.

Expertise is characterized by speed of action, forward-directed solutions, accuracy, enriched representations, and rich elaborations of knowledge in terms of depth and organizational quality. (p. 94)

Gudmunsdottir and Shulman (1989) investigated the teaching of social studies by a novice and by an expert teacher with thirty-seven years of teaching experience, both of whom had expert content knowledge in their disciplines. They observed that these two teachers differed in two respects. First, the expert teacher had developed a comprehensive overview as well as a clear point of view about the subject matter, whereas the novice teacher had not. Second, while the expert teacher had plenty of opportunities to re-define his content knowledge to construct pedagogical content knowledge, the novice teacher did not. The expert teacher knew a number of ways of segmenting and structuring the curriculum and was aware of the pros and cons of each approach. The novice teacher, by contrast, knew only one way and could only visualize one unit at a time. Gudmunsdottir and Shulman (1989, p. 33) summed up the difference as follows:

The most dramatic differences between the novice and the expert are that the expert has pedagogical content knowledge that enables him to see the larger picture in several ways, and he has the flexibility to select a teaching method that does justice to the topic. The novice, however, is getting a good start in constructing pedagogical content knowledge, starting small, and progressing to seeing more and larger possibilities in the curriculum, both in terms of unit of organization and pedagogical flexibility.

Wineburg and Wilson (1991) examined how two expert history teachers transformed their knowledge of history to make it accessible to students. They observed that these two teachers used diverse methods to convey their subject matter knowledge, including examples, analogies, demonstrations, role-plays, stories, and debates. All of these methods, however, shared the common feature of functioning as a bridge between the teacher's sophisticated understanding and the developing understanding of the students. They remarked that it was in the pedagogical content knowledge of these teachers that their expertise was best seen. Wineburg and Wilson concluded that

> Knowledge of subject matter is central to teaching but expert knowledge of content is not the singular determinant of good teaching.... Both teachers possess rich and deep understandings of many things, understandings that manifest themselves in the ability to draw from a broad range of pedagogical possibilities. In fact, it may be their very ability to alternate between different modes of teaching that earns them the designation "wise practitioner." (1991, p. 336)

The above studies show that understanding the knowledge bases of expert and novice teachers, particularly their pedagogical content knowledge, is crucial to understanding expertise in teaching. Grossman (1990), drawing on various models of teacher knowledge, especially Shulman's model, proposed four general areas of knowledge as the cornerstones of professional knowledge for teaching: general pedagogical knowledge, subject matter knowledge, pedagogical content knowledge, and knowledge of context. In her model, pedagogical content knowledge is presented as a central component that interacts with the other three components of knowledge. In addition to Shulman's conception of pedagogical content knowledge, which includes knowledge of students' existing knowledge, misconceptions, and preconceptions about the subject matter and effective means of representing the subject matter, Grossman adds knowledge and beliefs about the purposes for teaching a specific subject discipline at a specific level and knowledge of the curriculum as important subcomponents of pedagogical content knowledge.

To summarize, the studies of teachers' content knowledge reported above show that central to successful teaching is pedagogical content knowledge, which is the transformation of subject matter knowledge into forms of representation that are accessible to learners. The transformation process requires an adequate understanding of the subject matter, knowledge of learners, curriculum, context, and pedagogy.

4.4 Reconceptualizing Teacher Knowledge

4.4.1 Teacher knowledge domains

In the studies of teachers' content knowledge reviewed in the previous section, there seems to be a consensus that teachers' subject matter knowledge is something that can be clearly identified as such, and that it can be set apart from other components of teacher knowledge. However, this view has been questioned by various researchers. McNamara (1991) observes that subject matter knowledge is inextricable from pedagogic content knowledge. Calderhead and Miller (1986) maintain that the distinction between procedural knowledge and subject matter knowledge is often made, but it is more analytical than real. In their study, the student-teachers in primary schools indicated that they found subject matter knowledge useful and mentioned the ways in which it helped them to plan lessons, to diagnose pupils' difficulties, and to respond to pupils' questions and unexpected classroom events. However, these student-teachers never referred to their subject matter knowledge or their degree studies in their planning protocols, nor did they mention it in interactive stimulated recall and student assessment. Calderhead and Miller suggest that student teachers' planning could be influenced *indirectly* by their subject matter knowledge, but it is doubtful whether subject matter knowledge influences their practice through conscious processing. They point out that the categories of teacher knowledge provide a useful analytical framework for thinking about teaching, but in the complex task of teaching the boundaries between these knowledge bases may be less easily distinguishable and less meaningful because they constantly intermesh in practice (see also Bennett, 1993). Grossman herself, despite her categorization of teacher knowledge, cautions that the components of teacher knowledge are less distinct in practice than in theory (see Grossman, 1990).

Similarly, Feiman-Nemser and Parker's (1990) study of the conversations between experienced teachers and novice teachers found that although subject matter concerns permeated the tasks of teaching, teachers rarely spoke directly about the meaning of the subject content. Subject matter was always discussed in relation to students' thinking and understanding and in relation to classroom management and organization. The suggestions given by most of the experienced teachers often reflected an integration of knowledge of subjects with knowledge of students, contexts, curriculum and pedagogy. As Feiman-Nemser and Floden point out, "in practice, teacher's knowledge functions as an organized whole, orienting the teacher to her situation and allowing her to act" (1986, p. 513; see also Eraut, 1994). It is the melding of these knowledge domains that is at the heart of teaching (see McDiarmid, Ball, and Anderson, 1989).

4.4.2 General pedagogical knowledge and pedagogical content knowledge

Discussions of teacher knowledge and classroom practices often make a distinction between general pedagogical knowledge and pedagogical content knowledge. While it is true that there are pedagogical principles and skills that are general to the teaching of all subject disciplines (for example, taking roll-calls, collecting homework, and so on), much of the so-called general pedagogical skills are governed by the specific subject content being taught. For example, classroom organization, which is often considered a kind of general pedagogical skill, is very much governed by the specific curriculum content of each lesson or unit for a specific grade level, and even for a specific class. For example, in an ESL speaking skill lesson, a teacher is likely to organize students to work in pairs or groups in order to maximize the opportunities for speaking. However, if the teacher is introducing phonetic symbols for the first time, it is likely that there will be a fair amount of lockstep teacher-fronted instruction so that the teacher can demonstrate how the sounds are produced. In other words, how the classroom should be organized and managed in order that student learning will be maximized is inextricably linked to teachers' knowledge of the subject matter. The so-called general pedagogical skill, which should be more appropriately referred to as the *management of learning*, is as much part of pedagogical content knowledge as the effective representation of the subject matter being taught, which can be referred to as the *enactment of the curriculum*.

4.4.3 Pedagogical content knowledge as integrated and situated

Another consensus that is implicit in the discussion of teachers' content knowledge is that pedagogical content knowledge is a separate component and that it interacts with other components of teacher knowledge (see Grossman, 1990). However, if pedagogical content knowledge is the effective representation of subject matter knowledge to learners, as Shulman puts it, it involves not only an understanding of the content itself, but also an understanding of the learners, their preconceptions and misconceptions, and the teaching strategies for dealing with them, as well as the specific contexts in which the teaching takes place. Hillocks (1999) argues that the categories of knowledge do not exist as separate entities from which teachers draw when designing and planning their curricula; they interact with each other. I would argue that pedagogical content knowledge, which is central to the teaching act, is an *integrated* and coherent whole. This kind of knowledge is situated and practical because it is closely tied to the specific context of the classroom and is embodied in teachers' classroom practices.

4.4.4 Understanding teacher knowledge: Teachers' metaphors, images, and beliefs

It has been suggested that very often teachers' knowledge can be better understood through the metaphors that they use or the images that they have formed of teaching. These metaphors and images are often derived from their past experiences, which shape their understanding of social situations (see Lakoff and Johnson, 1980). For example, Bullough, Knowles, and Crow (1992) found that one of the teachers in their case studies adopted the metaphor of "policeman" to give coherence of meaning to his experience of managing a class of students with behavioral problems and the teaching role that he was expected by the school to embrace. Another one of their teachers used the metaphor of "rescuer" to represent her understanding of her role as taking caring of students and protecting them from failure in order to build up their self-esteem. This metaphor was derived from her childhood experience of being "rescued" from a miserable home by her teachers. Grant's study (1992) of three teachers of different content subjects found that they used different metaphors to represent their thinking about the teaching of their subjects. The physics teacher used the metaphor of "magicland" to represent the excitement that science can offer to children. The history teacher thought of history as a "game" in which students could see historical events from different perspectives. The English teacher used the metaphor a difficult "journey" to represent the hard work but the gratifying outcome in the learning of literature (p. 433). As Schon (1979) points out, the metaphors that we use encapsulate the way we think about and make sense of reality as well as the way we come to see the world in a certain way. They are therefore a powerful tool for understanding teacher knowledge.

Closely related to teachers' metaphors are their images of teaching. Clandinin (1986) suggests that teachers' "images," such as "classroom as home" and "language as the key" are powerful ways of summarizing the way they think about their classroom. The term *images* has also been used to refer to the way teachers seem to have organized their knowledge (see for example, Johnston, 1990). It has been pointed out that student-teachers and beginning teachers start out with images of what teaching is like and should be. They may have positive or negative images of teaching, which are often influenced by their past experiences, especially their experiences in schools. More experienced teachers' images, on the other hand, are influenced by their own experiences at work and at home. These images permeate their practical experience in the classroom and shape their understanding of their work as teachers and their classroom practices (see Calderhead and Robson, 1991; Johnston, 1992; Powell, 1992).

Another notion that is often used in relation to explications of teacher knowledge is "teacher beliefs." In the teacher education literature, beliefs are equated with knowledge by some (see for example Kagan, 1990), or not easily distinguishable (see for example Calderhead, 1996) and considered distinct from knowledge by others. This is because of the different interpretations of the nature of teacher knowledge. If knowledge is perceived as propositional in nature and dependent on truth conditions, then it is distinct from beliefs because the latter do not have truth value and do not have to be agreed on as being true by a community of people (see Feiman-Nemser and Floden, 1986; Lehrer, 1990; Richardson, 1996). However, if teacher knowledge is considered as personalized, idiosyncratic, and highly context specific, as in teachers' "personal practical knowledge," then there is considerable overlap between the two, though they are not synonymous (see for example Elbaz, 1983; Clandinin and Connelly, 1987). Teacher beliefs have been given a great deal of attention in the teacher education research literature because of their important role in helping teachers to make sense of the complex and multidimensional nature of classroom life, to identify goals, to prioritize actions to be taken (see Nespor, 1987), and to shape their evolving perceptions of themselves as teachers (Johnson, 1994).

The term *belief* has been used together with terms such as *assumptions, conceptions, personal theories* almost interchangeably. They have been considered by some researchers as inextricable (see Pajares, 1992). Woods (1996), for example, proposes a hypothetical concept of "an integrated network" of beliefs, assumption, and knowledge (referred to as BAK) on the basis that they can be "posited in terms of interrelated propositions" in the sense that "certain propositions presuppose others" (p. 196). This network, he argues, affects the way a teacher interprets teaching events and hence the teaching decisions that are made. Similarly, Wood and Bennett (2000) subsume skills, experiences, beliefs, memories, and assumptions under teacher knowledge. They propose that such knowledge influences the way teachers construct their learning environment and curriculum tasks.

In this book, teachers' metaphors, images, beliefs, assumptions, and values are subsumed under a more general notion of teachers' conceptions of teaching and learning. Research on teacher learning has pointed out that the conceptions of teaching and learning held by teachers have a powerful influence on their classroom practices, what and how they learn (see for example, Calderhead and Robson, 1991; Richardson, 1994; Yung, 2000). In the studies reviewed in this chapter, we have seen many examples of how teachers' personal assumptions, values, and beliefs filter through to their classroom practices and the way they define problems and manage dilemmas in the classroom.

Connelly and Clandinin (1994) point out that teachers' personal values and beliefs are very much shaped by their personal experiences. Therefore, in understanding teachers' classroom practices and the knowledge embodied in these practices, it is important to understand their conceptions of teaching and learning and the sources of influence that shape such conceptions.

One often mentioned source is what Lortie (1975) refers to as an "apprenticeship of observation." Lortie points out that all teachers have had the experience of being a student, and this experience often provides them with an image of what teaching is and, in some cases, what teaching should be like. This source of influence is particularly strong for teachers who join the profession without professional training and hence have nothing but their past experience to fall back on, even when the experience was unpleasant (see also Brookhart and Freeman, 1992; Calderhead and Robson, 1991; Johnston, 1992).

Grossman (1990) points out that a further dimension of influence resulting from an apprenticeship of observation is that teachers' memories of themselves as students often shape their expectations of students as well as their conceptions of how students learn (see also Feiman-Nemser and Buchmann, 1986). For example, teachers often compare what their students are like now with what they themselves were like when they were students and expect the former to behave similarly.

Another source of influence is the academic background that teachers have. Studies on teachers' subject matter knowledge have focused on how the quality of teaching was compromised when teachers were educated in subject disciplines other than the one that they are teaching (see the review of studies of teachers' subject matter knowledge in the earlier sections of this chapter). However, little has been said about how their own disciplinary backgrounds affect their personal beliefs and values and how they in turn filter through to their conceptions of teaching and learning. For example, a teacher with a social science background may have beliefs and values that are quite different from a teacher with a science background.

A third source of influence is teachers' own teaching experience. It has been repeatedly pointed out in research on teacher education that teachers consider classroom experience the most important source of knowledge about teaching (see, for example, Lanier and Little, 1986; Anning, 1988).

The fourth source of influence is the personal life experience of teachers which shapes their "substantial self" (Nias, 1984), which is the person that they bring into the classroom context. Bullough, Knowles, and Crow (1992) believe that beginning teachers often enter preservice courses with partial but firmly held conceptions of themselves as teachers and a teaching schema that is developed over years of life experience (see also Lyons, 1990). These conceptions not only influence the way they begin to teach, but also act as life-long references for their identity as teachers (see, for example, Goodson, 1992a; Bell and Gilbert, 1994; Raymond, Butt, and Townsend, 1992). As Goodson (1991) points out, "Life experiences and background are obviously key ingredients of the person that we are, of our sense of self. To the degree that we invest our 'self' in our teaching, experience and background therefore shape our practice" (p. 144). It is this personal dimension that is being emphasized in Connelly and Clandinin's conception of teacher knowledge as personal practical knowledge. In recent years a number of studies have been conducted on teachers' lives and biographies and their roles in teacher development (see, for example, the studies collected in Goodson, 1992b; see Carter and Doyle, 1996 for a summary of studies in this area).

Despite the fact that teacher education courses have been criticized as a waste of time (Conant, 1963), studies of the interrelationship between teacher education courses and teachers' beliefs and classroom practices have shown such courses to be a source of influence. For example, Grossman's study (1990) showed that the three teachers with professional preparation shared striking similarities in their conceptions of teaching English. The importance of helping students to bring in their own experiences in understanding literature, using a process-oriented approach to writing, and providing scaffolding for students in literature and writing are three examples. All three teachers attributed their conceptions to the influence of the professional coursework that they attended. By contrast, the other three teachers with no professional preparation differ considerably in their conceptions of teaching English. For example, while one of them believes that teaching English is mainly an explication of literary texts, another one sees teaching English as communication. The kinds of influence that teacher education courses have on teachers' conceptions of teaching, however, are dependent on a multitude of factors (see Calderhead and Shorrock, 1997). Similarly, Borg (1998) found that the initial teacher training course had a powerful impact on the personal pedagogical system of an experienced EFL teacher, so much so that even negative classroom experience did not bring about change in his work.

To summarize, one can say that teachers have their own personal conceptions of teaching and learning, which are influenced by their personal life experience, beliefs and values, their disciplinary training, their teaching and learning experiences, and their professional training, if they have any. These conceptions have a powerful influence on the way teachers make sense of their work (see Calderhead, 1988). They may be changed or modified as teachers gain experience or as they encounter critical incidents that challenge them. They may also be very resistant to change. The interaction between teachers' knowledge, conceptions of teaching and learning, and the world of practice, is an important dimension that should be taken into consideration in understanding teacher knowledge.

4.4.5 Dialectical relationship between teacher knowledge and context

As I have pointed out before, many of the expert-novice studies reviewed in the previous chapter were based on information-processing theory, which assumes that the cognitive processes that teachers engage in take place in their minds and are independent of the context. However, as we have seen, philosophical and anthropological approaches to knowledge as well as ethnographic case studies of teachers' work and teachers' lives show that the knowledge that teachers develop is jointly constituted by the acting teacher and the context in which they operate. Lave (1988) points out that "A dialectical relation is more than a declaration of reciprocal effects by two terms upon one another.... A dialectical relation exists when its component elements are created, are brought into being, only in conjunction with one another" (p. 146). That is to say, teacher's knowledge and the practices in which it is embedded jointly constitute the context in which they operate, and this in turn is an integral part of the knowledge so constituted. As Putnam and Borko (1997) remark, "How a person learns a particular set of knowledge and skills, as well as the situation in which a person learns, become fundamental parts of what is learned" (p. 1254). Teachers' knowledge therefore must be understood in terms of the way they respond to their contexts of work, which shape the contexts in which their knowledge is developed. This includes their interactions with people in their contexts of work, where they constantly construct and reconstruct their understandings of their work as teachers (see also Grimmett, MacKinnon, Erickson, and Riecken, 1990). Freeman (2000) observes that "The knowledge that animates language teaching can – and needs to – be found within the activity of teaching itself and not beyond it, in work about teaching" (p. 1). By "the activity of teaching," Freeman is referring to "the teacher and learners as participants: to the ways in which they conduct their work together; to the background of that work; to the tacit norms and the explicit rules they evolve to do the work in the classroom, institution, and wider community; and to the tools they use to get the job done. All this together constitutes knowledge" (ibid.). In understanding teacher knowledge development, therefore, it is important to understand how teacher knowledge is jointly constituted by the contexts in which they operate and the way they perceive and respond to them.

The reconceptualization of teacher knowledge discussed in this section, that is, the integrated nature of teacher knowledge and its dialectical relation with context of work, as well as the powerful influence of conceptions of teaching and learning on teacher knowledge, will be used as an interpretive framework for understanding the knowledge that is embodied in the classroom practices of the four ESL teachers in the case studies.

4.5 Summary

In this chapter influential conceptions of knowledge and characterizations of teacher knowledge have been reviewed. Echoing Ryle (1949) and following Polanyi (1966), Schon (1983) sees professional knowledge as 'knowing-in-action' and emphasizes the nature of teacher knowledge being embedded in the teaching act which is tacit and often not easy to articulate. His characterization of the professional as the "reflective practitioner" highlights the importance of reflection in the development of professional knowledge and professional expertise. The characterization of teacher knowledge as practical knowledge by Elbaz (1983) emphasizes the practical dimension of teacher knowledge – practical in the sense of its being closely tied to the teachers' experience and the specific contexts of the classroom and in the sense of its action and decision-oriented nature. Similarly, the characterization by Connelly and Clandinin of teacher knowledge as personal knowledge emphasizes the importance of personal experience in shaping teachers' understanding of teaching and their stories of teaching. This personal dimension has also been pointed out by Elbaz, who sees the knowledge of self, which includes personal beliefs and values, as an area that integrates other areas of practical knowledge. Shulman's characterization of teacher knowledge as comprising various distinct components (the most important being subject matter knowledge and pedagogical content knowledge) brings in a different but complementary dimension of teacher knowledge that provides a useful analytical framework for understanding teaching. In the analysis of the teaching act, however, it is often difficult to distinguish among them.

All of the above characterizations of teacher knowledge perceive teacher knowledge as as related to the world of practice. Teachers' knowledge shapes their classroom practices, but their classroom practices in turn shape their knowledge, as they reflect on their practices during and after the action, and they come to a new understanding of teaching. This kind of reframing of teacher knowledge is particularly evident when teachers come across problems and puzzling situations.

Drawing on the insights provided by the various characterizations of teacher knowledge, this chapter draws attention to four aspects of teacher knowledge. First, teacher knowledge as manifested in teachers' classroom practices is often an integrated whole that cannot be separated into distinct knowledge domains. Second, teachers' personal conceptions of teaching and learning play a very important part in their management of teaching and learning. These personal conceptions are influenced by their personal life experiences, their learning experience, their teaching experience, their academic background, as well as the opportunities for professional development, including professional courses. Third, teachers' pedagogical content knowledge, which is embodied in the act of teaching, can be perceived as mainly two intertwined dimensions, the management *of* learning and the enactment of the curriculum in the classroom. Fourth, there is a dialectical relation between teachers' knowledge and their world of practice. As teachers respond to their contexts of work and reflect on their practices, they come to a new understanding of teaching and learning. The knowledge that they develop in this process constitutes part of the contexts in which they operate and part of their world of practice.

5 *The Case Studies*

The study reported in this book adopted a case study methodology. The case study approach is more about a unit of analysis than about data collection strategy. This study took as a unit of analysis what Lave (1988) refers to as the "whole person in action, acting with the settings of that action" (p. 17). It focuses on the ways in which the teacher, as "teacher-acting," following Lave's "person-acting" (ibid., p. 180), relate to their specific contexts of work, how they make sense of their work as a teacher, and how their knowledge, perceptions, and understanding of their work develop over time. It sees a dialectical relationship between teachers' contexts of work and the way teachers respond to them, which entails that the knowledge so constituted would be different. In order to make a rich and thick description of this situated knowledge, multiple case studies were used. Four ESL teachers teaching in the *same school* were selected for the study in order to highlight how teachers relate differently to what would be considered very similar contexts and how the knowledge can be constituted differently.

Yin (1994) points out that case studies do not aim at making generalizations about populations or universes, but rather at expanding or generalizing theoretical propositions. The study reported in this book does not aim to generalize how ESL teachers, as a population, develop expertise in teaching or how ESL teachers at different levels of expertise differ from one another. Rather, its aim is to explore the concept of expertise in teaching and to further our understanding of expertise as a process, using ESL teachers as cases for investigation. For each case study teacher, data is collected from a variety of sources and by a variety of means (see 5.3). From the data, key features and themes in individual cases are identified and used for cross-case analyses. The interpretation and discussion of the data are made in the context of the theoretical propositions that the study aims to generalize.

5.1 The Linguistic Context of Hong Kong

In order to understand the four case study teachers' lives and how they make sense of their work as ESL teachers, it is very important to bear in mind the larger context in which schooling is situated as well as the specific contexts in which teaching is situated. For the former, the linguistic context of Hong Kong is crucial. In Hong Kong, 96 percent of the population is Chinese, the overwhelming majority being Cantonese speakers (Tsui and Bunton, 2000). Only 1.3 percent are native-speakers of English (see Bacon-Shone and Bolton, 1998). In recent years there has been a steady increase in the percentage of the population who reported that they knew English well, quite well, and very well, rising from less than 10 percent in the early eighties to nearly 40 percent in the late nineties. English is used in most written business communications, and both English and modern standard Chinese are used in all official communications. However, English is not widely used for social interaction or for oral communication in business and government. For this reason, it has been argued that English is a foreign language rather than a second language in Hong Kong. However, because English is one of the official languages, even after the change of sovereignty in 1997, and is widely used in written communication, it is regarded as a second language. In Hong Kong, English has always been considered a prestigious and important language because of its role in business and international communication. The situation has not changed after 1997 although its role in government is not as important as before.

Before 1998 most of the secondary schools used or claimed to use English as a medium of instruction. In reality, most of the so-called English medium schools used a mixture of English and Cantonese for instruction when the teachers felt that their students could not follow the lessons in English. The use of mixed code in teaching was disapproved by education policy-makers on the ground that sustained use of mixed code by learners who are still trying to master the target language will prevent them from making the effort to express themselves solely in that language, hence adversely affecting their target language development. Consequently, in 1998, Chinese was mandated as the instruction medium for three quarters of the secondary schools which failed to demonstrate that their students had the ability to learn content subjects through English. Schools that were allowed to use English as the medium of instruction were required to observe strictly the rule of using only English in the classroom. In social interaction, however, mixed code is widely used. Most publicity materials are bilingual, and it is very common to see slogans written in mixed code. There are also Chinese and English television and radio channels. In other words, although English is not required for a wide range of communication purposes, it is not difficult to access materials in English.

5.2 The School Context

Marina, Ching, Eva, and Genie are four ESL teachers teaching in the same secondary school, St. Peter's Secondary School, in Hong Kong. A large number of schools in Hong Kong are run by religious orders, such as the Anglican Church, the Methodist Church, the Catholic Church, Buddhists, and Taoists. St. Peter's does not belong to any particular religious order but is run by a Protestant organization formed by a group of Protestants with a mission to spread the Protestant faith through education. Some of these schools give preference to teachers who are either Protestants or Catholics when making appointments. At St. Peter's, all teachers are Protestants, but they prefer to call themselves "Christians" because of the negative connotation associated with the word *protestant* historically. St. Peters is located in a relatively old housing estate, which consists of closely packed blocks of government subsidized public housing that charges very low rent for low-income families. The school is medium sized with twenty-four classes and slightly more than 900 students. It is one of the older school premises that is very small and compact. It consists of a T-shaped six-story building and an open-air playground where physical education lessons take place. Apart from the home classroom for each class, there are very few special purpose rooms and no activity rooms. The physical environment of the school is far from satisfactory. Like most classrooms in Hong Kong, the classrooms in St. Peter's are very small and can barely house thirty-six to forty desks put either in double rows or single rows, and a teacher's desk. There is one big staff room in the school, which houses most of the teaching staff, and a small staff room where the vice-principal and the head teacher for guidance and counseling sit. In the big staff room, each teacher has a small desk of three feet by four-and-a half feet on which textbooks, the students' exercise books and teaching materials were put. There are a few public bookshelves and three computers for common access at one end of the room. When teachers need to talk to students individually during recess or lunchtime, they usually have to do so standing in the corridor outside the staff room.

The majority of the students at St. Peter's come from the housing estate and are working-class children. Their parents have little education and do not speak English. Therefore, the students have very little exposure to English at home, and they seldom watch English television programs. They will not get support for their academic work from their parents. The banding[1] of the school is about two to three, which indicates

---

1 In Hong Kong, secondary schools are divided into five bands, with band one having students of highest academic ability and band five having students of lowest academic ability. Most schools have students of two consecutive bands. In 2001, the government merged five bands into three.

that the academic ability of the students is about average in the whole secondary school student population in Hong Kong. The school is an English medium school. When the study was conducted, the new policy for medium of instruction was not in place yet. Therefore, mixed code was prevalent in classrooms, except for English classrooms. Unlike middle-class children, the students of St. Peter's cannot afford to travel abroad for holidays. Therefore, the English classroom is almost the only place where they have exposure to English and where they are forced to use English for communication. Most students live in the housing estate where the flats are very small, ranging from three to five hundred square feet, with one or two bedrooms. They often have to share a room with their siblings and there is very little space to do their homework properly. The home environment is often very noisy at night because their parents and grandparents will have the television on for the whole evening. In other words, apart from not being able to get parental support, the home environment is also not conducive to academic study.

St. Peter's is well known for its supportive, collaborative, and collegiate culture. The school principal is very supportive of her staff and respects its professional judgement. She is always ready to make, or to allow her staff members to make, adjustments to their teaching schedules in order that they can pursue further professional development. She is highly regarded by her staff. The school has set up what they call a double class-teacher system, whereby each class is looked after by two class-teachers, one being an experienced teacher and the other a new teacher. Normally, one would expect the new teacher to be an assistant to the experienced teacher. In this school, however, the new teacher is given the responsibility of being a class-teacher with the assistance and guidance of an experienced teacher. In addition to the double class-teacher system, they also have an agreement among experienced teachers that they can be assigned to a new teacher for pastoral care if need arises. Since the majority of the teaching staff sit in one big staff room, experienced teachers are seated next to or near new teachers to facilitate interaction between new and old teachers.

5.3 The Four ESL Teachers

As mentioned at the beginning of this chapter, all four case study teachers are from the same school. In most schools in Hong Kong, teachers teaching the same subject form a "subject panel," and each panel is headed by a senior teacher, referred as the panel chair, who is responsible for the organization of teaching and assessment of a particular subject and for quality assurance. The expert teacher in this study, Marina, is the chair of the English panel (which is equivalent to a head teacher in schools in the United Kingdom, or the head of the English Department in the United States school system). The other three teachers are members of the English panel. All four teachers entered teaching with no professional training.

To understand the development of expertise in teaching, I focused on Marina, whom I first met when she enrolled in the in-service teacher education program at the University of Hong Kong, called the Postgraduate Certificate in Education program (PCEd). She was in her fourth year of teaching, and I was her tutor as well as her teaching practicum supervisor throughout the two-year program. Her performance in the course was outstanding, both in theoretical courses and in the practicum, and she graduated from the program with a distinction. All her course tutors considered her a teacher of great potential. In the second year of PCEd training, she was appointed chair of the English panel in St. Peter's after an inspection by the Education Department (the equivalent of the Ministry of Education). Marina and I have kept in touch since she graduated from the program. I invited her school to join a computer network, *TeleNex*, which I set up in the early nineties to provide professional support to ESL teachers in schools. She responded very positively and actively contributed ideas and materials to help other teachers on the network. She also shared her own problems and asked for advice with them. In the latter half of her sixth year of teaching, Marina attended a six-month refresher-training course organized by the Education Department. In her eighth year, she enrolled in a Master's program in ESL teaching at the university, and I was her course tutor again. (See Chapter 6 for a detailed account.)

Marina was identified as an expert teacher on the basis of the very positive comments on her as a teacher from her course tutors, her principal, her colleagues, and her students, as well as the reactions of fellow teachers on *TeleNex*. Having known Marina for five years and being well aware of the progress that she had been making professionally was another reason why she was selected as an expert teacher.

In order to understand the differences between an expert teacher and teachers who are in different phases of professional development and have attained different levels of teaching competence, I invited three teachers in Marina's school to join the study. When the study started, two of them, Ching and Eva, had five years' teaching experience and would be considered either proficient or competent teachers in the novice-expert literature. The fourth teacher, Genie, had only one year of teaching experience and was still very much a novice in the field. As mentioned at the beginning of this book, the data collection spanned a year and a half (see 1.3). Therefore, by the time the data collection was completed, Genie was already in the middle of her third year of teaching. I was therefore able to get her to talk about her professional development not only in the first two years but also the beginning of the third year as well. In the cross-case analyses, not only were they compared with Marina, but they were also compared with one another. This kind of comparison is very useful in furthering our understanding of what expertise in teaching means and its developmental processes.

5.4 Data Collection

A commonly used methodology in most expert-novice studies is to give novice and expert teachers vignettes of classroom events – either presented in writing, on slides, or on videotapes – and ask them to describe and comment on those situations and in some cases the corresponding actions that they would take. This method has the advantage of comparability because teachers are given the same stimuli that could be absent in data collected from real-life classroom teaching since each classroom is unique. However, a disadvantage is that teachers are either responding to fabricated classroom events (no matter how much they try to approximate real classrooms), or to other teachers' classroom events. Their analyses and solutions could be quite different if the events took place in their own classrooms when they had access to all the background information that is missing in these vignettes. Their knowledge of and relationship with the students would also be an important factor in their decision-making. (See also Copeland et al., 1994.)

Another commonly used methodology is to compare the cognitive processes of novice and expert teachers. The comparison is based on interviews conducted about their lesson planning and their reflections in postlesson observation interviews. Very often, "stimulated recall" (Bloom, 1954), in which teachers are asked to recall their thinking at specific points in the lesson, with the help of replaying the recordings of the lesson soon after is used. (See Clark and Peterson, 1986, for a brief summary of modes of inquiry in teacher thinking; and Calderhead, 1984, for the use of stimulated recalls for research on teacher thinking and their possible disadvantages.) Questions have been raised about teachers' verbal reports. Some point out that teachers' words may not accurately represent their thinking and understanding; others observe that teachers' reports may be post hoc rationalization of their behavior (see Yinger, 1986; Calderhead, 1996).

In this study data are collected by what Wolcott (1992) refers to as "watching," "asking," and "examining," that is, lesson observation, interviews, and curriculum materials including teaching plans, teaching materials, and students' work. Nonparticipant observations of real classroom teaching were conducted of these four teachers, following them through their teaching of one specific class. For the expert teacher,

Marina, the observation period spanned a period of three months during which every ESL lesson that she taught in S2 (grade 8) was observed and recorded. This enabled me to familiarize myself with the school environment and the students. It also allowed me follow her through two complete units of teaching, as well as to focus on specific areas of teaching that I am particularly interested in. For the other three teachers, Genie, Eva, and Ching, the observation period of their teaching spanned one complete unit, which lasted about a month. The rationale for conducting observation in this manner is twofold. First, a unit in their scheme of work includes all four language skills, grammar, and vocabulary teaching. It also includes any other aspects of ESL teaching that they consider important, for example, newspaper reading and reporting, and extensive reading. Following these teachers through at least one complete unit enabled me to gain a comprehensive picture of how they dealt with the ESL curriculum, the routines that they had established, and their repertoire of teaching strategies. Second, following these teachers through one specific class enabled me to see the extent to which they established continuity and integration among the various components in the curriculum, and the rapport that they established with their students.

The observations were video- and audio-recorded, supplemented by field notes, taken as I was observing the lessons, on aspects of the classroom that were likely to have been missed by the recorder. Because of the busy schedules of the teachers, it was impossible to interview them before and after their teaching for every single lesson. Therefore, the methodology adopted was a mixture of interviews and "conversations" as expounded in Woods (1985). Lengthy semistructured interviews lasting from forty-five minutes to one-and-a-half hours were conducted at regular intervals, about once a week. In between, whenever the teachers had a less busy day, I would grab ten minutes before class to ask them about their plans for teaching, and fifteen minutes after class to ask them questions about what was observed in the classroom. Occasionally, I made use of opportunities like giving them a ride home, having a soda with them during recess, eating our lunches, or walking them to another class and chatting with them while they were waiting for another teacher to wind up his or her lesson. After I got home, I recalled and recorded what we talked about and put it down in writing. In Marina's case, one of the interviews took the form of a recorded conversation in my home over Chinese New Year followed by lunch. Another took place in a restaurant.

The interviews adopted a progressive focusing approach (Woods, 1985). The first interview provided a general overview of the family background, life history of the teachers, and an overview of their teaching practices. The follow-up interviews zeroed in on issues and themes that emerged from the conversations. Issues that emerged from classroom observations were also brought up.

In addition to classroom observations and interviews, teachers' lesson plans, teaching materials, and student work were also collected and examined. I also had the privilege of attending and recording an ESL panel meeting at the end of the school year to review the implementation of process writing in the past year.

For Marina, semistructured interviews were conducted with her students to investigate the impact of her teaching on students' learning. Altogether there were six students in S5 (grade 11) who had been taught by her for 3 years. Five students in S2 (grade 8) were interviewed to investigate their reactions to her teaching, and their perceptions of good teaching. Marina readily agreed to these interviews because of the very comfortable and trusting relationship that we had established. Ideally, data should have been collected from the students of the other three teachers. However, I was aware that asking the students to talk about their teacher and their teaching, which inevitably involves evaluation of some sort, would be too threatening for these three teachers who I knew less well. Therefore, only informal conversations were conducted with students before and after the class to get a feel for the class as well as to establish rapport with them.

It has been pointed out that it is impossible for the researcher to obtain genuine data in research of this nature because the questions asked by the researcher are likely to cause the teachers to reflect and reorganize their thinking, hence "contaminating" the data. As Sabar (1994, p. 119) points out "obtaining teachers' knowledge from their stories entails some kind of intervention." This happened in my data collection process. For example, I asked Marina whether she thought of the class as a whole group or as individual students when she prepared a lesson. She replied that it was the former. In a subsequent interview she referred to the same question again and said that she had begun to think about specific students when planning lessons. While I accept that this is an inevitable limitation, this kind of "intervention" did not change the thrust of the data fundamentally as far as the present study is concerned.

5.5 Data Analysis

All interviews with teachers and students were conducted in Cantonese in order to eliminate any barrier created by a second language. The data were all transcribed and translated into English by research assistants and checked by me at least once to ensure that there was no distortion in the translation. In order to retain the flavor of what the teacher said, I tried to strike a balance between literal and semantic translation. It was only when literal translation affected the meaning of the utterance that the translation was modified syntactically and semantically.

Classroom recordings were transcribed verbatim and supplemented by field notes taken during observation which provided a wealth of information that could not be captured by even a video-recorder.

The analysis of the data was an ongoing process that was carried out in tandem with data collection. As soon as an interview was conducted or a lesson was observed, a rough preliminary analysis of the interview or the lesson was done and this often generated further unanticipated questions that were asked in subsequent interviews, or alerted me to certain phenomenon in the classroom to which I paid more attention in subsequent observations. Sometimes, further questions were generated even during an interview or a lesson observation. The whole process of data analysis was an emerging understanding of what I was learning about these teachers (see Rossman and Rallis, 1998). For each teacher, the interview data was analyzed initially to formulate a skeleton of their professional development, the key features in their classroom practices observed, and the knowledge embedded in these practices. The interpretive framework outlined in Chapter 4 (4.4) was used as the basis for making sense of the data. Salient features and themes describing their phases of professional development, conceptions of teaching and learning, sources of influences, and classroom practices were identified through repeated readings. An information tree outlining the phases of development and classroom practices were drawn and the transcribed texts were analyzed with the help of NUD*IST. A similar process was applied to the follow-up interviews, some of them without the help of NUD*IST. However, instead of letting the categories dictate the interpretation of data, I adopted a grounded approach and allowed the data to inform me with regard to whether the categories indeed captured what the data was telling me or whether any new themes and features emerged after each reading. Within-case comparisons were conducted to identify changes in teachers' perception of their work, and cross-case analyses were conducted to identify emerging common patterns. The analysis of data collected from one teacher often triggered a reanalysis of data from another teacher. In other words, the interpretation of the data was an iterative process in which interpretations were checked against a number of readings and "hearings" in the case of audio-recorded data and "watchings" in the case of video-recorded lessons. This often resulted in a new or a more enriched understanding of the data (see also Miles and Huberman, 1994).

The analyses, especially their stories about their own professional development, were given to the teachers for their verification of the accuracy of the information provided as well as the interpretation. Any gaps in information were filled in by the teachers themselves. The teachers were also asked to correct any misinterpretation of what they said in the interviews or misinterpretation of their work.

5.6 Ethical Issues

5.6.1 Being obtrusive

There were two phases in my data collection. The first phase, which focused on collecting data on Marina, involved being in the school every day for three consecutive months. The second phase of collecting data on the other three teachers involved being in the school every day for one month. I was fully aware of the obtrusive nature of being resident in a school for such a long time, especially when the school has a small campus and the staff room is already very crowded.

In order to be as unobtrusive as possible, I told Marina not to make any effort to give me space or to entertain me while I was visiting her. In the first phase I was not provided with a desk in the staff room, nor did I request one. When I was not observing lessons, I stayed in the playground and sat on benches with my laptop to write up my field notes and to formulate questions for follow-up interviews. During recess, I would chat with the students. In order not to disturb other teachers, interviews were conducted either in special rooms or on the playground. In the second phase, as I got to know a number of teachers in the school better, they made room for a small desk next to the computers for me to place my tape recorder and my laptop. I was able to stay in the staff room, and this gave me a feel for the atmosphere in the staff room and for the busy life teachers had in this school.

5.6.2 Teacher-researcher relationship

When collecting data, I was very much aware of treating teachers not as "subjects," but as "people" who have feelings, values, and needs (Elbaz, 1983). I was also mindful that the study, which requires teachers to make close self-evaluation, is very threatening, as Stenhouse (1975) points out, and that building up a relaxed, comfortable, and trusting relationship that can "transcend the roles and dissolve fronts" is crucial (Woods, 1985, p. 14). In the case of Marina, this did not pose a problem because we had known each other for a long time. For the other three teachers, however, I had to work on the relationships. In soliciting their consent to join the study, I had an initial conversation with each of them to explain the objective and the value of the study. Some researchers maintain that in order to minimize the effect of bias on the teachers, only part of the real objectives of the research should be revealed (see Sabar, 1994). However, I felt that it was literally impossible and even unethical to follow a teacher so closely and yet not disclose the aim of my research. I also felt that in order to understand teachers' thinking, their problems, and anxieties, as well as their developmental path, it was necessary to develop an equal relationship with them, to develop mutual trust and understanding with them. Therefore, after the teachers shared their life stories, the ups and downs in their career development, I reciprocated by sharing with them my family background, my learning experience as a student, and my anxieties as a schoolteacher in the past and as a university teacher at present. Sometimes, my own life accounts served as a "catalyst" which helped teachers to recall their past experience (see Woods, 1985, p. 16). As the research progressed, we became friends and they were willing to share private sides of their lives with me.

5.6.3 Reciprocity

Besides getting teachers to identify with the value of the research and establishing a trusting relationship with them, I was also aware of the need for the teachers to be able to benefit from their participation in this study. I gave them comments on their teaching and shared ideas and materials with them. In order not to contaminate the data, I made sure that the sharing would be confined to areas in which I had already completed the interviews and observations. This sometimes created problems. Genuine questions soliciting information were sometimes taken by the teacher interviewed as suggestions. For example, when I asked Marina, "Why didn't you give them the questions before you asked them to read the passage?" she responded, "Yes, maybe I should do that." This happened with the other three teachers as well. Whenever this happened, I immediately clarified the intention of my question as purely to obtain information. I also offered to pair up with a student when somebody was absent in class. When doing this, I tried to be as unobtrusive as possible and took the opportunity to get to know the student.

In short, the tools of my research were, in Elbaz's words, "shaped by the effort to regard the teacher as a person, to become aware of the reality of her work situation as she encountered it, and to give an account that was consistent with (though not identical to) her view of her work" (1983: 51).

5.6.4 Anonymity and interpretation

A study of this nature reveals a very private side of the lives of teachers, especially when trusting relationships develop between the researcher and each of the teachers. In each of the four cases, the teacher took me into her confidence and shared her problems with me. In some cases they specified that they did not want me to include the data in my analyses. To protect the teachers, I gave the teachers the analyses to read, particularly those pertaining to their life history and professional development, and asked for their consent in order to ensure that the study did not in any way compromise them or jeopardize their relationship with their colleagues, even with their family members, as well as their future prospects in their school. Since full credit could not be given to these teachers, I tried to make sure that at least the story is theirs rather than mine by asking them to indicate whether they agreed with my interpretation of their stories. When there were discrepancies between my interpretation and theirs, I always adopted the latter.

I preserved the anonymity of the teachers, the students, and the school by using fictitious names. In Hong Kong, English first names are commonly used. In order to preserve the cultural flavor of Hong Kong as a place where the east meets the west, when giving teachers and students pseudonyms, I used a Chinese pseudonym if they used their own Chinese names, and I gave them an English pseudonym if they used English names.

6 The Professional Development of the ESL Teachers

In this chapter I shall examine the professional development of the expert teacher, Marina, the two experienced teachers, Eva and Ching, and the novice teacher, Genie. In particular, Marina's development of expertise in teaching will be discussed in detail. In trying to capture the professional development of these four ESL teachers, I drew on studies of the teachers' professional and career development and in particular upon the findings of Huberman's (1993a) study of 160 Swiss teachers. When drawing on Huberman's as well as other researchers' delineation of the phases in teachers' professional life cycle, I adopted an open-minded approach and allowed the rich data to inform me of possible variations of the phases that they outlined. In the following section, I shall outline briefly their delineations before reporting on the four case study teachers.

6.1 Teachers' Professional Life Cycle

Studies of teachers' professional and career development have identified phases, sequences, or stages that teachers go through in the course of their careers (see for example Field, 1979; Burden, 1990; Fessler and Christensen, 1992; Huberman, 1993a). Typically, beginning teachers go through a "survival" phase where they are preoccupied with their own survival in the classroom. They feel diffident, inadequate, and ill-prepared. Some of the well-documented problems and concerns in this phase are those of reconciling educational ideals and realities, maintaining classroom discipline, establishing an appropriate relationship with students, playing the role of a teacher, and having an adequate mastery of knowledge as well as instructional methods (see also Fuller and Brown, 1975; Adams, 1982). Huberman (1993a) observes that it is also a phase of "discovery" where teachers are excited by the fact that they are now a teacher with their own students. The survival and discovery elements often go together, with one or the other being more dominant. He refers to this phase as "exploration" (p. 5).

Positive experience in the first phase usually leads to a phase of "stabilization," where teachers consolidate their experience from the first phase, gain confidence in teaching, and master teaching skills. They are more flexible in their classroom management and better able to handle unpredictable situations. This phase is marked by a move away from concerns about self to concerns about instruction and the impact of their instruction on students. In other words, teachers' focus changes from self to students (see also Field, 1979; Lightfoot, 1983). It is also in this phase that, typically, teachers become committed to teaching. Negative experience in this phase, however, could lead to a phase of self-doubt.

Following the stabilization phase, Huberman (ibid.) observes that some teachers go through a phase of "experimentation" and "diversification." Motivated by the wish to increase their impact in the classroom and to seek new challenges, they conduct personal experiments using different instructional methods and materials as well as a variety of classroom management skills (see Feiman-Nemser, 1983). Sikes, Measor, and Woods (1985) point out that teachers going through this phase are highly motivated, enthusiastic, ready to confront issues that they took for granted before, and to take on new challenges. This phase corresponds to what some teacher-development studies have referred to as a "renewal stage" where teachers look for innovation (Katz, 1972). As Sikes et al. (1985) observe, the desire to increase one's impact in the classroom often leads to a heightened awareness of problems with the system and the desire to go beyond their own schools to bring about change. For some teachers, disappointment with the outcome of reforms, particularly structural reforms, in which they have participated energetically, could lead to a phase of self-doubt and uncertainty with regard to one's commitment to teaching. For other teachers, this phase of self-doubt could follow the "stabilization" phase, which can be caused by factors like the monotony of classroom teaching and unpleasant working conditions. Huberman (ibid.) refers to this phase as "reassessment."

A phase of uncertainty or even a crisis can lead to another phase, or rather a state of mind, where teachers come to terms with themselves and hence have more peace of mind. They are less vulnerable to others' perceptions of them. This is a phase of "serenity" in which teachers speak of "being able to accept myself as I am and not as others would have me be." (Huberman, ibid., p. 10). It is marked by a decline in professional investment and enthusiasm, but also greater confidence, more tolerance, and spontaneity in the classroom. It is also a phase where teachers' relationship with students become more distanced, largely caused by the widening gap between themselves and their students (see also Lightfoot, 1983; Prick, 1986).

Some studies observe that a phase of "serenity" is followed by a tendency towards conservatism, which is characterized by resistance to and skepticism about innovation and change, increased complaints about students and colleagues, and a craving for the past (see Prick, 1986). In other cases conservatism follows a phase of self-doubt and results from reactions against failed attempts at structural reforms (see Huberman, 1993a). Though conservatism is closely related to age in most cases, the Swiss data in Huberman's study show that this is not necessarily the case; the most conservative teachers in his study were actually the youngest teachers.

Studies in human life cycles observe that near the end of a career, people disengage themselves from professional commitments and allow more time for their own personal engagements. Similarly, a phase of "disengagement" has been identified in teachers' career cycles. However, the disengagement can take the form of withdrawing and investing their time and effort elsewhere, as a result of disappointment with the system, or reconciling the discrepancy between what they had set out to achieve and what they have actually achieved. In Huberman's words, the disengagement can be "bitter" or "serene" (1993b, p. 110).

The phases of development outlined above, however, are not linear. As Huberman (1993b) points out, attempts to delineate teacher development as a discernible sequence of phases is problematic because they tend to ignore the factors such as personal experiences, social environment as well as organizational influences which shape teachers' development. Indeed, researchers have found that teachers move in and out of the various phases (see for example Fuller, 1969; Sprinthall, Reiman, and Sprinthall, 1996; Field, 1979). For example, Fessler and Christensen (1992) found that involvement in professional development and assuming new roles such as being a mentor teacher can result in teachers moving back into a phase of enthusiasm and commitment. Similarly, new problems can make a teacher lose self-confidence while success can have the reverse effect (see Field, 1979).

The question is: what are the factors that contribute to teachers' moving in and out of a certain phase of professional development, how can their professional enthusiasm be sustained, and why do some of them become expert teachers while others remain experienced nonexperts?

In studying the factors predictive of career satisfaction, Huberman (1993b) found that teachers who engaged in classroom-level experimentation were more likely to be satisfied with their career later on than those who were heavily involved in structural reforms. He identified three other factors predictive of career satisfaction. First, teachers who sought diversity in classroom teaching or a shift in roles usually attain a higher level of satisfaction. The diversity can be in the form of teaching higher grade students or teaching a different subject. Huberman observes, "...without recurring episodes in which the demands of the situation are slightly beyond one's existing repertoire, be it for children or adults, there is no development" (1993b, p. 112). Second, when teachers were asked to describe their "best years," they typically mentioned specific classes which they enjoyed teaching, where apathetic students became enthusiastic about learning, and where the class was constantly engaged in purposeful activities. He observes that career satisfaction was high "... when teachers felt 'pushed' or 'stretched' beyond their customary activity formats or materials and met this challenge through systematic revisions of their instruction repertoire" (1993b, p. 113). Third, significant improvement in students' learning because of one's efforts also contributes to teachers' job satisfaction. Huberman's observations were made from the perspective of career satisfaction. However, they strongly echo Bereiter and Scardamalia's (1993) theory of the development of expertise in teaching, which is central to teacher development. It is when teachers work at the edge of their competence that they develop their expertise. It is when they refuse to get into a rut and seek new challenges going beyond the "customary" that their performance becomes exemplary.

In the rest of this chapter I shall examine the professional development of the four ESL teachers in the light of Huberman's delineation of teachers' professional life cycle and Bereiter and Scardamalia's theory of expertise, and discuss the factors and sources of influence that have shaped their development.

6.2 Marina

Marina was in her early thirties and in her eighth year of teaching when the study started. She comes from a working-class family. Her father is a construction worker, and her mother is a housewife. She studied in a primary school in a housing estate where the students were all from working-class families. Her academic results were outstanding in the public examination for secondary school entrance. She placed first in all three key subjects in the primary curriculum in Hong Kong: Chinese, English, and Mathematics. She was the only one in her school who was able to get such good results and was awarded a government scholarship. She recalled having a teacher who was very kind to her and gave her a great deal of additional help. "I had a teacher who was very nice to me. She was not a good teacher; she used mixed code,[1] but she helped me. She gave me additional exercises to work on to help me. My primary school teachers liked me a lot and were very nice to me." Because of her

---

[1] "Mixed code" refers to using English and Cantonese in teaching, which is a common practice in many schools in Hong Kong because of students' limited ability in understanding instructions in English. The use of "mixed code" in teaching was frowned upon by the Department of Education (the equivalent of the Ministry of Education elsewhere) and it has made repeated attempts to stamp it out with little success.

good results, she entered a very prestigious secondary school where the majority of the students came from middle-class families and the medium of instruction and communication was English, even in school assemblies.

The first two years in this school were "very tough" for Marina. She described an "unforgettable" incident:

I remember an incident when I first entered St. John's [fictitious name]. It was in the assembly, I couldn't understand a single word that the principal was saying. I couldn't even understand her instructions to turn the book to a certain page. My classmate sitting next to me had to help me. That was unforgettable.

This experience was unsettling for her because all of a sudden, Marina, who used to be top of the class, had to be helped by her peers. She had to do something about it.

I felt that my English was inadequate. The school gave us a book list and I climbed to the fifth floor where the library was to look for books. The children's books were very nice; they weren't graded readers like what we have now, but books by Enid Blyton, C. S. Lewis. They are very thick. I often couldn't finish them because they were difficult to read. I didn't know about extensive reading, and I looked up every word that I couldn't understand. So I got through very few pages in two weeks' time and I had to return the books because the loan period was two weeks. Sometimes I renewed them and sometimes I returned them.

She started off by following the list of books recommended by the teacher and gradually she branched out and read a great deal, mostly fiction. Reflecting on her secondary-school experience, she observed that although it took her several months to get used to English medium instruction, it took her several years to build up her self-confidence. It was only in Secondary Three (grade 9) that she began to feel a bit more comfortable with English, and it was not until her preuniversity years that she felt confident about her English. What is interesting is that instead of congratulating herself on her own success, she remarked, "Now looking back, I think if I had read other types of books (apart from fiction), I don't know if it might have been better because my scope would be broader."

Marina did not have an English environment at home; her parents do not speak English. So in addition to reading voraciously, she tried to maximize the opportunities for learning English. She paid attention to the English around her, including the media, posters, labels, signage, and so on. She said, "To survive in St. John's, I have to work on my English." Marina's struggle for survival at St. John's had a strong influence on her conception of learning English and the strategies that she developed for teaching English, as we shall see in Chapters 7 and 8.

After St. John's, Marina entered Hong Kong University and took translation as her major discipline. Teaching had always been her aspiration since she was a child. Her image of teachers was that they should be kind to students and have authority. She remarked, as she puzzled over why she had always wanted to be a teacher:

...teaching has been my aspiration since I was a primary pupil. I don't know why. I wasn't like one who would become a teacher, I was a fierce child.... Maybe apart from my family, the school and teachers were people I had contact with most.

Upon graduation, she did not go into teaching immediately because she felt that she needed more work experience before entering the profession. Her first job was working in a government department. She did not like the job and left after a year. She explained why:

I didn't like it. It was very boring. It's all desk-work.... That year, they managed to double their staff size. There was not enough work to go round. So I had plenty of free time. There were only three days when I had to work. For the rest of the days, I just read newspapers and magazines. It was a very secure job but there was no job satisfaction. So I left.

She left the civil service and took on a fund-raising job in a hospital, out of interest rather than for its prospects. She had to contact a lot people and she found the experience enriching. However, there were a lot of office politics. So she left the job after a year and went into teaching at St. Peter's.

I saw in the papers that a Christian Hospital was looking for somebody to raise funds. In June I took on this new job.... There were no prospects in this job, but it was a very good experience. I had to contact people, and I learned a lot. But the personnel relationship was very complicated. [meaning "there was lot of office politics"]. I didn't like it. So my third job was St. Peter's.

Her experience of working in nonschool settings and dealing with people from different walks of life enabled her to handle problems better. She said:

I remember once I had a chat with my principal and we were talking about new teachers having problems adapting to the environment. She made a remark that when I first joined the school, she felt that I was better able to deal with "things," incidents, and students. This could be because of my past experience.

When Marina decided to go into teaching, her mother advised her against it because she felt that it was very tough going and that the longer she stayed in the profession, the harder she would have to work. When Marina applied for a teaching post in the school, she had no idea what it was like. Being a Protestant, she believes in having a religious element in teaching, and so she decided to join St. Peter's, which is a Protestant school.

6.2.1 Learning teaching

SURVIVING IN THE CLASSROOM AND RELATING TO STUDENTS

In the first two years of teaching, classroom management and her relationship with students were two recurring concerns for Marina. She said, "I felt that what was difficult was not dealing with the daily business of teaching, but dealing with students; how to help students tactfully and how to manage them in class." She elaborated on this:

> ... in my first year of teaching, I had problems dealing with students. Students do not respect new teachers (in general). I was OK with most of them, but some of them said I was unfair behind my back.... Some thought that I was lenient, but I was also sometimes very strict, particularly in handling disciplinary problems. They couldn't accept that.... For example, they told me that I tended to pick on a certain group of students when they talked in class, and did not pick on others who were also talking. As a teacher, I found it very difficult because it was impossible to keep an eye on the whole class all the time. But I might have done that unconsciously.

Like all new teachers, she found it difficult to handle the multiple dimensions of classroom teaching, the large number of students, and to exercise her judgment on when to be lenient and when to be strict. She simply followed the advice given to her when she first joined the school.

> In the summer of the year that I joined the school, we had a retreat camp and the principal chatted with the new teachers. I remember her telling us that you must be strict first and then lenient later. So in the first year, I tended to be strict, but I am not a strict person, I didn't know how to do it. That's why I had this feeling of not being able to handle students and not being consistent.

After the first year, Marina did not feel that her classroom management had improved; there were still disciplinary problems. She decided that she ought to be "more firm," "more serious" so that the class would not "get out of control."

> In the second year, I was really strict. My colleagues noticed that too. I was lenient in the first year, in fact the second and third year, possibly the fourth year as well, but definitely the second and third year were the two years in my eight years of teaching that I was strictest. I scolded students. I would gave them dirty looks, I seldom smiled in class.... In the recent two to three years, it became better. It was part of my development, but it was also because students had disciplinary problems, I felt that I had to be more strict with them.

For Marina, being very strict with students was effective in terms of classroom management. Her S3 (grade 9) students were very noisy in all lessons except hers. The successful experience was a positive reinforcement for her. She said, "Maybe that's why I continued to be strict – because it worked." On reflection she felt that she was too strict and unable to see things from the students' perspectives. She cited the following two incidents which she described as "regrettable."

> There was an S3 [grade 9] student, and I taught him English. He copied his homework and I found out. I penalized him by giving him a demerit. He pleaded with me to let him off once and give him an opportunity to rectify his mistake. I refused. Looking back now, I felt I was wrong. If I had given him the opportunity, I might have helped him to mature, to forgive and to see things from other people's perspective. When I refused, he looked very upset. I think I was too strict. There was another case. It was also a male student. His writing was terrible; it was illegible. I made him do it again. But he was the kind who wouldn't succumb to pressure. He disliked me, and the dislike was there even when I wasn't his teacher any more. I think it affected his attitude towards English as well. These are regrettable things.

The problem of classroom management and handling her relationship with students persisted in her second year of teaching. She described herself as "having double standards." She was more lenient with S6 students (preuniversity year) because she had been teaching them for two years and she knew them well. However, she was still very strict with S3 students.

MAKING LEARNING FUN AND INTERESTING

Contrary to managing students, in teaching methods, Marina was able to see things from her students' perspective even in her first year of teaching. In the first two years she was engaged in exploring ways to improve her teaching: how to make her teaching fun and interesting to the students.

Going into teaching without professional preparation, Marina relied heavily on the way she was taught, that is, what Lortie (1975) refers to as the "apprenticeship of observation." Marina said:

> I think it has to do with my previous learning experience and the school culture.... In my secondary school some of my teachers, not all of them, some of them, were very boring, just reading aloud from the readers, but some were very lively. In S2 we had public speaking, in S3 we had debates, we had a lot of group discussions. So I thought that learning English didn't mean that the teacher had to do all the talking. Students should be involved.

Marina also picked up from her colleagues the concept of working on tasks. "I feel that students need to produce things. We must give them the opportunity to work together, to produce."

Another source of influence was her German teacher at the Goethe Institute when she was an undergraduate.

> In my final year I went to Goethe [Institute] and I had a very good German teacher. He was German. His methods were very communicative. There was a lot of talking, pair work, group work, discussion, and he was very funny. If students spoke very softly, he would open a [Chinese] paper fan, which meant "speak louder." For teaching intonation, he brought a musical

instrument. He had a lot of influence on me. When I started teaching, I borrowed a lot of his methods. For example, information gap activities. I actually learned information gap activities from him. Of course I had to make adaptations, but I learned the method from him.

Apart from communicative activities, Marina specifically mentioned grammar teaching as the area that she is most comfortable with. In her secondary education, grammar was never consciously taught. Students just picked it up when using the language. However, the German teacher taught grammar systematically and she modeled her own grammar teaching on his.

When he taught grammar, he would select sentences with similar patterns, put them on a transparency and get you to deduce the rules. It was very clear to me, easy to follow. I use this method, too, when I teach.

From her own experience of learning German, she is convinced that one can learn another language through that language without using the mother tongue. Therefore, in her classroom, students are not allowed to speak a word of Cantonese. They will be penalized if they do so.

I learned German from scratch, and this teacher used very little English, and yet I could follow what he was saying. So in my lessons, I seldom used Cantonese. It was only in the last year or two that I allowed them to use Chinese for certain words. It was because in my experience I didn't feel that it was necessary to use the mother tongue. Also, when I was a student, we never used mother tongue.

In addition to relying on her past experiences, she paid attention to anything that was related to teaching. She went to seminars frequently, no matter whether they were organized by the government Education Department (equivalent to a Ministry of Education), publishers, or educational bodies. She also attended extramural courses offered by the University on specific teaching skills like reading, pronunciation, and vocabulary. Although the seminars conducted by the government have always been criticized by teachers as a waste of time, Marina did not simply dismiss them. She found some of them useful and worth going to because there would be some useful ideas or materials that she could use. She would keep the teachers on the English panel informed of new seminars so that they would not miss good ones. Apart from going to seminars, she bought a lot of reference books and resource books on teaching. She felt that "there was a need to do that" because the teachers in her school were very positive about changes and always felt the need to adapt new things to their own teaching. She was very much influenced by the school culture and the attitude of her colleagues.

I find that there is a need to do that. Our school advocates an activity approach. In our pilot scheme [a scheme where the school got rid of textbooks and used materials produced by their own teachers], we used a lot of activities. In my first year of teaching, I also followed an experienced colleague who used a lot of group work. I experienced difficulties in conducting group work. Putting students in groups does not mean that they will use the materials actively. I still face the question of how to get students interested and how to get them to participate. I felt in the first few months [of my teaching], I didn't learn anything in this aspect, and I didn't know how to do it. So I started looking for reference materials. I remember the first book I bought was *Teaching English through English* [Jane Willis, 1980]. It was for beginning teachers, and I found that the things covered in the book were things that I had no knowledge of, so I started buying more and more books.

Marina loves reading and she can read for hours and hours. Apart from reading up references and resource books, she would put them in the resource library in the staff room. Her experimentation with different activities and different ways of designing activities gave her immense satisfaction, especially when she saw students enjoying the lessons and improving.

6.2.2 Self-doubt and reassessment

Although being very strict with students helped Marina to maintain discipline in class, she was not happy with the effect this had on her relationship with her students. She said:

Actually, I didn't feel good about being so strict. The students were scared of me. They would listen to you, and would do what you asked them to, but that doesn't mean they were willing to learn. Because they were scared of you, the atmosphere was not very pleasant in class.

At the end of the third year, Marina was frustrated by the fact that despite her efforts, she was still unable to exterminate disciplinary problems.

After the third year, I told my principal that I didn't want to teach any more. It was very difficult. I think the difficulty was mainly with handling relationships with students. I found that although I was strict with them, there were still disciplinary problems. I remember I still found several students copying each other's homework. I found it very frustrating and told the principal that I wanted to quit and study librarianship.

When I asked her what made her change her mind, she said there were a host of factors. The first one had to do with her family. Her brother, who had completed a master's degree in the U. K., decided to stay on, and she felt that if she went overseas, there would be nobody to take care of her parents.[2] The second one was that she applied for the in-service Post-graduate Certification in Education (PCEd) program at the Hong

2 At that time, there were no librarianship programs offered in Hong Kong.

Kong University and was accepted. The third and most important factor was the support from her principal.

> My principal [who was then vice principal] gave me a lot of support. That was very important. I couldn't remember her exact wording, but she said even if I changed jobs, would I be able to get more job satisfaction from it than from teaching? She didn't actually help me directly in handling students, but she cared about me. She knew what happened and she cared.

Apart from the care and concern from the principal, the school culture and the support system for new teachers that the school has established was an important factor. The school has a double form-mistress (i.e., class teacher) system as well as pastoral care for new teachers.

> New teachers become form-mistresses from the very beginning. The experienced teacher acts as a helper.... In addition to the form-mistress system, an experienced teacher is responsible for a new teacher. This is not done explicitly, but there is an understanding of who is look after whom, and sometimes we also arrange for an experienced teacher to sit next to a new teacher.

In the first year she teamed up with her principal (who was the vice-principal then) as form-mistresses. She received a great deal of help from her, particularly in settling disputes with students, and they became very good friends. The moral support from her colleagues, her principal, and a pleasant working environment helped her to make the decision to stay on. This phase of self-doubt and uncertainty about her commitment to teaching did not last very long. She told herself, "This is not the end of the world," and she moved on.

6.2.3 Understanding and mastering teaching

Deciding to stay on marked a turning point in Marina's professional life. In describing her own development, Marina repeatedly referred to the fourth year as the turning point.

> But it is funny though, in terms of teaching methods, I started to see it from the students' perspective even in the first year of my teaching – how to make it interesting and fun for students. But it was not until the fourth year that I really dealt with their disciplinary problems, how to see school regulations from their point of view, what are the things that I didn't have to be so strict and would help them. These are two different stages.... In the fourth year, I started to see things from students' perspective.

The "two different stages" refers to the first three years as a stage and the period after the fourth year as a different stage. It was in the fourth year that she applied to do a two-year in-service PCEd program at the university. When I asked her why she wanted to enroll in the program, she said:

Because I believed that if I were to stay in teaching, I needed to study PCEd. Moreover, I started to assist my panel head [Head of the English panel]. I thought it was about time I did it. I could afford the time because I was in my fourth year of teaching already, I would not be so busy. I considered teaching my career.

The PCEd program confirmed a lot of her own practices and provided the rationale for them. "In the PCEd program, a lot of the ideas were interesting. I was already using these ideas but I didn't know why they were good before."

An example that she cited was using information gap activities that she had borrowed from her German teacher and had been using since her first year of teaching. It was not until she attended the PCEd program that she understood the rationale behind these activities.

When I first taught, I borrowed a lot of his methods [referring to her German teacher]. For example, information gap activities. I actually learned information gap activities from him. Of course I had to make adaptations, but I learnt the method from him.... It was not until in the PCEd lectures, I think it was one of your lectures, when you explained what was good about these activities, I remember you used an activity from Penny Ur, there was a diagram of the zoo, that I knew why they were good. But I had already been using them in my teaching.

Another example was the teaching of reading comprehension. A very common routine observed in Hong Kong classrooms is that the teacher goes over the reading passage in class, explains the meanings of words, and asks students to answer the questions on the passage without giving them guidance on how to answer the question or on the reading skills involved. In the teaching of reading comprehension in the PCEd program, attention was drawn to the difference between "teaching" and "testing," and this confirmed Marina's belief about the need to distinguish the two.

As for reading comprehension, the difference between testing and teaching was emphasized in PCEd. This confirmed what I believed in. So now when I teach a reading passage, I look at the questions first and see if they are appropriate and if students know the purpose of those questions. These are confirmed in the PCEd program.

The PCEd program also introduced instructional practices, such as the teaching of writing and text analysis, of which Marina was not aware.

There were also new ideas that I wasn't aware of. For example, writing, Peter [a course tutor] talked about text organization, situation, problem, solution; it was then that I realized that I needed to teach the framework [structure of text]. Before that, I just taught compo [composition] in the way that everybody teaches. At that time, the books that I bought were more on grammar [teaching of grammar]. Discourse, I find discourse very interesting; the lectures that you gave on discourse. I took out some of the exercises in your handouts and gave them to students. For example, the newspaper editorial that you used in the PCEd lectures, I gave it to my students to work on.

The use of group work is another example. She was made aware of the need for a purpose in group work.

Group work. The need for a purpose in group work. In the PCEd program, I was made aware of this. Previously, when I asked students to do group work, the purpose was to get them to talk in English. This is still one of the purposes now, but I'd ask myself something more – what is the aim of this group work? I know that I should tell students what the aim is.

Apart from instructional practices in the classroom, the PCEd program also helped her to understand wider educational issues. She mentioned specifically that the program had helped her to understand why streaming could have a negative effect on students.

Teacher as a gatekeeper, schooling and society, and streaming are things which I came across in the PCEd program. Even before I joined the program, I had been wondering about streaming [putting students in different classes according to academic abilities]. Streaming was originally intended to help students, but I had been doubtful about its effectiveness; it made students feel that they were no good. It was only after I had studied *Schooling and Society*[3] that I realized that it had a labeling effect. I began to realize that we really need to think carefully about streaming.

Another aspect that she mentioned was how the course on psychology of learning had helped her to think positively and to see things from students' perspective.

I think positive thinking is important. And that has something to do with the PCEd program. It talked about students' psychology of learning and the factors that contributed to their sense of failure. Then I felt that I needed to see things from students' perspective. You need to empathize. There is a need to think positively.

Thinking positively is something that she often refers to when she talks about teaching and about her colleagues as an important element. What she learned from the program not only helped her in her relationship with students, but also in coping with stress and depression.

Teaching is a very heavy responsibility, but there are also other aspects of teaching that make you very happy.... When you look at the huge pile of compositions that you have to mark, you feel depressed. So I start to think of more positive things, like the students are lovely, even the naughtiest student is in fact lovely.

Her colleagues' positive attitude to work also helped her to think positively.

3 *Schooling and society* is a module offered in the educational theory component of the PCEd course.

When I look at the new colleagues, they are like that as well. They find the work load very heavy, sometimes the students are very naughty, but when they see the positive side of their work, they put effort into it. If you are talking about making money, then there are other jobs where you can make more money.

This phase, which consists of the fourth and fifth year of teaching, was a period when Marina, having had three years of teaching behind her, had built up a repertoire of instructional practices. She was able to draw on this repertoire for her teaching, thus allowing her the time to explore new ideas, to "tinker" with her existing practices (Huberman, 1993b, p. 112), and to think about wider educational issues. Reflecting on her own development, she said,

...if we are talking about being able to draw on my existing ideas, I think it was about the fourth year that I was able to come up with ideas for teaching fairly quickly. This is because there are certain things that I have mastered already. It was about the year when I started doing my PCEd.

6.2.4 *Taking on a new role*

In the fifth year, when Marina was still doing the second year of the PCEd course, she was appointed Head of the English panel (referred to as Panel Chair in Hong Kong) because the incumbent emigrated to Australia. She accepted the appointment on the basis that she had already been an assistant to the English Panel Chair for two years, and the principal thought that she had been doing very well. She said, "I only thought that somebody had to do it, and I took on the job." However, she had no idea of what was involved. She said:

When I became the panel chair [of English], I actually did not have a clue what was involved. Although I was an assistant to the previous panel chair, there were not many extra duties for me. I thought I was the most suitable one within the English panel and so I agreed [to take on the job] but I have no idea that being a panel chair was in fact quite complicated [meaning not easy], there're a lot of administrative duties and other chores. When I was an assistant [panel chair], my partner did all these, so I didn't realize he had done so much. I just thought that somebody had to take up the position, it's just a matter of who. I was an assistant at that time, and the principal thought my performance was good and my teaching was good too. So she thought I was the suitable person, and asked me [to take up the position].

Her understanding of the responsibilities of a panel chair at the time was to carry out routine duties such as holding meetings, dealing with circulars, checking students' exercise books and examination papers, and paying class visits to new colleagues. Gradually she realized that there were a lot of responsibilities and that the role of the panel chair was very important. She also realized that she had to "deal with human relationships," which was "very complicated" to her. She did not like the job because she found administrative duties such as taking stock of the headsets and machines in the loop room [a room with loops for listening] very time-consuming. Had she known that a panel chair had to take on such administrative chores, she would have been more cautious about taking on the job. She said, "I prefer spending the time on teaching rather than on administration."

In her sixth year Marina completed her professional training. She had one year behind her as English panel chair. She began to move from just handling "administrative chores" to introducing changes in teaching in small ways. In her capacity as panel chair, she went beyond her own teaching and started to involve the whole English panel to make changes to their teaching. She started with small changes. One was the specification of teaching objectives in the scheme of work. She recalled, "The need for clear objectives and lesson plans was much stressed in the (PCEd) program, and I felt the panel needed to set objectives too." Previously, in the scheme of work, there were no teaching objectives. She suggested that teachers teaching the same level should discuss and arrive at a list of teaching objectives. However, she was unhappy with what she had achieved. She felt that some of the objectives were still very general and needed some work. The other change was to introduce the teaching of phonetics in oral English lessons. Phonetics was not widely taught nor systematically taught in schools at the time. She found that many of the students were tongue-tied in class – not because they did not know the words, but because they did not know how to pronounce them. In other words, instead of making a host of drastic changes, she focused on change that was manageable and "within control" as well as much needed. She is, in Huberman's words, "tinkering with" her own teaching as well as the teaching of other English teachers, and experimenting with ways to improve English teaching in the school. It was after the introduction of phonetics teaching that she realized a panel chair could do more than merely deal with administrative chores. She felt that she could bring about change not only in her own teaching but also in other teachers'. However, she could not theorize about her role until she attended a refresher course for panel chairs in the following year.

In this same school year, she was visited by the Advisory Inspectorate of the government Education Department. This is a formal inspection procedure which all teachers had to go through before they could be promoted to Senior Graduate Mistress, a rank above the Graduate Mistress.[4]

---

4 Graduate Mistress and Graduate Master are ranks given to teachers who are University Graduates by the Education Department of the Hong Kong government when they join the profession. The former is for female teachers and the latter for male teachers.

6.2.5 Opportunities for reflection

In the second half of Marina's sixth year, in order to perform better the role of a panel chair, she requested leave for half a year to participate in a refresher course for panel chairpersons. This was a course funded by the government, and teachers were released on full pay to attend the course. Her request was approved by her principal, who was very supportive of any measures to enhance the quality of teaching.

In this course she was introduced to the concept of the panel chair as "an agent of change." She said:

> It was then that I learned that I play a key role in the professional development of my panel. I still remember the exact wording "an agent of change" now... [This] shows how impressed I was when I first heard the phrase. The reason was that I identified with it. At that time, I had already had the actual experience of introducing changes, however, small a scale they were, in my own panel. So I saw [and still see] myself as the agent of change.

In the first reflective journal that she wrote, she specified three goals for attending the course were "to streamline the work of the panel so everyone has breathing space to reflect on their teaching," "to think of a more schematic program for staff development," and "to explore means to promote independent learning." She also had the opportunity to read up on references on educational change and teacher development. Among them is Pamela Grossman's book *The Making of a Teacher*. Marina also had the opportunity to reflect on her own development. In the reflective journal that she wrote during the refresher course, she said:

> This [Pamela Grossman's book] reminds me of my first few years of teaching. I didn't do the PCEd until the fourth year of my teaching profession. The reliance on past experiences was predominantly heavy, particularly in the first few months of teaching. Luckily, I came from a background where drama, role-play, and discussions were the norm. The greatest influence on my style and approaches of teaching was the school culture. It was a time when St. Peter's was still having the pilot scheme and everyone was expected to select, adapt and evaluate teaching materials. When I did the PCEd course, I found that the methods recommended were in line with the approaches I adopted. In retrospect, wasn't that staff development? One of the objectives that I set in attending this course was to think of a more systematic program to help staff development. I began to see that one way of achieving this goal is to engage my colleagues in school-based materials development.

Marina's reflection on her own professional development helped her to decide on getting teachers involved in school-based materials development as a milieu for professional development. She zeroed in on the teaching of writing and grading students' writing as an area to start. She continued:

> This involves greater changes and has to be initiated by the panel chair, with the support of panel members.... I've narrowed down my objective next year

to trying out "process writing" in S1 and involving basically S1 teachers in developing materials. The tryout will throw more light on approaches to writing adopted in other forms. I'm going to talk to S1 teachers, enlist support, examine S1's scheme of work and work out a tentative plan so that all S1 teachers can work on it and make modifications.

She read several books on writing and she sent messages to *TeleNex*, an English-teacher support network, to discuss her ideas and to consult other teachers.

Though Marina was absorbing new input like a sponge, she had problems in relating theory to practice, especially in the management of a panel. She said:

But on management, it was very theoretical. After listening to the lectures, I thought, How on earth could we put that into practice? They told you how to manage the colleagues, we must have autonomy and the like. But we didn't know how to apply this.

She also learned that for teachers to be committed, it was important to give them a "sense of ownership" by allocating responsibilities to them. However, she had difficulties reconciling that with overburdening teachers with responsibilities. She expressed her concern as follows:

I don't know, asking them to be a coordinator might foster a sense of ownership, but it might also make them feel that they are given jobs to do again. It's a kind of duty.... I am in a dilemma when I have to ask teachers to do things on top of their teaching. For example, I paired up with a colleague to be the panel chair. We have form coordinators. So everybody has some responsibilities. For some teachers, if I ask them to work on resources [for teaching] together, I feel that it would be a burden to them. But I would agree that, for example, Genie is now S3 coordinator, she's taken on this responsibility, and she does have a sense of ownership, and it's the same with Eva; their attitude is very positive.

Marina felt that apart from assigning duties, she needed to give her teachers something more, though she was not very clear exactly what that something was, and she had not been able to do that.

The question is, do I have something additional to give them to foster a sense of ownership? I haven't done that, I just threw them into the water and let them struggle, and they learned how to swim.

Spending half a year away from the classroom to attend the refresher course was considered by Marina as essential to her professional development. It gave her the opportunity to read journals, references, and resource materials in the library; to think of ways to improve her own teaching as well as the teaching of the whole English panel; and most important, to reflect on her work in a wider context. It gave her the time and breathing space to read up on education policy issues like curriculum change, which took her beyond her school and her classrooms.

6.2.6 Reinvesting resources

SEEKING MORE PROFESSIONAL INPUT

Attending the refresher course provided Marina with fresh input, particularly on current theories of English language teaching. At the same time, it made her crave for more. A year after she resumed teaching, she enrolled on a two year part-time master's program on Teaching of English as Foreign Language (TEFL).

> If I really want to learn how to teach, it [the PCEd program] is not enough. The PCEd is very practical.... When I am doing the MEd [Master of Education] this year, there are lots of names that I have never come across. I know nothing about the writers who are famous in particular fields. I don't need to learn about them [in the PCEd program]. So I enrolled on the MEd program because I want to know more about teaching. I've completed the first year now, and it's very good. I have more knowledge about the theoretical basis of my work and I have learnt to read critically.

One of the examples that she gave was the critique of textbooks. In the past she intuitively felt that some activities were not very good, but she did not know why. After studying more about pedagogic grammar, she knew more about the nature of the activities. For example, some of them require students to notice certain patterns and regularities. She also learned how to proceduralize her knowledge of grammar. So when she looked at the exercises provided in the textbooks now, she could see more clearly what the problems were. Things that she found boring when she did her PCEd program, such as classroom language, she now found very interesting. Group work was another example. She had formerly thought that group work would get students to participate in conversations, but now she knew that doing group work would provide students with the opportunity to engage in the negotiation of meaning with their peers.

Doing a masters' program was very tough for Marina, though. She often had to stay up very late to do her assignments and thus had only one or two hours of sleep. Her students knew about this and called her "superwoman." So did her colleagues such as Genie and Eva. Marina did extremely well on the course, often getting the top grade for her assignments. She chose topics that were related to her teaching tasks at school and addressed issues about which she had always wanted to know more. For example, she studied the learning strategies of good learners in her S5 class, and critiqued the textbooks. In other words, the master's program was a way of helping her to gain more theoretical input for her work as a teacher, rather than a way of gaining another paper qualification.

EXPLORING THE ROLE OF A PANEL CHAIR

In her fifth year, when Marina took on the role of a panel chair, she treated it more as taking on administrative chores on top of her teaching.

However, after she came back from the refresher course in the seventh year, Marina had a different understanding of her role. She said, "I think the most important role of a panel chair is to decide the English panel's directions and aims of teaching and to help the colleagues to develop professionally. This is more [important] than dealing with administration and the loop room." At one point, she thought that she could achieve those two things even if she were not the panel chair. However, her views changed after trying out process writing; she realized that she could not have brought that about if she were not the panel chair. She said:

> I've been thinking, I don't know, if I'm not panel chair, how much I can do about exploring process writing. I'm now in a position that I can introduce change, so I must grab the chance to try.

In steering the direction of the English panel, Marina worked hard to keep up the tradition of modifying and adapting textbooks. This was not easy because this practice had been questioned by some colleagues who thought that it would be simpler just to follow the textbook. Marina had to insist on being critical about textbooks and improving them. If they gave up this practice, the English panel would stagnate, she felt. To set an example, she adapted the materials and shared them with colleagues. She said, "It is very tough going to require myself to do that. But we have kept up the spirit."

In helping colleagues to develop professionally, Marina was faced with the dilemma of setting targets and goals for them and not over-burdening them. She said, "My colleagues are already exhausted, I just do not have the heart to push anything more down their throats." She did not have any formal plans for staff development. Her management of the panel was more on "a personal basis." By this, she meant talking to colleagues individually to find out if they have any problems and to give them advice and assistance. For colleagues who were teaching the same level as Marina, she felt that she could do a lot more by sharing materials and discussing their teaching with them. For example, she would try out new ideas herself and then share her teaching with the panel members in meetings. She would also approach them individually and invite them to try out these ideas.

Another important aspect of the work of a panel chair is quality assurance. The school has in place the practice of panel chairs observing teachers in their first and second years of teaching. At first, Marina did not think there was much use in doing this because she would not be able to see what the teacher was really like behind closed doors. Instead of just rejecting the practice, she consulted the history panel chair. He pointed out to her that the class visit would enable her to see what a teacher could achieve, and she agreed. After conducting some class visits, she encountered the problem of what she could do when she observed lessons that did not go well. She believed that teachers knew when their lessons did not go well and that it would be much better for them to see good teaching in action than just to tell them their shortcomings. Therefore, she invited them to observe her teach, and she also acted as the middleman by referring them to observe other colleagues who were good. For example, when she heard that Genie wanted to find out more about group work, she suggested that she observe another colleague who used group competition a lot. Marina's willingness to open her classroom to anybody at any time changed the nature of the class visits. It was no longer a quality assurance mechanism but rather an opportunity for learning. It also enhanced the culture of collegiality and collaborative learning.

Another quality-assurance measure was the checking of the grading of homework and compositions by the panel chair. At first she focused on whether teachers made any mistakes in marking and whether they were able to pick out students' mistakes. However, as she learned more about genres and genre structure, she turned her attention to the students' writing – whether the style and genre were appropriate to the writing task. When she spotted problems in students' writing, she would discuss with teachers how they could help the students. For example, she read Genie's students' writing and found that some students produced unnatural interview reports, which used indirect speech throughout. Marina shared with Genie an assignment that she had just completed on indirect speech in the MEd program on pedagogic grammar to help Genie understand the misconceptions that textbooks proliferate regarding the use of indirect speech. She also lent her a journal article on indirect speech. In fact, Marina shared with her colleagues a number of her MEd assignments, which she thought would be relevant to their teaching. She said, "When I decide whether I'll show them [an assignment], I think of whether it is useful to them, relevant to their teaching, and whether they'll find it difficult to understand." In other words, in the process of exploring her role as panel chair, she reinterpreted her role from one of watching over her colleagues to one of helping them to develop professionally.

Handling relationships with colleagues when she received complaints from students was problematic. She recalled an unhappy incident in her sixth year of teaching when students in S6 and S7 complained about a certain teacher and told her that his teaching style was straight lecturing and that they were not learning anything. Marina, being very close to the principal, told her about this. Subsequently, the principal talked to the students and followed up on their complaints with this teacher. He reacted very strongly to this and told Marina that she should have talked to him directly rather than going straight to the principal. He was so upset that he suffered from insomnia. At the time, Marina did not realize that there was a difference between the teacher getting negative feedback from the principal and getting it from her. Marina found out subsequently from talking to him that this was not the first time that this had happened to him. There was a previous incident when the students complained about him to the form master who related this to the principal. He was very upset that the students did not talk to him directly and instead went around him and related their complaints to a third party. Both the principal and Marina spent some time to assure him that Marina had no ill intention and that she was merely trying to help. This was a good learning experience for Marina. When a similar problem recurred two years later, she handled it differently. She discussed the problem with the form master, and they agreed that the form master should first ask the students to discuss among themselves what they would like this teacher to do to improve his teaching and also what they would do themselves to help the teacher to conduct his teaching more effectively, such as coming to class fully prepared. The students took the advice, and the problem was resolved satisfactorily. The teacher's style improved, and the students reported that they were getting more out of his lessons. Marina feels that she has learned a great deal in performing her role as the panel chair, but there is still a long way to go. She feels that she is not good at handling "complicated" matters, such as human relationships, and she has yet to explore better ways of enhancing staff development.

Evaluating her work as a panel chair, what she deplored was that the administrative chores of writing reports and program plans for the Education Department, as well as the many meetings, were taking her away from her work with the students. However, when she looked at what her panel had achieved, she felt that it was all worthwhile. She said, "The English teachers in my school are forward-looking and receptive to innovations. We have a very good relationship and have good morale, despite the heavy workload. Inspectors from the Education Department applaud our work, and I think we have excellent records. I am very proud of my panel."

6.2.7 Taking on the challenge: adopting the process approach to writing

The six-month refresher course gave Marina time to step back from her teaching and ask questions about existing practices. In Bereiter and Scardamalia's (1993) words, she "problematized routines" and asked questions about practices which had been taken for granted. In particular, it provided her with the opportunity to seek answers in an area that had been troubling her – the teaching of writing. She read a lot about this and wrote about it in her reflective journals.

What induced her to think about this topic was her own experience in teaching writing. A very common practice among teachers in Hong Kong is to give students a composition topic, sometimes provide them with some vocabulary items related to the topic, mark the composition in great detail, and ask students to do corrections. She was very much aware of the enormous amount of time that teachers spent on marking compositions, which she described as 'very painful,' considering that it had so little impact on the students. She commented:

> ...marking compositions is very painful. After all the marking, you find that the students are still the same, the content is very limited and uninteresting. This made me feel that students need to go one step further to improve their writing, and that is, if they took one step further, it would help their thinking and how to assess other people's writing.

She also observed that her colleagues had the same problem. She said:

> ...I looked at my colleagues, they were all suffering from marking compos [compositions]; marking is no fun. The students produced the ideas. These ideas ought to be very interesting, especially when students are in their teens, and they should be very creative. But why did they have to do it merely as a piece of homework? The third thing is students ought to be able to do it better. The question is whether we are giving them the opportunity to do so. Their understanding of composition is that they have produced a piece of writing. The teacher's responsibility is to correct the mistakes, and then their job is to do the corrections and hand it in. But this is not what writing is about.

She read up on references on the teaching of writing, for example, Harris (1994) *Introducing Writing*, and White and Arnt (1991) on *Process Writing*. She found the ideas useful because they corroborated her own experience in writing. She said, "even in my own writing, I don't have just one draft. I think if you want to produce good writing, it is not possible to accomplish it at one go."

Although there were many research articles on process writing, there were not many resource books on the teaching of writing. This did not deter Marina from experimenting with it. On the contrary, she found it challenging. She said, "It's precisely because there aren't many [teaching resource] books on writing that I wanted to work on it. I wonder why there aren't many [teaching resource] books on writing. Is it because it is an aspect that has seldom been touched on?"

After a year's incubation, and in her eighth year, Marina embarked on a major experiment with the process approach to writing. Typically, she did not ask her panel members to try it out at all levels, but started with junior forms. The experiment took place throughout the whole school year, where all colleagues teaching S1 to S3 (grades 7 to 9) were involved – some to a fuller extent than others. (See Chapter 9 for a detailed account.) In a panel meeting in which I participated, when the teachers reviewed the effectiveness of the implementation, it was clear that there was marked improvement in students' writing. The meeting ended with the teachers in high spirits agreeing that the tryout was a success and a move in the right direction.

Looking back at the changes that she introduced, Marina felt that she was lucky to have colleagues who would support her whenever she introduced changes. Few colleagues would see these changes as a waste of time. Marina attributed this to the school culture – that the school strongly advocated making changes and this was accepted by colleagues as the norm. Apart from the school culture, she felt that there were other factors as well. She said, "My colleagues and I have a very good relationship. I try to be supportive and give my colleagues as much help as I can, like sharing good resources and ideas. I also show appreciation for their hard work. I try not to be bossy, and I don't put on airs. My colleagues feel that I'll stand up for them and fight for them when necessary."

She also tried to be reasonable in her assignment of workload. She said, "I try to make sure, though not always possible, that everyone has a lighter teaching and marking load once in a while, like teaching two junior form classes and one senior class instead of two senior classes and one junior class once every few years." When she initiated process writing, she was very much aware of the extra work that needed to go into the marking. She persuaded the school authority to accept process writing. Because teachers had to spend more time going over the various drafts of the students' composition, it was reasonable that they could require students to write fewer compositions a year.[5] She consciously avoided a top-down approach when introducing innovative practices. She tried them out first and invited colleagues to observe how she implemented them in her own classrooms. There was a great deal of informal sharing of ideas, and she felt that was very useful in changing beliefs.

Reflecting on her own professional development, Marina saw three broad stages. She said:

The first year is a stage when I was very green. [I] didn't know what was going on. I just observed and followed others. The second to the fourth year, I was already developing my own style of teaching. From the second year onwards, I used a lot more group work in teaching, which was [a] more active [style of teaching]. It was a period when I learned how to handle students. The years following up to now, . . . because I am a panel chair and I have to run the [English] panel, I have entered a stage in which I am not just responsible for my own teaching, but I also have to give advice to other colleagues. I think I will divide it [my professional development] into these three broad stages. The last stage began in my fifth year [of teaching]. I had already established something about teaching, and I just built on that. And the other thing is how to get along with my students. I know how to handle it skillfully and tactfully. My new role in the panel is the thing I need to develop.

5 In Hong Kong, the Education Department gives schools a rough guideline of how many compositions they should expect a teacher to give to students. Schools have the flexibility to decide on the number of compositions that they give to students, but they will be asked to justify the number when the Education Department conducts an inspection.

6.2.8 Synopsis

Marina entered teaching with a personal conception of teaching and learning. Her primary school experience contributed to her image of a teacher: she should have authority and yet should be kind and caring to students. She should also have experience working in settings other than a school. This served as a reference for her as she explored her role as a teacher (see Bullough et al., 1992). The development of her relationship with the students is one where the seemingly conflicting qualities of the teacher as having authority versus being kind and caring were reconciled. She is no longer a figure of authority who has control over her students. She is seen by students as a friend who they feel free to ask questions and can turn to when they have personal problems. An expression often used by her students to describe her is that she is "totally integrated with the students." Yet at the same time she is someone they respect and from whom they can learn a lot. In the past two years, Marina has become the "agony aunt" for her students. They wrote her letters to tell her how miserable they were, their dating problems, and which teachers were not good, and so on. Marina said, "I can feel my own development through my relationship with my students."

Her own learning experiences had a strong influence on her conception of what language learning involved. They were the basis on which she formulated her own practical theories of teaching. Her experience of going from a housing estate school to a very prestigious middle-class school and having to struggle very hard to survive in the school had a strong influence on her personal beliefs about learning in general and English language learning in particular. Reading and maximizing the available resources for learning English figured importantly in her teaching (see Chapter 6). Moreover, it influenced her personal belief in the importance of maximizing time for learning. This was reflected in her insistence on punctuality in attending classes, both for herself and her students. She felt that as a thirty-five minute lesson is already very short, if class started late, there would be very little time left for teaching and learning.

Her own learning experiences together with the professional input that she obtained from reading, from attending the PCEd program, as well as from attending seminars, helped her to understand and to master teaching. The master's program that she was attending when the study was conducted gave her theoretical input that helped her to probe deeper into questions relating to students' learning, the curriculum, and language policy. While her learning experience helped her to develop techniques and strategies for learning, the professional and theoretical input that she obtained helped her to theorize her practices.

The school context in which she worked and the way in which she responded to it played a crucial part in her professional development.

The school culture was supportive, and she was able to benefit from the principal's guidance and emotional support, which helped her to overcome her doubts about her commitment to teaching. She was also able to integrate her own learning experience with the teaching approach advocated in the school. This led to strong student involvement in her teaching.

The development of teaching expertise in Marina was a process where she was continuously working at the edge of her competence (Bereiter and Scardamalia, 1993). She was constantly reflecting on her teaching, making further improvements by seeking professional input and trying out ways to improve her own classroom practices. In handling teacher-student relationships, she was unhappy about merely maintaining control over students; she was not content with her class being the best behaved class in the school. She wanted something more than that: she wanted to develop a relationship in which students were disciplined not because they were scared of her, but because they wanted to learn. She also wanted to make learning enjoyable for them. The achievement of being able to "integrate with the students entirely" was the result of Marina's effort over the years.

In the development of expertise in classroom teaching, we can see a persistent search for renewal of teaching in small and big ways. There was constant questioning of what she was doing and how she could make it better, and an awareness of what she needed to know in order to do her job well. Reflecting on her professional development, she felt that she was expanding her repertoire of teaching skills, but there were still areas of teaching that she needed to think about more. For example, can reading skills such as skimming and scanning really help students to read better and read faster? Does vocabulary learning involve long-term and short-term memory? Her oral lessons received very good feedback from students, but she was not satisfied. She felt that there was a need to reexamine the materials that she developed three years ago and see what needed to be changed. Do students benefit from being forced to hand in their homework? These are questions that she is asking herself now. Questions that she would not have asked in the past.

In playing her role as a panel chair, Marina's understanding of her role changed from being a caretaker to an agent of change and a mentor through the experience of leading her teachers to implement a new approach to the teaching of writing, as we shall see in Chapter 9. In other words, she is extending her impact from her own classroom to other classrooms in her school, and even to teachers in schools on the teacher support network, *TeleNex*. It is through this process of constant renewal, meeting as well as looking for challenges, that Marina became the expert teacher that she is now.

6.3 Eva

Eva, a university graduate in Sociology, was 27 and in her fifth year of teaching when the study started. Eva comes from a working-class family of three children. Her father died when she was in primary six. Her mother became the sole breadwinner, working over the years as a factory worker, a clerk in a restaurant, and a saleslady in an electrical appliance shop. Eva learned to be very independent because her mother was unable to spend much time with her and her siblings. After her father's death, Eva was determined to work very hard to get a university degree for the sake of her mother so that they could have a better life. Eva and her siblings all like jobs that provide them with opportunities to meet and interact with people. They find it easy to build good relationships with people, and they all enjoy teamwork.

Eva loves her job as a teacher, but initially, teaching was only her second choice. Social work was her first. Yet, she chose sociology instead of social work as her major discipline at The Chinese University of Hong Kong because it was less demanding in terms of assignments, and this gave her the "space" to think and to ask questions. The year she graduated there was a big cut in the employment of social workers in the government Social Welfare Department, but a great shortage of English teachers. After waiting in vain for one and a half months for a position in social work, she accepted a late offer in July from a school, St. Peter's, where she stayed on for six years. She enjoyed her work at St. Peter's despite the fact that it was very hard work, and she was perpetually exhausted.

Eva went to an English medium secondary school where the teaching method was described by her as "very old fashioned." By that, she meant that the teacher was talking all the time, there were no activities, and little student involvement. All she could remember about English lessons was the recitation of new words, dictation, and reading aloud. She liked English because she had good results and was praised by her English teacher. The strongest influence on her, however, was not her secondary but university education.

6.3.1 Conceptions of teaching

THE "SPACE" OF TEACHING

Eva's academic background in sociology and her religious background have had strong influences on her personal beliefs and values as well as her personal conceptions of teaching. She felt that sociology made her think and discover problems: "It [Sociology] always says that things are not as simple as they appear to be." Central to her beliefs about teaching are the concepts of "creativity" and "being humanistic." She always reminds herself to maximize the space for creative and humanistic approaches to teaching. The metaphor of space was used frequently when she talked about teaching. She referred to having space for curriculum development and space for reflecting on her teaching. She liked English teaching because it provided her with space for creativity. She explained:

> Up to now, I still find teaching English fun because there's a lot of *space* for development. There are not a lot of restrictions in the curriculum.... Even when teaching reading comprehension, when you set questions,... you could introduce different perspectives.

Eva would compose her own texts for reading comprehension and the topics could be about religious beliefs, moral values, and even the disciplinary problems in school that she felt unhappy about. Sometimes she would use students' names and write descriptions about them when designing cloze passages or grammar activities. She particularly enjoyed doing that because, according to her, "this is creative writing, which has to do with people." She felt that students would find them interesting and that was her top priority in teaching.

STUDENTS AS INDIVIDUALS

Eva came across Marx's theory of alienation when she studied sociology. This made her more aware of the importance of seeing students as individuals and as people rather than as groups. This is why, even though teaching was not her first choice as a career, she knew that she would like the job because she could "explore the talent and nature of every individual." She related an incident when she heard, indirectly, in her first year of teaching, that her students thought that her teaching was not good enough. What upset her was not her students' criticism, but the fact that she might never be able to make it up to them. She said:

> Feeling that my teaching is not good enough is not the source of pressure, but the fact that there is no time to improve, that there is no way I can improve within a short period of time. By the time I have improved, I will not be teaching the same group. The ones who will benefit from my improvement will be some other students. This makes me feel uncomfortable and pressured. Each student is not a group; they are individuals. If I can't teach them well this year, maybe after this year I will never have the chance to teach them again for the rest of my life, especially teaching them "how to be a human being."[6] I take this to heart.

She felt that she may not be a good teacher with a lot of good teaching techniques, but she cares about her students, and for her, this is most important.

6 This is a common expression in Chinese that refers to the moral conduct and the values that a human being should have.

Her conception of students as individuals played an important part in her emphasis on developing a close relationship with students as an important aspect of teaching. To do that, she tried to find out more about each student. When teaching, she would pick up the remarks that her students made and develop a dialog with them: "I like to develop a conversation with them and to respond to them. I like to ask how they feel about things and ask questions about themselves.... When you teach, you should develop a relationship with them...you should find out more about them." Eva's classroom discourse was characterized by the interpolation of a one-to-one dialog between herself and a student. She said, "I pay attention to the human side, human relationship, and I think this is my personality. Studying sociology brought out this element in me." This kind of dialog, however, could be distracting at times and could make it difficult for the rest of class to follow the lesson.

SOCIAL AWARENESS IN TEACHING

Another strong influence that she came under was her social and political involvement in her university days. In her days, student bodies in universities were politically active and very vocal. She was an executive member of the students' union and participated actively in social and political discussions in the Chinese Literary Study Club. She read a lot of Chinese literature and novels written about people who have experienced the turmoil of the Cultural Revolution. She came under the influence of her peers whom she described as "very mature people who were going to do big things." She joined the demonstrations and rallies after the Tianman incident. She felt that it was important to make students aware of things happening around them. In her teaching she tried to relate the teaching content to things that were close to the students, especially social events. She said, "English is already an alien and unfamiliar language and culture. If we talk about things which are unrelated to them, then the teaching is meaningless." For her, students had to be able to relate to the content that the language was used to express. The social dimension of her teaching was realized by the way she built social, political, and moral issues in her materials. She would give the senior form students newspaper articles to read and ask them to discuss these articles or to conduct role-plays. She would also use political figures and government officials as her characters in the teaching materials. The examples that she used in class were often related to current affairs.

MORAL VALUES IN EDUCATION

Her evaluation of whether she was successful as a teacher and whether she had achieved her educational aim was based on the moral values that she wanted to inculcate rather than the language skills that she wanted her students to master. She cited an example of teaching a unit on a native African who acted as a guard to prevent people from poaching elephants' trunks. She asked the students to discuss his personality and what insights they gained from the story. She also asked them to write down their thoughts on this story afterwards. She said, "I think in terms of education, I have achieved my ideal. Education is not just about learning the language. From the point of view of moral education, I have achieved the aim." She felt a greater sense of achievement when the text that she gave to the students was related to their daily lives and would thus make students reflect. Another example she gave was a writing task, "the secret door," where students were shown the picture of a door and they were asked to imagine where the secret door would lead to. Eva was happy with the task because her students could express their ideals in life. She said, "according to my criterion, I am successful, and it [the writing task] is meaningful."

IMAGE OF A TEACHER

For Eva, the teacher is not and should not be a figure of authority. She does not mind students pointing out her mistakes. In fact, she feels that it is quite important for teachers to be able to accept having their mistakes pointed out by students. She remarked, "Teachers nowadays are no longer the authority. Teachers who are authoritarian are no longer accepted by students." Not only does she hold such an attitude, she also thinks that it is important for students to have this attitude. She recalled an incident when she mispronounced the word "kindred" and one student pointed out her mistake. She gladly accepted the correction and thanked the student. However, the students' facial expressions showed that they were a bit surprised that even the teacher would make mistakes. She found this worrying. She said, "How come this class believes everything the teacher says? I think this is not right. They are very nice and very good students but this is worrying because if students grow up to be like this, then it will be problematic." So she encouraged her students to correct her when they found her making mistakes. She feels that in fact it helped her to build up her self-image and confidence by being not authoritarian.

6.3.2 Beginning teaching: disintegrated, chaotic and torturous

In her first year of teaching, Eva was overwhelmed by the new working environment. She described the first year as basically trying to catch up with other colleagues and getting through the teaching materials. In that year the school started a pilot scheme in which they discarded textbooks and produced their own materials. She was given a list of topics to be covered and a set of materials. However, she could not relate to them and see the materials as an integrated whole. She was preoccupied with keeping order and discipline in the classroom, learning how to run class business, and getting used to the school environment. She was bogged down by things such as getting students to stick the hand-outs onto their exercise books so that they would not lose them and checking whether they had done that. To Eva, this was not helped by being given the "worst" class, commonly referred to as a "remedial class," where students were weak and the classroom discipline was poor.

To maintain order in the classroom, Eva was very strict with her students. If students forgot to bring their homework, they would be put on the snake list (lazy bones list; *snake* is a metaphor in Chinese for laziness). Sometimes, when students forgot to bring their homework, she would penalize them in the same way that she would for not doing their homework. If the offense was repeated more than seven times, she would give them a black mark for misconduct, which, according to her understanding, was the received practice in the school. She remembered an incident when she gave a black mark to a student and the whole class got very angry and complained to their form mistress. Eva reflected on it and came to the conclusion that "that's not the way to teach." Later, she talked to the student about his behavior, and in the end she decided to delete the black mark. She felt that it would be more helpful to the student to state what she expected of them more clearly, rather than giving them a black mark. She later found out that her colleagues did not actually follow the rules as strictly as she did. She said, "I was new. I didn't know the whole picture. I thought that other colleagues followed the rules. If I had asked them, I would have found out that I should not have done that." We can see that in her first year of teaching, Eva, like all new teachers, was going by the school rules rather than her own conception of how disciplinary problems should be handled. Her deletion of the black mark was more a realization that there was a difference between what the rules said and actual practice and that she should have exercised her own judgement rather than just going by the books. She summed up her first year of teaching as "disintegrated" and "chaotic."

Not having been trained professionally, Eva had nothing to fall back on except her past learning experience. She came from an "old-fashioned" school that was teacher-centered, with the teacher lecturing at the class all the time. All Eva could remember about the English lessons were recitations (memorization), dictation, and reading aloud. In grammar lessons the teacher merely wrote sentences on the board and asked the class to copy them into their notebooks and make sentences. For vocabulary learning, students had to write down the meanings of the new words in English and produce a sentence. The vocabulary items had to be memorized by heart, and students would be tested on those items. There was very little she could draw upon from her learning experience.

Eva herself found that her teaching was very boring, and what was worse, her students could not understand her because her teaching was not systematic. They did not pay attention to her. She was most bothered by grammar teaching. She felt that her students were not learning even though she spent a lot of time on it. She felt "lost" and that she was ineffective as a teacher. She remembered that none of the "remedial class" students could stay on after S3, a point at which further screening takes place, and she attributed that to her own ineffective teaching. The words *disintegrated* and *chaotic* cropped up every now and again in Eva's accounts. She did not want to "torture" herself and her students, and so she formulated a motto for her own improvement, "It [My teaching] must not be boring. I should be able to teach students something. The students should be self-motivated to learn and to take their learning seriously."

6.3.3 Gaining a sense of ownership and trying out things

In her second year Eva was assigned to teach S2 and S3 again. Eva was a bit more confident because she had already taught the course once, and she was given the "best" class, in terms of academic ability, and that helped. She was able to pay more attention to detail. For example, when she taught reading comprehension, she asked herself questions like "should I go through the questions first, or should I cover the vocabulary items first?"

She also began to have a sense of ownership, both about the school and the students. Coupled with this sense of ownership was a sense of responsibility. She began to think seriously about how she could improve her relationship with her students. She said, "I began to think of my interaction with the students after I got used to the school environment. I felt that this was an area I could develop. This is my place... I am responsible for the students' achievement. The students are mine." She began to take responsibility for her own actions rather than just rely on the received practices of the school. She felt that there was space for her as a teacher in how she managed the classroom for teaching. There was also potential and space for development for the teacher despite the heavy workload. She felt that S2 students were malleable and within that year she could try things out. She exploited the space opened up by the freedom to produce her own materials for trying out new things. She said:

I'd write a story which is educational. I have written a piece for S3 where I put in religious beliefs which talked about the difference between Satan and God. It was very short. I have also put down something about counseling and discipline problems.

6.3.4 Exploring teaching

In her third year Eva was appointed coordinator for S2. Instead of just using materials prepared by other colleagues, she became involved in materials design and preparation. She basically followed her predecessor's very detailed plan and the objectives that she had laid down. Though she was the coordinator, she had very little idea of "how much could be taught and how students could learn." Therefore, she asked Ching, who was the S1 coordinator, for the course outline for S1 to see what was covered in the previous year, and she also looked at what was covered in S3. Eva noticed that there was little continuity between the different levels. She began to formulate her own conception of the need for continuity in the curriculum. She considers S2 and S3 as comprising a unit and S4 and S5 as comprising another unit. She also developed her own theory of "integration." She would use a reading text as input for writing. She explained, "I always think of integrating things. I have tried integrating listening, writing, and comprehension as one unit. The feedback from colleagues was good. They felt that it saved time and was more practical." This was a principle that she worked on when she decided on the scheme of work as a coordinator. To obtain input for her teaching, she attended refresher courses organized by the Education Department. She also sought advice from her colleagues and invited them to comment on the teaching materials that she had designed.

For Eva, S2 is the best time for trying out new things: "S1 is an induction to a new environment. Students need a lot of help to adapt to switching from Chinese to English medium instruction.[7] In S3, things are 'getting serious.' Therefore, S2 is a transitional stage, where she could try out a lot of new things. She disagreed with her school's view that if teachers wanted to try anything, they should do it in S1. So in that year, with two years of experience under her belt, Eva started to think about what she could work on. Grammar teaching was an area that she dreaded, and she decided to work on it, making it more lively, effective, and fun. She looked at the materials that Marina produced and observed her teach. She recalled,

She [Marina] helped me a lot. Vocab, grammar, how to teach. She would take me through how she actually taught a lesson, and also told me her students' reactions, and she shared the teaching materials and the posters that students produced. The games she also shared. Anything you could take away, she'd let you take away. For a new teacher, you can really learn a lot. Yes, she's willing to coach you. This is very important. As somebody new to the job, you are scared.

---

[7] Secondary schools in Hong Kong either use Chinese or English as the medium of instruction. Before 1997 the majority of the schools were English medium. After 1997 about one-third of the schools used English as the medium and two-thirds used Chinese as the medium of instruction.

Apart from being very generous with her time, Marina also gave Eva a great deal of encouragement. Eva recalled Marina telling her from time to time that she had improved. This kind of moral support made life less difficult for her. Eva also consulted Ching when she had questions about grammar. She wanted to read up on grammar teaching, but often found herself running out of time when preparing lessons and then later on other things took over.

In her fourth year Eva was promoted to be the coordinator for S3. This promotion was a source of pressure, and she became very tense and often fell ill. Fortunately, she had the guidance of the former S3 coordinator, who was very thorough and helpful. In describing her, Eva used the Cantonese term *si fu*, which means that Eva took herself to be Marina's apprentice from whom she learned teaching skills. In these two years, she was better able to relate to students, and her teaching improved. She introduced more game elements in her teaching. "They had games, they worked in groups, they needed to produce something and they learned something."

At the end of her fourth year, Eva still felt that she had not come to grips with teaching junior forms. She was still getting feedback from her students that indicated that they could not understand her when she was teaching. She said, "I feel that for S2 and S3, it [teaching] can be very free, but it can also be very confusing. I felt that I was creating chaos." However, she had difficulties explaining how and why she created chaos and confusion. She remarked, "This is just a feeling. Things that I have taught are forgotten easily like vocabulary, and reading comprehension skills. May be they did not have much practice, and they forgot." Not being systematic enough when she taught was another possible reason that she gave. Eva hastened to add that she was not putting all the blame on herself, but she felt that she could improve.

6.3.5 Looking for challenges and asking questions: "I have to try; otherwise I know so little."

At the end of her fourth year, Eva was asked to be the coordinator for S2 again in the coming school year. While Eva gladly took on the assignment, she wanted some new challenges. She asked the principal to "promote" her to teach S4. She planned to follow the same class of students to S5 so that she could find out what the requirements were for the Hong Kong Certificate in Education Examination, a public examination for graduates at S5. This would enable her to better prepare the junior form students for the public examination. Normally, teachers with no relevant disciplinary training would not be given senior forms. However, the principal, who was always supportive of new ideas and initiatives, agreed and assured her that she could do the job.

When she took on a senior form in her fifth year, Eva felt that she had a lot to learn. She said:

This year, there are things that I want to come to grips with, and there are a lot of areas that I am not clear about. For example, syllabus design, what is the main emphasis? We set objectives each year and the objectives are more or less the same every year, but how do we achieve these objectives? This is important.

She was unhappy with the objectives that were put in the scheme of work year after year. She felt that it seemed as though the objectives were put down for the record and for other people's eyes but not for the students. She said, "When you face the students, you really want to be able to teach them things which are useful, and you want to be effective."

She felt ill-prepared. "I had to teach before I could finish going over the textbook myself. I hadn't finished analyzing the themes and the relationship between the themes and yet I had to teach. It was a mad rush.... It's really terrible to be teaching such senior classses and public examination classes." Her teaching was still "not systematic enough." She said, "I feel that I didn't really teach them much. Maybe in the end they would have to rely on themselves for the Hong Kong Certificate in Education Examination."

Teaching S4 was a big challenge to Eva because the students were more mature, and they were more vocal in expressing their complaints. She heard indirectly through her friend at church that her students complained about her teaching – that she was not a good teacher. She was demoralized. She planned to follow S4 to S5, in line with her view about continuity. However, the negative feedback from students affected her badly. In view of that, she thought that it might be best not to follow this group of students to S5; she felt that her students were not learning much from her. Her confidence was undermined. She said, "I don't have confidence.... I feel that I am inadequate in everything." Eva faced this challenge with mental strength. She said that it was a new job, and therefore she was not afraid of not being up to scratch. She wanted time to reflect on her teaching. She made use of long vacations to think about her teaching. "Every time after a long vacation, I will revise something, both my expectations for my students and myself, and the teaching focus, I will make some changes. But I have to wait for long vacations."

In that year, she applied to enroll on a professional training course. She was hoping to obtain input not only from the course but also from the course members. She felt the need for professional training because her teaching was ineffective. She said, "There are far too many areas where I need input. For example, phonetics I am learning. Teaching oral, how do I teach intonation, I have to learn. How to teach vocabulary. These are areas I am weak in." Unfortunately, she was unsuccessful because there were a large number of applicants and priority was given to English major graduates. At the same time, she talked to her colleagues a lot and shared her teaching experience and teaching notes with them in order to improve herself.

6.3.6 Coming to grips with teaching junior forms

Although on the one hand Eva felt that she was a bit stretched and that she was not coping well with teaching senior forms, on the other hand, she felt she had made progress in teaching junior forms. There was more integration in the materials. When she looked at the lesson plan, she was able to imagine what was going to happen in the lesson. She was more flexible in her teaching and was able to make interactive decisions to change her lesson plan in response to students' needs. For example, she changed class work to homework when there was not enough time to get through the activity. "It is more important to make sure that students have learned something. This is a consensus among all teachers. If we catch up next time, it would be OK. Sometimes we also cut down the materials. We do that all the time." What is interesting is that instead of finding the work of coordinating S2 easier the second time around, she found that it was more hard work. She explained:

There are certain things that I feel that I ought to do and there is no excuse not to because I am already more familiar with the job. I cannot bear not to improve on the overall direction [of the curriculum].

She reworked the old materials that were not very good. She also tried out process writing under Marina's leadership and put a great deal of effort into it.

She received positive feedback from students; her lessons were always lively, and students liked them. However, Eva was far from complacent. She was aware of her inadequacies in classroom teaching. There were certain areas in which she lacked confidence. Teaching phonetics, for example, was an area about which she did not know anything and was trying to learn. She was sensitive to students' reactions in class and she knew whether the class was well managed. She said, "You knew when students could not follow your teaching. They [the students] won't deceive you." In particular, she was aware of her lack of clarity in giving instructions. Her students could not follow her instructions. Sometimes she would give homework in the middle of the lesson and sometimes at the end. She kept referring to her teaching as not systematic and that she needed to improve on those aspects.

Reflecting on the past three years since she became a coordinator, Eva felt that "there was potential and space in those three years for [her own] development."

Eva summed up her current phase of professional development as follows, "I am coming to grips with how to make use of the resources available and how to make use of them in the space that I have. When I have this overall improvement, then I can make changes at the micro-level."

Reflecting on her professional development, she felt that she began to gain confidence in the second year. Teaching was no longer as chaotic as the first year. Being the coordinator for S2 in the third year was a challenge. Taking on teaching S4 in the fourth year was yet another challenge because the students were more mature, more direct with their criticisms, and she heard more complaints. This was something she was still trying to deal with. However, she was not put off by the problems. She said, "I feel that this is something new to me. So I am not afraid of not being up to scratch.... In the process [of dealing with the problems], I really want to be able to stop and reflect on my teaching." In the past five years of teaching, Marina has been a constant source of help and encouragement, and her comments have been the yardstick by which Eva judged her own performance. She said, "I remember Marina saying, 'You have improved again from last year.'... Very often, I rely on what my boss tells me. She said my writing is getting better. I am more organized, especially in terms of the curriculum and classroom management." Despite the difficulties that she encountered, she felt that on the whole she was making progress. She felt strongly that there were many areas that she needed to work on. She was also contemplating moving to another school in a year's time because she felt that working in a different school context and teaching students with different backgrounds would be a new stimulus for her.[8]

6.3.7 Synoposis

Eva's professional development is marked by the heavy influence that her sociology background has on her conceptions of teaching and learning. She is acutely aware of the social and moral values that permeated her interaction and relationship with her students, which is very much part of teachers' professional thoughts and actions (Goodlad, Soder, and Sirotnik, 1990). She is a teacher who finds the inculcation of values, which has been referred to as the "pedagogical side" of teaching more important than the "didactic" and "subject-matter side" of teaching (Beijaard, Verloop, and Vermunt, 2000, p. 752). Her understanding of students as individuals and not as a group has shaped the way she handles her relationship with her students. Teaching has been a process in which she explores how this conception can be realized in the classroom. Eva went from simply following the school rules in dealing with disciplinary

---

8 After the sixth year of teaching, Eva did move to another school where the students were of lower socio-economic background and much lower academic ability.

problems to developing her own style of handling misbehavior. She has also developed a very special way of relating to her students through the questions that she asks, the remarks that she makes about the students, the examples that she gives, as well as the tasks that she assigns to the students.

Eva's professional development is characterized by her constant reflection on classroom events and her own practices in order to make sense of and assign meaning to them, and to formulate principles that can guide her future actions. Eva is aware of her own weaknesses and is also able to pinpoint the specific areas of weakness. She judges her own performance by looking at how effective she is. She said, "Judging from effectiveness, I feel that there is a need [to improve]. My ineffectiveness has affected my confidence. It has not affected my will to strive [for improvement]."

Her will to strive for improvement is characteristic of her development. This is evidenced by her positive attitude in trying out new things, and trying to interpret and theorize new experiences in her own way. It is also evidenced by how she treated her work as a coordinator the second time around. Instead of reducing the demand of the task by simply recycling what she did before, she set a higher standard for herself and problematized what could have been treated as unproblematic, such as reworking the teaching materials and the teaching of writing (see Chapter 9). Her search for new challenges to extend her competence was evidenced by her request to teach senior forms that were not normally assigned to teachers with no relevant disciplinary training. In the face of difficulties, she was able to see her own strengths.

Eva shares many of the characteristics that Marina has. However, there are clear differences between them. As we shall see in Chapters 7 and 8, while Marina has developed clear principles about ESL teaching which are theorized practice, Eva's actions were very much guided by her knowledge in sociology, her learning and teaching experiences, as well as her intuition, rather than by theories of language, language teaching, and learning. We can say that Eva has developed expertise in some aspects of teaching. The "pedagogical side" in handling relationship with students is one example. But she still bears the characteristics of a novice teacher in other aspects, especially in the "didactic and subject-matter side," that is, in the enactment of the ESL curriculum, as we shall see in Chapters 7 and 8.

6.4 Ching

Ching comes from a working-class family and grew up in a very protected environment. Her father is a leather-factory worker and her mother is a cleaner in an airplane cleaning company. As blue-collar workers, they were keen that their children did not follow in their footsteps. They tried their best to provide for their children's education and to offer them the best they could. Ching has three siblings, but she was the only one who could get into university. Her elder sister was once a nursery-school teacher, but she quit teaching because of ill health. Her brother is a technician, and her young sister a secretary. For Ching, life has been smooth sailing. She entered an English medium secondary school where the students were of average ability and mainly from working-class families. Ching did very well in school and entered the same university as Marina, majoring in English linguistics. When the study started, Ching was 26 years old and was in her fifth year of teaching.

Ching became a teacher "by elimination," that is, by eliminating what was not suitable for her, like management and administrative jobs, rather than by choosing what she would like to do. Having spent two summers working in business offices, Ching decided that the business world was too competitive for her. Moreover, she had to socialize with people inside and outside the company. This was too much for her quiet personality. Unlike her university peers, she did not go for positions in the civil service because they were too "cushy." She said, "I didn't feel that I would like a job that you don't have to do very much and yet you get a good income." She had a group of close friends from secondary school days, all of whom chose teaching as their career. She said, "We weren't interested in the commercial sector and therefore preferred something 'simple' and 'easy.' This had much to do with our personalities – quiet, unsociable, and introverted."

Her parents were happy for Ching to join the teaching profession because it is stable and the pay is good. For them, school is a well-protected environment where there is no risk involved, unlike the business world. Ching herself felt that teaching was meaningful, but she was not sure if it was the right kind of job for her. She decided that until she had made up her mind about teaching, she would not enroll in a professional training course.

6.4.1 Beginning teaching: a journey on an emotional roller coaster

Ching entered teaching with an image of a teacher being knowledgeable, "qualified," academically competent, and able to help students academically. This image did not change much over time. She felt that she was neither well-prepared nor well-equipped for teaching. She did not have any vision or a sense of mission because she was so concerned about being able to manage her job as a teacher that she did not have any spare capacity to think of other higher goals. She said, "I stressed so much that I had to be academically competent and be able to present what I had in mind in my lessons.... I was only trying to be a teacher, with teaching as the focus most of the time.... Any long-term or far-sighted goals were out of my mind then." She saw teaching as first and foremost being able to present knowledge clearly to students.

The first month of teaching saw a very nervous Ching who found it daunting to speak in English in front of forty students. She said, "I couldn't even begin to think of teaching methods. I had to overcome the problem of having to speak English in front of so many people." She was assigned to teach S1 and S4. The latter was a class with low self-esteem and an inferiority complex. The students took an immediate dislike to Ching because she was seen as an inexperienced teacher for the academically poor. Her relationship with several students was particularly tense and unpleasant. Classroom management was a problem. Like all novice teachers, dealing with the multiple dimensions of classroom teaching was a problem. She could not deal with misbehavior and keep the class going simultaneously. When one student misbehaved, all her attention would be focused on that student and the rest of the class would be neglected. She recalled an incident when a senior form male student misbehaved in class and she decided to talk to him during recess. However, instead of being repentant, the student walked away from her in the midst of their conversation. Ching felt very hurt and could not understand why he behaved in such a way. She wondered if she was not tactful enough or whether her words were too provocative, but she did not have a definite answer.

With no professional training, Ching had nothing to draw on except her own learning experience. She did not remember very much about her school learning experience apart from the impression that the teacher was the authority and the lessons were teacher-centered with little student involvement in activities. The students "sat and listened rather than engaged in using the language together." Individual work predominated. Similarly, Ching's lessons were teacher-centered, dominated by teacher talk with little student participation. There was also little variation in her teaching. She attributed this to her own personality. She said, "I am not a lively person, and I am not creative, and so my teaching reflects my personality." She found it very difficult to motivate low-ability students to learn a language and to communicate with them in a language that they had problems even understanding. She could not see obvious improvement in her students and she had little sense of satisfaction. She wanted to do something about this. She said, "On the one hand, I wanted to inject more fun elements to make my students enjoy the lessons. On the other hand, I was not that kind of person. I was in a dilemma."

In her students' eyes, she was "cold" because she seldom interacted with them outside of class. They found talking to her difficult. Ching felt that this was due to the policy of the English panel, which stipulated that students should talk to their English teachers in English even outside the classroom. "There is a [language] barrier between the students and the teacher.... It is relatively difficult to build a close relationship with students." Ching was unhappy about the situation but she did not know what she could do about this. The opportunity to observe Marina teach and to discuss her work with more experienced colleague were a panacea for Ching. They shared materials, and tried them out together, and discussed how their lessons went. She would interact with colleagues whom she knew well, such as those sitting near her, but she found it difficult to talk to other colleagues. The opportunities for learning from other English panel members were mostly in panel meetings and form meetings (that is, when teachers teaching the same level met).

The first two years of teaching was a journey on an emotional roller coaster for Ching. She cited what her colleague said as mirroring how she felt: "When a lesson went well, she would step out of the classroom saying 'teaching suits me'; but when she had a lousy lesson, then the minute she stepped out of the classroom, she would say 'no, teaching doesn't suit me.'" She often questioned her own competence and aptitude to be a teacher, and wondered whether she should quit teaching. However, she seldom shared her anxieties and problems with her friends or colleagues. She said, "I didn't think my friends who taught in other schools could understand my school and my situation. As for my colleagues, I did not know them well enough to share my feelings with them." Her discussions with colleagues on the English panel was confined to classroom teaching. In other words, despite the support system that was set up in her school, Ching was not able to take full advantage of it and obtain emotional support. When I asked her what made her stay on, she said, "There's no other field I could fit myself into! I also thought I could improve!"

6.4.2 *Gaining confidence and improving teaching*

Having been assigned "remedial classes" for two years, Ching was given a brighter class as well in the third year. She welcomed the assignment and felt more "balanced": "When all my students were low-ability students, I was affected emotionally." With two years of teaching behind her, she became more confident and less inhibited in speaking English in front of the junior students, but not the senior students. She wanted to make her teaching more enjoyable and to relate better to her students, both for their sake and for her own sake. She started, in S1 classes, to vary her teaching a bit more by introducing more activities such as class competitions and the dramatization of stories, and she could see a difference in the students' reactions. Her relationship with her students improved. She was not sure, however, whether the improvement was because of the students or because of her. She said, "I don't know whether it was

The Professional Development of the ESL Teachers 119

because the students were different, or because I have changed; my relationship with my students became closer. I could relax; the atmosphere is more relaxed, and I have a stronger sense of humor. Students are willing to chat with me in English." However, as I probed the reasons for the improvement, she said:

Well, I think basically I didn't encounter major difficulties in managing the classes, except for the S5 class where there were a number of low achievers. The S1 students were cooperative on the whole, and they participated quite actively. More class competitions also worked, which could arouse their interest in the lessons.

In other words, the improvement was due to factors external to herself. There was no reference to whether her understanding of her students or her work as a teacher had changed.

At end of the third year of teaching, she decided that she liked teaching. She said, "When I had completed three years of teaching, I was quite sure I liked teaching although I was exasperated by the students, and teaching was hard work." She was fond of her students, especially the younger students at S1. They are, in her words, "teachable" and "obedient." In addition, she felt that she had come to a different understanding of what teaching was about. She said, "Teaching is not just a job, a duty to fulfill, but guiding and witnessing the growth of my students.... I started to realize that being a teacher should be a matter of teaching, learning, guiding, counseling.... That's to say, it's far more challenging than I thought." She began to concern herself with the causes of students' problems, either academically or psychologically. She was also able to share her thoughts more with her colleagues and to learn from them.

6.4.3 Facing new challenges and struggling for a balance

TEACHING SENIOR CLASSES: "A MOUSE PULLING A TORTOISE"

In her fourth year of teaching, Ching was given a new and more demanding task: to be the form mistress of preuniversity year students, S6, whom she would follow to S7 in the fifth year. Most of the students were new entrants from other schools who could not stay in their own schools because their public examination results were not good enough. Because of this, they were unfavorably disposed to the school, and they challenged the school regulations. Though there were no explicit confrontations, the atmosphere was unfriendly. Ching felt that they were particularly hostile towards less-experienced teachers. When going through reading comprehension questions, for example, the students often challenged her answers and demanded an explanation of why her answers, and not theirs, were correct. She found it difficult to respond to challenges like this: "I find the explanation process or having to think of a way of explaining the answers very difficult." Having grown up in a protected environment where she never had to "face a lot of challenges," this was very trying for her.

Teaching the preuniversity curriculum for the first time, she was floundering. She described the situation as "the mouse pulling the tortoise," a Cantonese expression meaning one does not know where to start. She was very unsure of herself, especially when she disagreed with the guidance given in the Teacher's Notes that went with the textbook. She did not know whether she ought to present her own view to the students or to stick to the textbook. When the students put forward reasonable arguments to support their answers and to refute her answers, she was lost. She said, "When I feel that they [the students] have good reasons for their answers, do I insist that mine are correct? Or should I make some adjustments to my answers and then everything would be OK?" She had a feeling that the students did not see her as a competent teacher, and she lost confidence. She saw things in a negative light.

BALANCING TIME FOR FAMILY AND TIME FOR WORK

In the midst of trying to cope with defiant students, she got married. Trying to strike a balance between family life and school work posed another challenge. Before she got married, she used to work for long hours after school. This was no longer possible. She stayed back until five, but in the evening, she still had to get her marking and lesson preparation done. Though her husband was teaching in the same school, he did not have as much marking to do, and he was not happy that Ching should be spending so much time on schoolwork. They discussed this and there was a period of tolerance and conciliation. But conflicts reemerged. Her husband often reminded her thus, "You have only one husband, but you have many students." Though Ching agreed with her husband that family life was important, she tended to forget this once she got into her work. "When I get engrossed in my work, I tend to forget, and I won't stop and the alarm goes off."

Also in her fourth year, despite her unhappy experience with the S6 class and her unresolved conflict between family life and professional work, Ching decided that she wanted to stay in education, though she was by no means sure whether she wanted to stay at St. Peter's. She enrolled in an in-service PCEd program at The University of Hong Kong. She wanted to get input to improve her teaching rather than to just obtain a paper qualification. She said, "I feel that in these four years, I have been producing a lot of output, but not enough input.... I feel inadequate. So I thought I should get some insight from the course to help me teach more effectively."

LOOKING FOR PROFESSIONAL INPUT

The input that she was looking for was mainly teaching methods and techniques. She was able to get new ideas, for example, in the teaching of vocabulary, reading, and grammar. However, when she tried them out, not everything worked. Yet, she had no time to reflect on what worked and what did not. Nor was there time to read up on references, though there were plenty in the school cabinet. She relied on her own intuition when preparing materials for teaching, rather than the theoretical input that she received in the program. She emphasized that whether the techniques worked or not depended on the students' cooperation. "If it is a cooperative class, it doesn't matter what method it is. I can try it out. If the method requires the class to cooperate and they are not cooperative,... then it would be very difficult." She tried to move away from teacher-centred teaching and involve students more by conducting group work. However, it did not always work, and Ching attributed it to the students not being well-disciplined or having difficulties following the instructions.

RELATING TO SENIOR STUDENTS: THE PROBLEM CONTINUES

Enrolling in a professional course competed against her time for family life and her time for schoolwork. The tension with her husband was always lurking in the background. It would build up and break into confrontation. The stress arising from course work and family life was not helped by Ching's following last year's S6 up to S7 and being their form mistress for the second year. The problem of managing senior form students was still not solved. The students would miss school when there were lessons they did not want to attend. Treating them as mature and responsible students, Ching was not very strict with them. However, this was taken by the students to mean the offense was acceptable. There was disagreement among staff members about how matters like this should be handled. Ching was in favor of penalizing students for breaking school rules, no matter whether they were junior or senior students. However, other colleagues disagreed and argued that being too strict would generate resentment among students. She was very frustrated that she did not have the support of the school to discipline her students. This made her job as form mistress of S7 even more difficult. Her students were less respectful of her because she was less experienced. She observed, "In their heart of hearts, they wondered if you have enough "substance" to be a teacher of senior forms. I can feel that." The biggest problem she had was that she could not build a relationship with them. She could not reach out to the students, save a few, even when they went on a school picnic. Her students would not crowd around her and ask a lot of personal questions. They were "strangers" to her. Ching dismissed this by saying, "Students nowadays are very different from what we were like in the old days. They like to get together with their own buddies and would not pay attention to anybody else." However, when she found that her own students bought a bunch of flowers for a subject teacher to celebrate her birthday, she felt very unhappy. She realized that she must work on her relationship with her students. She took her principal's advice and talked to her students in free lessons and tried to understand them and be supportive. But time was an important factor; she was not able to put in as much time as she wanted.

Meanwhile, Ching continued to explore ways to improve her teaching in junior forms. She gave a questionnaire to her junior students to obtain feedback at the end of the school year. She asked them which lessons they liked best and why. She wanted to find out in which areas of teaching she needed to improve. What is interesting is that she chose to obtain feedback from the junior students, with whom she felt comfortable; but not from the senior form students, where there was an even greater need to find out what the students wanted.

At the end of her fifth year, Ching was still very diffident about handling senior students even though she had taught them for two years already. She had not come to grips with the difference between teaching junior and senior forms. She felt that the experience was so bad that from then onward things would be better because "nothing could be worse."

There were several colleagues who had a good relationship with the senior students. They were very humorous in class, and the students were ready to listen to them. However, Ching never asked them for advice. She felt that she did not know them well enough to do so. Instead, she came up with her own explanation: it could be these colleagues were more experienced, or one of them was the head of the school discipline section, and so she could do a better job.

Looking back at her fourth and fifth years of teaching, Ching felt that she had gained more confidence in teaching junior forms and her relationship with the students had improved. She was more relaxed and her students were willing to chat to her in English. She was also better able to improvise. She did not have to put down in great detail what she was going to do, including what example to give. She was more flexible in coordinating S1 and would make adjustments to the scheme of work according to the needs of the students. However, she still had not overcome her inhibitions when teaching senior forms. She said, "I'm still exploring.... I have a lot to learn." What bothered Ching most was the struggle between her personal life and professional life. She had been looking for a "balance" but could not find it. She said:

I felt that I've lost balance.... I felt that I should improve on my teaching, but when I thought about it further, I realized that I don't have much time, and I stopped going any further. This is the biggest struggle that I had in these two years.

The fifth year of teaching ended with Ching feeling inadequate and diffident about herself as a teacher, because she wasn't able to relate to senior students and still desperately trying to balance family life and school work. Yet she was convinced that education was the field in which she wanted to be involved. She tried to think of ways to solve the problems, such as teaching in a bisessional primary school (that is, a school which operates either in the morning or in the afternoon only), and working in educational settings but not teaching. At this critical moment, the principal intervened. In the following school year, Ching was assigned to teach S6 students who were their own graduates rather than new entrants from a number of different schools. When Ching found that the students had better learning attitudes and the classroom atmosphere was much better, she gave up the idea of leaving the school and stayed on.

6.4.4 Synopsis

Ching entered teaching with an image of the teacher as one who is well qualified and knowledgeable academically and who has an understanding of a teacher's role as "teaching," which is imparting knowledge effectively to students. Having had no professional training, she felt ill-prepared and ill-equipped. She was so anxious about having to manage forty students all at the same time that she could not think beyond getting through the day and making sure that she was able to present knowledge clearly to students.

Her life experience of being brought up in a protected family and having things working out very well for her, as compared to her siblings, also contributed to Ching's preference for things proceeding in an orderly and well-disciplined fashion. Her own learning experience in school, where the teacher was the authority and the classroom was teacher-centered, had a strong influence on the way she managed her own classroom and her teaching. She taught very much the way she was taught, with little student involvement and little variation. The lack of obvious improvement in her students gave her little job satisfaction. She found it difficult to make her own teaching lively and interesting because of her quiet personality. She could not reach out to the students, and she attributed this to the language barrier set up by the policy of the English panel of requiring students to speak to teachers in English at all times. The first two years of teaching were emotionally unsettling for her, and she had doubts about whether she was meant for teaching. Though she was able to share teaching materials and ideas with her colleagues, she was not able to open up herself and share her problems with friends or colleagues. She stayed in teaching and went on to the third year of teaching for lack of a better alternative.

Having had two years' teaching experience of managing a class of forty gave Ching the confidence to think of how she could introduce more variety in her teaching. She was better able to relate to her students as well as to her colleagues. She started to see that teaching was more than just imparting knowledge effectively – that it also involved caring for students' emotional growth. In this phase, we witness two major developments in Ching's professional growth: her relationship with students and her understanding of her role as a teacher. Ching attributed the improvement of her relationship with the students to the fact that the students were different – they were "cooperative," "teachable," and "obedient." There was no reference to how her own understanding of her students had changed.

In her fourth year of teaching, the new task of taking charge of a senior form posed a fundamental challenge to her image of a teacher and her conception of the role of a teacher. Her authority as a teacher was threatened by defiant senior students, and she felt that she was no longer able to live up to the image of being knowledgeable and academically competent. This undermined the confidence that she had built up over the previous three years. It is interesting that again Ching attributed her poor relationship with the students to an external factor: the students were prejudiced against the school and they were different from "what we were like in the old days." It was not until she found out that her own students did have a nice relationship with her colleagues that she realized that she could too, and that she should work on the relationship. As Huberman (1993a) observes, for many teachers, the relationship with students is at the heart of motivations as well as difficulties, frustrations and even crises experienced by teachers. The transition from one phase to another phase was also typically marked by a shift in their rapport with students. The setback that Ching suffered coupled with the challenge typically faced by women teachers of having to balance professional life and family life, as well as doing a professional course, which also competed for time, led to a period of serious self-doubt and reassessment of her commitment to teaching. It was the principal's assigning a high-ability class to her that helped Ching to make the decision to stay on the job.

It seemed that after five years of teaching, Ching never really got off the emotional roller coaster that she had embarked upon. One characteristic that seemed to emerge is that she never had the opportunity to engage in deep reflections of her work and her role. In the face of failures as well as successes, there was a tendency for her to attribute the causes to factors that seemed to be beyond her control, such as her personality, her students, her family situation. With no fundamental changes in her image of a teacher, her conceptions of teaching, her knowledge of students and how best to help them to learn, the progress that she has made in teaching was easily thwarted by changes in external circumstances. Another characteristic was her reluctance to open up herself and seek advice from her colleagues. Unlike Marina and Eva, Ching was unable to take full advantage of the supportive and collaborative school environment. Therefore, though she moved beyond the survival phase and was discovering more about teaching, she suffered a setback and was not quite able to move out of the self-doubt phase.

6.5 Genie

Genie comes from a devout Protestant family of two children, herself and an elder brother. Her parents were retired businesspeople. Her grandmother has been living with her family since she was a baby and has had the greatest influence on her regarding religious beliefs and moral values. Genie has great admiration for her grandmother as a very competent and wise person, and feels that she can talk to her just about anything. Genie herself is a very devout Protestant and has a strong sense of religious mission in spreading the gospel.

Like Marina, she studied in a Chinese medium primary school and then got into an English medium secondary school that is also prestigious. However, unlike Marina's school, it was a government school in which the teachers were civil servants who were generally considered by students as "old fashioned." Changing from using the mother tongue to using English to learn was "very tough," according to Genie. "Everything was in English, including the school assembly and all announcements." She had to work hard to fit into the school. Fortunately, she liked English and loved reading aloud and talking to herself in English to play with the sounds of the language. Her school learning experience was not particularly exciting, and she seldom made reference to it when she talked about her teaching.

At university she majored in English. Teaching was not her first choice nor was it a conscious choice. Upon graduation, she joined a commercial organization as an executive officer but did not like the work there. She did not like sitting in the office and doing paperwork all day. She quit after a few months and looked for another job. However, she could not find one that she really liked. A friend who was working at the Hong Kong government Education Department suggested that she could try being a supply teacher, which means substituting for a teacher who has taken leave, to see if she liked teaching. She did and liked it. In the following year, she joined St. Peter's as a full-time teacher. She saw this as God's will that she become a teacher.

6.5.1 First year: Coping with the pressure of "real" teaching

Upon joining St. Peter's, Genie was assigned to teach S3 and S4 and to be the form-mistress (class teacher) of S3. The first two months of teaching did not go well for Genie. Like all new teachers, Genie had problems coping with the multifaceted nature of teaching. She found herself "very busy," "confused," and "forgetful." She found class business time-consuming and distracting. She often forgot to deal with class business until the lesson was over. On the following day, as soon as she started teaching, she forgot about class business again.

For the first time in her life, she felt under pressure because unlike being a supply teacher, she was engaged in "real" teaching, and the students were her students rather than somebody else's. She said, "When I was a supply teacher, there was no pressure. If the students did not listen, I would not take it to heart. But here, these are *your* students." Unsure of herself and the practices in the school, she followed doggedly what was laid down in the scheme of work and the schedule. In order to cope with the very tight schedule, she spoke very fast in class. She said, "I was scared. I didn't know what was going to happen [if I didn't cover everything]." Her colleagues were surprised that she could cover everything in the scheme of work and keep to the schedule. They gave her a pat on the back and told her that she was very capable. This kind of positive feedback was reassuring for Genie but did not help her to take a critical look at her work. Her students complained that she spoke too fast and the words she used were too difficult. Instead of taking the students' complaints at face value, she wondered whether the complaints were merely a camouflage for their disrespect and nonacceptance of her as a new teacher.

6.5.2 *Image of the teacher and the classroom*

When Genie entered teaching, she thought that a teacher had to be very strict and stern and have a sound knowledge of his or her subject. Her image of a teacher was that she or he was boring, out-dated, and not enterprising. This is why she did not want to be a teacher when she graduated from university. When she became a teacher, the last thing she wanted to do was to play out this image. Yet, she was advised by her colleagues to be strict with the students. She said, "Some colleagues told me that if I was strict at the beginning and then became more lenient a bit later on, it would work better." This was very much against her wish, but she followed their advice. She would demand an explanation for not handing in homework and would make students do it immediately. For misbehavior, students were also sent to detention right away. To make sure that her students would not become "uncontrollable," Genie hid her "true self" behind a stern front. This did not go down well with the students.

What she had hoped for was a close relationship with her students. She used the image of "home" to describe the classroom. She saw the teacher and students as sharing the same home, and thought that their relationship should be as close as members of a family. When there were visitors to her class, she asked the students to welcome them in the same way that they would welcome visitors to their homes. Her conception of the teacher-student relationship as family came from her belief that since the students and the teacher would be spending time together for at least one year, their relationship should be as close as members of a family. She believed that if the teacher and the students had a good relationship, the lessons would be more enjoyable, and the students' academic results would be better.

Genie saw her role as providing guidance to students rather than giving instructions and imparting knowledge. She also had a sense of mission of imparting her personal moral values and beliefs to her students. She would select articles on social and political issues and get students to read and discuss them. She was keen to get students to participate in class because she believed that it was through active participation that students learn. She said:

I believe that learning means my *providing guidance for them to think and act*, and they should think and produce. If they are passively taking things in, it is meaningless.... When they enthusiastically participate in class, I can *guide* them more smoothly, and the lesson would be livelier. (My emphasis)

For example, when teaching vocabulary, instead of telling students what the words meant, she would ask them to look up the meanings of words in the dictionary. She said, "I feel that things that they do on their own they will remember better."

However, her students were not responding to her, especially those in S4. These lessons were described by Genie as "the water is still and the river flies," which is a Chinese expression that means the place is very quiet and still. The students were reluctant to volunteer answers, and when she made specific nominations, what she often got was "I don't know" for an answer. She was badly affected. She asked herself, "Was it because they could not understand me? Was it my fault? Was my teaching so boring that they were not interested in participating?" She was bewildered, and there were a lot of "ups and downs in [her] heart." She asked for advice from colleagues and found them "a great source of help and reassurance." They gave her many practical ideas and materials for teaching. They consoled her and pointed out that S4 students were at an awkward age where they felt that they were more mature than junior students, and so they would not get all excited in class and fight for the floor to give answers. However, in many respects, they were not really very mature. This helped to ease Genie's mind a bit but not entirely, because according to a colleague who was their former teacher, this was a very lively and creative class, and yet they were not relating and responding to her. She felt that her teaching needed to be improved. She did not know "how to present the materials" to the students in a variety of ways. She knew that if this continued, both the students and she would "suffer." She tried to read more teaching resource books to get ideas for teaching, but she also accepted the fact that it would take time for her to grow and mature as a teacher.

6.5.3 A breakthrough

A breakthrough came after two months or so when she decided to talk to the students whom she knew well and trusted. She asked them what problems they found in her teaching. In order to see whether the students were serious or just wanted to have fun in class, she asked them to give her advice on how she could improve. They told her that their former teacher put them in groups and did group work. Genie took the suggestion on board and the atmosphere in the classroom turned around. She described what happened as follows.

> It was not just me talking all the time. I would ask them questions, and they would look for answers from books and handouts and compete against each other. They also competed in looking things up in the dictionary.... they would do [the exercises] together and discuss among themselves.... The distance between the students and me became much closer. It was no longer a big class of thirty to forty people sitting there. The atmosphere was very different.

Genie did not feel that asking students for advice would compromise her authority as a teacher. She said, "I expected them to help me because they had been taught by different teachers. So I wanted to find out how they would like to be taught, and I also wanted to find out if there was anything they really liked from their past experience. If they told me, and if I could do it, I would try."

Once the atmosphere turned around, Genie felt that she could reach out more to students. She would play games with them after class and would participate as their peers rather than as their teacher. She was pleased when the students told her that she was "a big kid," and "one of them." She talked to her students (in Cantonese) whenever she had time. She did not just talk about learning English, but their lives, their religious beliefs, their family, friends, and school life.

In addition to talking to students, Genie often went to her colleagues for advice. She also observed Marina and other experienced colleagues teach. She was very open about her problems in teaching, and she received a lot of support from her colleagues. At the end of the first year, Genie had established a good relationship with the students. She asked them to evaluate her teaching in their diaries. She received very frank comments. For example, one student told her that the minute she opened her mouth, they knew that she was a new teacher and inexperienced. They also felt that sometimes she was not in control of things and did not know what she wanted to do. Genie did not mind these comments at all because they were, in her words, "from the students' hearts."

In the course of her first year of teaching, her image of a teacher changed. She found that many of her colleagues were enthusiastic about teaching. They were energetic and willing to try new things, and were a lot of fun. She realized that she did not have to put on a stern face all the time; she could be playful with them, and she realized that having a sense of humor is also very important. The first year ended with Genie feeling much more positive about herself, about the teaching profession in general, and able to relate to students much better than at the beginning. Her image of a teacher had changed, and she was able to achieve more congruence between the teacher that she aspired to be and the role that she actually played.

6.5.4 Second year: Making teaching interesting and getting students involved

In her second year, Genie followed the S4 class up to S5 but remained the form mistress of S3. From the very beginning of the school year, she put students in groups and asked each group to choose a name for the group. This was to give students a sense of belonging rather than a way of organizing learning. The group size was about six or seven instead of four or five because she thought that bigger groups would generate more ideas and would be more fun. However, as soon as the novelty of sitting in groups wore off, the problem of lack of student participation relapsed. Her colleagues told her not to put all the blame on herself and that interaction was a two-way process. Genie was not satisfied. She did not want students to be quiet: "Just me talking with no student participation is very boring. I am bored and the students are bored. I believe that learning means me providing *guidance for them to think and act*, and they should think and produce. If they are passively taking things in, it [*teaching*] is meaningless." (My emphasis) She tried to address this problem by spending more time looking for and designing teaching materials and asking for advice from colleagues.

As she gained experience, she began to move away from following the schedule as doggedly as she did in the previous year. She also heard from her colleagues that it was better to cut out things that she could not cover, and focus on those that were important for students to learn.

In her second year of teaching, she was beginning to develop a comfortable relationship with her S5 students, having taught them for a year at S4. With S3 students, however, she was still having problems. She did not relate particularly well to the class as a whole, and the students were generally apathetic. She lost her temper with some of them when they were not attentive, and they felt that she was "picking on them" all the time. This bothered her. She tried to open herself more to them and tried to see things from their perspective. At the end of the second year, she asked the S3 students to evaluate her teaching. They gave her very frank comments. Some of them said that she had improved and others said that her teaching was still very boring. They also told her that as they got to know her better, they found out that she was not that strict, and when she had games with the students, she was really into it. Genie enjoyed reading these comments. She said, "What they wrote was really from their hearts and that's what I like about them."

The second year saw Genie suffering a setback from the breakthrough that she achieved in the first year. She continued to make an effort to reach out to her colleagues as well the students and discuss her problems with them. The central question that she wanted to address but was not quite able to was how she could make her teaching interesting enough to engage the students' attention.

6.5.5 Third year: Dealing with a difficult class

In her third year of teaching, Genie was presented with a big challenge of teaching a very difficult S3 class. She described the beginning of school as "fighting a battle." She felt that she was not in control, especially when students were engaged in group work. She said, "In normal classes when they are sitting up straight (that is, in teacher-fronted classes) it is easy to see them because everybody faces you.... But starting the lesson [is always a problem because] some of them are not with you and you have to repeat.... Group work is even worse." She found the boys in that class particularly problematic. Except for a few who were described by Genie as "OK," the rest were "exasperating." They were either talking all the time, or daydreaming. She did not know whether they understood her. The phrase "I don't know what they are doing" kept recurring in the interviews. She said, "I have to be very long-winded and to keep them under control. That's hard work.... I am exhausted." She did not know how to tackle the problem except to "keep an eye on them all the time." If they went overboard, she said, "I would not give face." "To give face" is a Cantonese expression meaning "to save face" (Goffman, 1971). For Genie, it was very hard work, and it was frustrating to keep them "under control" and to have to repeat instructions all the time. They were not willing to speak up, and she felt that she "wasted" a lot of time getting them to speak loudly, especially the girls. She also became impatient because she was already behind schedule. She said, "I never thought that I would have had to deal with this [getting students to speak up in class] as well." She was badly affected by this class, and she felt that "things were not going as she wished."

There was a boy named Kenneth in this class who was particularly difficult to manage and was seen as the rotten apple in the class. He was disruptive in class and often tried to distract students sitting near him from their work. He had been sent to the disciplinary master who made him sign contracts to behave himself. Genie would reprimand him in front of the class and make him leave his group and sit on his own. Genie's relationship with him was clearly strained.

Halfway through the first term, a critical incident occurred that changed the relationship. I was observing Genie teach, as part of this study. As usual, Genie started the lesson by collecting homework from the students. Genie found that some students had identical homework, and she was trying to find out who had copied from whom. Kenneth was among them. When Genie questioned him, his attitude was defiant and rude. Genie was very upset and in the middle of questioning Kenneth, she went quiet. She walked to the windows and stared outside. Tears were rolling down her cheeks. There was stony silence in the classroom. I went up to Genie, offered to take over the class for her, and walked her to the staff room. When I went back to the classroom, a quarrel had already broken out between Kenneth and several students, including the class monitor. Before I could call the class to order, Kenneth and the class monitor had broken into a fight. With the help of some strong students, I separated them and stopped the fight. I asked Kenneth to go and wash his face, calm himself down, and come back for class when he was ready. Kenneth rushed out of the classroom and banged the door closed. It was a relief to me when he did come back after five minutes. After the incident, Genie and I discussed how to deal with Kenneth. We agreed that Genie should have a serious talk with him. If Kenneth showed that he was repentant and promised to improve, then he should be given the opportunity to improve rather than simply punishing him in public, though he fully expected that already. In the course of the conversation, Genie found out that Kenneth came from a troubled family and had a rough family life. He admitted that he behaved badly and was relieved to hear that he did not get a black mark on his conduct from Genie. Since then, Genie tried to find time to interact with Kenneth at a personal level, and he tried to improve not only his behavior in class but also his work. He was enjoying school more than before, though academically he was still struggling. This critical incident not only changed Genie's relationship with Kenneth, but also helped her to realize the importance of trying to understand her students. This guided her in the way she handled what she might have considered "disciplinary problems" in the past. For example, she was absent one day and she asked her colleague to have them work on some vocabulary exercises in the textbook. When she returned after sick leave, she found that a number of students had not done the exercise. In the past she would have reprimanded them for not doing their work. However, this time she checked first with those who usually completed their homework to see if they had done their work. She found that they had not done it either. So she concluded that there must have been some miscommunication between the teacher and the class, and perhaps even between herself and her colleague. She also tried to stop herself from getting frustrated when the students had not done their homework. She made contingency plans for different scenarios. For example, if she planned to go over the answers to homework, she would also have ready some other materials in case the students had not done their homework. She said, "To prepare more is better than less."

With a new understanding of how to build a relationship with her students, she also began to work on her relationship with her S4 students. Half of the class was her former students in S3 who did not have a particularly close relationship with her. She described a breakthrough occurring in the second term when she had a frank talk with the class and shared with them her feelings about them and her expectations. The conversation also helped her to understand that students expected her to be consistent in what she required of them. She said, "Because our relationship had improved, the lessons also went more smoothly, and I started to feel the satisfaction of teaching. The class atmosphere was more relaxing and enjoyable."

In terms of teaching, she was more critical of the materials provided. For example, for reading comprehension, instead of using the questions provided in the textbook, she provided a framework to guide the students when they read the text. She said:

If I listed the main aspects covered in the text so that they are like sub-headings, the students can find the relevant information according to these sub-headings to help them understand the passage. I feel that this helps them to understand the passage better than these (reading comprehension) exercises.

She was also able to start making interactive decisions about her teaching. When there was time left in a lesson, she would have something else that she could do with the students, such as going through newspaper articles. She was also able to make changes to her plan on the spot on the basis of students' reactions. She was more aware of the need to exercise her judgement on the amount of materials she should and could cover. Reading up on resource materials and trying out activities suggested by colleagues made her feel that ideas came more easily to her. She had a greater variety of teaching techniques, and her teaching was improving. However, she was still at a stage when she was not quite able to articulate the principles that guided her decisions, and even when she could, she was not sure of herself. She often cited Marina or her other colleagues as a source of authority when she was providing justifications for her actions and practices.

Though she was much better at relating to students and understanding their problems, at times, she still used her own learning experience as her reference for judging her students. For example, having been a self-motivated student herself, Genie could not understand why her students needed such close guidance and monitoring. Similarly, when she talked about the trouble of getting students to speak up in class, she compared herself as a student with them and said, "I was not like that. I find them [the students] very troublesome."

Looking back at her professional development, Genie felt that she had learned that "a teacher must be open-minded and sincere towards her students." She also felt that

> the most important thing in teaching is to build up a good relationship with students. Once it is built up, the lessons can move on smoothly, and a teacher's satisfaction mainly comes from that as well. A teacher does not only impart knowledge to his students but also has to be a role model to influence students' values and beliefs.

6.5.6 Synopsis

Genie entered teaching with a negative image of what a teacher *is* and her own image of what a teacher *should be*. The former was very much influenced by her own learning experiences in school and the latter by her own religious background. However, when confronted with the reality of managing classroom discipline and keeping students "under control," she hid her true self behind a stern front. The conflict between the persona that she assumed for pragmatic reasons and the image of the teacher as a family member providing guidance preoccupied her in her first two years of teaching. Like many novice teachers, she turned to her colleagues for emotional support and advice. However, unlike most novice teachers, she also turned to the students for advice. Her sincerity, open-mindedness, and humility won the students over, and she was able to get closer to them. With the moral support of her colleagues and her own efforts in resolving the conflict between the two images of the teacher, she was able to survive the first year of teaching and feel more positive about herself and the profession.

The relationship that Genie managed to build with students in the first year did not involve fundamental changes in her understanding, however. The problem recurred every time she took on a new class in the second and third year. She went through periods of exhilaration when she thought she had achieved a breakthrough and depression when she suffered a setback. She was frustrated and exhausted, but she did not give up. She tried to sustain a frank dialog with her students. Paradoxically, the students were both a source of frustration and exasperation as well as a source of motivation for her to persevere.

Coming from a middle-class family, having studied in a prestigious English medium school, and having been a highly motivated learner herself, she found it difficult to empathize with working-class children. Her sense of frustration was often caused by comparing herself as a learner with her students and failing to understand why they could not be like her. She was very keen to improve her teaching, and she picked up ideas from colleagues and resource books and tried them out. However, the improvement of teaching was understood as gaining technical skills. There was little reference to her understanding of how students learn and how to structure their learning experience in such a way that would engage their attention. Students' participation in class was used as the criterion for success rather than the learning outcome. As Calderhead and Shorrock (1997) point out, there is a persistent belief among student teachers or beginning teachers that learning is unproblematic. If the teacher presents interesting activities and students are involved, then they will learn.

The critical incident in the third year of teaching had a strong impact on Genie. She reflected on the incident and began to see the importance of being able to see things from her students' perspective and to empathize with them. She began to see that building a good relationship with students was very important for successful teaching. She has yet to understand that effective teaching is also an important element in building a strong relationship with the students.

6.6 Summary

In this chapter I have given biographical accounts of the professional development of the ESL teachers. The accounts show that there are certain similarities among their developmental paths. Like all beginning teachers, they were overwhelmed by the multifaceted nature of classroom teaching. The initial years were particularly challenging for these four teachers because all of them went into teaching with no professional preparation. They all went through the process of negotiating their role as a teacher, and in this process their family background, their learning experience, their life experience, and their disciplinary background had a powerful influence on their conceptions of teaching, learning, and the image that they had formulated for themselves as teachers. The initial years were painful and unsettling for all of them. There were tears and joy, frustration and satisfaction. Genie, having only completed slightly over two years of teaching, was going through this phase. The other three teachers all went through periods of "self-doubt." However, despite the fact that they were working in largely similar contexts, their paths diverged soon after the initial years. While Marina and Eva were able to move out of the phase of self-doubt and on to another phase, Ching did not seem to be able to get off the emotional roller coaster. It was clear from the biographical accounts that each teacher responded differently to their contexts of work. Marina and Eva were able to benefit from the supportive culture in the school and were able to see possibilities for teaching and learning within the contextual constraints, whereas Ching had difficulties opening herself up for interaction with her peers and transcending the constraints. There was also a difference in the way they handled the problems that they were confronted with, and a difference in the problems that they chose to confront. When they encountered difficulties in teaching, Eva and Marina both engaged with exploration and experimentation. The satisfaction that they gained upon seeing positive learning outcomes sustained their enthusiasm in and commitment to teaching. Ching engaged in relatively less experimentation because of her concern for keeping order and discipline. Both Eva and Marina problematized what appeared to be unproblematic, such as the way they handled disciplinary problems, and they were able to reframe their understanding of their work and their roles as teachers after reflection. However, while Marina's explorations and experimentation, as well as her problematization of her work as a teacher, involved an interaction between theoretical input *and* personal practical experience, Eva's were largely based on the latter. Both of them looked for challenges and tried to extend their level of competence. In the process of taking on challenges, Marina seemed to go from strength to strength whereas Eva suffered setbacks from time to time. This suggests that the kinds of challenges that one takes on and whether one is able to benefit from these challenges are important factors in the development of expertise. Later, in Chapter 10, we will focus on the differences outlined above and discuss in detail the ways in which they are critical to the development of expertise.

7 Teacher Knowledge and Managing the Classroom for ESL Learning

In this chapter I shall examine the classroom practices of the four ESL teachers and the knowledge embedded in these practices. The investigation of classroom practices will be done under two broad areas: the management of the classroom *for* learning, and the enactment of the ESL curriculum. The latter refers to the way the ESL curriculum is being given meaning by the teacher and the students (see Synder, Bolin, and Zumwait, 1992). As pointed out in Chapter 4, these two broad areas are intermeshed and often difficult to disentangle. Their division is more for the convenience of organizing the discussion than real. In this chapter I shall focus on the management of the classroom for learning, or "the management of learning." The enactment of the English curriculum will be the concern of the next chapter.

7.1 ESL Teacher Knowledge

While there are a number of studies on the knowledge of L1 English teachers (see, for example, Grossman, 1990; Hillocks, 1999), not much has been written about ESL teacher knowledge (see, however, Woods, 1996; Tsui and Nicholson, 1999). In ESL teaching, the target language is both the medium and the object of learning. While there seems to be a consensus that the ESL teacher's ability in the target language is part of teacher knowledge, it is not evident that there is consensus regarding what constitutes the subject matter knowledge of ESL teachers and whether such knowledge should be explicitly taught. For example, whether the grammar of the target language should be taught explicitly has been debated. It has been proposed that a second language, like a first language, can be "acquired" and not "learnted" (see, for example, Krashen, 1982). In the past two decades, however, the explicit teaching of grammar has been given more prominence in the ESL curriculum (see, for example, the collected papers in Bygate, Tonkyn, and Williams, 1994 and James and Garrett, 1991; Ellis 1998; Rutherford, 1987; Schimdt, 1994).

Woods (1996) outlines the assumptions underlying language, language learning, and language teaching. He points out that language has been perceived by some as a single unified entity and by others as a cluster of entities or genres, such as general English versus scientific English. Language has also been perceived as knowledge as well as abilities. The former consists of knowledge about phonology, syntax, lexis, and discourse as well as sociolinguistics, communication strategies, and strategies for the four language skills. The latter consists of the four language skills; the microskills in each of the four skills, such as guessing meaning from context when reading or listening; and composite skills such as note-taking (see p. 187).

Tsui and Nicholson (1999) represented the knowledge structure of ESL teachers according to Shulman's categories of teacher knowledge and conceptualized ESL subject matter knowledge as knowledge about the language system, which consists of phonology, lexis, grammar and discourse. They also subsumed the teaching of the four language skills, language learning strategies, and language teaching strategies under pedagogic content knowledge. Knowledge of language learning strategies includes knowledge of strategies such as risk-taking, tolerance of ambiguity, and self-monitoring, whereas knowledge of language teaching strategies includes knowledge of strategies such as using different activity types, focusing on accuracy or fluency, and adapting materials for different ability levels. The management of learning and the management of resources are subsumed under pedagogic knowledge. The management of learning refers to aspects like student motivation and learner empowerment. The management of resources includes aspects like the authenticity, accessibility, and appropriateness of the materials used. This delineation, as pointed out in Chapter 4, is more analytic than real. One could well argue that knowledge of second language learning strategies, which involves knowledge of theories of second language learning, should be part of the subject matter knowledge of ESL teachers. Similarly, the management of resources for learning involves knowledge of the language system in order to understand the advantages and the potential disadvantages of using authentic language materials for teaching. Therefore, in discussing the knowledge embodied in the management of learning and the enactment of the ESL curriculum by the four ESL teachers and how their knowledge is developed, no attempt will be made to categorize them. Rather, teacher knowledge will be discussed as an integration of the various aspects of knowledge involved in ESL teaching and learning.

7.2 Management *of* Learning

The term *management of learning* is used in a wider sense than the term *classroom management*. The latter is frequently used to refer to aspects of classroom organization, such as conducting individual, pair, or group work; maintaining order; dealing with disruptive behavior; and handling daily business, such as collecting assignments and taking roll calls. While these are important aspects of a teacher's work as a classroom manager, they are only part of it. As Calderhead (1984) points out, classroom management is inextricably linked to instructional objectives. The teacher not only has to maintain discipline in the classroom, but he or she also must manage the classroom in a way that will best facilitate learning. Therefore, when examining the work of the four case-study teachers, I shall look at the way they manage the classroom *for learning*.

Studies of teachers who are effective and ineffective classroom managers have pointed out that the difference between the two lies not in the ways these teachers deal with disruptive behavior, but rather in how they prevent disruption. Well-established classroom norms and routines are important means of preventing disruption and managing learning in the classroom (Kounin, 1970; Anderson, Evertson and Emmer, 1980; Calderhead, 1984). Norms are rules governing what constitutes acceptable and unacceptable behaviors, and routines are procedures that have been established over time to control and coordinate specific sequences of behavior (Yinger, 1979). Norms and routines are necessary because of the very complex and relatively unpredictable nature of classroom teaching. The teacher has to deal with a large number of individuals with different social and possibly different cultural backgrounds. He or she also needs to respond to a multitude of events that happen simultaneously within a very short time. (See 3.2 for the discussion on the multidimensionality, simultaneity, immediacy, and unpredictability of classroom teaching). As pointed out in Chapter 3, by making the timing and sequencing of teacher and student behaviors predictable, and by making clear what constitutes acceptable and unacceptable behaviors, teachers reduce their cognitive load as well as management load so that they will have the spare capacity to deal with the unpredictable. With established classroom routines for dealing with recurrent events in the classroom, such as collecting homework and handling students who have not done their homework, the teacher does not have to waste time in dealing with them individually. More time can then be devoted to teaching. The use of routines is a very important part of interactive decision-making and is considered an essential element in classroom survival: routines create and manage the learning environment (Calderhead, 1984; Doyle, 1986; see also Woods, 1996). Studies of expert and novice teachers have observed that the former have available a repertoire of routines that enable them to handle a variety of situations (see Leinhardt and Greeno, 1986). Similarly, expert teachers establish norms that are made known to students so that they know what is expected of them. Routines and norms are developed over time.

Hence, it is hardly remarkable that expert teachers, when compared to novices, have more routines at their disposal. For as Olson (1992) points out, embedded in the routines and norms are complex ideas of how the classroom should be managed to facilitate learning. Therefore, the kinds of routines available and whether they facilitate the management of learning distinguish expert and nonexpert teachers.

Calderhead (1984), citing the study of Anderson et al. (1980), observed that effective classroom managers often outline classroom rules in detail on the first day of school and spend considerable time at the beginning of the school year explaining classroom procedures. In order to give the reader a flavor of these four teachers in their management of learning, I shall start reporting on each case study teacher with a description of the first two lessons that they conducted at the beginning of the school year when the study began. The features identified in these two lessons will be elaborated on, and further features will be added in the subsequent discussion.

7.3 Marina

In Chapter 6 we have seen that when Marina first started teaching, she faced the same problem as all novice teachers of being overwhelmed by the complexity of classroom teaching. Over the years, however, she has been able to negotiate a set of classroom norms with her students and to establish routines that enabled her to conduct lessons smoothly. In the rest of this section, I shall characterize the ways in which Marina managed the classroom for learning, the conceptions of teaching, and learning and knowledge that are embedded these practices.

7.3.1 Management of learning in action: Marina's first two lessons

Marina and Eva were teaching the same level, S2 (grade 9), and they agreed that the instructional objectives of these two lessons were twofold: to get the students to use adjectives to describe themselves, and to get to know each other by describing themselves to their classmates. Marina and Eva also exchanged ideas on how the lessons should be conducted.

Marina started the lesson by using three adjectives to describe herself: *hard working, punctual, talkative*. She told the students that she worked fourteen hours a day. She then asked if they knew the meaning of *punctual*. When explaining the word *punctual*, she established the first house rule: Be punctual when you come to class.

M: What is *punctual*? When does school start every morning? When does school start every morning?
Ss: Eight o'clock.
M: Eight. Right. Yes. Eight. And I am punctual. I am always here at eight. Are you punctual? Are you punctual? [*pointing at a student*]
S: [*very softly*] Yes.
M: Sorry? Yes. Anybody knows you? Which class do you come from? 1A. Right. Who's punctual in 1A? OK. Is he punctual? Yes or no?
Ss: Yes.
M: Yes. So he is punctual, and I am punctual too. So I am always punctual for lesson. *Now everybody, if, after the recess time, you come in late, I won't let you in because I am punctual.*

After *punctual*, Marina pointed at the word *talkative* on the board and asked about the student who was most talkative in class and whether girls were more talkative than boys. She noticed a student speaking in Cantonese, and she established the second house rule: No Cantonese in English lessons.

After introducing herself, Marina asked the students to use three adjectives to describe themselves. She asked them to take out their dictionaries and exercise books, and in the meantime she counted up to five, indicating that by the time she finished counting, the students should have carried out her instructions. This is a routine that she employed whenever she asked her students to carry out an action, for example, getting into groups, going back to their seats, or taking out books. The aim was to let students know that they should complete the action within a time limit and that they should not waste time.

When the students had their dictionaries and exercise books ready, Marina asked the students to write down their names and three adjectives to describe themselves in the vocabulary book, but they should not let their neighbors see what the three adjectives were. This was because later she was going to ask them to tell each other about themselves and she wanted to make sure that there was an information gap between them. Two minutes were given for the task. She moved on to another task and gave instructions. Before she did that, she told the students to listen to her instructions carefully, and she would ask them to repeat the instructions. At this point, she established another routine: after listening to her instructions, they would be asked to repeat her instructions. And she did ask them to repeat her instructions.

Marina instructed students to work in pairs and to tell their neighbors their names, the adjectives they had put down to describe themselves, and why they used those adjectives. Three minutes were given. Marina set the alarm clock for three minutes. When the alarm clock went off, Marina asked them to write down their neighbor's name and the three adjectives they used in their vocabulary book. She reinforced the rule of speaking in English in the lesson.

M: Now I would like you to write down your neighbor's name and the three adjectives in your book. Open it [the vocabulary book] now. If you can't remember, ask your neighbor, *in English*.

The first lesson ended after the students completed this activity. In the second lesson, on the following day, before she started teaching, Marina went over the answers to the exercise that she asked them to do the night before. She spent a lot of time going over the pronunciation and the meanings of the adjectives. In the course of doing so, she heard Cantonese being used several times, and she reminded the students that they would be punished if she heard Cantonese again. For homework, she asked them to learn the pronunciation and the meaning of the words by heart, and to choose three adjectives from the list that she went over with them to describe themselves and give reasons. After giving the instructions for homework, she called on a student to repeat the instructions. This reinforced the routine that she established in the first lesson. Near the end of the lesson, Marina invited volunteers to help her set up a routine for collecting homework and handling students who had not done their homework.

From the above description of Marina's first two lessons, we can see a number of striking features in her management of learning. First, while most teachers would spend the first lesson in the school year going over rules and regulations and day-to-day management matters, Marina maximized time for teaching and learning by integrating the establishment of norms and routines with teaching. Norms and routines were spelled out explicitly when the teaching situation lent itself to their formulation. This shows that in Marina's conception of teaching, context is very much part of the teaching act. As we shall see in Chapter 8, being able to see the various aspects of the teaching act as an integrated and coherent whole is an outstanding feature of Marina's teaching in both the management of learning as well as the enactment of the curriculum. Second, the choice of using adjectives to describe oneself as the instructional objective of the first two lessons was very much integrated with the communicative need for the students to get to know the teacher as well as their fellow students at the beginning of the school year (recall that some of them came from different S1 classes). Third, Marina was able to establish a number of important routines and norms very early on in the school year, all of which were consistently reinforced throughout the school year. In the following sections, we shall deal with each of these one by one.

7.3.2 *Handling classroom discipline*

Marina's lessons were characterized by a high level of student involvement in doing things with and in English. Therefore, her classrooms were often very noisy, but the students were enjoying themselves, and they were learning. However, there were also times when she wanted absolute silence and attention. She articulated her guiding principle in keeping discipline in the classroom as follows:

If I'm talking about something that I need the attention of the whole class for and that everybody must follow what I am saying before I can carry on [with the lesson], then I want them to be quiet and to pay attention. But if I give them tasks to work on and they are talking noisily, then I don't mind that at all. But once I think [the topic] is important, then I need them to be quiet. And I will also ask them to repeat what I just said to make sure that they understood what I said.

Underlying the norm that Marina established for acceptable and unacceptable noise is her knowledge of English learning as a process in which students "should be involved" and must be given the opportunity "to work together, to produce." As we have seen in Chapter 6, this conception came partly from her own learning experience in school and partly from the professional course she attended.

She discriminated between on-task noise, which was tolerated and even encouraged, and off-task noise, which was not tolerated. It also embodied her knowledge of the importance of giving clear instructions, which she explained as follows: "Once they started working on the task, it would be disruptive to ask them to stop and explain [the instructions] once again if I found that some students did not get them. And if they did not understand the instructions, it would be impossible for them to carry out the task." Therefore, when she was giving instructions, no matter whether the instructions were for homework or classroom tasks, no noise would be tolerated. As we have seen in her first two lessons, in order to make sure that the students did understand the instructions, she built in a routine of asking them to repeat what they were supposed to do, especially when the instructions were complicated or when she noticed that some students were not paying attention.

Asking students to repeat what has been said, either by the teacher or by fellow students, became a routine for ensuring that students were listening, either out of necessity or courtesy. She said, "If I notice that the students did not pay attention, I would ask them questions so they know they need to pay attention. This is respect [for others], this is courtesy."

Marina's expertise in handling classroom discipline is realized not only in establishing routines but also in her ability to judge when the noises made foreshadowed disciplinary problems and must be curbed, and when they could be usefully exploited to achieve instructional objectives. As Tripp (1994) points out, having routines does not make a good teacher; it is the judgement that he or she exercises in the use of the routines. For example, it was common to see in Marina's classroom students shouting out answers in a joking manner or students making a funny remark – but instead of ignoring or reprimanding them, she would turn the remark into a teaching point. The following is an excerpt from a writing lesson in which Marina was helping them to enrich an account of a robbery.

> Marina asked the students to elaborate on the description of the robber.
> M: ... Imagine, what sort of person will that robber look like? Give me some adjectives.
> S: Ugly.
> M: Ugly, OK. Ugly. Yeah. How ugly? How ugly?
> S1: Three eyes.
> M: Three eyes?
> Ss: [laugh]
> M: Where is the other eye? Where is the third eye then?
> S1: Forehead.
> M: Here in the forehead?
> S1: Yes.
> M: Wow, that's... that's not a man, it's a monster. It's an E. T. OK, so, maybe this person has got three eyes, one more eye, a special person with an eye on the... on the forehead. Any anything else you can you can use?
> S2: Four... four ears.
> M: Wow, with four ears! OK. Four ears. And where are the other two ears then? Where are the other two ears?
> S3: On the face.
> M: Sorry?
> S3: On his face.
> M: On... on his face!

From the above excerpt, we can see that some students were deliberately trying to be funny by suggesting that the robber had "three eyes" and "four ears." These suggestions were not in line with what Marina wanted them to do, that is, to give a more vivid description of the robber. Nevertheless, they served the purpose of adding more details to the appearance. Therefore, instead of ruling them out of order, Marina took them on board and asked the students to elaborate on where the extra eye and ears were. Soon after these exchanges, the students were back on track and suggested that the robber was tall, wore a T-shirt, and so on. Marina therefore successfully achieved her instructional objective of getting students to provide more details to enrich their descriptions.

Being able to make judgement on whether the students were trying to be disruptive or whether they were offering a serious answer requires knowledge of the students and their background. Otherwise, what would be a serious answer could be taken as a cheeky answer. The following excerpt is an example.

Marina was checking the replies that the students wrote to a letter on the problem page. The letter was from a student who had had problems doing his homework because he shared a room with his younger brother and baby sister, and they were very noisy. One of the students suggested that he go to the library.

M: How many of you have suggested this thing, going to the library?
Ss: [several students put up their hands]
M: OK. What other suggestions have you got?
S: Go to the toilet.
M: Go to the toilet.
Ss: [laugh]
M: Or bathroom and shut the door and stay there the whole day.
Ss: [laugh]

The suggestion of doing his homework in the toilet was by no means a cheeky answer. Apartments are very small in Hong Kong, and it is very rare for working class children to have a room to themselves. Studying in the toilet is not unheard of. As we can see, Marina accepted the answer as appropriate, though she half-jokingly added that he could stay in the toilet for the whole day.

Marina was also clear about what remarks to sanction, which indicated that the students had gone too far, for if not curbed they could go wild. For example, when students used acronyms that stood for foul words in Cantonese, like *P.K.*, or if they used *S.M.* (which stood for "sexual maniac"), Marina immediately sanctioned them. The following is an excerpt from a grammar lesson in which Marina drew a face on the board and asked the students to write a sentence to describe the face and give a reason. Some students said that he was yawning because he has breathed in some poisonous gas.

M: ... "He has breathed in special poisonous gases." I am still looking for Albert's sentence. Mr. S. M. – Who is Mr. S. M.?
Albert: Superwoman! [The class roared and became very noisy.]
M: Oh no, class, I know the meaning of S. M. [The boys roared.] No, no. Sorry, hush! Don't – don't use it. It's not good – sorry, hush, hush! It's not a good – it's not a good – a good thing to say, OK?
Albert: Mr. P. K. [The class roared again.]
M: All right. So now – hush! No, no, no. For the last time, please. No more, no more S. M. or P. K.[1] or what. OK, now –
Albert: Sentence Making ah!
M: Um Mr. – Mr. Sentence Making, OK? (The class laughed again.) Mr. Sentence Making is what? What's the word?
Ss: Moaning.
M: Is moaning? Moaning is m-o-a-n-i-n-g. (M spelled out the word.)
Albert: M-o-a-n-i-n-g.
M: OK. 'Is M-o-a-n-i-n-g'. (M wrote moaning on the blackboard.) Is moaning.

Albert was the rowdiest and most vocal student in the class. He often came up with cheeky answers, but many times they were appropriate. As we can see from the above excerpt, Marina detected the potential disorder

1 "S. M." stands for "sexual maniac" and "P. K." stands for the Cantonese words *poke kai*, which is a swear word equivalent to telling people to go to hell. The former is a taboo topic in schools and the latter is a taboo phrase that is considered vulgar.

that could set in if she did not put a stop to Albert's attempt to produce sentences using the acronyms. After class Marina told me that when she first heard these acronyms from the students, she smelled something fishy. She asked around and found out from her male colleagues what they referred to.

Marina's judgement was made on the basis of her knowledge of the students, their culture and what the shared jokes were. Calderhead (1984) points out that it is the prevention of disruptive behavior that characterizes experienced teachers. For Marina, her expertise in handling classroom discipline lies in her ability to prevent disruptive behavior and to differentiate disruptive and nondisruptive behavior. An S5 (grade 11) student, Fanny, observed: "There was no need [for Marina to be strict]. When she stopped talking, we knew what to do. She did not have to scold us; all of us knew: 'Oh no, Miss Tam is not speaking now. We need to start our lesson.'... She was not strict to us and she didn't scold us. But she could still control the class. We talked a lot during the lesson, but we still paid attention to her when she was teaching."

When disciplinary problems got really serious, such as half of the class not having done their homework, Marina would deal with these students after class or after school instead of using up class time. When she had to deal with them in class, she would draw a line between dealing with disciplinary problems and teaching. One of the S2 students, Wendy, observed:

She [Marina] could get very upset when many students did not hand in their homework. But she would not let her emotions rub off to the rest of the lesson. When she was teaching she would quickly switch to the teaching mood and have a lot of fun with students. She would not pick on students who did not hand in their homework. She gives [equal] opportunities to everyone and she cares for everyone.

This was echoed by several other students, both in senior and junior forms. Underlying this practice is her belief about the importance of maximizing time for teaching and that learning should be fun.

Many disciplinary problems in the classroom are due to boredom and frustration. When students feel that the materials are uninteresting, irrelevant, and lack variation, or that the task is too difficult or not challenging enough, they become fidgety and their attention fades. The management of learning encompasses two major aspects, the organization of learning and the management of resources.

7.3.3 Organization of learning

Marina's teaching was described by both senior and junior students as lively and characterized by a lot of activities and student participation. Group work and pair work was a feature mentioned by many students.

Initially, Marina's perception of group work and pair work was simply a means of getting students to talk to each other in English (see 6.2.3). As she gained experience and received input from professional training, Marina began to see pair work and group work as a vehicle for collaborative learning. Moreover, there should be a purpose for students to work together, and students should be working on a task with an outcome that they could share with the rest of the class.

A commonly observed routine in her classroom is that when students were asked to work on tasks, they would go out and get a poster from her, a set of felt pens and some blue tack. The students would write on the back of the poster, and when they finished they would put their "product" on the board using the blue tack. To give them a sense of ownership of the product, she asked students to sign the product with their own names or a name that they invented for their group. Marina would then go over the production from each group with the whole class. For example, in a grammar lesson on the passive voice, each group of students was required to produce a riddle using some passive structures. Their riddles were then posted on the board, and Marina went over the riddles, pointing out grammatical mistakes, and then got the rest of the class to guess the answer.

Embodied in this routine is Marina's knowledge of managing the classroom and time for learning. Many teachers ask the students to either write their productions on the board or to read them out orally. The former is very time consuming and the latter often results in students not being able to hear what was reported verbally. Marina's routine saves time and ensures that all students can see what each group has produced. It allows Marina to go over the productions very efficiently and provides another opportunity for her to consolidate what was taught in the lesson.

In organizing group work, Marina sometimes assigned different tasks to different groups. For example, when getting students to find out the meanings of words in the dictionary and their pronunciation, she would assign different words to different groups. When one group had completed their task, Marina would put their answers on the board and would go over all answers with the whole class. This not only shortens the time needed to go through the entire list of words, but also allows students to work at a different pace. Her students liked this routine and remarked, "If it's the whole class who has to look up the same words, some may do it faster [than others] if they are used to looking up words in the dictionary – and they will shout out the answers or write them on the blackboard. And those who haven't will stop looking up their dictionaries [because the answer has already been given]. So it's good to divide into groups."

Decisions on whether different groups should be assigned different tasks or the same task requires the teacher to exercise his or her judgement on the nature of the tasks and whether the whole class will be able to make sense of the outcome of different tasks. Otherwise, when one group is presenting the product, the other groups would be at a loss. For example, when Marina was teaching "giving advice," she gave the students five letters on the problems page in a magazine and went over all of them with the class. Then she asked each group to write a reply to one of the letters. At the end, each group presented their reply to the letter. Since Marina had gone over all five letters with them, they had the contexts for making sense of the replies produced by each group.

7.3.4 Management of resources for ESL learning

MAXIMIZING RESOURCES

Marina's management of resources for teaching was typified by their variety, authenticity, and relevance. She was able to exploit materials for teaching in a creative way. Influenced by her own language learning experience in which she had to maximize her opportunities for learning English in order to survive at St. John's, she made use of junk mail, pamphlets, and brochures for teaching (see 6.2). She would collect them and put them in a box. She would collect materials even when she was traveling. For example, when she went to the United Kingdom as part of the refresher training for panel heads, one of things that she collected for teaching materials was a pamphlet from Sainsbury supermarket. Her selection of materials is guided by her knowledge of the difference between authentic language, which is found in real life situations, and language, which is artificially produced for teaching purposes. Marina's selection of materials is also influenced by her belief that students are more likely to see the relevance of this kind of material to their everyday lives. Apart from providing students with realia, she would also ask students to collect samples of realia. She explained as follows:

Yes, I like using that because they are authentic. This is the main reason. Texts, which are fabricated, are not as good. Another thing is, if I use realia, students would feel that [the realia] is closer to their lives, then they would pay more attention to the things [language] around them because these realia are taken from things around them. For example, the patients' charter, I am sure every student has a copy. I kept my copy.

She paid a lot of attention to junk mail, letters, school circulars, and newspapers, collecting them and filing them. This she did for both junior and senior forms. When she ran out of ideas for teaching, she would go through these materials.

When she taught instructions in S2, she asked the students to go to the supermarket and look at instructions on the packaging and bring some back to the school. The students brought back a lot of things, such as instant noodles packages, tin labels, recipes, and so on. She then helped the students to identify the common structures in these instructions. When teaching vocabulary on stationery, she gave them some Chinese words, for example, *stapler and hole puncher*, and asked them to find out the English equivalent in stationery shops. This kind of activity provided an experiential dimension to language learning and enhanced the students' sensitivity to the English around them.

Lillian, an S2 student, said, "I became more interested in the language... I paid more attention to English. When I spotted an English sentence, I would take another look, just out of curiosity. I would also memorize interesting sentences that I came across." Fanny, an S5 student, paid attention to the advertisements in the MTR stations, and when she watched advertisements on the English television channel, she would compare them with the Chinese version. She also watched English serials and documentaries. Wendy, another S5 student, also said that she paid a lot more attention to the English around her. She said:

Sometimes on the streets, say in Tsim Sha Tsui, when foreigners ask the way, I will volunteer to help them. I always take those opportunities [to practice my English]. When I cross the harbor, some writings are in English only and not bilingual. I will try to guess their meanings, though I am not sure. If I can remember the words, I'll look them up in a dictionary when I'm home. When I eat out in a restaurant and the menus are in English only, I'll pick up new words like *cappuccino*, words that I didn't know before, but now I know.

For her Master's assignment, Marina studied a good and a poor language learner in her own S5 class. She found that the good language learner, among other traits, paid a lot of attention to the English around her. The student reported to her thus: "When I go out, I often look at the street signs, billboards. Sometimes there are very big Chinese characters, with tiny English words below. I still crane my neck to read the English words and check them against the Chinese characters." She also found that this student felt positively about herself and her own English ability. The poor language learner, on the other hand, found language learning "painful" and had little sense of success. She said, "I feel that no matter how hard I try, I still can't learn languages well." This study confirmed her practical knowledge about how and what resources she could exploit for teaching. The research literature on learner variables and learning strategies, such as the work of O'Malley and Chamot (1990), provided Marina with a theoretical basis for her future teaching actions.

Using students' work as a resource for learning is another characteristic of Marina's teaching. The bulletin board at the back of the classroom is often full of students' work. For example, after teaching the use of passives to write riddles, she posted on the board the riddles that her students wrote for the rest of the class to guess. After teaching the use of the past participle form as adjectives, such as *annoyed, scared, excited,* she put faces expressing such feelings drawn by students on the bulletin board. These posters served as a way of consolidating what had been taught. Good work was put on the school bulletin board both as a form of encouragement and a resource for learning for students in other classes.

Marina is very alert to resources that are made available to schools by the government Education Department. When the Extensive Reading Scheme was first introduced to schools by the government, Marina grabbed the opportunity and joined the scheme. She set aside two lessons per week for students to read the books in class. Instead of getting them to write book reports, which to her is a recipe for killing students' interest in reading, she asked them to tell her about the book. She would reward them with a sticker if they gave a good summary. Some of her students had read more than eighty books by the end of the school year. Because there was no such scheme for senior forms, Marina made available to senior students her personal library. A number of S5 students borrowed books from her because they found her books more interesting than those they could find in the library.

St. Peter's is not a particularly well-resourced school. Apart from the standard subsidy that it receives from the government, it does not get additional funding from donors. The school does not require parents to put in additional resources because of their low income. The equipment in each classroom is the basic board and chalk. While there are several overhead projectors for common use, there is no overhead projector in the classroom. The teachers have very little funding for buying teaching aids such as overhead transparencies. Given the poor resources, Marina came up with her own teaching aids, which consisted of felt pens of various colors, any big pieces of paper that she could lay her hands on, and some blue tack for sticking the papers on the board. The big pieces of paper are package wrappings of photocopying papers that she saw lying around in the general office, large monthly calendars, and advertising posters that had been taken down from school bulletin boards. She said that it would be much more economical and environmentally friendly to make use of "waste papers" than to buy big poster papers from stationery shops. These big posters are for students to put down their group work productions so that Marina can go over them with the whole class efficiently and effectively (see 7.3.3).

MAXIMIZING TIME

For Marina, time is an important resource for learning. She was never late for class because she felt that thirty-five minutes for a lesson was already very short. If the lesson started late, she would not be able to cover very much. One of her S5 students, Howard, observed, "Every time when the bell rang, within almost one minute she would turn up for class. She is different from other teachers.... She said, 'If we start [the lesson] on time, I can teach you more.'"

In the first few years of teaching, Marina got very upset when the students came to class late. Howard recalled an incident when he was still an S2 student. His class was five or ten minutes late going to the "loop room" (the listening laboratory). Marina was very upset and cried as she scolded them for not taking their lessons seriously. Since then, Howard said, the students knew that they must be punctual. Marina reflected on this and realized that although she was able to get the students to be punctual, her emotional reactions had had adverse effects on the learning atmosphere (see 6.2.2). To tackle this, she laid down a rule for punctuality at the beginning of the school year and reinforced it throughout the school year, as we have already seen (see 7.3.1).

To ensure that no time is wasted, she always brings an alarm clock to class, and when she gives a time limit for working on tasks, individually, in pairs or in groups, she sets the clock to remind herself. She seldom allows more time after the alarm has gone off, unless it is absolutely necessary. According to Marina, this routine was set up because she knew that it would be very easy for a teacher to forget the time. If the teacher did not keep to the time limit given, students would be spending more time than was needed on a task. They were also more likely to be off-task if they felt that they did not have to finish the task on time. The time that she allocated to activities was often accurate, and she seldom ran over or finished much earlier than the bell. Wendy (S5), observed, "... her timing was excellent. Really. When she has said everything, then I would count, 'ten, nine, eight, seven, six, five, four, three, two, one.' Then the bell rang. She kept it so accurately that you wouldn't think time was wasted."

Getting students into groups can be rather time-consuming, especially if it is not well planned. In Marina's lessons, whenever students have to do group work, she will count up to ten, at the end of which all students will be in their own groups. This is because at the beginning of each school year, Marina asks her students to form groups and stay with the group for the rest of the year. She also trains the students to get into groups within the shortest possible time. This results in a brisk pace in her teaching.

MAXIMIZING THE CLASSROOM FOR LANGUAGE LEARNING

Marina's classroom is typified by the prevalent use of English once the lesson has started, no matter whether the students are bantering with one another or engaging in serious discussion. There is an understanding in her English panel that students should be encouraged to use English in all English lessons. However, some teachers are more successful in implementing this than others.

To implement this policy, apart from making it clear right from the beginning of the school year, as we have seen in 7.3.1, Marina developed a simple system for rewarding the use of English and penalizing the use of Cantonese in the classroom. If a student was found using Cantonese in class, no matter whether it was whole-class teaching or group or pair work, his or her name would be written on the board and one mark would be deducted from their oral English mark. If however, they used English all the way through group or pair work, two bonus marks would be given. A crying face next to the name on the board denoted mark deduction, and a smiling face denoted mark addition. In addition, she also asked the students to monitor each other's use of Cantonese. Seldom did she ignore any instance of violation.

In addition, she encouraged teachers to provide opportunities for students to use English in extra-curricular activities. For example, some of her colleagues set up a story-telling corner at lunchtime in which the junior form students have to tell stories in English to senior forms students, who would give them a grade for their performance. For the school Open Day, Marina set up an English room where all students on duty had to use English to introduce their school activities to the guests.

Besides creating a language-rich environment in the classroom, she also tried to make use of extracurricular activities as opportunities for students to use English. For example, she set aside certain rooms in the school Open Day where the students had to use English to introduce their work to visitors. She also asked students to write English riddles as games for visitors.

Her insistence that students use English in the classroom is guided by her knowledge of English language learning that was formulated as a result of partly her own learning experience (particularly her secondary school learning experience) and partly of her German learning experience, as we have seen in Chapter 6. This knowledge was supported by the theoretical input that she received in her PCEd course and especially in the Master's course. In a document that she submitted to the school administration on measures for improving students' language proficiency, she argued strongly against the use of mixed code (English and Cantonese) in the teaching of English and other content subjects. She wrote, "This [an English-rich environment] can only materialize when English, not mixed code, is used as the teaching medium."

7.3.5 *Motivating students and establishing rapport*

Marina's students described her lessons as "fun" and "lively." Many of them said that they became more interested in English after they had been taught by Marina. Two of the S2 students interviewed said that they were not interested in English when they were in S1 because it was boring and difficult. But in S2, they found that "it [learning English] was fun." Winnie, a student of average ability, said that she found that lessons enjoyable particularly when there were games and she could learn a lot through games. The S5 students interviewed unanimously said that Marina's teaching was different from other teachers – that it was more fun, with lots of games and activities, and very enjoyable. An S5 student, Jerry, said, "She doesn't just teach. It's lively. She cracks jokes with the students." Fiona, an S5 student, said, "I am motivated to learn English because the lessons are fun. At least because the lessons are fun, I am now taking the initiative to read storybooks." When she was in S1, she did not like English at all. She would say, "English? I don't really give a damn."

Apart from making the lessons fun by using a lot of activities and games, the comfortable relationship that she established with her students and her commitment to teaching had an important part to play in motivating them to learn English. Wendy, an S5 student, said that she was "inspired" by Marina. She said:

> I think she's lively by nature, so her lessons are so enjoyable. [When I was] in Form Two, perhaps because we were young then, she gave us posters and asked us to write sentences on them and put them up [on the board]. I think apart from learning the structures... this encouraged us to be imaginative. So I felt very happy. And she loved to laugh. This gave us a feeling that she really appreciated our work, no matter whether it was good or bad, right or wrong. So as a student you would feel happy and you wouldn't feel inferior in front of her.... Also when a teacher seems to appreciate you, you'll think to yourself, I have to work harder! So you'll try your best to improve yourself.

Wendy recalled that when she was taught by Marina in S2, learning English was really "learning through games" and they were given stickers[2] when they won a game. As they moved to higher forms, Marina stopped giving them stickers and there were no more games, but she could still maintain the students' interest in English. Wendy explained why:

> It's her attitude.... What's important is her attitude, not whether she gave me stickers... While she was teaching, she seemed to be learning with us.... She became one of us; she was totally involved in the whole lesson. She wouldn't separate herself [from us] like, 'I am the teacher and you are the students. I teach you and you listen to me.' It's not like that. She would join us when we played. She would redress our faults through playing with us. That I think is marvelous. I don't know how to put it into words. I mean I felt she was whole-heartedly engaged in it. Even when it was a double-lesson, I wouldn't feel [bored].

Wendy observed that because the students liked Marina, they wanted to make her happy and so they worked harder. She said, "If you want to

2 Stickers were very popular among younger students in Hong Kong schools. Students were given stickers of cartoon animals, people, or patterns as a kind of encouragement for good performance.

make a teacher happy and you like her, surely you will participate more and get more involved in her lessons." Wendy's remarks were echoed by Gwen, an S2 student, who was touched by Marina's persistence in helping students understand. She said:

If you couldn't understand [something], even if it was abstract and difficult to explain, she would still spend so much time on it, even thought it was a small point. She'd tried her utmost to clarify it for you. She did not mind. Sometimes when I got her point already and she was still going on about it, I'd even feel annoyed. She would still be explaining from different perspectives, using gestures. That's so enjoyable because you could feel her enthusiasm. You'd think, if the one who teaches (us) is not bored, we, who are being taught, should not be.

Fanny, another S5 student, saw Marina more as a friend than a teacher. She would go to her if she had personal problems and family problems. Marina would listen to her patiently and would help her to tease out the problem, but she would not impose any solution on Fanny. She said, "While she understands, she will also make a full analysis for me.... She will say, 'it's going to be like this, and I leave you to judge.' Like this." While not all students interviewed said that they would go to her for personal problems, most of them said that if they had questions, they knew that they could go to her and that she would be very willing to help them.

Another important way to motivate students to learn is to give them a sense of achievement and to let them know that they are making progress and improving. In her eighth year of teaching, at the very beginning of the school year, Marina's S2 class ranked last among the five classes of S2 in the first test. This was very demoralizing to the students. She thought about how she could encourage her class, and she came up with the following solution. She gave each student a record of his or her own scores in tests and examinations, and showed them how much their scores had improved or declined from one score to another. Those who had improved were given a smiling face and those with declining scores received a crying face. She hoped that by doing this, students who had improved would be encouraged and those who did not would have to think about why. She said:

My aim is I don't want them to think 'oh dear, I've only got forty-something, I've failed again.' And that's it. I want them to know whether they have improved or not. If they have improved, then that's already quite good [even if their marks are low].

This kind of record was particularly encouraging for students who did not get high marks but had made some improvement, even if the improvement was very slight.

7.3.6 Developing knowledge of management of learning

In this section we have seen how Marina managed the classroom for learning. By establishing norms that made clear what was acceptable and unacceptable behavior as well as what was expected of students, she was able to minimize disruptive behavior. By establishing management as well as teaching routines, she made some of the classroom events predictable, hence allowing more room for the students and herself to deal with the unpredictable. Drawing on her knowledge of the students and their family backgrounds, she was able to differentiate disruptive from nondisruptive behavior and preempt the former.

The apparent ease with which she handled the disciplinary problems and the excellent rapport that she established did not come automatically with experience, however. In Chapter 6 we saw how Marina struggled with disciplinary problems, particularly in her first three years of teaching. She found it difficult to cope with the multiple dimensions of classroom teaching: she was unable "to keep an eye on the whole class all the time," and to exercise her judgement on what was permissible and what was not. She tried to be "firm," "serious," to keep students under "control," and she was highly successful in maintaining order. However, this was in conflict with her image of a teacher as being kind and caring to students and being able to inspire students to learn (see 6.2). Her mastery of classroom discipline and rapport with students was a process of trying to resolve the conflict between her image and her practices by constant reflection on experience, as a result of which she reframed her understanding of how her image of a teacher should be played out. For example, her reflections on critical classroom incidents – like the "regrettable" events of being unforgiving and inflexible in dealing with disciplinary problems – helped her to come to a new understanding of not only how she should handle these problems, but more importantly the impact that a teacher could make on more profound aspects of student learning such as learning attitudes and moral values.

Governing the strategies that Marina has developed over the years is her belief that it is important to maximize time, opportunities, and resources for learning. This belief is formulated as a result of her own learning experience as a student from a working-class family and her knowledge of the students as working-class children. It shaped the way she formulated the norms and routines, such as punctuality, finishing tasks on time, dealing with disciplinary problems after class, organizing group work, and so forth; and it guided her creative ways of providing opportunities for learning.

Embodied in each of the strategies that she used in the management of learning is a rich integrated knowledge of students, context, subject matter, pedagogy, and curricula. For example, her use of realia for teaching started as a creative exploitation of materials for teaching that was based very much on her own experience of having to "survive" in one of the most prestigious English-medium schools (see 6.1). This knowledge is oriented to the specific context of working-class children in a city where English is hardly used at home or in daily social interactions but, paradoxically, can be found everywhere. As Leinhardt (1988) points out, it is "contextually developed knowledge that is accessed and used in a way that tends to make use of characteristic features of the environment as the solution tools" (p. 146). Subsequently, as Marina obtained input from the professional education course and the master's program, she was able to formulate and articulate the theoretical bases of this contextually developed knowledge. For example, acquiring knowledge about text analysis enabled her to theorize her preference for using realia containing authentic texts over fabricated texts provided in textbooks. Theories of second language acquisition and language awareness provided the theoretical motivation for asking her students to pay attention to the English around them and to "notice" the linguistic features and patterns. Theories of language learning strategies and her own investigation into strategies used by her students helped her to make explicit the tacit knowledge embedded in many of her classroom practices.

This body of knowledge, which is practically oriented and situated, was developed as Marina responded to her specific context of work by finding ways to maximize what is realistically achievable, given the limited resources available to teachers and the tight schedule that teachers have to meet. A very good example is the very simple teaching aids that she developed for getting students to produce language on big posters so that she could provide corrective feedback efficiently and effectively, and so that the productions could be used for consolidation after the lesson. Providing corrective feedback and consolidation are both important aspects of language teaching.

In the context of the phases of professional development that Marina went through, we can see that the "state" that Marina has reached in her management of learning is the result of a "process" in which she problematizes what might have been considered by other teachers as routine or acceptable, and tried to find solutions congruent with her conceptions of teaching and learning. As she reflected on her experience, she gained new insights and understanding of her work as a teacher. Marina's development of knowledge in managing the classroom for learning is a process of responding to the constraints imposed by the context of work by opening up whatever possibilities for learning that she could find and continuously searching for improvement by trying out new ideas, by learning from experience, and by theroizing her actions and practices.

7.4 Eva

7.4.1 Management for learning in action: Eva's first two lessons

Like Marina, Eva started the lesson (S2, Grade 8) by introducing herself and using two adjectives to describe herself: *optimistic* and *happy*. She gave each student a piece of yellow paper for writing their English name, and a piece of white paper for putting down two adjectives to describe their classmates. When the students had finished, she asked them to pass the papers to the front. As she was collecting the papers, she counted up to ten. By doing this, she established the house rule: complete the action before the teacher finishes counting.

After collecting the papers, Eva put the yellow papers in one bag and the white papers in another bag. She then pulled out a name from one bag, invited a student to come to the front and asked him or her to pull out a piece of white paper and read out the two adjectives written on it. The class was asked to indicate whether they agreed that the adjectives appropriately described this student. For homework, she asked the students to write down three adjectives to describe themselves and give reasons in the grammar exercise book.

In the second lesson on the following day, she began by asking students to name adjectives to describe God. She asked the students to form eight groups of five and give their own group a name. She set up a reward system to encourage participation in class. For each correct answer from a group member, the group would get one mark. The marks would be totaled every two weeks, and the group with the highest score would get a prize. After explaining the reward system and setting a time limit for forming groups, she went over the list of adjectives that was given on the previous day and asked students to classify them as positive or negative adjectives.

As mentioned before, because Eva and Marina were teaching the same level, they used the same materials and often discussed the lesson plans. This is why there were a number of similarities between their lessons. Like Marina, Eva started teaching right away by introducing herself with some adjectives. The students were also immediately involved in activities. The house rules were established as the teaching progressed. Eva organized the students and introduced the reward system very early on. One can see a strong influence of Marina on Eva through the routines and norms established.

What is interesting is that Eva's lessons may appear to be quite similar to Marina's, but in fact the activities that Eva introduced did not quite achieve the objective of getting to know each other, which Eva and Marina agreed on. In Marina's lessons, students were asked to write three adjectives to describe themselves and then to tell their partners what those three adjectives were and why they would describe themselves as such. The activity served the purpose of helping students to get to know each other by telling each other about themselves using adjectives. The subsequent activity of asking them to write down their partner's name and the three adjectives that their partners had used to describe themselves served the function of consolidating their knowledge of their partners.

By contrast, Eva's activity of asking students to pull out two adjectives from the bag and indicate if they agreed with the description was not appropriate as the first activity in the school year because some students did not know each other and were therefore not in a position to agree or disagree with the description. The activity would have been much more appropriate for consolidation after the students had been introduced to each other. The activity of using adjectives to describe God departed from the objective of the lesson because it did not help the students to get to know each other. Practicing the use of adjectives for describing people became the end rather than a means to an end. In the following section, we shall discuss in greater detail the routines and norms that Eva established to manage the classroom for learning.

7.4.2 Handling classroom discipline

Like Marina, Eva's classroom was relaxed, full of noise and laughter. Students were happy to see her, and they often greeted her effusively when she turned up at the door. Eva seldom talked to the students harshly when they forgot to bring their books or their homework. She felt that putting on a stern face did not help. Rather, she believed that if she tried to explain to the students what they needed to do, they would listen to her. When she checked homework, she would ask students to redo it if they had not done it properly. She would differentiate between those who were willing to redo their work and those who were not and only penalize the latter.

A striking feature was Eva's jocular way of handling disciplinary problems if they were not too serious. She would draw a tortoise on the student's hand and not allow them to wash it away until they had come to see her after class. The word *tortoise* has a negative connotation in Chinese, and Eva used it as a means of indicating negative evaluation. This was an effective way of making students aware of their mistakes. As I observed Eva drawing the tortoise on students' hands, I often found that students responded to it with a mixture of fun and embarrassment. If the problem was really serious, such as when more than half the class did not complete their homework, she would not use the jocular penalty. Instead, she would give the whole class a serious talk. To make sure that the students got the message, she would switch to Cantonese. However, if there were only one or two students who committed the offense, she would deal with these students individually after school in order not to waste class time. What comes through clearly in Eva's handling of disciplinary problems is her conception of students as individual human beings who are reasonable and should be respected. Her knowledge of her students also enabled her to exercise her judgement on the gravity of the disciplinary problems and the appropriate measures to deal with them.

7.4.3 Group work and seating arrangement

Like Marina, Eva used group work frequently. Eva's personal approach to teaching came through strongly in the way she exploited the additional physical space in oral lessons when the class size was reduced to half to allow more opportunities for students to speak in class. She would put students in five groups and rotate their locations in the classroom so that there would not be some groups sitting at the back all the time and consequently not getting as much attention as those sitting in the front. Eva's actions were guided by her conception of students as individuals and the importance that she attached to maintaining a personal relationship with the students. She wanted to be able to establish eye contact with her students and not let any student feel neglected. When she could not see the students sitting at the back, she would ask them to show their faces.

Her sensitivity to students as individuals was manifested in the way she arranged the seating in oral lessons when they were not doing group work. For example, in an oral lesson in which consonants were taught, Eva asked the students to arrange the desks in a semicircle. She explained why:

I think they will find it difficult to pronounce consonants. So I want them to see how others pronounce them so that they won't just sit there not knowing what to do and feeling afraid. I want them to be able to watch their peers. Like when you do tai chi, or learn to dance, you follow other people when you don't know how to do it.

When the students looked tired and their face muscles were a bit tense after practicing the consonants for a long time, she made up some sentences on the spot using the students' names, such as "Sam is very thin. Wallace is not thin. Wallace wants to be thin. So Wallace eats less ice-cream." This woke the class up immediately. Eva explained that she loved doing this because this was her way of relating to them: "to develop a conversation with them and to respond to them."

Underlying Eva's seating arrangement was her knowledge that consonants were difficult for the students and her awareness of the students' anxiety when they found the task daunting. Allowing students to see what their peers were doing was a kind of emotional as well as learning support. The smaller size of the split class, therefore, gave Eva not only the physical space but also the metaphorical space to try out different seating arrangements, which were guided by her understanding of how best to manage the classroom to facilitate learning.

7.4.4 Maximizing the classroom for learning

USING ENGLISH IN THE CLASSROOM

In Eva's classroom one could hear English used nearly all the time. Like Marina's classroom, her students used English even when they were joking with each other. She did not allow the use of Cantonese and deducted marks if students were caught using Cantonese. However, instead of deducting marks from individual students for speaking Cantonese, she deducted the marks from the group. She did this for two reasons. First, deducting marks from individual students would be too personal and offensive. Second, if the marks were group marks, then there would be group pressure to speak English. Eva explained, "By doing this, I am handing back the responsibility to the students, and they will monitor each other." This was quite effective because very often when one student used Cantonese, the whole group would censor him or her. Consequently, the classroom became an English-rich environment where English was heard and used by students.

BENEFITING FROM EACH OTHER'S CONTRIBUTIONS

A norm that Eva established is that everybody must speak loudly when answering questions or making presentations in class. She told the students that because class time was limited, anybody speaking would be taking up other people's time and space. Therefore, they must speak loudly so that everybody could hear what was said and could benefit from it. In addition, when a student had answered a question, Eva seldom responded by saying whether the answer was correct. She would direct the students' answers to other students for evaluation. This, according to Eva, was to inculcate in students the concept that the teacher was not always right. Students should be responsible for their own learning and not always look to the teacher for the answer. However, this was not always positively responded to by the students because they felt that they needed the final word from her and when that was not forthcoming, they felt a bit frustrated.

"TEACHING-LEARNING"

To ensure that time was effectively spent on learning, whenever Eva asked her students to work on tasks, she would demonstrate how to do it first. She cited the Chinese word for "teaching," which is literally translated as "teaching-learning," and said, "You must teach the students first before you can expect them to learn." For her, it would be a waste of time and would not be fair if students were just left floundering without the teacher teaching them how to do it.

This routine was developed in response to students' criticism that her instructions were unclear. In order to make sure that they knew what they were supposed to do, she demonstrated how to do it. Despite this routine, her instructions were still unclear at times. She felt that she was too impulsive and spontaneous, and she tended to digress. As a result, her students found it difficult to follow her. For example, she would give homework orally in the middle of the lesson. Her students requested that she put the homework instructions on the board. She was receptive to their suggestions, and she said, "My students are training me up."

ENCOURAGING PARTICIPATION

Eva tried to encourage student participation by setting up a system to reward participation in class in junior forms. At the beginning of each lesson, a student would be assigned to draw a chart on the board for recording marks for each group. For each student who volunteered to speak in class, one mark would be awarded to the group to which the student belonged. In order to encourage more students to volunteer, she allocated an extra mark to new volunteers. At the end of the lesson, the marks would be added up and the group with the highest mark would get two stickers and the second highest would get one. There was a chart on the bulletin board where the students put the stickers. At the end of the term, the group that collected the highest number of stickers would get a prize. The students responded very well to this scheme and competed hard to get the highest number of stickers.

Eva started introducing this system in her third year of teaching. In the subsequent three years, the reward system underwent some modifications. For example, initially only one prize was given to the group with the highest score at the end of term. She found that she needed to give more immediate incentives and so she gave them the stickers at the end of each class and allowed more than one group to get the stickers. In order to foster team spirit, she made the students stay in one group throughout the term so that they would work together to get the prize.

From the above account, we can see that a great deal of thinking had gone into the formulation of the routines, norms, and strategies for maximizing the classroom for learning. Embedded in Eva's practices is her personal conception of "teaching" as encompassing "learning" and the presupposition of learning in teaching. Also embedded in her practices is her belief that she should maximize the opportunities for learning for all students, help them to take responsibility for their own learning, and not to be subservient to the teacher.

7.4.5 Creating a positive and supportive culture

In managing the classroom for learning, Eva attached a great deal of importance to building a positive and trusting culture in which students were mutually supportive. She frequently made positive statements about her students when she gave examples to illustrate a grammar point or explained a vocabulary item. When designing test items, she would write about students and their good behavior. For example, in a writing lesson, she used the revisions made by a student on his first draft as an example for teaching. The writing was about a robbery and on the top of the page, Eva wrote, "'A Robbery,' by a hard working, careful, attentive, and cheerful student in 2A." This was a conscious attempt on her part. Eva explained that it is important for a teacher to be encouraging and positive about their students. Moreover, students would remember the examples better if they contained positive statements about them or their peers.

When students had worked hard in a lesson, she would praise them for being very attentive, and if the tasks were difficult, she would tell them not to give up. When students gave a wrong response or could not answer the question, Eva would try to put the student at ease by explaining to the rest of the class why he or she could not give an answer or why he or she gave the wrong answer. For example, in an oral lesson when Eva was going over vowels and consonants, one of the students, Charlotte, did not know how to pronounce the vowel /ə:/ and was embarrassed. Eva knew that this was because some dictionaries used the phonetic symbol /ɜ:/ instead. She came to Charlotte's rescue by explaining to the rest of the class why the student had a problem with this sound.

Besides being positive about students, Eva would censor any negative remarks that students made of one another. For example, in an oral lesson one of the students, Peter, called another student, Sam, a stupid boy. Eva stopped him immediately and asked him to see her immediately after class. Fostering mutual trust among the students was also something that Eva strove for. For example, in one lesson, the students were totaling the marks for each group, and some groups got more marks than they should have. They broke into an argument, and there was an implicit accusation that some groups were cheating. Instead of trying to witch-hunt, Eva said, "I know you all are honest, but you might make mistakes sometimes. So can you please check once again to see if you have made any mistakes?" This calmed down the students and the mistake was sorted out very quickly.

7.4.6 Developing knowledge of management of learning

The most outstanding feature of Eva's classroom is the positive atmosphere. In the first two lessons, the two adjectives that Eva introduced to describe herself were "happy" and "optimistic." While they reflected Eva's personality, they also encapsulated the ethos that she wished to promote in her classroom. Eva's classroom was one where anxiety was low and students were ready to ask questions and contribute ideas. However, as we have seen in Chapter 6, Eva went through difficult times, especially in her first year of teaching, when she was unable to exercise her judgment on handling disciplinary problems. Eva's reaction to her students' complaint about the way she handled misbehavior was not to put the blame on her students, but rather to reflect on the situation. It is interesting that the conclusion that she drew from the negative experience was "that's not the way to *teach*," rather than "that's not the way to *handle misbehaved students*." Eva was thinking of her relationship with the students in the larger context of teaching. The remedial action that she took, however, was motivated by bringing her own practices in line with other colleague's practices. It was not until her second and third year of teaching that she began to feel confident enough to take responsibility for her own practices. We have seen the personal approach that she adopted in managing the classroom for learning, which is geared towards to the specific context of teaching. For example, Eva's strategies for organizing the seating arrangements in oral lessons were oriented to the physical space that was available only in oral lessons because of split-class teaching. In other lessons when she had a full class, she had to adopt a different set of strategies for establishing contact with students and giving them individual attention.

Embedded in Eva's management of the classroom for learning is an integrated knowledge of students and context, and, to a lesser extent, subject matter knowledge. The way this knowledge was held and realized in classroom practices was strongly guided by her conception of students as individual human beings who should be respected and given equal attention and equal opportunities for learning; by her image of the teacher not as a figure of authority, but rather as somebody who is willing to take advice from students and to stand to be corrected by them; by her understanding of the inherent relationship between teaching and learning; by her perception of the primary role of the teacher as imparting moral and social values; and by her belief in the fostering mutual trust and support among students. These conceptions, however, were by no means fully and explicitly formulated. It is in the process of putting them into practice over the years of her teaching experience that she theorized them as she reflected on her classroom practices.

There were times, however, when she was faced with the dilemma of living up to her personal beliefs and the realities of teaching. For example, the system for rewarding participation in class conflicted with one of her educational goals of helping students to become self-motivated to learn. Yet the reality that she had to face is that her students were mainly working-class children who had very little support from their families and whose living environments were so noisy and crowded that they were not conducive to studying at home. She said, "If the students were to be self-motivated, then I would need cooperation from their parents and the teacher-student ratio should be lowered. But I know that these are unachievable." Eva admitted that the reward system was a compromise. As Lampert (1985) points out, there is often no neat and simple solution to pedagogical problems. Eva tried to manage the dilemma in the hope that eventually she could do away with the reward system altogether.

7.5 Ching

7.5.1 Management of learning in action: Ching's first two lessons

Ching's students were all new entrants from different primary schools. Most of them did not know each other. Her first two lessons can be roughly divided into five segments. In the first segment Ching dealt with the collection of homework that she had given them when they registered in the summer. She asked students who had forgotten to bring the summer holiday homework to write their names down on a piece of paper. She then introduced some house rules.

C: ... *If you forgot to bring your textbook today, you will not be punished* because I will tell you something about what you have to do in English lessons.
[Ching then asked them to hand in their summer holiday homework.]
... And if you [referring to the student sitting in the first row] find that someone has not brought their summer holiday homework, please pass out these pieces of paper to that one and then he or she should write down his or her name on this piece of paper. OK? *I do not tell you whether you will be punished, but if you fail to hand in your homework today*, please write down your name first. Do you understand?
Ss: No.
C: Some of you don't understand. Raise your hand now. If you really don't understand, please raise your hand. OK? I will try to repeat it. *When I am trying to tell you what to do, I want you to keep noisy or quiet?*
S: Quiet.
C: Of course quiet. For you know it. OK? I will give pieces of paper to the students sitting in the front.... *Don't ask questions until I have finished, OK? Don't ask questions until I have finished.*

The first segment set the general tone for Ching's classroom – that there are certain rules that must be observed, and violation of these rules will lead to punishment. The first house rule is that there will be penalties for not bringing their textbook and not handing in homework. The second house rule is that students are expected to be quiet when the teacher is talking, and they should not interrupt the teacher until she has finished.

In the second segment Ching moved on to give students the timetable for the nine English lessons in a six-day cycle-week. She then went into great lengths about what they would do for each lesson, and what books they should bring for which lessons. She also discussed the handbook, usage book, and dictionary that they should have ready for all lessons. In order to remember students' names quickly, Ching asked the students to give themselves English names and to bring their photographs for her to put on the seating plan.

The third segment was taken up with getting to know the students. Ching gave the students a piece of paper on which the students were required to answer some questions that she asked them verbally. She posed four questions. First, which primary school they came from; second, whether their English teacher spoke English [in class] most of the time; third, whether they liked English and why. At this point, she asked a student to repeat the two parts to the third question. Here she introduced another routine: when she gives instructions, she may from time to time ask them to repeat the instructions. The fourth question was what they hoped to learn in English lessons this year. When the students had handed in their answers, she told them that she would keep them and give them back at the end of the school year so that they could see whether they had achieved what they hoped.

In the fourth segment Ching spoke at length about the importance of the second house rule; that is, paying attention when she is talking.

C: ...I would like to remind all of you, *usually if you started talking when I am talking, I will stop*.... If I tell you, "I am serious" that means I am now very grave, I am talking about something very important. [*She repeated this in Cantonese.*] When I am serious, I need your attention. Do you understand?

The last segment, segment five, of the lesson was taken up with asking students where they lived and how they came to school. This was followed by giving them instructions on what students should do if they had not finished their book reports and setting a deadline for late submission. Before she gave the instructions, she enacted the second house rule by saying, "I am serious now. Can you hear? I am serious now," to get the students' attention. She warned them that if they could not meet the deadline, then she would not treat it lightly.

Like Marina and Eva, Ching took care to lay down rules and norms at the very beginning of the school year. However, instead of going right into teaching and integrating the rules into her teaching, she spent most of the time on establishing classroom norms and rules, and specifying the detailed requirements for each lesson. Therefore, time for learning was not maximized. There was also a strong emphasis on order, discipline, and the punitive consequences of not observing house rules. Usually, in the first two lessons for S1 students, opportunities would be provided for students to get to know each other. In the third and fifth segments, we can see that Ching basically took the time to get information about the students from her own perspective; that is, what the teacher wanted to know rather than what the students wanted to know about each other. What came through strongly was that Ching is a serious teacher who expects compliance from her students.

7.5.2 Norms and routines

Ching's classroom was characterized by the predominance of teacher talk, teacher-centeredness, order, and control. The students were generally very well-behaved. One gets a strong sense that the teacher was the figure of authority and that the students were respectful to the teacher. Students raised their hands when they wanted to ask or answer a question, and they waited to be called upon before speaking. When students were asked to get into groups, they did it very quickly and quietly. Unlike Marina and Eva's classrooms, students seldom responded to the teacher spontaneously or shouted out the answers in their seats. There was not as much laughter as there was in Marina's and Eva's classrooms, and the reactions from students were more restrained.

Like Marina and Eva, Ching set up routines for managing general classroom business such as cleaning the board, collecting homework, and getting into groups. However, the routines that she established were more often based on punitive principles than positive reinforcement. While imposing penalties on students for misbehaving was something that the majority of teachers practiced, what was striking about Ching's management of learning was the pervasiveness of the penalties that she imposed on students. For example, she usually collected homework near the end of the lesson, and students who reported that they had forgotten to do their homework would be asked to remain standing as a kind of penalty. Another example is that when students did not follow her instructions, she would appoint them to be "on duty;" that is, to make sure that the blackboard is cleaned after every lesson and that the classroom is tidy. Ching explained that she felt that most of her students are "teachable." "Teachable" is a Chinese expression commonly used by Chinese teachers to mean that a student is receptive to the teacher's guidance and is willing to change undesirable behavior. However, she felt that there were some students with whom she had to "use negative means, like detention, to get them to follow instructions and do their homework."

7.5.3 Handling classroom discipline

Despite the fact that teaching seemed to proceed in an orderly fashion, there did not seem to be a large variety of routines that Ching called upon to deal with different aspects of classroom life in order to keep the students "under control," as it were. Classroom discipline seemed to be managed by her authority over her students. She was very conscious of getting all her students' attention. When some students were not paying attention, she would stop talking and look at them until they became quiet. According to her, this was a very effective means because whenever she did that, the rest of the class would notice and they would inevitably turn their eyes to these students. This put pressure on these students to stop talking or to stop fooling around. Ching attached a great deal of importance to having all students pay attention to her and do their work in an orderly fashion. She said:

I am easily disturbed emotionally, and I am seriously affected if they do not pay attention or when they mess around with their pen or correction fluid. When I noticed them, I got very impatient and I wanted to bring them back to what we were doing in class. My anxiety was quite strong.

Besides the authoritative stance that Ching assumed, she was also able to maintain order in the classroom because of the effective way of giving instructions, which she had developed over time. She usually broke down her instructions into manageable chunks instead of giving them all at once. She would also check students' comprehension of these instructions by asking them to repeat them, as we have seen in the first two lessons.

Ching set up rules and expected the students to stick to them. If her rules were not adhered to, she saw it as a disciplinary problem. For example, when the students made a great deal of noise in class, she did not or could not distinguish between whether the students were testing her limit or whether they were just talking very excitedly about the task. Unlike Marina, she did not distinguish between on-task noise and off-task noise. When students made a lot of noise in group work and came up with ideas which were funny, she felt that the students were "too relaxed." She said, "I would accept interesting ideas, even though sometimes some ideas surprised me. But perhaps because of my own character, I thought it [the lesson] was rather disorderly."

When a task did not work as well in one class as in another class, Ching would attribute it to the characteristics of these classes. In explaining why the task worked better in another class, she said "to a great extent, it is characteristic of that class – most of the students pay attention, they have relatively longer attention span, and their learning attitude is really positive." In other words, instead of asking herself whether the same task should have been given to two different classes, and how it should be modified, Ching attributed the success or failure to students' attentiveness and learning attitudes.

7.5.4 Organization of learning: Group work vs. individual work

Like Eva, Ching put the students into groups of six. Students were allowed to give their own group a name, and they came up with names like "Supersonic," "Speed," "Adidas," "Winner," and so forth. The students enjoyed the freedom of naming their own group. The organization of the class into groups was more of an incentive for students to participate in class rather than to get them to engage in collaborative learning. The groups competed to answer questions and marks were awarded for each correct answer.

When Ching started teaching, she was very reluctant to use group work for fear that the class would get out of control. As she gained more confidence in herself, particularly after she enrolled in the PCEd course, she was willing to use more group and pair work. However, in her heart of hearts, Ching still preferred individual and pair work. This is consistent with her conception of teaching as the teacher taking control of the class. In comparing the two S1 classes that she was teaching, she often used the words "well-disciplined" and "obedient" to describe what she considered to be the better class. She had two worries about using group work and games in teaching. First, she was not sure if she could keep the class "under control" and second, she was concerned about the learning outcome. When I asked her whether she found that she had any success using group work and games for teaching, she said:

It depends on how you see it. If you look at the students' responses, you know that they really liked it. They were very lively and they liked moving about. But if you look at its effectiveness, it [the game] may not have achieved the teaching goal. The students might not have learned what I wanted to teach by playing the game.

In other words, for Ching, fun and learning outcome, and group work and keeping discipline in class were each a dichotomy. She could not see that disciplinary problems are often related to the organization of learning. There could be a number of reasons for students not paying attention or being disruptive. When they cannot follow instructions, when they fail to see the purpose of an activity, or when they find that the materials are not challenging, their attention will wander, and they are likely to be disruptive. For example, it is commonly found that students do not pay attention when other groups are reporting the outcome of their discussions. This is because they have not been given a purpose for listening.

The students are simply reporting to the teacher instead of to their peers. This is why Marina's use of big posters for students to present their language productions was so effective. The big posters with big characters allowed everybody in the class to see what had been produced by each group and to respond to them as well.

Ching, having observed Marina using large posters for group work production, tried to use that in her classroom. However, she did not quite understand the purpose of doing this. When she could not find large poster papers, she just used A4-size papers. She said, "I thought the difference between a larger poster and a sheet of paper was just the size of the words. There's not a big difference. So in the end I used A4-size worksheets instead." At the end of group work, students just presented their work orally. It was difficult for the students to follow the presentations, and Ching was not able to go over their productions. Consequently, the opportunity for reinforcement was lost.

7.5.5 Using English in the classroom

While Ching was strict about keeping order and control, she was more relaxed about getting her students to use English for communication in the classroom, especially after the first two years of teaching when she felt that English was a barrier to building a close relationship with students. She encouraged her students to use English in group work and pair work and she would remind her students from time to time that they should not use Cantonese. However, she was not as persistent as Marina and Eva. She did not impose any penalty on students when she found them speaking in Cantonese. Ching's rationale was that her main task in dealing with S1 (grade 7) students was to acculturate them into secondary education. Helping them to change over from Chinese to English medium instruction was first and foremost. She was aware of the difficulty that the students might have in switching over from Chinese to English immediately. Therefore, she was more tolerant of the use of Cantonese than Marina and Eva.

7.5.6 Developing knowledge of management of learning

The most striking feature of Ching's classroom was its orderliness and discipline. The teacher was the figure of authority and the students were, or at least were expected to be, respectful of the teacher. Most lessons were teacher-fronted. Students paid attention to her when she was giving instructions, and her instructions were clear and systematic. From time to time, there would be group or pair work. Students were also very much aware of what was permissible and what was not. For example, too much noise in group work and when playing games would mean a sanction. Students knew that violation of these rules and norms would result in penalty.

The rules and routines that Ching established for managing the classroom corresponded to her image of the teacher as well-qualified and academically competent, and her conception of a teacher's role as focusing on "teaching," which was understood as presenting knowledge clearly to students. This conception governed the importance that Ching attached to organizing her lessons systematically and making her instructions clear and accessible to students. Going into teaching with no professional training, Ching had nothing on which to rely except her own learning experience in school as models of teaching. The orderly and well-disciplined manner in which her lessons were conducted was something that she achieved after two years of struggling with the multifaceted nature of classroom teaching and overcoming the anxiety of standing in front of a class of forty and speaking in English.

Ching was able to exercise her own judgement with regard to using English in the classroom after the first two years and did not stick to the policy recommended by the English panel. She was also able to provide a sound rationale for not enforcing it in S1 classes. Embedded in this flexibility is her knowledge of the difficulty and anxiety experienced by students switching from Chinese to English medium education, having gone through the same experience herself. However, she was not able to exercise flexibility in aspects such as noise tolerance, which conflicted with her image of teaching. Unlike Marina, she was not yet able to discriminate between on-task noise and off-task noise and to judge when noise foreshadowed disciplinary problems and when it indicated high levels of involvement.

Her attitude towards group work was perhaps an epitome of Ching's conception of teaching. On the one hand, she wanted to make her teaching interesting and enjoyable to the students, to get students to participate more, to build in more variety. Group work is a means of achieving all of those. On the other hand, she wanted teaching to proceed in an orderly and disciplined fashion, and to produce effective learning outcomes. Group work cannot guarantee both. In the first two years, when Ching was still very much in the survival phase, she seldom used group work. It was after her reassuring experience in the third year, and with encouragement from the professional course in the fourth year, that Ching started using group work. Ching's use of group work indicated her willingness to take risks, albeit in a small way. As we shall see in Chapter 8, the way Ching tried to use group work represented an interesting dichotomization of fun and learning.

Over five or six years of teaching, the development of Ching's knowledge in managing the classroom for learning pertained more to the technical aspects of classroom management than to her knowledge of students and student understanding. For example, when talking about the improvement of her relationship with students, Ching attributed it more to improvement in her teaching techniques than to her understanding of them. She seldom referred to changes in her knowledge of students. Her frequent reference to the difficulties she had in handling both S1 and S6 students who were so different was a case in point (see 6.4). While she shared some common classroom practices with Marina and Eva, she seldom theorized about her actions.

7.6 Genie

7.6.1 Management of learning in action: Genie's first two lessons

Genie's first two lessons can be divided into four segments. In the first segment she laid down some general rules and routines. They included what students should bring for the English lessons, including the kinds of exercise books, files, pens, dictionary and so forth. She also laid down the routine of handing in newspaper work on every Monday. In the course of doing this, Genie tried to put the students at ease by telling them not to be shy and encouraging them to ask questions if there was anything they did not understand. She assured them that she would give them help and guidance. She also tried to establish the house rule that they should speak English in class by repeating the instructions.

In the second segment she collected homework and book reports. Again, she reminded the students not to speak in Cantonese. Several students did not have the book report with them. Genie spent some time dealing with each of them individually and negotiating a time for handing in the report. As she was doing this, the rest of the class got very noisy. The following extract gives a flavor of how she dealt with the problem.

G: Next, it's the time I collect something from you, right? Your homework, please.... So please write down your name and pass it up to the front.... *Don't speak in Cantonese.* And please erase the blackboard.... Pass it up to the front, right. *Don't just always turn your head around.* Have you all handed in your homework? Who hasn't? Yes? What's wrong? Sorry?
S: Book report.
G: You haven't done the book report? Did your teacher ask you to do it last year? [*Students nodded their heads.*]
G: *So why didn't you do it then?* ... You forgot it. So when can I have it? *When can I have your book report? Tell me a date.* Don't tell me next year, next summer holiday. Yes?
S: Next Monday.
G: Next Monday? No. A week! So do you think it is fair now? Hmm?
S: I forgot –

G: You forgot to bring [your] storybook report? Have you done it? Really? But when will you bring it then? OK. Tomorrow. Before eight o'clock. Come to the staff room and see me and give me the homework. How about you? ... Now I hope all of you are honest, right? *Tell me really why, and don't just think of the reason to deceive me.*

In the above excerpt, we can see that Genie was trying hard to manage classroom discipline as well as to get on with the class business. Her classroom management style was typically reactive. She did not discriminate between what demanded immediate attention and what could be dealt with later or what demanded individual attention and what could be handled alltogether, such as when a number of students had forgotten to bring their book reports.

In the third segment Genie asked the students to form groups, for which she had specified group size and a mixture of boys and girls. She gave them three minutes to do so and to find a group representative. As the students were looking for their group members, Genie kept reminding them not to speak in Cantonese and to be quiet. After the students had gotten into their groups, Genie explained the rationale for putting them into groups: that they would feel more comfortable sitting with friends, and they would have a chance to discuss questions among themselves. She laid down the a number of house rules for group work. They included penalty in the form of deducting conduct marks for improper behavior and speaking in Cantonese, and incentives in the form of awarding marks for participating in discussions and answering the teacher's questions. At the end of the school year, the group with the lowest mark would have to buy a present for the winning group. She also encouraged the groups to be vigilant of each other. The group that reported another group using Cantonese would get marks. She built in a caveat that these rules could be changed if she found other unforeseen problems with the marking system. And indeed, she subsequently did.

Having laid down some house rules and organized the class, Genie started teaching. She told them that there were other house rules, but she would leave them to a later stage when need arose. This allowed her to leave a good part of the second lesson for teaching. As the lesson progressed, Genie implemented the house rules that she laid down. Groups talking in Cantonese were warned and marks were deducted. Groups that answered questions were given positive marks.

The above account of Genie's first two lessons shows that there are some similarities between Ching and Genie. Both emphasized the importance of proper behavior in the classroom and the penalty for breaking rules. However, in contrast to Ching, Genie also provided the rationale for the practices that she introduced to the students. And it is clear that alleviating students' anxiety and making the lessons enjoyable were very much on Genie's mind. Asking students to be vigilant of each other in the use of Cantonese is an interesting one. Although it was intended as a way of encouraging students to use English, it had a tendency of encouraging students to find fault with other groups in order to get ahead. This stood in stark contrast to Eva's strategy of encouraging collective responsibility to achieve the same goal: a group member speaking in Cantonese would have marks deducted from the whole group. By doing this, as Eva pointed out, she handed the responsibility back to the students. The two different approaches reflect a different orientation to classroom management, Eva's orientation being more positive and Genie's orientation being more negative and punitive. More important, it reflects a difference in the extent to which they were aware of how their moral values shaped and were shaped by their everyday classroom practices. Also unlike Ching, Genie started teaching early on in the second lesson and left the introduction of other rules until later. However, compared to Ching, Genie was much less "in control." She was busy dealing with individual student's problems while desperately trying to keep the rest of the class in order.

7.6.2 Handling disciplinary problems

Genie's classroom was typified by noise and laughter as well as frequent interpolations of "Shhh" from Genie to stop students talking. There were also calls for students to pay attention and to stay on task. In Genie's words, she was "fighting a battle." She described the way she dealt with classroom discipline as follows: "I keep an eye on them all the time and for those who are getting too much, I would not 'give face'" (See 6.5.5). By not "giving face," Genie meant that she would reprimand and penalize students publicly for disruptive behavior. When the discipline got really bad, she would switch to Cantonese and crack down on them. The penalties that she had used were asking the misbehaving student to leave his group and sit in a corner, and deducting marks from groups that took too long to get into groups. She also called on students who were not paying attention to answer questions, and if they could not, she would ask them to remain standing.

What Genie was trying to do was to deal with every single instance of what she perceived to be unacceptable behavior. This is why she said that she felt "exhausted." She had not yet developed the ability to discriminate between disciplinary problems that were obstructive to the achievement of instructional objectives, and those that were not and hence could be either ignored or dealt with later. Being able to maintain classroom discipline was one of Genie's major concerns. In the interviews, the concern to keep students "under control" came up several times. She was afraid that she might be looked upon as professionally incompetent if she could not even keep order in her own classroom.

7.6.3 Norms and routines

As we have seen in Genie's first two lessons, she was aware of the importance of laying down rules and norms, and setting up routines for dealing with class business. However, she was not able to stick to them consistently. This could be due to two reasons. First, in managing the classroom to facilitate learning, Genie faced a dilemma. On the one hand, she wanted to make the classroom a place like "home," where the students see themselves and the teacher as members of the same family. Her own religious background led to her belief that the teacher and students should love and care for each other. On the other hand, she was confronted with the reality of having to manage the classroom so that teaching and learning could take place effectively. Therefore, sometimes when she felt that she might be a bit harsh on the students, she would drop the rules or norms established. One example was not implementing the penalties that she laid down for violation of rules. Another reason was that some of the rules that she laid down proved to be impractical, and she had to drop them. For example, she established the rule that students must speak English in English lessons. She imposed a penalty on students who broke the rule by requiring them to go and speak to her in English for five minutes. She soon found that she was not able to cope with doing that for three classes. There were far too many students violating the rule. So she changed the rule and asked the students to talk to each other in English for five minutes. However, she soon found that the students were simply saying things in English for the sake of it instead of engaging in a meaningful conversation. Eventually, she had to abandon this penalty.

Apart from the above two reasons, in other practices such as the allocation of marks to groups, there were inconsistencies as well. Sometimes bonus marks were given for a good sentence provided or for being the first group to answer the question. The students had no idea of the rationale for the allocation, and they simply cheered or moaned depending on whether the marks allocated were high or low. Sometimes random bonus marks did not help her in managing the classroom for learning. As Calderhead (1984) observes, "establishing classroom norms often presents difficulties for beginning teachers." If the teacher was inconsistent in enforcing the norms, it becomes very difficult for the teacher to renegotiate.

7.6.4 Organization of learning: The interpretation of group work

When Genie first joined the school, Eva was the coordinator for S3 (grade 10) and she shared her experience and practices with Genie. One idea that Eva passed on was to organize the class into groups and give each group a name. Genie allowed the students to form their own groups of five to seven and to give each a name. For double lessons, students would sit with their group members, whereas for a single period, they would remain in their own seats. The groups would compete against each other in answering questions in class and working on tasks. Very often, the students sat in groups even though the task given was individual work or when it could be done in pairs. In other words, whether students worked in groups was determined not by instructional objectives, but by the duration of the lesson.

In one sense, Genie's conception of grouping was similar to Eva's. It was more a way of organizing the class and a seating arrangement rather than a way of organizing learning. However, Genie hoped to achieve more than just a way of organizing the class. She explained that first, she wanted to give the students a sense of belonging. So she modeled it on the "house system," which is commonly adopted by schools in Hong Kong, and by her own alma mater as well, in which the whole school was organized into several houses, and each house was made up of students from different academic classes and levels. She wanted the students to stay with the same group throughout the year so that they could get to know each other better. Second, she wanted to use grouping as a means of making students feel safe because they would be sitting with friends and would have the chance to discuss problems with them. Third, by introducing group competition, she could make her lessons more interesting and motivating.

Because group work was understood more as a way of organizing the class than as a way of organizing learning, Genie never considered the question of how to design the tasks in a way that would make it necessary for the students to collaborate for task completion. Nor had she pondered the question of the optimal group size for carrying out the tasks. She explained, "I feel that bigger groups will be more fun. If you have only three or four in a group, there are too few people. There are not enough ideas." She also asked the students whether they liked bigger or smaller groups, and they confirmed her preference for bigger groups because with more people there would be more ideas. However, when she conducted group work, she experienced difficulties: some of them did all the work and others sat there and did nothing. This, however, was interpreted by Genie as some members being too dominating and other being unable to collaborate with others. In fact, the mere physical distance between the group members sitting around four or five desks in a row made it difficult for everybody to participate in the discussion. When I raised this point with her, she said, "I was only thinking that too few people is no good. I didn't see it [group size] from the point of view of division of labor [in group work]."

Like Ching, Genie found it particularly difficult to maintain classroom discipline when students were conducting group work. She felt more comfortable and at ease when she was doing whole-class teaching because she was able to see everybody's face and she could keep an eye on all of them. The classroom was also less noisy. In order to make sure that all students listened to her instructions, Genie had to be very "long-winded" and she found this "hard work." When Genie asked them to get into groups, there was a major reshuffling of desks and chairs, and the students took a long time to settle down. Instead of addressing the problem fundamentally by reducing the size of the group and hence minimizing the moving of chairs and desks, Genie introduced a system of awarding five marks to the group that settled down first and deducting ten marks from the last group to settle down. There were so many criteria for rewarding and deducting marks that the system soon became fairly meaningless to the students.

7.6.5 Developing knowledge of management of learning

In this section we have seen how Genie managed the classroom for learning. We have seen that Genie, who was in the survival and discovery phase of her professional development, was still very preoccupied with maintaining order and discipline in the classroom. She was still experiencing difficulties in coping with the multiple dimensions of classroom teaching, and had not yet gained enough knowledge about classroom events in order to be selective in dealing with them (see Clark and Peterson, 1986; Doyle, 1977; Sabers et al., 1991).

Genie's conception of the classroom as "home," with the teacher and students as family members, permeated her management of the classroom learning. This was best reflected in her own interpretation of "group work," which should be more appropriately called "grouping," as a kind of support system that would make students feel safe and cultivate a sense of belonging. When Genie first used group work in her first year of teaching at the suggestion of the students, she saw it as a way of breaking the monotony of her teaching and getting more students to participate. In the process of implementing it, she theorized her actions and was able to formulate the reasons explicitly. Embodied in the use of group work was also her understanding of what students wanted and what would best suit them, which she strove very hard to achieve. What is interesting is that, like Ching, she found it difficult to maintain discipline when conducting group work; yet on the other hand, she used group work regularly for the reasons outlined above. Here we can see Genie's willingness to take risks and to explore ways of improving her teaching. What Genie had yet to come to grips with was how group work should be organized and designed in order to facilitate language learning.

Genie was still at the stage of experimenting with rules and routines and, like many novice teachers, was not always consistent when implementing them. As we have seen in the previous sections, such inconsistencies reflected the dilemma she faced in playing out her role as a guide to her students rather than as an authoritarian figure and in maintaining order and discipline so that learning can take place. She was not always aware of the practicalities of implementing the measures that she had introduced, nor of the moral implications of getting students to monitor each other. The practices that she had introduced are still in flux, unlike Marina, whose routines are fairly well-established. Therefore, much of Genie's attention and energy was still focused on dealing reactively – rather than proactively – with unruly behavior and stopping it from occurring (see Reynolds, 1992; Westerman, 1991). This took her away from the more important task of achieving instruction objectives (see Berliner, 1994).

8 Teacher Knowledge and the Enactment of the ESL Curriculum

In Chapter 7 we investigated how the four ESL teachers managed their classrooms for learning. We have seen that Marina has built up a rich repertoire of routines to handle the multifaceted nature of classroom teaching. We have also seen that embedded in what appears to be a mundane routine is Marina's situated knowledge about teaching, learning, and her students. Such knowledge, as Elbaz (1983) points out, shapes teachers' world of practice and classroom life. Compared to Marina, the other three teachers have a much less-rich repertoire of routines and norms, with Genie still trying to establish routines and norms that would reconcile her own beliefs and the realities of the classroom.

In this chapter we shall be looking at the knowledge embedded in these four teachers' interpretation and implementation of the ESL curriculum and how their knowledge developed over the years. In the review of novice-expert studies in Chapter 3, we have examined studies conducted on the preactive and interactive decision making of novice and expert teachers. While curriculum or lesson planning and the actual teaching constitute two different phases of teaching, the decisions made in the preactive phase of teaching are often intertwined with the way learning is managed in the lesson. Therefore, in this chapter, I shall simply organize the discussion according to the planning and the enactment of the ESL curriculum.

8.1 Planning the ESL Curriculum: Scheme of Work

At St. Peter's, the English language curriculum does not encompass literature. Although there is a set of textbooks prescribed for each level, teachers have a great deal of flexibility and autonomy when making decisions about the curriculum. At the beginning of the school year, those teaching the same level will agree on a common scheme of work for the whole year. A scheme of work specifies the number of units that will be covered, the duration of each unit, its components, and the number of lessons required for each component. Teachers teaching the same level decide on which units and which components of those units they wish to use from the textbook and what kind of supplementary materials they wish to add.

Curriculum planning is an interactive process that involves top-down goal-directed procedures in which activities are generated and bottom-up procedures in which activities and resources are picked up and matched against the goals (see Woods, 1996). In this process, teachers draw on their knowledge from a number of domains. Knowledge about students and student understanding as well as previous experience of what worked best in their classrooms and the school contexts – what materials are available, and what can be achieved realistically – all play an important part in teachers' instructional planning. As Calderhead (1993) points out, it is a pragmatic as well as a creative and interactive problem-solving process.

8.1.1 Marina

Marina believes that in order to help students learn, they should be given the opportunity to work together and to produce things using language. Hence, to help students to learn English, they should be engaged in tasks that require them to produce the target language. She also believes that language must be learned in meaningful and communicative contexts. (See 6.2.1) For her, grammar and vocabulary are the building blocks of a language, and therefore, grammar teaching is a very important part of the curriculum as is, to a lesser extent, vocabulary. These beliefs figure prominently in her planning of the scheme of work.

For Marina, a unit in her scheme of work is a coherent whole in which the various language skills are embedded in the language tasks that students are required to complete. She does not see the four language skills as discrete skills to which specific time-slots in the timetable should be allocated. For example, when planning a unit on traveling, she started with a reading passage on the traveling itinerary of two tourists. The passage served as the context for teaching grammar, which was the present perfect tense, as well as for teaching vocabulary. The topic, vocabulary, and target structures covered in the reading passage served as input for the writing task at the end of the unit. She talked about her planning for a unit after I observed the first lesson in this unit:

> The topic of Unit eleven is about traveling, and the grammar focus is present perfect. Today,... I asked them to extract from the reading passage some points like "they (the tourists) have done X", "they haven't yet done Y." There are two purposes here. They [the students] have to find the main points [in the reading passage]; second, these sentences are in present perfect, which we will cover soon. I think the itinerary given here [in the passage] is very inadequate. So I have asked them to come up with their own itinerary.... A lot of them have chosen Ocean Park, Lamma Island, and some talked about going to the

Science Museum. And then Activity nine is a small activity which asks them to match the names of places [to what they are famous for] so as to broaden their knowledge [of local places]. I want them to write a composition related to travel.... Last year, they were asked to write a letter to a friend and it seemed to be unrelated [to this unit]. I think it can be a larger scale activity this year. I plan to ask them to go to the Tourist Association and look for some pamphlets. I will give them a [writing] topic like this: the Hong Kong Tourist Association will publish a newsletter for young visitors, and the students will need to write an article to introduce something [about Hong Kong]. They can choose to write about special foods, places to visit, interesting games or activities. I also want to teach them to write in a special tone, positive and persuasive, to encourage visitors to come to Hong Kong. I have this idea because when we used the product writing approach, students had little opportunity to explore how to write. Now that we have used the process writing approach, we can do it in a different way. I discussed this with Eva this morning, and we agreed to think about it a bit more. I'm planning to go to the Hong Kong Tourist Association myself to look for some information. So the [activity on] itinerary today gave them the opportunity to think about it first. I hope they'll learn more as they go to the Hong Kong Tourist Association to collect information and prepare for writing. I will concentrate on vocabulary in the next lesson. There are some vocabulary activities for them to do. Then I'll cover the present perfect tense....

We can see from Marina's planning thoughts that the teaching of the language skills, grammar, and vocabulary was organized around the language tasks that students had to perform. She did not attempt to teach discrete skills for their own sake. There was coherence among the tasks in the sense that each one prepared the students for the final writing task. For example, the activity on drawing up their own itinerary together with Activity nine, which required them to match the tourist spots with the special features of these spots, helped students to get to know more tourist attractions in English. Marina drew on her experience in the previous year and improved on the writing task. The new writing task, which involved the production of several drafts, was described by Marina as "explor[ing] how to write." This view is congruent with her belief in the experiential dimension of language learning. Students need to be exposed to a language-rich environment in which they need to do things with language. Going to the Tourist Association to look for information and making decisions about what would be useful for their writing task is a good example. Noting down the names of tourist attractions in Hong Kong is another.

It is interesting that the reading passage was used not so much for teaching reading skills per se, but rather for the teaching of grammar and vocabulary. She in fact omitted the reading comprehension questions. She said, "I don't think it's necessary to go through the questions to help them understand the passage. I want them to do the vocabulary exercises first.... I think the main points in the reading passage have already been covered today.... I feel that I need to spend more time with them on vocabulary." This is characteristic of the way Marina handled the reading comprehension passages in the whole scheme of work. Although she also dealt with reading skills in some units, the reading passages primarily served as the contexts for teaching grammar and vocabulary. This shows the importance that Marina attached to grammar and vocabulary. Closely related to this is her stronger emphasis on the productive skills, writing and speaking, especially the former.

An important part of curriculum and lesson planning is the selection of teaching materials. As Marina talked about how she made decisions regarding which sets of textbooks to adopt for the school and what materials to use for each unit, three criteria emerged. First, whether the activities are contextualized and communicative. She explained why she selected one set of textbooks over other sets as follows, "... the activities have clearer contexts, and they are more communicative." Second, whether the textbook is well organized in terms of levels of difficulty, and whether the materials are of interest to students. She said:

We think that [name of textbook] is a bit difficult and there are problems with its organization.... Sometimes they have very difficult units coming before easy units, and sometimes the materials are very boring.... So we tend to skip these units.... We didn't follow the book that much, and we made a lot of changes. For books four and five, we mainly used the reading passages and seldom touched other sections.

The third criteria is whether the explanations of grammar points provided are valid. For example, in a critique that she wrote on the teaching of reported speech in textbooks, she pointed out that the explanations provided often centered on the formal aspect of the structure, whereas reasons for back shifting of tense and time or reference changes were seldom given. The examples and the exercises given were all transformations of decontextualized sentences from direct to indirect speech or vice versa. Marina pointed out that this kind of contrived form-focused exercise does not help students understand how language is used in real-life situations. In her concluding statement, Marina wrote,

Knowledge cannot be proceduralized without a conscious awareness of the language function and meaning and considerable practice in language use. Neither of these requirements can the textbook grammar fulfill. It is then clear that textbook grammar and exercises have to be supplemented and adapted to create real needs for grammar use in context.

We can see from the above account that Marina's planning of the scheme of work and the selection of materials were guided by an integration of her knowledge of the subject matter, which includes linguistics, communicative language teaching, the teaching of writing, and language learning as well as her knowledge of the students and the context(s) in which they operate. Marina's planning scheme and selection of materials also realize her conception of how resources for language learning can be maximized.

8.1.2 Eva

Eva's approach to planning the scheme of work is close to Marina's. This could well be because they taught the same level and they often shared their lesson plans and materials. Underlying her curriculum planning are two principles: continuity and integration. As mentioned in Chapter 6, she feels that the S2 curriculum should not be taken as independent of the S1 and S3 curricula. She conceptualized the S2 and S3 curricula as a unit, and S4 and S5 curricula as another unit. Therefore, when drawing up the scheme of work for S2, she referred to the schemes of work for S1 and S3. She also tried to integrate the language skills whenever she could. She explained, "I always think of integrating things. I have tried integrating listening, writing, and [reading] comprehension as one unit." However, her principle of integration was pragmatically rather than theoretically motivated. She explained her thinking behind this principle: "It's because of the lack of time.... I don't know, I just felt that it was easier that way and also less fragmented. The feedback from colleagues was good. They felt that it saved time and it was more practical." It also has to do with her predilection for simplicity. She explained:

I think it has to do with my personality and my way of thinking. For example, to me, clear and simple is good.... I like organizing materials. I am not used to having a lot of materials piling up. When I write papers, I spread everything on my desk and then deal with them slowly. I enjoy the process.

Eva's conception of integration can be seen from the way she planned Unit 5. Like all units in her scheme of work, Unit 5 was based on the textbook, but Eva made a number of modifications. The reading comprehension passage in this unit is about a local television station. It provides some background information, such as the number of channels it has and the size of its audience. It also tells stories that are passed on among the staff. Before going into the reading passage, Eva designed some pre-reading activities to familiarize students with vocabulary related to television, such as the names of television programs and their channels. She gave them a television schedule and asked them to discuss who watched which program. This was followed by a guessing game in which each group was given at random the name of a program and asked to act it out for the rest of the class to guess. The aim of this activity was to give students an opportunity to practice their speaking skills as well as to highlight vocabulary items like *television stations, channels, audience, broadcast,* and *producer*. After this, she moved on to the reading passage.

She gave the students the main topic of each paragraph and focused on helping students identify the key words. For homework, students were asked to use the questionnaire provided in the textbook on television watching habits, interview one classmate, and report to the class. This was followed by a debate on the motion "It is bad to watch too much television."

The above account shows the interrelationship between some components of the unit. Some activities prepared the ground for the next activity. For example, the prereading activities familiarized students with the names of television programs and channels and ensured that they had the necessary background knowledge and vocabulary to conduct the questionnaire activity on television watching habits. The questionnaire findings in turn provided input for the debate. For each activity, Eva emphasized the different language skills involved. For example, for the questionnaire, she emphasized the importance of understanding the questions and the vocabulary. She also required the students to report the findings orally. She gave the following instructions to the students:

Find one classmate and ask him or her the questions. But before you do that, you must make sure that you understand everything in this questionnaire. And then you must make sure that you understand the meaning of the words. OK? So, try to ask one classmate and then tomorrow, I will ask some of you to stand up and report [the results] in the next lesson.

While Eva was able to achieve integration of language skills in the performance of language tasks and some coherence between some activities, she was not able to achieve coherence with regard to the unit as a whole. For example, in Unit 5, as well as for some other units, the grammar focus was not related to the reading text. She just followed the grammar focus suggested in the textbook, which was the present perfect tense. Yet, in the reading passage, the present perfect tense was seldom used. Instead, the simple present tense was used to describe the television station and the simple past tense was used to relate the stories. For teaching the present perfect tense, she used a completely different set of materials that was not related to the unit even in terms of topic. Neither the grammar tasks nor the reading tasks were related to the final writing task, which was a piece of narrative writing describing a robbery involving the use of the past and past perfect tenses.

When making decisions about the teaching materials, Eva mostly relied on her past experience of how things went in the classroom as well as her own intuition of what worked and what did not. For example, for the above unit, Eva did not find the reading passage useful. However, she was unable to say why. She was aware of her lack of a theoretical basis for making judgements about curriculum planning, and she voiced her concern in the interviews. She said:

This year, there are things that I want to master, and there are a lot of areas that I am not clear about regarding syllabus design. What is the main emphasis? We set objectives, and the objectives are more or less the same every year. But how do we achieve these objectives? This is important. Sometimes the objectives that we wrote are a bit like just for the record, for other people's eyes. When you face the students, you really want to be able to teach things which are useful and effective.

Embedded in Eva's curriculum planning is her conception of the importance of integration and continuity, which was very much formulated as a result of her own practical experience of what worked best, and further reinforced by the positive responses that she received from colleagues. Eva's curriculum planning also had to do with her own personal enjoyment of the process of organizing things. The integration that she partially achieved in a unit was guided by her practical knowledge of language skills and her knowledge of the kind of preparation that students needed in order to carry out a task. However, she was unable to achieve an overall coherence of a unit because, unlike Marina, she does not have an adequate knowledge of English linguistics (as we shall see in 8.3.3) and a coherent framework with which to relate the different components of a unit.

8.1.3 Ching

Ching followed the textbook very closely when drawing up the scheme of work, and nearly all the activities provided in the textbook were used. For some units, there would be supplementary exercises taken from another grammar exercise book. Only very occasionally would Ching design her own activities. For some units, the reading passage served as meaningful contextualization for grammar. Ching was happy with that and used the reading passage as input for the writing task. There were, however, some units that lacked coherence. The activities were unrelated and dealt with discrete language skills for their own sake. Ching was aware of the problem. She observed, "It is difficult to link up the activities smoothly so that they are not unrelated and independent." However, unlike Marina and Eva, who tried to achieve coherence and integration by adding activities of their own, Ching found it difficult to do so and largely allowed the textbook to determine the curriculum. Ching's planning was therefore done at the micro rather than the macro level.

When making decisions at the micro level, we can see an interesting interplay between her knowledge of linguistics and her knowledge of the students. In a unit in which the grammar focus was the use of *will* and *going to* (future fulfillment of present intention), her decision on whether to focus on one or both was initially based on linguistic considerations. She found that the difference between *will* and *going to* is very subtle and there is no hard-and-fast rule regarding when to use which. She explained, "Very often, when we use them [that is, *will* and *going to*], it seems that the line [that is, the boundary] is not very clear. In some situations, both of them could be used." In light of this, she wondered if it would be less confusing for student to focus on one form. She said:

> Shall we just teach them *will* and tell them that there is more than one way to use *will*? I mean it [will] can have two different functions, one to predict and the other to tell people about your intention. It may be better [to focus on the same form with two different functions] than tell the students that there are two forms [for the same function].

However, what concerned her most was not which alternative would be easier for students to understand the language system, but rather whether she could find any interesting activities for the two functions. Finding interesting activities has been one of her major concerns since she started teaching. She herself found learning easy and enjoyable but had difficulties making students feel the same way. Finally, she decided to focus on the expression of intention with two linguistic forms, *will* and *going to*. This was because firstly she could think of activities that she felt would interest her students and second, because in the scheme of work, they were supposed to teach both *will* and *going to*. In other words, how to represent grammatical knowledge to students in an interesting way, and following what was laid down in the scheme of work were important criteria for Ching.

The following is another example in which we see Ching letting her concern for student interest take priority over the linguistic objective of the lesson when selecting materials for teaching. The grammar focus of this unit was comparatives. To make grammar teaching more interesting to her students, Ching decided to use a game called Top of the World. She put the students into groups and asked them to send one representative from each group to join a series of competitions. For each competition, after the representatives had come to the front of the class, Ching would tell them what they were competing for, for example, who was the tallest, who had the longest hair, and so on. During the competitions, many superlatives were used, but not comparatives. When planning for the lesson, Ching was well aware of the mismatch between the game and the linguistic objective, but she selected the game nevertheless for two reasons. The first one has to do with motivation. She said:

> Before [playing the game] I was well aware of that [the mismatch]. But I thought that the game could motivate the students and get them involved [in activities]. After the game, I would draw their attention to comparatives. I didn't think that that would be too much of a problem.

To make up for the mismatch, she asked the students to take the same adjectives used in the game to write comparative sentences, for example:

Samuel Wong is shorter than Fred Tang. The second reason was that in the end-of-the-year evaluation of her teaching, the students told her that they would like to have more activities during grammar lessons.

From the above examples, we can see that while Eva's planning decisions were largely based on past experience and her knowledge of the students, Ching's planning decisions were informed by both linguistic knowledge and knowledge of the students' interests. Students' interests sometimes took priority over the linguistic objective of the lesson. When Ching could not integrate the two, she tended to cater for students' interests even at the expense of the linguistic objective. In the lesson on comparatives, the competition game was used as a means of livening up the classroom atmosphere, rather than as a meaningful context for achieving the teaching objective. This resulted in the unnecessary dichotomization of learning and fun.

8.1.4 Genie

As coordinator for S3, Genie was responsible for drawing up the scheme of work. She largely followed that drawn up by her predecessor, which was largely based on the prescribed textbook. She gave an account of how she planned the scheme of work:

First of all, I based it on [name of the prescribed textbook]. We selected a number of units [from the textbook]. For each unit, I will cover all aspects of English teaching.... We'll try to cover reading comprehension, and... we'll have dictation.... We'll have writing on different topics.... There's also grammar. There are about five to seven lessons for teaching different grammatical items. For oral, there are different topics. The colleague responsible for a specific unit will have to look for materials. Oral will include reading aloud the reading comprehension passage. For listening, there are different skills that they can learn. There is newspaper work. For S3 students; they have to read the *South China Morning Post* [a local English newspaper].

From Genie's account, we can see that she did not have a conceptual framework, in either linguistics or language teaching, to guide her when making decisions about the curriculum. She saw language teaching as teaching the four language skills and grammar; and a scheme of work as a sequence of activities. When I asked her on what basis she determined the grammar focus of each unit, she said, "I never thought of that." I referred to a unit in which the passive voice as well as the past and present perfect tenses were the grammar focuses and asked her for the rationale. She explained that in the previous year, the passive voice was taught at the end of the school year and so there was very little time for practice. Therefore, her colleagues suggested that it should be taught earlier on. She further added, "From my experience last year, the passive voice is messy. So I want to, from the very beginning, refresh their memory of how the passive voice is used and review the use of the passive voice when they read newspapers." As for the two tenses, Genie explained that the decision was based on the number of periods available. She said, "There are five periods altogether [for grammar] and I want to cover something light. So I thought of these two tenses. The students have already been taught the simple past tense. Now they have to learn the present perfect and in what way it is different from the simple past. So I thought that they should be able to learn these two tenses in two periods."

The same rationale of time was used when I asked her about a unit in which the grammar focuses were reported questions and the past and past perfect tenses. The two tenses were put in that particular unit because they could be covered in two lessons. When I asked if she could have been thinking of relating the two tenses to the backshifting of tenses in reported speech, she said:

No. The composition is related to what they covered in the text and the grammar items. When I planned, I was thinking along the direction of getting them to use the grammar items and the content of the reading text in their composition. So I chose news report [as the writing topic]....

The fact that students often confused the use of the past tense with the use of the past perfect tense was also a reason for putting the two tenses together.

Genie's explication shows that she was aware of students' problems and past experiences, and she did take them into consideration when making decisions on the scheme of work. However, Genie could not see the linguistic or language learning motivation for determining the grammar focuses of each unit and its sequencing. Consequently, she used the number of lessons as the criterion. Woods (1996) observes that there are two types of concurrent course structures: chronological and conceptual. The former, determined by the calendar and the clock, is not part of teachers' decisions but plays a crucial role. It could also be constraining. The latter is made up of conceptual units or elements at different levels of abstraction; they can be content, goals or methods. In Genie's case, it seemed that the chronological structure was part of Genie's decisions about the curriculum.

Genie was aware of the need to integrate the various components of a unit. For example, she tried to relate the reading passage and the grammar focus(es) to the writing task. She was able to do that more successfully for some units than others. There were some units where the activities for the various language skills were tenuously related or unrelated. For example, in a unit on the Royal Society for the Prevention of Cruelty to Animals, the grammar focus was the passive voice. Yet, the passive voice was used only scantily in the reading text. The writing task, which was writing an advertisement urging people to adopt pets, was related to the topic of the reading text but not to the grammar focus. In a unit discussed above, reported questions and the past and past perfect tenses were the grammar focuses, and there were instances of such target structures in the reading text, which was an interview of a pop singer. However, Genie did not exploit the text for the teaching of these structures. Instead, she used grammar exercises taken from other textbooks.

When she took over as coordinator of S3 in the second year, she simply followed what was laid down in the scheme of work and past practices. She had some partially formed conceptions of the need for coherence and integration of skills in a unit. However, she was not always clear how integration and coherence could be achieved. Her own classroom experience and consultation with her colleagues were the two main sources on which she drew to make sense of the curriculum. When accounting for her plans and the materials that she had chosen, she often used reasons like "it was used last year" or "my colleagues taught me." For example, initially, when she selected articles from the newspaper, her sole consideration was whether it would be interesting for the students. Subsequently, her colleagues pointed out to her that the articles could be exploited to consolidate the grammar focus of a unit, and she took their suggestion on board. Henceforth, students' interest and grammar focus became her criteria for selecting newspaper articles. Genie had not yet formulated her own guiding principles for curriculum planning. As Westerman (1991) observes, the inability to see the overall coherence of the curriculum and how the components in curriculum interrelate is typical of novice teachers.

8.2 Lesson Planning

Studies of teachers' planning processes and planning thoughts observe that experienced teachers seldom start with aims and objectives when they plan a lesson. Rather, they will start with materials or content, and think about students' interests and the activities that may be required. They are more efficient in lesson planning and they often plan their lessons mentally with only brief notes as reminders. Their planning thoughts are much richer and more elaborate than novice teachers. Novice teachers, on the other hand, tend to start with aims and objectives, and to stick closely to the prescribed curriculum guide. They tend to spend a long time preparing for lessons and have detailed lesson plans, which may include what they are going to say, what action they intend to take, and even what they will put on the blackboard. The differences observed between expert and novice teachers have been attributed to the fact that expert teachers have rich past experience on which to rely, and they have mastered a repertoire of routines from which they can draw, whereas novice teachers have not (see for example Calderhead, 1984;

Borko and Livingston, 1989). In the rest of this section, we shall see if such differences were also found between the four ESL teachers.

8.2.1 Marina

Marina never goes to class without preparation and a lesson plan, no matter how busy she is. "I would not be confident that the lesson would go well if I did not do that," she said. Much of Marina's planning decision is conscious rather than routine, especially if the lessons cover a new topic (cf. Calderhead, 1984). She said, "For certain ideas, they come to me very easily. For others, I had to think for several evenings, especially if I have never taught them before." Her planning could take place anywhere and she often engaged in a mental dialog in her planning thoughts. She said:

> I would think about it when I am on a bus. Sometimes I would shake my head as I was thinking about it. I think the person sitting next to me must have been wondering if I'm crazy. Sometimes, in the middle of a meal, my mother would say, 'Are you thinking about your teaching again?' and I wasn't even aware of it. Maybe I was shaking my head.

In her lesson plans she would jot down an outline of what she would do, with a brief description of the steps and examples as well as the drawings she would put on the board. In her planning thoughts, she would think about what her students would be interested in, and she would go over the steps mentally. She said:

> I would think about what students would be interested in. I would rehearse the steps in my mind. What I would do for this step and what I would do for the next step and then modify them. So when I plan the lesson, I break it down into very small chunks. I would even think about what instructions to give and how they should be given.

She would also plan what questions she would ask, and even whom she would call on to answer the questions, and jot them down. When planning the questions and examples, she would draw on her knowledge of her students, including their family backgrounds, their interests, and so on. For example, when she planned the introduction of negative sentences using the present perfect tense, she initially jotted down a question asking whether they have stopped kissing their parents goodnight. However, she felt that this was too westernized for Chinese working-class children. Therefore, she changed it to whether they have stopped saying good morning and good night to their parents. She explained that saying good night and good morning to parents was not alien to them but was probably something that they did only when they were very young. Hence, it was very likely that she would be able to elicit a negative sentence.

Marina files her lesson plans and modifies them every year. Therefore, they contain notes that she has jotted down over the years. In these notes there were questions, illustrations, even names of students. She usually looks at the lesson plan again the night before as well as immediately before the lesson. She explained that she did this habitually because she wanted to make sure that she knew the steps by heart so that she could move from one step to another smoothly. "If I'm not familiar with the steps," she said, "I may get lost suddenly." When a lesson did not go smoothly because she was stuck at some point or she had made some mistakes, she would blame herself for being ill-prepared or "slow." An example that she gave was a writing lesson in which she took the students through a writing task. The task was to write a letter to encourage young visitors to come to Hong Kong. In her lesson plan, she had already put down "discuss the 'tone' of the letter" at the beginning of letter writing. Thinking that she would have no problem explaining what *tone* meant, she did not prepare ways of presenting tone to the students. However, when going over the various parts of a letter, she forgot to discuss the tone of the letter at the very beginning until she was talking about the second paragraph of the letter. As she carried on with the rest of the writing task, she kept thinking of when and how she should explain what *tone* meant. Finally, she decided to go back to it at the very end. She put down several adjectives on the board, *friendly, unfriendly, funny,* and *interesting*, to illustrate what was meant by *tone* and asked the students to choose the appropriate adjective for the tone of the letter. This episode was cited by Marina as an example of "being stuck" because she did not prepare thoroughly enough and did not know the steps by heart.

Marina was largely able to follow her lesson plan. She would put down the time allocated to each activity on her lesson plan. Her timing for each activity was remarkably accurate, even for activities she had never used before. However, she was also very sensitive to the students' responses and was able to make spontaneous adjustments to her plan without disrupting the flow of the lesson. For example, in a grammar lesson on present perfect and the adverbs *yet* and *already*, she put down *revision* for present perfect tense and allocated fifteen to twenty minutes to it in her lesson plan. However, as soon as the students showed difficulties understanding the use of the present perfect tense, she made an interactive decision to spend more time on it and postponed the teaching of the adverbs *yet* and *already* to the next lesson. She said:

I had to act according to my students' reactions immediately. I also had to think about whether I should still teach *yet* and *already*, whether I should leave them until later, whether I should spend time to go over it [the present prefect tense] again or whether I should just remind them of its usage and ask them to revise it themselves. I decided that understanding the usage of the present perfect is more important than understanding *yet* and *already*. Therefore, I just focused on the present perfect [for that lesson].

She emphasized that it is very important to be sensitive to students' responses. If there were any gaps between the students' responses and her expectations, she would slow down.

From Marina's account, we can see that like other expert teachers in the novice-expert literature, Marina's planning thoughts were very rich and elaborate. She engaged in "mental dialogs" in which she rehearsed the whole lesson in small chunks. Also, like other expert teachers, she was able to respond to students' needs and problems and to adjust her plans very quickly (Brown and McIntyre, 1992). However, unlike the reports about expert teachers in the research literature, Marina's planning often required conscious decisions, and she had to spend a lot of time preparing for topics which she had never before taught (cf. Calderhead, 1984). She had both mental and written plans. Her written plans, though in note form, contained information such as the names of students that she would call on, the pictures that she would put on the board, and the examples that she would give (cf. McCutcheon, 1980). Moreover, despite the years of experience that she had, she would go over the lesson plan the night before as well as right before the lesson to ensure that her lessons would be conducted smoothly. Knowing the procedures and the content of the lesson by heart allowed Marina to free up her mental resources to deal with the unpredictable in the classroom, to respond to students' questions and problems.

It is interesting that even with eight years' teaching experience and with the rich repertoire of teaching strategies that she had built up, Marina still spent a lot of time preparing for her lessons, especially when they covered topics that she had never before taught. Marina's approach to lesson preparation would be what Bereiter and Scardamalia (1993) referred to as "progressive problem solving" (p. 156). Instead of trying to fit the new task into her existing repertoire of teaching strategies, and reducing the problems of planning to a minimal by recalling routines that she had already established, she problematized it and tackled it at a higher level. Underlying the apparent efficiency and automaticity with which Marina was able to conduct her lessons was the high standard that Marina set for herself and the hours of preparation that had gone into these lessons.

8.2.2 Eva, Ching, and Genie

Compared to Marina, the planning thoughts of Eva, Ching, and Genie were not as rich or elaborate. All three of them used the materials and the activities available as the starting point of their planning. Although Eva said that she started with objectives, her description of the objectives of a lesson actually revealed a mixture of objectives and activities.

For example, she described the objectives of a lesson as getting across the main idea of a passage to students, helping students to identify key words, to understand some vocabulary items, and to note some sentence structures that the students could use in their writing. All three teachers wrote outlines for their own lessons. Eva would jot down everything she wanted to do in the lesson first and then reorganize it. She would also put down the questions that she would pose to the students, the vocabulary items that she would cover and the exercises that she would give for homework. Sometimes she would also jot down how she would explain some new words to her students, including cartoons. Like Marina, Eva would go over her lesson plan the night before as well as on the day of teaching. She would make adjustments to her lesson plan if necessary.

Ching's lesson plans followed closely the sequence of activities in the textbook and were systematic. When she had time, she would put down more detailed lesson plans. However, if she was busy, she would just "think on her feet." Genie wrote lesson plans according to what she would ask her students to do. Similar to Ching, Genie's lesson plans followed the textbook closely. For Genie, the purpose of writing the lesson plan was to get the plan into her head so that she could be more "free," "more flexible," and not have to refer to the written plan when she was teaching.

In terms of how well they could anticipate student questions and student problems when planning the lessons, there were clear differences among them. Eva felt that she had no problem envisaging how the lesson would proceed and what was likely to happen in the classroom. She could also anticipate responses from students and the questions that they were likely to ask. She had no qualms about not being able to stick to the lesson plan or the schedule in the scheme of work. "It is more important that students have learned something," she said. In fact, once she became the form coordinator, she held a number of meetings with her teachers, and they reached a consensus that they should not rush through the syllabus. Eva was ready to modify her lesson plans in response to cues from students. However, as we have seen in Chapter 6, sometimes, her indiscriminate responses to students' questions, comments and requests, led to digressions that took students away from the focus of the lesson.

Ching, on the other hand, appeared to be the opposite of Eva as far as this aspect of teaching was concerned. Ching's lesson plans were very much drawn up from her own perspective. She planned the lesson according to her own assumptions about student knowledge and student understanding, and what she would like the students to do. This is why sometimes the lesson did not turn out as she expected. When one task worked well in one class but not another, she attributed it to the students. She said:

I think to a great extent it is the characteristic of the other class. Most of the students [in that class] pay attention. They have longer concentration spans, and their learning attitudes are positive. They can also perform and behave well in class.

Alternatively, she attributed it to herself as not being suited to teaching.

Unlike Eva, once Ching had laid down her lesson plan, she was unwilling to change it during the lesson even when she found that her assumptions were wrong. For example, in a lesson on the use of *will* and *going to* to indicate intention, she anticipated that students had already covered *shall* in their primary curriculum and that they had been taught to use *shall* for futurity, but not *will* and *going to*. When she started the lesson, contrary to her expectation, the students were able to produce all three forms indicating futurity. However, instead of drawing out what students already knew about these three forms, Ching stuck to her own lesson plan and explained the form and function of *will* and *going to* nevertheless. In the postlesson interview, she said:

If I started to think about what I should do, now that I had anticipated wrongly, it might be even more confusing [to the students]. So I'd rather continue and ask for their feedback when the lesson is finished, like, were these forms taught in their primary schools, was this lesson just a repetition of what they had learned in the past. I might not have taught according to their needs. But at that moment, I couldn't change the plan too drastically because I had not prepared beforehand.

Genie had problems anticipating students' reactions in class. When she prepared for a lesson, she would try to get materials that she thought would be interesting to her students, and she got very excited about it. However, very often, the lesson did not turn out to be what she expected, and she was deflated. When I asked her whether she made any plans for dealing with possible student questions, she said, "That's impossible. I wouldn't know what they would ask. Also, I am not sure of their [ability] level." Though she put down time limits for the activities, she either did not observe them or did not make the time limit known to the students. Sometimes, halfway through the activity, Genie would announce the amount of time left for the students to complete the activity. This invariably led to groans and moans from students and resulted in tasks only partially completed.

We can see from the above account that although Eva's planning thoughts were not as rich and elaborate as Marina's, they bore some similarities. They both spent a great deal of time preparing for their lessons. Their knowledge of the students enabled them to conjure up a rich picture of teaching in action. Eva's rehearsal of the lesson by drafting the plan, going over it twice, and making modifications to it is somewhat similar to Marina's "mental dialog," only to a less sophisticated extent. They were both keen to make sure that they knew the lesson by heart. Unlike Marina, however, Eva was not able to both respond to students' questions and firmly steer the lesson so that it would not be "derailed" by the students (Allwright and Bailey, 1991). This is partly because of Eva's conception of teaching as establishing relationships with students as individuals in which engaging in a dialog with a student when he or she raised a question or made a remark was considered an important part of teaching. It is also due to Eva's indiscriminate attention to students' questions and comments whether or not they are related to the instructional objectives. As pointed out in Chapter 3, selectivity in attending to classroom events enables a teacher to be responsive to students and yet at the same time keep the lesson on track (see Berliner, 1994; Borko and Livingston, 1989; Reynolds, 1992; Sabers et al., 1991). This is one of the characteristics of expertise in teaching that is still wanting in Eva.

As far as being able to see things from students' perspectives and responding to students' needs are concerned, it appears that Ching and Genie are similar. Genie was unable to put herself in the position of the students, to anticipate students' questions and to preempt the problems that they might have. Studies of teacher knowledge have pointed out that novice teachers often have problems understanding the subject matter from the students' perspective and anticipating their problems and difficulties (see Grossman and Richert, 1988, Wilson, Shulman, and Richert, 1987). Why was Ching unable to respond to students' needs despite the fact that she was more experienced than Genie? The interview data cited above showed that this might have been due to her emphasis on keeping things under control in the classroom. Her fear that any change in her plan would cause confusion prevented her from addressing students' needs by taking risks. In other words, her conception of teaching as conducting lessons in an orderly manner prevailed. The choice that Ching made to stick to her own lesson plan was a conscious decision whereas that made by Genie could well have been unconscious.

8.3 Enactment of the ESL Curriculum

In 8.1 we have seen how the four ESL teachers approached the scheme of work and their conceptualization of English language teaching. While all of them recognize that coherence and integration of skills are important organizing principles, some were able to achieve them with greater success than others. We have also seen the criteria that these four teachers use when they plan the curriculum or a specific lesson. While Marina has clearly formulated principles that are supported by theories of language teaching and learning, Eva and Ching rely more on past teaching experiences as well as their own learning experiences. Although Ching has a linguistics background, she has problems in effectively representing that knowledge to students. Genie is still at the stage where she is trying to make sense of the curriculum, and trying to apply the principle of integration to it. She has had to draw on her experience in the past year as well as advice from her colleagues.

To explore further the pedagogical content knowledge held by these four teachers, in the rest of this chapter I shall examine their classroom instructions. Since it will not be possible to discuss their instructions in all areas of ESL teaching because of the limitations of space, I shall focus on specific areas for each of them. In the interviews I asked each of them which area of ESL teaching they thought was most important, which they felt most comfortable with, and which they found most difficult. All four teachers attached a great deal of importance to grammar and writing. Both Marina and Eva said that vocabulary is the other important area. Marina felt most comfortable teaching grammar. There was not an area that she found particularly difficult, but she paid least attention to listening skills. This is congruent with her emphasis on the productive skills rather than receptive skills. Both Eva and Genie felt most comfortable teaching reading but found grammar teaching most difficult. Ching did not feel that there was any area that she was confident in teaching but if she had to select an area, she would say grammar teaching is more manageable. She was most diffident about the teaching of reading. In the interviews, they tended to talk more about areas that they were most or least confident about, and their reflections revealed more about their conceptions and their knowledge.

In the rest of this chapter I shall examine the classroom instructions of all four teachers in grammar teaching since it is an area that all of them see as very important in the curriculum. For Marina, I shall examine her vocabulary teaching because this is another area that she feels is very important. For Eva, Ching, and Genie, I shall examine their teaching of reading, an area which Eva and Genie find easier to handle, but Ching finds difficult. I shall look at the knowledge and conceptions that shape their classroom instructions and practices. The teaching of writing, which is also another important area, will be dealt with in detail in Chapter 9 in the context of how process writing was implemented in junior forms.

8.3.1 Marina: grammar teaching

As mentioned in Chapter 7, Marina believes that grammar is central to language learning. For her, if a student has mastered the usage of a grammar item or structure, he or she will be able to use it correctly in the appropriate context. She also believes that learning should be outcome oriented and that there should be evidence to show that learning has taken place. Grammar teaching is an area where she believes it is relatively easy to see the outcome of learning as compared to teaching other language skills. In Chapter 6 we learned that as a student in school, she was never taught grammar, but her experience of learning German had a profound influence on her. The inductive approach that her German teacher used to help students to identify sentence patterns and formulate rules was one characteristic of her grammar teaching. Her own learning experience in school of being exposed to English in meaningful contexts also contributed to her conceptualization of the importance of teaching language in context. These atheoretical conceptions were later confirmed and theorized as she received professional and theoretical input from the courses that she attended.

GUIDING PRINCIPLES FOR GRAMMAR TEACHING

When I asked Marina how she approached the teaching of grammar, she gave the following account:

I try to integrate reading and grammar. The first thing I have to do is to see whether the grammar item [to be taught] has anything to do with the passage, whether the grammar item is based on the passage or not, because the treatment would be different. If it is based on the passage, then after going over the passage, I'll draw attention to the grammar items.... If not – if it is independent of the passage, then I'll use other materials to introduce the item. I usually start with something they are familiar with. For example, when I taught the use of *may* and *can* in writing rules, I started with regulations that they are familiar with such as school rules.

I'll start off with presentation, to present the item. I'll try not to tell them the rules or the patterns. I give them more examples so that they can tell me what rules or patterns they can deduce from these examples. Then I'll give them some practice. The practice often draws on their personal experience.... For example, when I taught the present perfect, *have you ever* something, I asked them to write a short note to their neighbor and their best friend in class and ask whether they have ever done something. Their partners had to give an answer. This is some form of practice. After the practice, if I feel that they have mastered – no, not mastered – but have gained some understanding, I'll ask them to produce, in groups or in pairs. Very often, I ask them to produce on big posters, and then I'll go over [their productions] with them. As for [individual] exercises, it depends on what items or structures have been taught. Sometimes I ask them to produce at home after practicing in class. Sometimes, I can do all three in a double period. These are the steps. But every time I aim at having a focus. So I often select one, or at the most, two [items/structures] to teach. This is easier to do in junior forms. But in senior forms, because they have already covered most grammar items, I'll deal with more than two, but I'll try not to overload them. Even in S4 and S5, I'll ask them to do things, like in a group, to produce something. It depends on the item, how I can do it.

From the account above, we can see the following guiding principles.

- First, grammar items are always presented in meaningful contexts. This is often in the form of integrating reading with grammar teaching, or exploiting other materials for teaching grammar.
- Second, an inductive approach is used to raise the students' awareness of language patterns and rules.
- Third, students are taken from the familiar to the unfamiliar.
- Fourth, presentations are always followed by practice before students are asked to produce.
- Fifth, students are asked to produce in pairs and groups before they are asked to produce individually.
- Finally, one or two grammar items are focused on at a time to avoid overloading the students.

SELECTION AND DESIGN OF GRAMMAR ACTIVITIES

When selecting or designing activities for teaching grammar, Marina has certain criteria: they must be good, and there has to be variation. She defined *good* as follows:

To me, good means that it must be clear. The task must be clear, and it really requires them to use the grammar item. Another thing is fun. It must be interesting for them. These are important.... Things must be in context. Meaningful use. Sometimes if you make them produce an item for its own sake, it's not much use. Interest is very important. If it is not interesting, my students will say 'Boring!' to me.

We can see that Marina was very clear in her mind what she was looking for when she selected or designed grammar activities. The first criterion is that the task must be clearly outlined. She further elaborated that sometimes an activity might look appealing at first glance, but when she went through the instructions, she found that the instructions were not clear, and there were missing gaps. This kind of activity will not work well in class, she said. The second criterion is that the task must lend itself to the production of the grammar item(s) being taught. The third criterion, which is closely related to the second, is that the use of the target item must be meaningful. The last criterion is that it must be fun from the students' perspective.

The criteria that Marina spelled out are all very important. The second criterion is particularly difficult to satisfy. In many grammar activities designed by teachers themselves or textbook writers, contrived situations are given to elicit the production of the target language. This often leads to either the students producing language that sounds unnatural or completing the task successfully without having to use the target item at all. The third criterion captures the essence of communicative language teaching. People use language for communication purposes, not for its own sake. Therefore, to create a need for communication is very important. In the activities that Marina designed, she paid a great deal of attention to the creation of an information gap so that students need to talk or write to each other in order to complete the task. For example, when she taught the modals *should* and *ought to*, she asked each group to write down a problem about which they would like to seek advice; and after they had finished, she asked them to select one problem and write a response using the modals. The students were keen to read the advice that they received from another group.

The last criterion requires that the teacher knows the students very well and is able to see things from their perspective. Marina is able to do this particularly well. Her knowledge of the students and what appeals to them comes through clearly in the grammar activities that she designs. For example, when teaching bare infinitives, she used an old song called "They Made Me," taken from *Sunday Afternoons – Songs for Students of English as a Foreign Language* by Roy Kingsbury and Patrick O'Shea (Longman). This song is about parents making their children do many things that they do not like. She took away all the verbs after the bare infinitives *made* and *let* and asked the students to guess what the verbs were. After that she asked the students to imagine what they would do when they became parents and teachers; what they would make or let their children or students do. Many of them put down things that they were not allowed to do. Her students enjoyed the activity very much and were able to use the bare infinitives very well. Marina articulated her thinking behind this activity as follows:

I feel that students want to be adults. Sometimes, I'll think about what I would do if I were in their shoes. I think they would like to imagine what they would do if they were in my shoes. I try to see things from their perspective. I guess they would be interested to see how they could boss you around, if they had the opportunity.

In order to understand what young people are interested in and what appeals to them, Marina pays attention to books for children and young people whenever she goes to bookshops or travels.

STRUCTURING GRAMMAR INSTRUCTION

Leinhardt et al. (1991) observe that the systematic arrangement of experiences to facilitate understanding is a crucial element in the process of instruction and learning. This includes being able to use a variety of examples, analogies, and illustrations to represent the target information effectively to learners (Shulman, 1986). It is often not possible for any one representation to capture all the salient features or components of the concept, procedure, or meaning being taught. Therefore, whether the teacher is able to use multiple representations and to sequence them appropriately may be essential to students' comprehension. The arrangement of experiences also includes being able to organize the instruction in such a way that there is a progression in the complexity of tasks.

In grammar teaching it is important that the teacher structures the instruction in such a way that will help students to become aware of the grammatical items and be able to use the target structures appropriately in meaningful contexts. The ways in which the target structures are presented to students, the language tasks that they are required to complete, and the linguistic complexity of the tasks are important elements.

Ellis (1998) points out that there are four theoretically motivated options in grammar instruction. The first option is the presentation of the target structure in written or oral texts to help learners to identify its salient features, referred to as "structured input." The psycholinguistic rationale is that getting learners to attend to rather than to produce the target structure facilitates acquisition. The second option is the direct and explicit explanation of rules, referred to as direct "explicit instruction," or the indirect consciousness-raising, which involves learners working out the rules for themselves. The third option is the elicitation of the production of the target structures, usually going from sentence level to text level creation, referred to as "production practice" (see also Schmidt, 1994; Spada and Lightbown, 1993). The fourth option is to provide feedback to learners when they have made errors, referred to as "negative feedback." The argument is that this serves as a way of drawing learners' attention to the gap between their own production and grammatically correct productions (see, for example, Lightbown and Spada, 1990). Research evidence suggests that the use of more than one option is often more effective. For example, structured input used together with explicit instruction was found to be most effective in helping learners understand as well as produce the target structure (see, for example, Tanaka, 1996, cited in Ellis, 1998; cf Van Patten and Oikkenon, 1996).

Marina adopts an eclectic approach, and her grammar lessons often contain all four options. To illustrate how they are realized in the classroom, let us take, for example, her lesson on the passive voice.

Prior to this lesson, Marina asked her students to bring their science textbooks to class. She started the lesson by saying to the students that they knew more about science than she did and that she wanted them to tell her about photosynthesis, a topic that they had finished in the science lessons a few days earlier. She invited the students to tell her things that were needed by a plant, such as water, sunlight, carbon dioxide, and oxygen. As the students were providing the four elements, she drew on the board a picture with the sun, a tree with leaves, soil and water. She asked the question "What happened to X?" and elicited the following sentences:

Carbon dioxide is absorbed by the leaves.
Water is absorbed by the roots.
Light energy is absorbed by the leaves.
Oxygen is given out by the air holes in the leaves.

After putting these sentences on the board, Marina asked the students to identify the common features that they shared, and focused their attention on the verb form. In this segment, she used the "structured input," approach. Typically, her structured input consists of several examples in which she keeps the target form constant and varies the rest of the sentence in order to help students to "notice" it. Structured input was followed by "explicit instruction," in which she explained why the passive voice was used – because they were interested in finding out what happened to the carbon dioxide, what happened to the water, and so forth.

After providing "explicit instruction," she asked the students to copy the sentences down in their sentence-making books. Marina recycled the target sentences by getting as many students as possible to repeat the description of photosynthesis with and without the help of clues on the board. She did this by rubbing off from the sample sentences first the past participle, then the verb *to be*. Finally, she rubbed off all sentences on the board and asked the students to reproduce all of them. She asked them to describe photosynthesis to each other in pairs before telling the whole class. "Negative feedback" was given throughout the lesson whenever she found serious errors in the target structures produced by the students.

After production practice, she asked students to identify all the passive sentences in the science unit on photosynthesis. For homework, she gave them short excerpts of newspaper reports and asked them to draw illustrations for passive sentences like "Five people were tied up and blindfolded for almost seven hours at a Kwun Tong company by a gang of eight" and "A driver was killed and two passengers injured when their car rammed into roadside railings in Sai Kung early yesterday morning."

Marina's grammar lessons show a progression in the cognitive and linguistic complexity of the tasks that she gives. She usually starts by asking students to identify the target structure in a piece of text or by eliciting the target form or structure at the sentence level, or both. She then proceeds to ask students to produce a short piece of text in pairs or groups followed by individual production. The identification of target structures is linguistically less demanding than producing them. Production at the sentence level is linguistically less demanding than at the text level. In the lesson on the passive voice, the production of the passive sentences moved from production with clues to without clues, from pair work and group work, which are cognitively less demanding, to individual work.

When presenting the target structure, Marina uses a variety of contexts. For example, in the grammar lessons discussed above, the passive voice was presented in scientific texts as well as in news reports. Both contexts were familiar to the students, the scientific text being more familiar than newspaper reports. The students thoroughly enjoyed being more knowledgeable than their teacher and were keen to correct Marina when she made an inaccurate statement. For example, when Marina said, "Sunlight is absorbed by the leaves," the students all said it should be "heat and/or light energy is absorbed by the leaves."

8.3.2 Marina: Developing knowledge in grammar teaching

Embedded in Marina's teaching of grammar is rich and integrated knowledge. The aspects of grammar teaching discussed includes her guiding principles, selection of materials, and design of activities, to the way she structures the learning experience and represents the target structures. This knowledge covers a number of dimensions. The first dimension is her knowledge of the English language, language teaching, and language learning. This encompasses her knowledge of grammar as meaning and not as form, and hence grammar items are always presented in meaningful contexts. She finds it important to raise students' awareness of the grammatical patterns and help them to formulate rules based on their own observations. As Ellis (1998) points out, it is more motivating to get learners to discover the rules for themselves than to give them the rules. It also encompasses her understanding of communicative language teaching, in which language is produced for communicative purposes and not for its own sake. This can be seen from the way she organized the activities for using modals to give advice. They gave students a purpose and a real audience for giving the advice.

The second dimension is her knowledge of how learning should be organized. This includes what constitutes linguistically and cognitively more-demanding tasks; the need to have a clear purpose and an outcome when designing pair and group work; the distinction between "teaching" and "testing" and the importance of giving guidance; going over student production in an efficient and effective manner; providing opportunities for consolidation of what has been taught; and providing positive reinforcement by displaying students' work.

The third dimension is her knowledge of other curricula, which enabled her to relate the English curriculum with the science curriculum as well as with her students' daily lives, hence making their learning relevant.

The last dimension is her knowledge of the students' interests and the kinds of activities that are likely to engage their attention.

In Chapter 6 we saw that Marina's grammar teaching was initially just based on her own learning experience in school and in the Goethe Institut. She modeled her teaching on her German teacher and tried out the methods he used. She was not able to articulate the theory behind what she was doing, but she developed practical knowledge in response to what was realistically achievable, given the limited resources and the tight working schedule. It was only when she attended the PCEd course that she began to understand the theoretical rationale behind her classroom practices and to reflect on her teaching in a more systematic and principled way. The theorization of her own practices became the basis for her future pedagogical decisions. The more profound theoretical input in the Master's course in English language teaching enabled her to formulate her own theories of grammar teaching. For example, her analysis of the problems with textbooks confirmed her own conviction of using authentic materials for teaching, and her study of learner strategies provided the theoretical basis for enriching the experiential dimension of language learning.

Despite the fact that Marina enjoys grammar teaching very much and is very good at it, she does not feel that she can sit back and relax. It has been suggested in the expert-novice literature that expert teachers have a repertoire of teaching strategies and activities that they can draw on. However, this does not seem to be the case for Marina. She reported that she seldom has a number of activities at her fingertips that she can use. She explained:

It is often very difficult to have a number [of activities]. When you look at references, they may suggest a number of activities, but very quickly you narrow them down to just a few. *I have to select what is good.* Also, if I have already used a similar activity before, I have to modify it so that students will not feel that it is the same activity. I try to give them some variation. (My emphasis)

In other words, it is Marina's motivation to strive for excellence that explains why she does not seem to share the characteristics of expert teachers reported in the novice-expert studies.

8.3.3 *Marina: Vocabulary teaching*

Vocabulary is an area to which Marina attaches a great deal of importance because she feels that it is one of the building blocks of language. For each unit she selects a number of vocabulary items that she wants the students to learn. For example, in Unit 11 on traveling described in 8.2.1, Marina selected for teaching the following vocabulary items: *souvenir, recommend, decorated, itinerary, attraction,* and *terminus.* When I asked her on what basis she selected those items, she said that the words were all related to traveling. She believes that asking students to learn vocabulary items that belong to the same semantic field will help students to recall as well as to use them when writing. The concept of semantic field was introduced to her in the PCEd course. Before that, Marina said, she intuitively selected vocabulary items for teaching. She also tries to integrate vocabulary teaching with listening skills. In the same unit on traveling, she tried to introduce other sets of vocabulary in the context of shopping for clothing, such as *cardigan, scarf, shirt,* and *blouse.*

To help students understand these items, she took to class some souvenirs that she had bought when she was traveling, as well as pamphlets and brochures that she had collected from the Tourist Association for illustration. When she taught the word *itinerary,* she asked them to write down the places that they would like to recommend to tourists and to take note of special local shops that would be of interest to tourists over the weekend. Some students jotted down the names of shops in Chinese, and she helped to translate them into English – for example, Chinese herbal tea shop, and *dai pai dong,* which is a kind of open-air hawker food stall. On the basis of the names suggested by the students, she designed a worksheet on *itinerary* for them to complete. She helped students to understand the meaning of *itinerary* by actually making them go through the experience of drawing up an itinerary. This is congruent with Marina's belief in the experiential dimension of language learning and the importance of raising students' awareness of the language around them.

As I observed Marina's vocabulary lessons, I noticed a recurring routine. After having introduced new vocabulary items, Marina asked them to revise the items at home. On the following day, she started the lesson by asking the students to close their books. She asked for volunteers to explain each item. After going through all of the items, she asked them to open their textbooks and gave them two minutes to study the items again. She set the alarm clock for timing. When the alarm went off, she asked students to close their textbooks and nominated individual students to answer her questions.

The vocabulary consolidation routine is something that Marina has developed subconsciously over the years. I asked her the rationale for the routine and she explained as follows. Most of her students are working class children. They will not be able to revise their school work at home because the television will be switched on all night when their parents come home from work. Moreover, they are usually unable to get help from their parents. If she was to ask them questions individually from the very beginning, many of them would not be able to give an answer and they would be embarrassed. By initially directing the questions to the whole class, and asking for volunteers, she can be sure that those who volunteer know the answer. As they are giving the answer, those who do not know the words will have a chance to hear the explanation first. To consolidate the verbal explanation given by the students, Marina gives them another opportunity to read the explanations of the words in print. This helps them to remember the words better. She feels that after she has given them opportunities to listen to the verbal explanations given by their classmates and to read the written explanations, the students should be able to retain the meanings of the words longer. It is therefore less likely that they will be embarrassed when she calls on them individually to provide the explanations.

After a lesson where Marina used this routine, I interviewed the students. Their perception of what Marina did in class corroborated her intentions. Winnie, an S2 student, said, "Yes, Miss Tam always does that. I think she knows that we don't revise our work, but she does not want to embarrass us because she knows most of us won't be able to explain the words." The students welcomed the opportunity to revise the items before they were nominated to answer questions and found the routine effective. They were also appreciative of Marina's sensitivity to their feelings.

Embedded in this routine is Marina's knowledge of the students' family background and their life pattern. It also involves sensitivity to students' psychological well being and an understanding of the need for consolidation in learning. Reflecting on her practice in vocabulary consolidation, she said:

Teaching doesn't mean the students will learn what you have taught in the lessons. I have to think of ways to help them to consolidate their learning. . . . I don't think it's useful to ask the students to study at home because they won't. So I think it is worth spending more time to practice them in class. That's why I use lesson time to do vocabulary consolidation.

This routine emerged through what Marina described as a "gradual process." She realized the importance of recycling and consolidation in learning after her unsuccessful experiences in the first two or three years of teaching when she found that the students did not remember what was taught in class, did very poorly in tests, had very limited vocabulary, and constantly made the same grammatical mistakes, even though they enjoyed the lessons thoroughly and were interested in learning. At first, she addressed the problem by making them stay after school to learn the words. However, she did not feel good about punishing the students and the punishment was not effective. She reflected on this and came to the understanding that teaching is not equivalent to learning. She said, "You need to recycle [the materials]. Grammar and vocabulary need to be revised some time later. You cannot expect that they will remember." Having the right expectation helped her to accept students' forgetting what was taught without getting upset. She looked for alternative ways to help her students. She came across Gairns and Redman's (1986) book on vocabulary teaching, and that was the first time she was introduced to the idea of guessing meanings of words in context. She began to wonder if students would remember the words better in context. Attending the PCEd course helped her to think about the various teaching skills and reexamine her own vocabulary teaching. She started to incorporate the ideas about teaching vocabulary in context, vocabulary recycling and consolidation into her teaching, and a routine for vocabulary consolidation began to emerge. When she first started the routine, it was simply allowing time in class for consolidation. Pansy, one of the S5 students interviewed, recalled what Marina did with them when she was in S2. She said, "She (Marina) usually says, 'I allow you two minutes to read them and recite them.' Then she will ask us to turn it [the textbook or worksheet] over and question us on the meaning or pronunciation." Subsequently, the routine was refined and elaborated. When the students were able to recall the meanings of words that she had taught them before, even those that were taught several years back, she was heartened and knew that she was moving in the right direction. This approach to vocabulary consolidation routine became her personal strategy.

8.3.4 Eva: Grammar teaching

As mentioned in 8.3, Eva felt that grammar has an important place in the English curriculum. She said, "Grammar is something very systematic. It also affects a lot of things. It affects students' composition. It permeates everything. You can't ignore it." We can see that Eva had a vague conception of grammar being on the one hand rule-governed and yet on the other hand being closely tied to meaning. This was why it "affects students' composition" because she found that in students' writing, grammatical inaccuracies often hindered the proper expression of meaning.

SELECTION AND DESIGN OF GRAMMAR ACTIVITIES

Eva is critical of the exercises in the textbook that consist of merely manipulation of forms. To replace them, she tries to find from other resource books activities that provide meaningful contexts for the use of the target structures. She is also able to make interesting adaptations. For example, when teaching the question form of the present perfect tense, she started with an activity that required students to make statements in the present perfect tense. The activity was about a family preparing to go away on vacation and there were four pictures showing what they have and have not done to the house. The students were asked to look at the pictures for two minutes and then try to remember and write down the jobs that the family had to do before it went away. After the students had finished this activity, Eva gave them an extended activity. She asked the students to imagine that the family was visited by their grandparents who asked a lot of questions to check if they had done the jobs before they went away. The students were able to identify with the situation immediately and said that their own grandparents acted the same way. They were able to turn the statements into questions with little problem.

For another follow-up activity on the present perfect tense used together with the adverb *ever*, she gave them a list of personalities, all of whom were political figures, including dissidents from the People's Republic of China, local political commentators, and top government officials. She asked them to write down some questions to find out what they had done in the past. Eva took the opportunity to explain to the students who these personalities were.

In the context of evaluating her own teaching, Eva brought up the teaching of grammar in the following way:

Usually I feel a greater sense of achievement when the text is related to [students'] daily lives, about character, or even when it makes them reflect. When we work on the "secret door" [a writing task], I think about how they could express their ideals in life. Then according to my criterion, I am successful and it's meaningful. So I'm still thinking about how I can relate grammar to their daily lives.

Besides relating the grammar tasks to current events, and to social and political figures, Eva also tries to relate her teaching to students' daily lives by using examples that are about the students. She said:

I do this frequently, and the examples I use are normally related to them or about their classmates. They will be happier, and they will remember better.... Even when I design test papers, I write about things related to them and to their good behaviors. I sometimes use their names.

Whenever she writes about her students, she always says something positive about them.

From the grammar activities that Eva selected or designed, we can see that meaningful contextualization of target items, students' interests and relevance to students' daily lives are important criteria. Her grammar teaching is also influenced by her conception of teaching as inculcating moral values and social awareness, and her objective of fostering a supportive and positive culture in the classroom. (see 6.3.1; see also 7.4.5).

STRUCTURING GRAMMAR INSTRUCTION

Unlike Marina, Eva has not developed a clearly identifiable structure for grammar instruction. Sometimes "explicit instruction" takes place at the very beginning by explaining or by asking students to explain when a target item is used. Other times, she explains the structural pattern after "production practice." She seldom uses "structured input" to raise the students' language awareness. For illustration, let us take the grammar lesson on the present perfect tense described in the previous section, which is typical of Eva's grammar teaching.

Eva started the lesson with "explicit instruction" by asking the students to explain three situations under which the present perfect tense would be used. She moved to "production practice" by giving them an activity about a family going away for a holiday (see the previous section). For this activity, students were required to produce statements using the present perfect tense. Key words were provided. She asked the students to work in groups and provided feedback. Group work was followed by an extended activity in which she asked them to take on the personae of either the grandmother or the grandfather and change the statements into questions. Eva then gave "explicit instruction" again by drawing students' attention to subject-verb inversion and the insertion of the pronoun between the verb to have and the past participle, as in *Have you watered the plants?*

So far, the activities were controlled practice. Eva then moved to free production practice by introducing a game in which two students were asked to leave the room while the rest of the class made some changes to the classroom setting. These two students were to guess what changes had been made by asking questions using the present perfect tense. In the final part of the lesson, she introduced the use of the adverb *ever* to ask if people have ever done something in the past. This was followed by two "production practice" activities. One was to think of questions that they would like to ask some political figures that Eva listed on the board, using the adverb *ever* (see the preceding section). The second production activity was to use the same question form to ask their partners things that they had ever done. For each of the activities, Eva provided corrective feedback.

The above description shows that Eva also used a combination of options, except for "structured input," which she seldom uses. The overall approach that she used was intended to be deductive. She started with an explanation of three situations under which the present perfect tense would be used. The activities that followed should have been an application of the rules to use in the production practice activities. However, Eva did not explain which of the three situations the activities illustrated. The students simply completed the activities. Moreover, the explicit explanation of rules was not done as systematically as Marina did. For example, when Eva asked the students to explain the situations under which the present perfect would be used, they came up with explanations like, "A state of something we do up to now" and "Someone has done something before and then continue[s]." Eva asked the students to explain what *state* meant. One student came up with the following explanation:

S: She has been ill for months, meaning, hm, last month, ill.... Someone has been ill for months, meaning, hm, meaning, the man has just, just meaning that someone has has ill...

The student gave the right example but he was unable to explain *state*. Eva did not take the student's example on board and introduce the stative meaning of the verb *be* in the example. Instead, she asked the students to look up the meaning of *state* in the dictionary. One student offered *way of being*. This was not taken on board either. She stuck closely to the explanation given in the textbook and paraphrased it as, "You use the present perfect tense when we're talking about a condition up to now..." No reference was made to the example or the explanations that the students gave. In her explanation Eva did not distinguish between the use of the present perfect to denote a state of being that continued up to the present and its use to indicate an event that happened in the past but is extending into the present. She took them to be the same. The discussion in the "explicit instruction" left students quite confused about the usage of the present perfect tense.

In terms of task complexity, Eva broke down the task of asking questions using the present perfect tense into two subtasks. The first one was to get students to produce statements, and the second was to use these statements as a basis for forming the questions. She also moved from controlled practice to free practice. In other words, she was able to anticipate the possible problems that her student might have and try to preempt them by guiding students systematically. Like Marina, Eva used a number of activities in different contexts to represent the usage of the present perfect tense. All of these activities tried to relate to students' daily lives. However, some activities did not seem to have a communicative purpose. The last activity, in which students were to ask each other questions, is an example where the focus is on form rather than communicative function. While there is a place for activities focused on form, they should lead to activities that use form in communicative situations.

Eva's grammar teaching is apparently handicapped by her inadequate background knowledge in English linguistics and English language teaching. This affected the quality of her grammatical explanations, as well as her ability to distinguish between communicative and form-focused activities, and to judge the difficulty levels of the tasks in terms of linguistic complexity.

8.3.5 Eva: Developing knowledge in grammar teaching

In Chapter 6 we learned that grammar teaching has always troubled Eva, especially in her first year of teaching. She said,

> In the first year, I was most bothered by grammar teaching. I finished teaching an item very quickly, but students did not seem to have learned it after the lessons. Even if I spent a few more lessons on it, the students still did not seem to have learned it. This made me feel very lost. So I often thought about how to make grammar teaching effective.

Eva looked at Marina's materials and observed her teaching. Marina gave her very close guidance by going over the materials with her and sharing her students' work with her (see 6.3.4). This kind of apprentice-like guidance gave Eva many good ideas for teaching.

Eva is very much aware of her lack of linguistic knowledge, and she wants to read up on grammar. However, she finds it difficult to put aside time for it because there are so many other areas of teaching for which she needs input, and very often other duties take over. She tries to tackle this by asking for help from Marina and colleagues teaching the same level. Sometimes she consults Ching, even though they are teaching different levels. (See also 6.3.4)

In the meantime, she tries to cope with grammar teaching with the limited linguistic knowledge that she has. When going over reading passages, Eva selects some sentence structures that she feels will be useful for students and asks them to do substitution. For example, she took the sentence, *The veggy lion is one of the <u>funniest animals</u> in the world*. and asked the students to substitute the underlined parts with their own words. They produced sentences like, *The topic sentence is one of the most important things in a paragraph, Miss Lee [Eva] is one of the kindest teachers in St. Peter's Secondary School.*

When I asked Eva how she decided which parts of a sentence should be substituted, she said, "Take away those that can be changed. For example, adjectives can be taken away. So the main skeleton is still there." Eva was making use of whatever linguistic knowledge that she had to design these exercises in order to help her students learn the sentence structure. It is also interesting to see how Eva talked about the syntactic structures of the sentences, with minimal meta-language. For example, she described *the red plastic* as a "noun with adjectives included," instead of a noun phrase with a color adjective. When she asked students to use participial adjectives as classifiers, Eva said, "I asked them to write sentences with *-ing* serving as adjectives. They wrote something like *a barking dog, a sleeping beauty,* et cetera. Then they begin to understand that something can be included within the noun." Eva felt that this kind of exercise helped students to understand how meaning could be enriched by making changes to certain basic sentence structures.

Over the years Eva has built up a repertoire of interesting games and activities from which she can draw. She seems to be able to get into students' minds and anticipate what they are thinking about and what difficulties that they are likely to have. However, the decisions that she makes about whether the activities are good from the perspective of language teaching are largely based on experience rather than on language teaching theories. Her lack of linguistic knowledge also creates considerable difficulty for her when trying to help students understand grammar as a system of meaning.

8.3.6 *Eva: Teaching of reading*

Eva is more confident in teaching reading than other skills. She feels that it is easier to handle. As pointed out previously, she tried to integrate reading with writing by using some reading texts as models of writing that students could follow. For example, when she introduced the concept of a topic sentence, she reminded the students that in their own writing, they could use the topic sentence to introduce the main idea of a paragraph. She also demonstrated how they could elaborate on their ideas by adding supporting details. However, Eva's understanding of the teaching of reading comprehension is fragmented. She is aware of reading skills such as identifying the topic sentence and supporting details, predictive reading, inferencing skills, and so forth, and she taught them in her reading lessons. However, when I asked her what her objectives were in teaching reading and what the important skills were, she mentioned understanding the content of the reading passage, the meanings of new words, certain sentence structures, as well as the standpoint and attitude of the writer. This suggests that Eva does not have a coherent view of the objectives of teaching reading and how learners can be helped to become better readers.

Eva was taught in the traditional way, in which the teacher had the students read aloud and then answer the reading comprehension questions at the end. However, instead of simply relying on her past learning experience, she tried to make sense of the teaching of reading by setting her own objectives and assigning a new meaning to it.

Coherent with the metaphor of exploring the "space" in teaching, Eva often sets her own questions instead of using those provided in the textbook. By doing this, she hopes to get the students to read a passage from a perspective that is different from that offered by the textbook writer. This is the space that she feels that teaching can offer her.

Another way of creating space in teaching is to write her own text and set comprehension questions when she has time. She said:

> I love doing it. I have tried composing a text based on what was taught in oral and reading comprehension lessons, and then I wrote a story, which is educational. I once wrote a piece of text for S3, and I put in religious beliefs that talked about the difference between Satan and God. It was very short. I have also written texts where I include something about counseling and discipline problems, or something that I am unhappy about, to give vent [to my feelings] in these texts.

She sees this as creative writing on her part in which she can express her own beliefs and feelings. She enjoys creating these texts because they are about people (see also 6.3.1).

In addition to making space for herself in teaching, her text creation is also motivated by students' interests. She said, "I feel that students would find it more interesting. This is top priority. This is my personal concern. I feel that I may not be able to become a good teacher who is good at teaching. My concern for students is greater than my concern that students can learn something." In other words, Eva perceives her concern for the students and their learning as a dichotomy and that being a good teacher does not entail being good at teaching.

When the reading texts provided in the textbook concerns moral values, she will ask the students to reflect on the message conveyed and to write down the insights that they have gained after reading it. She considers herself successful in achieving the aim of education when the students are receptive to these moral values (see 6.3.1). Newspapers are another source of materials that she exploits for the teaching of reading. Sometimes she asks students to use the themes of the news article on social issues to conduct role-plays. Some students take on the role of a certain government official and others the roles of the people. She also asks them to respond to these articles and express their own views.

Eva's personal approach to the teaching of reading is something that has evolved over her five years of teaching. Embedded in this personal approach is her partial understanding of reading comprehension, which is handicapped by the lack of a coherent theoretical framework for understanding reading and the teaching of reading. Permeating the way she handles the reading text and the objectives for teaching of reading are her beliefs in the importance of creativity in teaching, and in being able to allow space for creativity and critical thinking. The powerful influence of her conceptions of teaching as inculcating moral values and social awareness, as well as being able to relate to students as individual human beings also came through strongly. This approach is coherent with her approach to the teaching of grammar and, as we shall see in Chapter 9, the teaching of writing as well.

In Chapter 6 we have seen that at the end of her fifth year of teaching, Eva was going through a stage in which she feels that she has made some achievements in certain areas of teaching, particularly in building a strong relationship with her students. Yet at the same time, she is well aware of her inadequacies, particularly in her knowledge of language teaching and teaching effectiveness. Her dichotomization of concern for students and students' learning as well as that of being a good teacher and good at teaching could well be an attempt on Eva's part to try to affirm her own worth as a teacher and counter her doubts about herself as a competent English teacher.

8.3.7 Ching: Grammar teaching

Like Marina and Eva, Ching feels that learning the grammar of a language is crucial to learning the language. She attaches a great deal of importance to accuracy. She monitors her own speech and self-corrects. Having majored in English linguistics at university, Ching believes that it is important to have a clear understanding of grammatical concepts. When preparing for lessons, she will check her own understanding of the target grammar items with reference grammars. Although she has adequate linguistic knowledge, she finds it difficult to make grammar interesting. She spends more time preparing for it than other areas of teaching.

SELECTION AND DESIGN OF GRAMMAR ACTIVITIES

Ching's major concern in grammar teaching is how to represent grammatical concepts and grammar usage to students in an interesting way. In 8.1.3 we have seen how Ching tried to introduce games in grammar teaching, specifically, in the teaching of comparatives, by using the game Top of the World. I have pointed out that even though Ching was fully aware that the game did not help to achieve the linguistic objective of the lesson, she still went with it because she could not find any other interesting game in which to contextualize the comparatives. In other words, students' interest took priority over the linguistic objective of the lesson. In fact, how to make learning interesting to her students is a concern that permeates all areas of her teaching. As we shall see in the ensuing section, this concern affects the way she structures grammar instruction as well.

When designing her own grammar activities, Ching also tries to make them relevant to the students. However, she has a narrow interpretation of relevance to students. She feels that in order to be relevant to students, activities must be set within the context of the school. For example, when teaching a lesson on the use of the simple present tense to talk about themselves and their family, she gave the students the situation of an interview for admission to the school. Another example is when teaching "giving directions," she used a map of the school building. When I asked whether she had thought of using materials like the plan of a shopping center, or the map of a park, she said that she thought that the school building would be more familiar to students.

STRUCTURING GRAMMAR INSTRUCTION

Like Marina, Ching often starts her lesson with "structured input" rather than "explicit explanation." She also gives students plenty of opportunities for "production practice" and provides feedback. In this section we shall take a typical grammar lesson and examine the way Ching structures the instruction.

This is a lesson on conditionals. Ching wanted to introduce two types of conditionals, one using the simple present tense in both the conditional clause and the main clause, the other using the future tense in the main clause. Ching started the lesson by putting some advertising posters on the board containing the first part of the conditional sentences. She took the students through each poster, but instead of eliciting the main clauses from them, she provided the main clause with an imperative structure in each case.

If you want to be a top runner, *wear Reebok sports shoes.*
If you want to lose weight, *come to our fitness centre.*
If your dog needs the best food, *buy Polo.*
If your hair needs more protection, *use Vidal Sassoon.*
If you want to save money, *open a savings account at our bank.*

After this she asked the students to work in pairs and produce conditional sentences which would appear in advertising or similar contexts. However, Ching did not model the task prior to this activity. Consequently, while some students produced sentences like *If you want to see dolphins, go to Ocean Park*, *If you want to get good marks, go to St. Peter's*, others produced irrelevant sentences that showed a lack of understanding of the task. After providing feedback Ching changed the main clauses in the five conditional sentences from imperative to declarative as an alternative way of writing advertisements. For example, *If you want to lose weight, our fitness center suits you.* Again, students were asked to follow the same pattern and change the conditional sentences that they produced accordingly. Some students produced sentences like *If you want to keep fit, TCBY[2] is the best!* Ching collected the work that they produced and moved to another stage of the lesson. Up to this point, there was no awareness raising of the structural pattern of these sentences.

2 TCBY is the brand name of a yogurt ice-cream that was getting very popular in Hong Kong.

Ching referred to the experiments in their science class and gave the students a pile of cards, some containing the conditional clauses and some containing the main clauses, and asked them to match the two parts. Some examples are:

If you light a Bunsen burner with the airhole closed, *the flame is yellow in color.*
If you put your finger into ice water, *it feels cold.*
If you put the same finger into tap water, *it feels warm.*
If you add salt into water, *it dissolves.*

This is followed by presenting another type of conditional using the modal will.[3]

If you don't leave my home, I'll call the police.
If Dad is free, he will visit his friends with me in August.

Ching drew the students' attention to the use of two different tenses in the main clause and explained that the present tense is used when one is certain that the event will happen and that the future tense is used when we are not absolutely certain that it will happen but we think that it is highly likely.[4] This was followed by asking students to complete a worksheet which has fill-in-the blanks exercises, two for advertisements and one for expressing possible future occurrences.

We can see from the above account that like Marina, Ching used a combination of all four options. When she provided "structured input," instead of getting students to identify the common structure exhibited, she highlighted it for them and gave explicit instruction on the forms and usage of the conditionals. During the interview and in her own written reflections, she said her original intention was to use the inductive approach by presenting more examples and asking students to identify the common structure exhibited in those examples. She also wanted to "use different contexts to let students discover the functions of conditional sentences instead of just telling them all the structures and tenses." However, she felt that this method would not work and decided to provide the answers herself.

Ching used different contexts to present the conditionals, one of which related to a science topic that the students had just covered. However, as Ching observed herself, the sequencing of the presentation was not

---

3 The modal will is often described as the "future tense" in Hong Kong textbooks. The Collins Cobuild Grammar of English refers to the use of will to indicate the future the "future tense" (see p. 255, 5.53).
4 Insofar as one cannot talk about future events with as much certainty as one can with present events, Ching is correct. Strictly speaking, however, the use of will in the main clause can also be an expression of what you *intend* to happen (see Collins Cobuild Grammar of English, p. 255, 5.52).

"systematic enough." This was evidenced by the students not being able to complete the final task very well. Unlike Eva, this was not because of her lack of linguistic knowledge. In the interview after the lesson, Ching demonstrated some linguistic awareness of the usage of the two types of conditionals. Commenting on the sentence *If you light the Bunsen burner with the airhole closed, the flame is yellow*, she said, "because it is [a] natural [phenomenon], we are sure that that is the consequence or the result. Therefore, I use present tense to indicate that the consequence is definite, as a result of [the fulfillment] of a condition." For the conditionals using the modal will, she explained that the main clause conveyed possible consequence, but not absolute certainty. She qualified her comments by saying that "it is not a 'must' to use future or present tense. There is no hard-and-fast rule." In other words, she was able to highlight the difference between using the present tense to indicate habitual occurrences or general truths, and using the future tense (that is, the modal will) to indicate the writers' judgment of the possibility of occurrence.[5] The qualification that she made showed that she was aware of the lack of one-to-one correspondence between form and function. She was also aware that conditionals are used in advertisements to achieve a persuasive effect. She said, "because advertisers want to make the advertisements more powerful, to appeal to the audience, they use the present tense or the imperative to make their products sell better." If the modal will is used, the advertisement will be less powerful. Ching's problem with sequencing in her presentation can be attributed to two reasons. The first reason has to do with her dilemma between whether she should use students' interest or linguistic demand or complexity as the criterion for sequencing. In the interview, she confessed that when she planned the lesson, she struggled over the sequence of presentation. She wanted to start with one that was easier for students. She thought of starting with conditionals with the future tense (i.e., the modal will) in the main clause because she had seen her students producing this kind of conditional before. However, she finally decided to present conditionals in advertisements as a way to start the lesson because advertisements would grab the students' attention. This is another example of the predominance of Ching's concern for students' interest over linguistic concerns.

The second reason has to do with her lack of awareness of the linguistic demands made on the students. Ching started with the use of the conditional for advertisements and moved onto its use in stating scientific truths. However, she did not explain to the students the difference between the two. The onus was on the students to figure out whether they

---

5 The future tense can also be used to indicate general truths, as in the case of *When peace is available, people will go for it.* (See Collins Cobuild English Grammar, p. 255, 5.54.) However, there is always the question of how much detail the teacher wants to go into.

were the same or different. It would have been linguistically less demanding if she were to start with conditionals that expressed scientific truths with which the students were already familiar, and then moved on to their exploitation in advertisements for persuasive effects. Her introduction of variations in the syntax of the first conditionals in advertisements, one where the main clause is a declarative, and the other an imperative, posed further linguistic demands on the students. Ching was not aware of this until she reflected on the lesson. She said, "... when it came to the end, when I wanted to give more examples, I was not aware that they already had so much to deal with. That's why they encountered problems when they worked on the task."

The biggest difference between Ching's and Eva's grammar teaching is that Ching does have the necessary linguistic knowledge on which to base her judgment with regard to selection of teaching materials and explanation of grammar rules and patterns to students. She is very conscious of the need to present the target structures in a way that will interest the students, and she tries her best to cater to that. In doing so, she is not always fully aware of the implications that different ways of representing the target language may have for student understanding. This results in achieving the purpose of arousing students' interest at the expense of proper sequencing according to linguistic complexity and linguistic demand.

8.3.8 Ching: Developing knowledge in grammar teaching

As we have seen in Chapter 6 and in the preceding discussion, the main difficulties that Ching has with grammar teaching is being able to engage students' interests. When Ching first started teaching, she was very apprehensive about moving away from teacher-fronted teaching, and allowing students to explore the patterns and rules of the English system. It was not until she attended the PCEd course, where the tutors encouraged using pair and group work that she began to be a bit more adventurous. Underlying Ching's reluctance to use pair and group work is a more deep-rooted conception of student learning. Apart from her belief that the teacher's role should be to transmit knowledge to students, there could also be a lack of confidence in students' ability to work things out for themselves. In the lesson on conditionals, we have seen that Ching made a considered decision to provide students with the main clauses in the advertisements because she felt that students would not be able to produce them by themselves. Her understanding of student learning outcome is another reason for her reluctance to use group or pair work. For her, it is very important that students are able to demonstrate that they have learned the target structure by being able to produce it correctly in writing. Therefore, when at the end of a game or group work, students are still producing grammatically incorrect sentences, Ching tends to negate the game or the task as an effective means of teaching and learning instead of trying to find out the factors that could have contributed to the unsatisfactory outcome, such as the complexity of the tasks and their sequencing, and whether there is congruence between the task and the linguistic objective.

Ching has been concerned about her inability to make her teaching interesting to the students, and she began working on it soon after she felt that she could keep her students under control. However, it was not until her fourth and fifth years, when she was doing the PCEd course that she began to bring more nonclassroom situations into her teaching and to use more authentic materials rather than simply follow the textbook. As we shall see in Chapter 10, such modifications in her teaching did not involve a change in her conceptions of teaching and learning.

8.3.9 Ching: Teaching of reading

The teaching of reading is an area in which Ching feels least confident, especially when she is teaching senior forms. She used the Chinese metaphor "the mouse pulling the tortoise," which means one does not know where to start, to describe how she feels about it. She shared her feelings about reading:

Sometimes when I teach a piece of reading comprehension, I don't know where to start – what I should teach first. It's like the mouse pulling the tortoise. Like I had a bad start and things didn't go smoothly, then I carried on for a bit, and before I knew it, I'd gotten to the end of the passage already. When I look back on what I have done, I feel that I didn't do a good job and that I failed again.

She is slightly more comfortable with setting reading comprehension questions because the PCEd course gave her some ideas. Apart from that, she largely teaches in the way she was taught as a student. She goes through a passage once to get the main ideas. For a more detailed analysis, she goes through the passage paragraph by paragraph; she also looks at the author's attitude and style of writing. She then goes through the reading comprehension questions.

When Ching talks about the teaching of reading, she is most concerned about whether the activities are interesting for the students. She feels that sometimes some passages lend themselves to interesting activities, but others do not. However, she seldom asks about the purposes of these activities and the kinds of reading skill being taught. For example, in one reading comprehension lesson, she gave a variety of activities to students like information transfer, matching headings with paragraphs and rearranging the sequence of events. The purposes of these activities were all understood as helping students to understand the passage.

What Ching finds most difficult is that not all reading comprehension questions have a right or wrong answer. She said:

When I was a student. I found reading comprehension difficult because not all questions have an absolutely right or wrong answer. It's not always that I am all wrong and you are all right. It's like I am right for a small part and you are right for a large part. For this reason, I find it difficult to teach. For example, when I give them the answer, a student will ask why my answer is correct, or why his answer is incorrect. I find the explanation process or having to think of how to explain it difficult. This is the problem with teaching reading comprehension in senior forms.

The difficulty that Ching experienced has to do with her inability to anticipate students' questions. For example, when her answers were refuted by the students, she felt that she was caught on the spot, and although she tries to explain her answers as best she can, she is not happy with it. Another source of difficulty is how to deal with students' refutations when she felt that they were well-grounded. She said,

Sometimes I feel that it has to do with logical thinking when answering reading comprehension questions. I feel that the students have reasons for their answers but I was unable to give them an instantaneous response or feedback. When I feel that they have reasons for their answers, do I insist that my answer is correct, or could I make some adjustment, and then everything would be OK?

Ching's remark, "... and then everything would be OK?", captures the conflict that she was not able to resolve. If she insisted that her answer was correct, which is congruent with her image of the teacher as a figure of authority, then her students would not be satisfied because they had "reasons for their answers." If she modifies her own answers to accommodate the students', then the students would be satisfied and in this sense "everything will be OK." However, it is not congruent with her conception that the teacher should be able to give the last word.

Ching's dilemma shows that she is still at the stage where she does not have the confidence to engage in intellectual inquiry with her senior students and accept that the teacher is not always right. She is afraid that accepting the students' answers as correct, or as a better alternative, is a sign of incompetence. When her own analysis of the text is different from those given in the teacher's notes, she is at a loss. She does not know whether she ought to stick to her own views or to follow the teacher's guide. She needs assurance from her colleagues to put her mind at rest.

Ching also experiences difficulties in explaining the writer's attitudes and style of writing to the students, something that she has to do frequently when teaching senior students. When she finds that her teaching materials do not turn out as expected, she questions if it is because she is not capable and that she does not have any talent for teaching. She spends more time thinking about her teaching and preparing lessons for senior forms than junior forms. It seems that while Ching has gained experience in teaching reading in junior forms, she is behaving like a novice teacher again when she is teaching senior forms, with which she has had little experience.

8.3.10 *Genie: Grammar teaching*

Genie described the way she taught grammar as being different from other people. She said,

> When I teach [grammar], you may find that my methods are different from other people. I teach the way I was taught. I'll give them some rules to follow. For example, for reported question, I'll get them to change the question to a sentence, and we have to change something in the question. If the question does not start with a *wh-* word, they have to add *if* or *whether*. If they do, then they just use it [the *wh-* word]. The positions of the subject and the verb have to be changed. For the subject, they need to look at who said it, that is, you need to look at the original question. The tenses will have to change because the time is different. Also, there are special words. Words about time such as *now* have to be changed because when you report it, it's no longer "now." Also the pointing words will have to change, like *this* becomes *that*. I'll tell them all this, and then ask them to do some exercises. That's it.

The reason why Genie declared that her approach to grammar teaching is different from other people is because she feels that teaching grammar rules is not an accepted practice. She had heard from colleagues that one was supposed to let students practice *using* the language and not talk about rules. However, from her own learning experience, she feels that knowing the grammar rules is essential. The grammar activities that she uses are just a way to make teaching more interesting.

SELECTION AND DESIGN OF GRAMMAR ACTIVITIES

Like Ching, Genie is most concerned about how to make her teaching interesting to the students, to get them involved in the lesson and in language production. In order to give students more practice in language production, Genie looks at a variety of grammar exercise books, apart from the prescribed textbook and grammar exercise book. However, most of the exercises that she selects are decontextualized sentence level exercises. Genie is well aware of the lack of variety in her presentation, but she does not have any idea how to improve on it. As we have seen in 6.4, this problem was most serious in her first year teaching. Genie tried to address the problem by getting the students to work in groups. For grammar teaching, Genie expects the students to be more involved when they worked in groups even though the tasks, such as sentence level exercises, can be completed individually. She said, "I always feel that when they are working together in groups, they should be very happy, very involved, happily discussing and collaborating to complete the task." She is more concerned about whether the students are actively participating than their learning outcome.

At the beginning of her third year of teaching, Genie began to take contextualized activities from grammar resource books, which gave her more ideas for teaching. Genie does not have any principles on which to base her judgement of whether the activities are well designed. If she feels that the activity works well in class, then it is a good activity.

STRUCTURING GRAMMAR INSTRUCTION

Genie does not have an identifiable structure in grammar instruction. Sometimes she starts with one or two sample sentences, which can be considered a kind of "structured input" and then moves on to explicit instruction. Sometimes she gives explicit explanations of the structural patterns after "production practice." The following lesson on modals, which is typical of other grammar lessons, may give some idea of how Genie structures the lessons.

Genie started the lesson by introducing the term "modal verbs." She presented two sentences, one containing *can* and the other *could* and asked the students what they indicated. The following is an excerpt.

> G: Under what situation – do we use the modals in the two sentences there? *"Last year I could see the island from my flat. I cannot see the island now; I can only see twelve new blocks."* So, a lot of new buildings. What do these modals show you? I can't see the island now. I mean I can see only twelve new blocks now. But in the past, in last year, I could see the island from my flat. So, what do *could* and *can* tell you?

When the students failed to provide the correct answer, she explained that the modals *can* and *could* indicated ability. (For problems with the presentation, see the discussion in the following paragraph.) This was followed by production practice. Students were asked to work in groups on a guessing game where they had to write riddles, using *can* and *could*, for the rest of the class to guess. There was, however, no pretask preparation by demonstrating to the whole class how the task should be done. To check their language production, Genie asked them to read out the sentences for the rest of the class to guess, for example, one group produced the following riddle for a parrot: "It can fly. It can learn to speak. It cannot swim. It cannot climb the trees. It cannot write. It can make the others laugh. It can sing." After checking the answers, she drew students' attention to the use of the infinitive verb form after the modal. She then moved on to introduce modals that indicate different shades of possibility – *can, could, may* and *might*. The instruction followed the same pattern of presenting sample sentences containing these modal verbs, explaining their usage, and giving students a task for group work.

From the above description of Genie's lesson structure, we can see that the input that Genie provided is not structured and differs qualitatively from that provided by Marina and Ching. The sample sentences were not presented in a context that would help students to understand the usage of *can* and *could*. In response to Genie's question, the students said that they indicated "past and now." This is hardly surprising because the juxtaposition of *can* and *could* in two sentences that contrasted past and present focussed students' attention on the difference between these two modal verbs rather than their similarity, which is, they are both used to indicate ability. In rest of the lesson, her representations of the use of *can* and *could* as well as *may* and *might* to indicate possibility consisted of decontextualized sentences. These sentences failed to highlight the salient features of the target items.

In Genie's grammar lessons, there are fewer contexts in which the target structures are re-presented in order to help students understand how they are used. The tasks given to students usually do not show a progression in task complexity. For example, sentence levels exercises do not necessarily precede tasks that require creation of texts. The tasks given are determined more by the teaching materials that Genie can find rather than by linguistic and language teaching criteria.

8.3.11 Genie: Developing knowledge in grammar teaching

Genie is most diffident about grammar teaching. She finds her own teaching boring and feels that the students are not with her. But grammar teaching has always been particularly problematic, especially in the first two years of her teaching. Students take a long time to complete the task. She is not sure whether it is because they do not know how to do it, or because they find the task boring and therefore are not motivated. When she prepares for grammar teaching, she feels good about it. She reads up on teachers' resource books and is excited by the ideas suggested. However, when she actually teaches it, her high spirits are dampened because the students are not with her and do not react in the way she anticipates. When she gives them grammar tests, many fail. She feels that she does not have "a good grasp of how to go about it."

Looking back at her teaching in the past two years, Genie feels that she has made some improvement in grammar teaching. She said, "At least, I have some more ideas. I picked them up from other people and I tried them out. I have also been reading up on grammar teaching resource books. I found some activities that I could use. So my teaching is not so boring." Yet, on the other hand, she still feels that "things did not work out according to my wish." She found that when she gave them group work, nearly half the class was not on task. There were one or two groups of students who were always daydreaming. This undermines her confidence. She said, "When I teach grammar, I don't know whether it is psychological, I don't feel so good.... I don't know whether it is because of disciplinary problems." Genie is still at the stage where she has difficulties seeing the relationship between engaging students' attention and the design of the learning experience.

8.3.12 Genie: Teaching of reading

Genie finds it easier to cope with the teaching of reading. When I asked her what she felt were the most important skills when she taught reading, she said:

The most basic thing is that students can understand what the passage is about. Comprehension means understanding. They must understand what the passage is about. Therefore, at the beginning I want them to read [the passage], and then I want them to get the main idea. Apart from understanding the passage, I want them to learn from the passage some sentence structures and some vocabulary items.... I want them to learn [these words] so that they can use them in their compositions. These are the two areas.

Like Eva, Genie sees the main objective of teaching reading as understanding the content of a piece of text. She further added, "I think students will learn something when they study a passage." She also tries to use the reading passage as input for writing and for vocabulary learning. Reading skills do not seem to figure in her objectives.

However, Genie is not entirely unaware of the strategies for teaching reading. In a lesson plan for a reading comprehension lesson on a passage called "White Gold," which describes how bird's nests are collected and why they are so expensive, she started with a prereading activity. In this activity she listed six aspects of bird's nests and asked students to put down all they knew about each aspect. She explained the purpose of this activity as follows:

Before I ask them to read the passage, I want them to think about how much they know about the topic.... This will arouse their interest. Then when they read the passage, they will find out about things that they don't know, such as the location [for collecting bird's nests] and why the location of the island is a secret. And also how bird's nests are collected, who the collectors are, and their intentions. These are the things that they don't know. They serve as a contrast to what they know. When they read the passage in detail, apart from learning the words, they also learn something [about the content].

What Genie tried to do was relate the students' existing knowledge to new knowledge presented in the text. Though Genie's explication was not couched in precisely those terms, she has partially formulated her own practical theory of the teaching of reading as a result of her teaching experience and consultation with colleagues.

In coping with the teaching of reading, as in other areas of teaching, Genie maintains a very positive and open-minded attitude to new ideas. She often picks up new ideas from colleagues and is ready to take risks and try them out in her own classroom (see also 6.4). However, she often does this without understanding their underlying rationale. In describing her approach to a reading text, Genie explained that one of the ways of checking whether students have understood the text was to ask them to draw pictures. For example, in the reading lesson on "White Gold" described above, Genie listed six main points in the passage and asked them to draw pictures for each point. She justified doing that as follows:

I think that it would be more interesting to ask them to draw pictures, and also they will be able to remember [the main points of the text] better. Also when I ask them to give a brief description of the picture by labeling it, that shows whether they have learned it, like *saliva, cliff*, and so on. I like to see them draw because I don't know how to draw myself. Then after presenting [the pictures], they are supposed to have understood the main content.

Asking students to draw pictures is a technique that Marina used from time to time, and she often shares her students' drawings with her colleagues. This technique was adopted by other teachers, including Genie. However, whether drawing pictures is an effective way of checking comprehension depends on what they illustrate. For example, Marina asked students to draw faces to express feelings when she was teaching the use of the past participle as adjectives, such as *bored, frightened, delighted*, and so forth. In 8.3.1 we have also seen that Marina asked the students to draw illustrations of the passive structures in news reports to see if they understood the agent and the subject. In Genie's case, however, students were asked to illustrate the processes and actions involved when collecting bird's nests, which was by no means easy. Indeed as the students were drawing the pictures, it became apparent that some of the ideas were difficult to illustrate. In other words, Genie adopted the form without a clear understanding of the relationship between the form and the objective.

Another example is giving students a purpose for listening to other groups when they are making presentations. This is a common problem that teachers face when they ask students to present their group work productions. Students are usually busily putting finishing touches to their own presentations when other groups are presenting. This is because they are not given a purpose for listening. Therefore, one effective means is to give them a listening task such as rating the presentation. Genie picked up this idea and asked the students to give marks to the pictures when each group was presenting the pictures to the rest of the class. She also gave marks herself. However, there were no criteria for mark allocation and students were not asked to justify their marks. The process of giving marks became an arbitrary and purposeless activity that could have been turned into a learning experience for the students.

Genie finds it easier to cope with the teaching of reading than other areas because there is a reading text that she can rely on, and there are exercises on the text that she can use. She feels safe. When Genie first started teaching, like all novice teachers, she stuck very close to the textbook. She was also able to stick to the teaching schedule, to the amazement of her colleagues. In the second year of teaching, she began to exercise her own judgement on the amount of materials to cover and the pace at which she should proceed. She was able to use more supplementary materials and to put more variety into her teaching. As mentioned above, she is keen to improve on her teaching, and she is receptive of any new ideas of which she can make use. However, she does not fully understand the rationale behind the techniques from the point of view of learning.

8.4 Summary

In this chapter and in the previous chapter, I have given accounts of how the four ESL teachers managed the classroom *for* ESL learning and enacted the ESL curriculum as well as the knowledge embedded in both. In Chapter 7, I focused on management of learning, the conceptions of teaching and learning embedded in the teachers' practices, and the ways in which they related to their specific contexts of work. In this chapter I focused on grammar teaching, which was considered the most important area of ESL teaching by all four teachers. In order to explore further the knowledge that they held in ESL teaching, I examined an area of teaching which they talked about most in the interviews, which is an area that they were either most or least confident about. I also discussed how their knowledge developed over time.

The discussion in both chapters shows that there are qualitative differences between Marina and the other three teachers. The knowledge held by Marina is much richer, more elaborate, and more coherent. She was able to see ESL teaching not as the teaching of discrete skills but as all interrelated in using language for communicative purposes. Her ESL teaching was also coherently related to the specific context of situation, and she was able to see and exploit the possibilities for ESL teaching and learning. Compared with Marina, Ching and Eva's knowledge were less rich and, most important, less integrated. They tend to dichotomize different aspects of teaching that are inextricably linked, such as fun and learning, student interest, and learning objectives. They were also more constrained by the limitations presented to them by their specific contexts.

Another qualitative difference among the four teachers is that Marina was able to clearly articulate her principles and criteria for making curricular judgement, and the curricular decisions that she made were often conscious decisions. Her principles and criteria were based not only on her personal experience, but also on the theoretical input that she was able to "interiorize" and realize in the teaching act. Compared with Eva, Ching was much better able to articulate her thinking in aspects of her teaching which are related to linguistic knowledge. By contrast, Eva was much more articulate about her thinking in aspects that are related to her personal conceptions of teaching and learning, and the values embedded therein. Genie's knowledge is not only the least developed and least coherent because of her lack of experience, but is also the least articulated.

The accounts of the four teachers presented in this chapter and in the previous chapter suggest three features relating to the critical differences between expert and novice teachers. The first feature has to do with the extent to which the ability to integrate various aspects of teaching and the extent to which the knowledge embedded in the teaching act is an integrated whole. The second feature is the way teachers relate to their specific contexts and are able to see possibilities they present. The third feature has to do with the relationship between being able to theorize one's practical experience and to "practicalize" theory. These three features will be discussed in detail in Chapter 10.

9 Taking on the Challenge: Exploring Process Writing

In Chapter 6 we saw that although the four teachers' teaching experience is varied and they are at different stages of professional development, they are all faced with challenges constantly. The nature of the challenge, however, is different. Novice teachers are faced with challenges that are very basic to classroom teaching, such as maintaining order and discipline and establishing rapport with students. The challenges that expert teachers face, or rather, those that they choose to face, often involve extending their influence beyond their own classroom; in some cases, to the whole school and in other cases, even beyond their own school. In her first two years when Marina took on the role of the chair of the English panel, she went beyond her own classroom and started to involve the teachers on the panel in experimenting with new ways of teaching, such as the introduction of phonetics in the teaching of pronunciation and the setting of objectives for each unit in the scheme of work. According to Marina, those were small scale changes. In her eighth year of teaching, she embarked on a much larger scale change in the teaching of writing. It is an area with which she is least satisfied and least confident. In this chapter we shall see how Marina rose to the challenge.

9.1 From Product Writing to Process Writing

For a long time at St. Peter's, teachers had been using the product approach in the teaching of writing, as in most schools in Hong Kong. Typically, a writing topic is given by the teacher followed by fifteen to twenty minutes of brainstorming with the whole class. The teacher will also provide them with a typical structure for writing: an introduction, a main body, and a conclusion. The students will then be given the rest of the double lessons to write, and the compositions will be marked as final products by the teacher. The teacher will go over common errors in class and students will correct their own errors identified by the teacher. This is a common routine adopted by many teachers in Hong Kong (see Sengupta, 1996). Some teachers, like Marina, will design exercises for the students on the common errors, especially grammatical errors, as remedial work.

As we have seen in Chapter 6, Marina is very dissatisfied with this approach to the teaching of writing for a number of reasons. First, it is ineffective. Despite the huge amount of time and effort that the teacher spends on marking students' writings, they do not seem to improve over time, and the same mistakes keep recurring. Hence, the efforts made by the teacher are not proportional to the results achieved. This is a feeling shared by all her colleagues. Second, students tend to think that it is their responsibility to write, but it is the teacher's responsibility to do the marking and spot the errors. The teacher's job, in Marina's words, is reduced to "proofreading." Eventually, students' writings are filled with red marks from the teacher, who corrected the grammatical mistakes. (See 6.2.7.)

To overcome the above shortcomings, Marina tried in the past to introduce some measures such as raising students' awareness of their own mistakes by asking them to do peer correction before handing in their writings. However, it was not taken seriously by the students because they saw the teacher as the person who was ultimately responsible for correcting the errors. Marina has always wanted to find an alternative way to make the teaching of writing more effective. As mentioned in Chapter 6, spending six months away from the classroom on a refresher course provided the space and the necessary resources for her to explore alternative approaches. She thought a great deal about how to improve the teaching of writing and read up on process writing. She was attracted to the idea of writing as a process in which the writer is engaged in producing more than one draft and, in the process of redrafting, clarifies and enriches his or her thinking. Marina liked it partly because it matched her own experience as a writer and partly because it was congruent with her conception of student learning. She said, "I always think that we need to give students a second chance to do things.... Their initial idea may be odd, but when they think about it again, they'll sort out the problem and try again.... This is the merit of process writing."

Initially, she wanted to start small by trying it out on S1 students only. However, because she did not teach S1 students, she would have no first hand experience and hence would not be in a position to provide guidance to her teachers. This means she would need to include S2, or perhaps all the junior forms. She decided to bring this up in the panel meeting in the summer. Prior to this meeting, Marina discussed the idea of process writing with the form coordinators and gave them two papers to read, one published by a schoolteacher, Julie, on how she adopted a process approach to story writing with her S3 students in Hong Kong, and a book chapter that I published that was a follow-up study of Julie's teaching of writing (see Li, 1991; Tsui, 1996). Both Eva and Genie were very impressed by what this teacher did, and thought that it was something well worth trying out on their students. During the meeting, there was a consensus that in the past too much emphasis had been put on accuracy and content had been neglected. There was also a consensus that opportunities should be provided for students to revise their writings. The concept and advantages of the process approach to writing were discussed. Subsequently, the panel agreed to try out process writing on all the junior forms first because these classes do not have to prepare for public examinations.

Marina gave the panel rough guidelines but did not propose a format that all of them should follow. The general spirit was that students should be given opportunities to revise the first drafts that they produced on the basis of the feedback that they received from the teacher as well as from their peers. When providing feedback to the first draft, Marina reminded her colleagues that the initial focus should be on content so that students would not be handling both content and form at the same time. It is only when reading the revised draft that the focus should be on accuracy.

The guidelines were rough because first, she had no prior experience of process writing, and she had no preconceived ideas of the best way to go about it. Second, she was anxious that her panel members might see this change as something imposed on them, that it was a top-down initiative. She emphasized that all teachers should try things out and review the effectiveness at the end of the year. Therefore, based on the general spirit of process writing, which is to provide opportunities for students to revise their writings on the basis of obtaining feedback from teachers and peers, Marina left it open to the panel members to come up with their own ways of implementing it in the classroom. In the course of the school year, Marina monitored the implementation by approaching her colleagues individually. She also shared with them what she did with her own class and invited them to try her ideas out when they worked well.

In other words, Marina herself was exploring how process writing should be implemented in the classroom and yet she also was trying to monitor and help her colleagues implement it in their classrooms. This was by no means an easy task. There were not many resource books on conducting process writing for ESL learners, although there were a number of research publications in this area. There were no resource materials for young ESL learners. It was therefore very much virgin soil on which Marina was treading.

In the rest of this chapter, I shall discuss how Marina explored process writing with Eva, the implementation of process writing in their classrooms, and the evaluation of the implementation by the students and Marina's colleagues. I shall also examine how process writing was reconstrued by the four ESL teachers.

9.2 Implementing Process Writing

In trying out process writing, Marina worked closely with Eva, who was the coordinator. The first writing task for the students was to write a description of their first impression of either their English teacher or one of their classmates. Eva, being the form coordinator, was responsible for drafting a plan for the implementation and preparing materials for all S2 teachers.

Eva's lesson plan contained what she perceived to be the essential components of a process writing approach. The first component consists of a prewriting task. There were two parts to this task: "data collection," in which the students were asked to put down some factual information about the teacher or the classmate whom they wished to describe and "observation," in which the students had to make their own observations about this particular classmate, such as their appearance, dressing style, the way he or she walks, speaks, and treats the teacher and other classmates.

The second component is writing the first draft, providing peer feedback, and revising the first draft to produce the second draft. Marina anticipated that the students might not have any idea of how they should provide feedback and what they should be looking for. She suggested to Eva that guidance should be provided to students by giving them something like a form to fill out. Eva took the suggestion seriously and looked up resource books on teaching writing for ideas. She came up with a simple form with two parts. In the first part she listed the main aspects to be covered and asked students to indicate whether each aspect was well written, difficult to understand, or whether it was simply missing. In the second part, they were asked to suggest ways in which their peers' writings could be improved. Again, a checklist and an open-ended question were given. The students were also given an opportunity to discuss in groups and report back to the whole class. The Reader's Comments Form proved to be helpful because many students incorporated the points on the checklist in their subsequent revisions. (See Appendix 1 for an example of a Reader's Comment Form for the second writing task.)

The third component consists of the teacher giving comments on the content of the second draft, students' revision of the second draft, and production of the third draft, which incorporates teacher's comments. The fourth component is the teacher going over the third draft, focussing on grammatical accuracy. The students, upon getting the teacher's feedback on accuracy, made corrections and produced the final draft.

While other S2 teachers, including Eva, just gave out the Reader's Comment Form and went over it verbally with the whole class, Marina selected a first draft and worked with the whole class on providing feedback on the comment form. This is very much in keeping with her practice of using students' work as a springboard for teaching and providing guidance before letting students work on their own. This kind of "learner training" is very important, and is often neglected by teachers (see Allaei and Connor, 1990; Leki, 1990, Stanley, 1992; Tsui and Ng, 2000). In her instructions for giving feedback, Marina wrote, "The following composition is written by your classmate. He has got some good ideas and some ideas can be even better." The instructions demonstrated her sensitivity to students' feelings by making sure that they would not feel that their work was being criticized or ridiculed.

On the basis of the experience gained in the first writing task, Marina modified the steps when she designed and prepared materials for the second writing task, which was to write a description of a mystery location for the reader to guess. Marina felt that text structure was very important for writing. Therefore, she built in an additional component that required the students to produce an outline first after the prewriting tasks and give comments on each other's outline. She designed a very simple checklist for students to provide feedback. This proved to be very useful to the students.

In addition to providing "learner training" for providing peer feedback, she built in "learner training" at the revision stage to help students to respond to teacher and peer comments and make corresponding revisions. She designed a worksheet in which she gave them a fabricated text containing comments from the teacher, and provided guiding questions to help students to rewrite the sentences by putting in more descriptive details and by changing statements into dialogs (see the worksheet in Appendix 2).

For all writing tasks, Marina included exercises on grammatical accuracy at the last stage, when students were asked to correct the grammatical errors identified by the teacher. She also gave them examples of good writing as models and motivated them to read. For example, for both the first and the second writing tasks, which were a description of one classmate and a description of a mystery location, she asked them to guess who and which location were being described.

The second writing task worked well, and the steps in what Marina subsequently called the "writing cycle" became more or less the blueprint for the writing tasks for the rest of the S2 school year (see Figure 9.1 for the writing cycle).

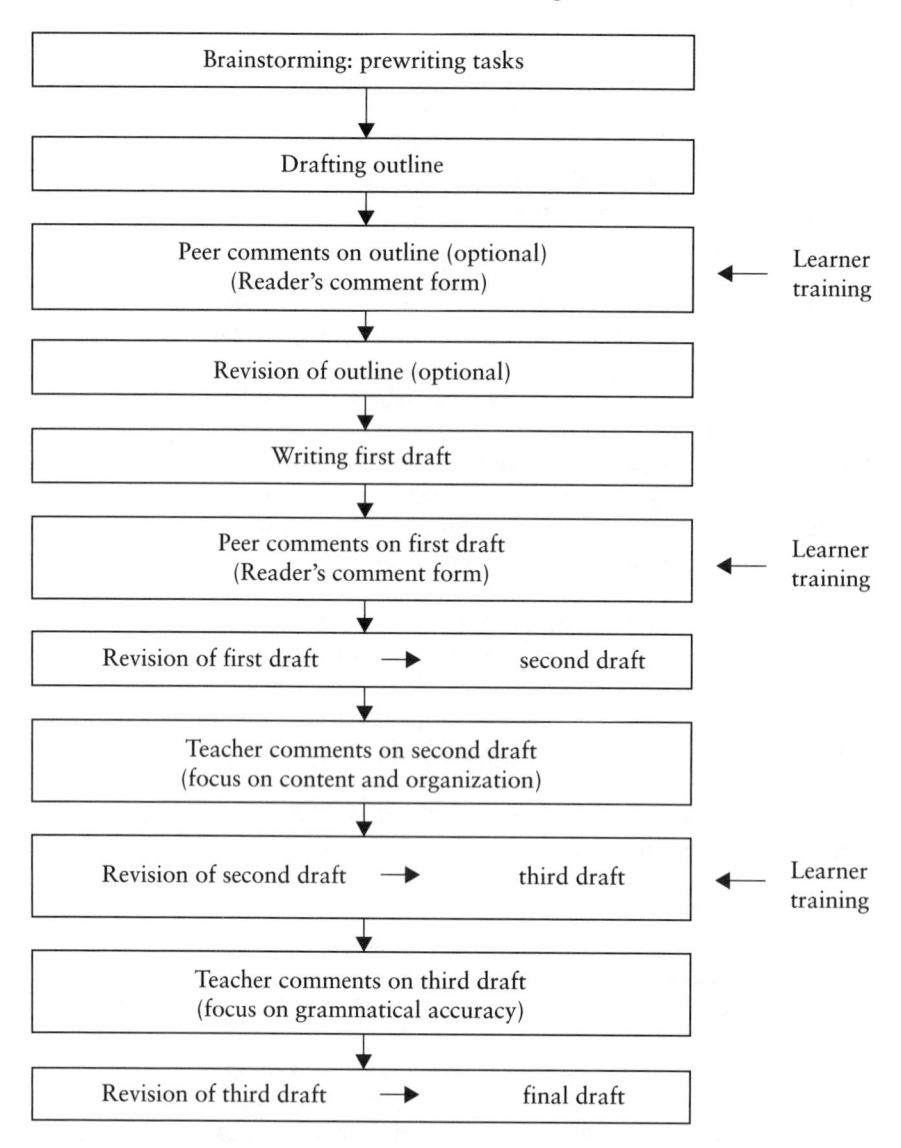

```
┌─────────────────────────────────────────┐
│     Brainstorming: prewriting tasks     │
└─────────────────────────────────────────┘
                    ↓
┌─────────────────────────────────────────┐
│            Drafting outline             │
└─────────────────────────────────────────┘
                    ↓
┌─────────────────────────────────────────┐
│   Peer comments on outline (optional)   │  ←  Learner
│       (Reader's comment form)           │     training
└─────────────────────────────────────────┘
                    ↓
┌─────────────────────────────────────────┐
│        Revision of outline (optional)   │
└─────────────────────────────────────────┘
                    ↓
┌─────────────────────────────────────────┐
│           Writing first draft           │
└─────────────────────────────────────────┘
                    ↓
┌─────────────────────────────────────────┐
│      Peer comments on first draft       │  ←  Learner
│        (Reader's comment form)          │     training
└─────────────────────────────────────────┘
                    ↓
┌─────────────────────────────────────────┐
│ Revision of first draft  →  second draft│
└─────────────────────────────────────────┘
                    ↓
┌─────────────────────────────────────────┐
│     Teacher comments on second draft    │
│     (focus on content and organization) │
└─────────────────────────────────────────┘
                    ↓
┌─────────────────────────────────────────┐
│ Revision of second draft  →  third draft│  ←  Learner
└─────────────────────────────────────────┘     training
                    ↓
┌─────────────────────────────────────────┐
│     Teacher comments on third draft     │
│      (focus on grammatical accuracy)    │
└─────────────────────────────────────────┘
                    ↓
┌─────────────────────────────────────────┐
│ Revision of third draft  →  final draft │
└─────────────────────────────────────────┘
```

Figure 1 The Writing Cycle

9.3 Monitoring the Implementation

After the first writing cycle was completed, Marina monitored the implementation by talking to individual teachers. Some teachers found that the students' writing improved, but not all students showed positive progress. There were some students whose first drafts were better than the revised drafts. At the end of first term, she inspected all the composition books, which is part of the duty of a panel chair. She paid special attention to whether the teacher gave comments, how the teacher did it, and whether students actually responded to the comments when producing revised drafts. From talking to teachers individually, she found that they had different interpretations of how they should respond to the second draft. An extreme case was a teacher who merely underlined all the mistakes and asked the students to correct them in the revised draft. Marina also found that while the S2 teachers asked the students to produce four drafts (including the final draft where grammatical errors were corrected), most of the teachers of S1 and S3 required only three. This was partly because there was not enough time for the students to produce four drafts, and partly because they found that students were unable to give useful feedback to their peers. The students took the teacher's comments much more seriously than peer comments. Therefore, after the students provided peer comments, the teacher gave comments on the first draft immediately. Students were asked to incorporate both kinds of comments in their revisions. This necessarily resulted in students attending to teacher comments and not peer comments. Some teachers even omitted peer comments altogether.

Besides talking to teachers individually, Marina discussed process writing in one of the form meetings after the second writing cycle. She found that most of the teachers simply asked the students to read each other's work and provide comments. Little or no guidance was given. For example, teachers did not read the compositions first and identify common weaknesses for students to pay attention to when reading their peers' writing. There was also no "learner training" in providing and responding to comments. In addition, most of them just gave oral comments to the whole class, without providing written comments for individual students. Consequently, the revised drafts were not much different from the first drafts.

For S1, Marina monitored the implementation mainly through Rosemary, the deputy panel chair, who was responsible for inspecting S1 teachers' marking. Marina and Rosemary inspected each other's marking. The S1 teachers were generally following the general spirit of process writing, and teachers were able to focus more on content than before. However, the students were responding to the teacher's comments as if they were simply answering questions. As a result of answering all the teacher's questions, their writing became much less focused.

Despite the anomalies that she observed, Marina did not push a panic button. She went around to each individual teacher, patiently listened to their problems, and shared her own experience with them. For teachers who were still very much oriented towards focusing on grammatical accuracy in the first instance, Marina emphasized the importance of focusing on content initially so as to encourage students to express their ideas. For teachers who provided only oral feedback to the whole class, Marina suggested that they provide written comments in the margins. Many of them took her suggestion, but the written comments that they provided tended to be very general. Marina showed them her own written comments to students and shared her experience of what kinds of comments worked well and what kinds did not. She also emphasized the need for "learner training."

Towards the end of the school year, Marina again inspected students' writing and talked to the panel members to get their reactions. Most of them responded very positively. The evaluation of process writing by the teachers and the students will be presented in the following section.

9.4 Evaluating Process Writing

9.4.1 Students' evaluation

In order to evaluate the implementation of this initiative, Marina, with my assistance, collected the following data. First, we administered a student evaluation questionnaire to S1 to S3 students. Not all the teachers were willing to participate in the evaluation, however. Typical of Marina's style, instead of stipulating that all teachers had to administer the questionnaire, she left it largely to their own choice. Seven out of ten teachers participated, and the questionnaire was administered to seven classes of S1 to S3 students. Second, we collected sample student writings from S1 to S3 to examine the kinds of comments made by teachers and peers, and the revisions induced.

The questionnaire scores showed a clear positive orientation to process writing. The overall evaluation comparing their experience with process writing and their previous experience with product writing showed a significant difference in the mean scores, rising from 2.69 to 3.02 on a Likert-scale of 4. The students liked having the opportunity to revise their writing. They took teachers' comments into consideration when revising their writing much more frequently and more seriously than comments from their peers. The students felt that their writing had improved in both language and content. The interviews that I conducted corroborated the questionnaire findings. The students interviewed all valued having their mistakes pointed out and having the opportunity to rewrite them. There was a strong consensus that the teacher's comments were helpful, encouraging, and gave them a lot ideas for improving their writing. However, their responses to peer comments were more varied. Some were more positive about reading peers' writings, and giving and getting peer comments, while others were less positive. Yan Ming, for example, found it useful to read peers' writings and provide comments, as well as obtain comments from his peers. He said that his peers helped him to write better sentences. He also found that reading the mistakes made by his peers raised his awareness of his own mistakes. He read faster and he wrote more and more. He said, "I don't know. It seems my hand wants to write... it writes whatever comes to my mind." Winnie, on the other hand, was disappointed that she was not getting useful feedback from her peers because all they did was to say that her writing was good. Martin enjoyed reading his peers' writing because he always found them interesting. Wing Yin liked the way the teacher gave comments in an encouraging manner. Like Winnie, she was unhappy that her peers did not fill the reader's comment form seriously. She was looking for further written comments apart from getting ticks and crosses in the boxes on the form, and she was disappointed that she seldom received any. She liked reading her peers' writings if they were good. Filling out the reader's comment forms helped her to improve her own writing because it raised her awareness of important aspects of writing. Wing Yin's feeling was shared by Patty as well.

The questionnaire and interview findings show that students responded well to the process writing approach. They liked being given the opportunity to revise their writings, and they benefited from the comments given by the teacher. When revising their drafts, they took the teacher's comments seriously. This suggests that requiring the students to revise their drafts after obtaining feedback gave them a purpose for reading the comments carefully and acting on them. In the past, no matter how much time the teacher spent in writing comments, the students would not pay as much attention to them because there was no need to act on them. As can be expected, students valued teachers' comments more than peer comments. This is especially so in Chinese societies where the teacher is very much a figure of authority. Reading peers' writings, however, received the highest rating among all items related to peers' feedback. The interviews revealed the reasons. To students, reading their peers' writings was an awareness raising exercise that alerted them to their own mistakes. Good writings produced by their peers also served as models for them to emulate. Providing feedback to peers could remind them of what they should include in their own writings. The findings also showed that learner training is very important. This includes training them how to provide comments as well as how to revise their writings on the basis of the comments.

9.4.2 Teachers' evaluation

At the end of the school year, Marina organized a year-end evaluation of the implementation and all ten teachers involved attended the meeting. The findings of the questionnaire were given to them and they were very pleased to see the positive responses from the students. Most of them evaluated this new approach to writing very positively.

Eva shared how she felt about process writing at the meeting. She said that she had come to see process writing in a new way. She liked reading students' writings more than before because there was more communication with the students. She said, "Communication is there, no matter whether the comments are given by their classmates or by me. So once we are connected, a relationship is established. I put my heart into it, and I am willing to put in more effort. Perhaps in the whole process, both parties put in more effort." She made an interesting comparison between product writing and process writing. She said, "In product writing, when a piece of writing is finished, it's like we both have finished the job, and no matter whether the writing is good or bad, we put a full-stop to it. In process writing, it seems that there is hope for further development in our relationship. I feel very good about this."

Lillian, an S3 teacher, echoed Eva and said that when she read students' second drafts, she looked forward to seeing what kind of revisions students had made after she had given them feedback. She found that their organization and the logical development of ideas had improved. This gave her a sense of achievement; she felt that she was fulfilling her responsibility as a teacher. This contrasted with the sense of failure that she had strongly felt in the past. She pointed out that it was a learning experience for her as well, and she changed from focusing on language to focusing on both language and content. Mark, an S2 teacher who was teaching English as a second subject, came to a different understanding of the purpose of getting students to write compositions. He said, "This year's practice helps me to better understand the purpose of teaching writing. It's not just to get the students to write sentences in English. Rather, it is to help them to fully express themselves and to organize ideas well.... Through the worksheets, we help the students to organize ideas systematically. I think this kind of training is important not only for English but also other subjects like geography and history." He found grading compositions "fun" and enjoyed teaching writing because most of his students showed progress when their final drafts were compared with their first drafts.

Genie shared Mark's feeling that it was much more enjoyable grading compositions than before. Previously, she had to correct every single grammatical error, which was tedious. Now, she just had to underline the errors, and the students would be able to help each other sort out some of the errors themselves. This made marking easier. She was particularly pleased that her students took the revisions very seriously. One student even volunteered to produce an additional draft in which she rewrote her story. The revised draft showed remarkable improvement.

Rosemary, the Deputy panel chair and May, an S1 teacher, felt that the experience was gratifying because students who took their work seriously showed great improvement. Rosemary found that when she asked her students to take on the role of a teacher, they took it very seriously and gave each other encouraging remarks like "good try." Chris, a teacher who felt that she started off with a very superficial understanding of process writing, gained a better understanding of its aim when she found that her students were very excited about reading the teacher's comments on their own writing as well as on their peers' writing, and that many of them took the comments seriously and improved their drafts.

The only teacher who expressed reservations was an S1 teacher, Jean. She was concerned that the marking load was heavier than before. She was also uncomfortable about students revising their writing according to the teacher's comments because the ideas were no longer their own. She felt that it was important that students used their own ideas rather than the teacher's. She was not sure that her students had really made any progress and wondered whether a disproportionate amount of time had been spent on writing.

In the meeting, there was a lively exchange of the problems and difficulties encountered and the different understandings of the functions of peer and teacher feedback. For example, in response to Jean's reservations about teachers giving comments for revision, Lillian pointed out that the teacher should not be telling students what to write, but rather to guide them to think about the logic of their arguments and the organization. With regard to the marking load, several teachers – Rosemary, May, and Eva – agreed with Jean that the workload was heavier than before because it was more time-consuming to provide comments than to simply identify or correct grammatical errors. Nevertheless, they found it worthwhile because of the progress that they saw students making. However, several teachers, including Genie, found that it was hard work going over the first draft, but the second draft was much easier to read. They also found that as students learned how to help each other in providing comments and correcting errors, they spent less time reading the drafts.

One commonly shared problem was getting students to provide peer feedback. A number of teachers found it difficult to get students to provide useful feedback, and as a result, they omitted this step. Another problem was getting students to revise their writing. Some students did not understand what revision meant and did not know how to respond to comments. There was also the problem of motivating students to revise. Some teachers felt that the choice of topic was important because if the topic was very simple, there was not much point in asking them to revise the first draft. Moreover, some students' first drafts were already very good, so there was no need for revision. A third problem was teachers themselves providing comments to students. Some teachers were not sure how to do it effectively and how to provide guidance. Some felt that the teacher should be asking students questions about the logic of the arguments and the organization. Others were apprehensive about asking too many questions, which might lead to a lack of focus.

To address the problems outlined above, the teachers agreed that in the future they needed to help students to give effective peer comments by using a kind of reader's comment form and to revise their own writings. The question about how teachers could give helpful comments was also asked. To address this question, Marina and I shared our analyses of the forty sample drafts with the panel. The teachers felt encouraged to read the analyses and felt that it gave them an idea of how they should provide comments and how they could guide the students. When the meeting concluded, there was unanimous support for adopting process writing in the following school year and to extend it to S4 as well.

9.5 Exploring Process Writing *with* Teachers

From the panel meeting, it was clear that most teachers were very positive about the effect that process writing had on students' writings. Although all of them had started off with a very vague idea of what process writing involved, and none of them had had a very clear idea of how it should be implemented and what the outcome might be – including Marina herself. The teachers were willing to explore the implementation of process writing in the classroom and to modify their practices as they went along. They were particularly pleased by the positive evaluations that the students had made and in the improvement in the quality of the students' writing.

When Marina started planning for the implementation, she felt that although she had theoretical knowledge of process writing, she had little idea how to put it into practice in the classroom. It was a much larger-scale project than previous attempts had been. She said, "Adopting process writing is more complicated. The role of the teachers is really important, unlike the teaching of phonetics where the most important part is designing the appropriate teaching materials." She was a bit apprehensive about what the learning outcome might be. However, she decided to forge ahead because she saw little value in the existing practice of teaching writing. She said, "You have to expect risks when you introduce something new, but it is worth trying."

Given all the uncertainties, it is remarkable how she was able to take the teachers along with her in an endeavor that involved ten teachers on her panel and fifteen classes of students. The success that Marina achieved had to do with her perception of her role as working *with* rather than *on* teachers. She was very conscious of the danger of adopting a top-down approach. She did not stipulate what teachers should or should not do. Instead, she worked closely with them, especially Eva, and tried to flesh out the important elements in process writing. The incorporation of the "learner training" element at different stages in the writing cycle is a case in point. Marina started with providing learner training only for peer comments. As she discovered problems in students responding to comments, she built in more learner training components. It is on the basis of her own classroom experience that she gave advice to colleagues. Although there was still one teacher who had great reservations about process writing at the end of the year, the general attitude was positive. This had to do with the personal approach that she adopted by talking to teachers individually and sharing her work with them. The sensitivity with which she handled teachers who were not willing to take part in the year end evaluation also contributed to the positive atmosphere. The year end evaluation provided important evidence that they were moving in the right direction. The qualitative analysis of the comments that the teachers gave and the revisions induced convinced the panel that they had achieved a great deal. Rosemary said to Marina after the meeting that she did not realize that as a panel they had done so much until she saw the analyses.

9.6 Reconstruing Process Writing

In this section we shall see how process writing was construed by the four ESL teachers, and whether, as a result of putting it into practice, they came to a new understanding.

9.6.1 Marina: Transforming the classroom context

When the idea of adopting process writing first came to Marina's mind, she understood it from a technical point of view – that it was a way of making the teaching of writing more effective and enjoyable for the teacher and the students. Getting students to give each other feedback and to revise their drafts was initially seen as a way of taking responsibility for improving their own writing and reducing the marking load of the teacher. After actually implementing it in the classroom, Marina had a much better understanding of how process writing can be realized in the classroom and of the role of peer comments in raising students' awareness of their own weaknesses in writing. In the following year, she took this as a research topic and tried it out on her S6 students. At the end of a six-month tryout, Marina gained a new understanding of the role of peer comments in process writing. She saw the incorporation of peer comments into the writing process not only as a means of raising students' awareness of their own weaknesses in writing, but also transforming the classroom context. By encouraging students to give feedback to each others' writing, collaborative learning in which the teacher is no longer the only source of knowledge is promoted.

One of her S6 students, Patrick, said, "You can treat the peers as your teacher; they can teach you things and help you." He even felt that he could benefit from working with weaker students. He observed, "[Even] if a peer is weak in English, ... he may know something I don't, ... he may spot something [that I can't] and tell me. Maybe we can't spot as many problems [as the teacher], but they [peer comments] are still useful." Another student, Wendy, felt that her peers' comments could be even richer than those provided by the teacher, especially when they had had experience responding to peer writing. She said, "With three peers giving comments in a four-member group, the comments can be very rich – much richer than those given by the teacher who has to rush through all the compositions in a short time." Incorporating peer comments also encouraged students to develop a sense of ownership of their own texts; they became more confident of themselves and took more control over their own learning (see Silva, 1990; Kutz, Groden, and Zamel, 1993; Tsui and Ng, 2000).

9.6.2 Eva: Exploring new meanings in process writing

Eva has always been interested in teaching writing. She said, "I think composition is to express something personal. It is interesting to explore the inner thoughts of each student." Before they started process writing, however, Eva described the teaching of writing as an "intensive" process in which writing and marking were to be finished within a specific period. She conceptualized it as going through some "working procedures."

After adopting process writing, she witnessed improvements in her students' writing. They wrote longer compositions with richer content and language. They also learned to interact with the reader by asking questions. They added interesting elaboration, and some students even rewrote the whole story after hearing or reading their peers' stories. Marking compositions became more interesting because she could compare the revised drafts with the first drafts to see whether improvements had been made. She commented, "Now, writing is meaningful. ... Students are more at ease. I think in the whole process, I could handle more, and students felt that they could handle more. We [the teacher and the students] are all more confident."

In the process of drafting and revising, Eva began to see the teacher as no longer "going through the procedures," but having an important role to play. She particularly liked the close guidance that Marina gave to the students by breaking down the revision task into manageable chunks. Eva said, "I think the teacher is a very important mediator. The kind of guidance and input provided by the teacher are important, if you want to achieve successful results in process writing." Her students became less afraid of writing, and this was an important indicator of success for Eva. Compared to her past experience in teaching writing, she felt that this was a real breakthrough.

What was striking, as Eva talked about her understanding of process writing, were the new meanings that Eva assigned to it as she went along. At the beginning, process writing was no more than asking students to go through more than one draft. Gradually, she began to see it as a process in which the students obtain feedback on their writing from peers and the teacher, analyze their own writing, develop their ideas, and make an effort to improve on previous drafts. When they have produced the final draft, it is something that belongs to them and not something that they just submit to the teacher. Like Marina, she felt that the students have a strong sense of ownership of text.

Eva also sees process writing as something that "gives students space, although the period of time is short, to think [about their writing] and learn to appreciate each other's work." Whether process writing is successful depends on whether students are able to learn about their own weaknesses in writing and to improve on them. In other words, the term *process writing* takes on a dual meaning of writing as a process of creating text as well as a process of learning how to create text.

At the end of the school year, as she reflected on her experience, Eva's understanding of process writing took on a new dimension of meaning. It has become a process of communication between herself and the students, and a means of developing a relationship with them. This is realized through her dialogs with the students, through the comments that she gave, and the revisions made by the students in response to her comments. As she said in the panel meeting, "In process writing, it seems that there is hope for further development in our relationship. I feel very good about this." The exploration of process writing by Eva, therefore, went beyond exploring a new teaching technique. In the context of discussing process writing, she said, "Every individual is unique and needs to be explored." Her conceptions of students as individuals and of teaching as being able to relate to students as individuals permeate the meanings that she has assigned and reassigned to her teaching of process writing.

9.6.3 Ching: Challenging conceptions of teaching and learning

Prior to the adoption of process writing, Ching's approach to the teaching of writing was very much a one-way process. She gave students a topic and told them what they could write about. When she marked their writings, she focused mainly on grammatical accuracy. Ching's initial understanding of process writing was a way of helping students to "develop an interest in writing, and through revising the different drafts, to learn how to develop and organize ideas." She also saw it as a way to reduce the marking load because she would not have to correct every single grammatical mistake.

For the first writing task, she spent a great deal of time brainstorming ideas with the whole class, writing ideas on the board, and grouping the ideas into different paragraphs. When students completed their first drafts, Ching put some questions for the whole class to think about in relation to the content. Though she emphasized the importance of peer learning and encouraged them to read each other's work, the peer feedback component was pushed out when she was pressed for time. She said,

I wanted to talk as much as I can in one lesson. I wanted to tell them all the problems in the first draft so that they can write better next time. But one lesson is not enough, so there's very little time for them to read each other's work.... And even if there is time for them to do that, I wonder if they have the ability to assess their peers' writings.

Ching explained that the S1 students had low English proficiency and so she had to spend much time helping them to understand her comments. In the entire school year, there was only one writing task in which she asked them to read each other's writing, but it was more for proofreading than for providing comments.

Despite the fact that she provided the opportunity for students to revise the first drafts, she found that there was not much difference between the two drafts. She explained why: "I think it could be because everything is ready in the first draft. They don't need to make an extra effort [to work on the content]. When I gave them feedback on the first draft, I might have emphasized more on grammar. So, besides correcting grammatical mistakes, there was not much change in content." In other words, it was her emphasis on grammatical accuracy that shaped her students' understanding of the purpose of revision.

Ching was keen to explore ways to motivate students to write and to improve on their own writing. She consulted various teachers, including Eva and Rosemary. In order to overcome the language barrier, she allowed students to draw pictures or to put down words in Chinese and even an "X" if they did not know how to express an idea in English in the first draft. She would provide them with the English word for the revised draft. In order to involve students more, she changed from teacher-directed brainstorming to brainstorming in groups. The students came up with ideas that she had not thought of before, and she was pleased. She also tried writing stories in pairs or groups of three, and her students loved it. However, Ching had nagging doubts about whether the writings that they produced could be regarded as the students' own work because the ideas came from a group, not from individual students.

At the end of the year, Ching positively evaluated process writing. She found that the marking load was in fact even heavier than before because she had to spend more time writing comments, but the marking was more focused. The students liked this approach because they had opportunities to read and rework their compositions. The way they responded to her comments also improved. Initially, they responded to her comments as though they were simply answering questions. However, in the last writing task, they were able to go beyond answering questions and elaborated the content more.

The implementation of process writing was a struggle between Ching's own conceptions of teaching and learning and those embodied in process writing. Throughout the implementation, she played a central role: from brainstorming to drafting revision. She tried to move from teacher-centered brainstorming to group brainstorming, but she still saw the teacher as the most important source of input. This can be seen from the fact that peer feedback never figured in the entire process despite her repeated emphasis on the importance of peer learning when she talked about process writing. Though time constraints could well be a factor, it was obvious her doubt about the ability of the students to provide useful feedback was an overriding factor. She encouraged students to focus on content. Yet, she could not help focusing on grammatical accuracy. She helped students to write freely by allowing them to put down pictures and even Chinese words. Yet she wanted the teacher to be in control. In a fairy tale rewriting task, she put restrictions on the length of the essay and what students could include in the story. She put a word limit of three hundred words and she gave the following rationale: "I'm afraid that they can't stop once they start writing.... If they write too much, they may put in too many unnecessary details." She also specified what characters they could not include in the story, one of them being the teachers. She was afraid that the students might say wild things about them. In addition, Ching said, "If there is no control, they may come up with many unexpected things. It would be more difficult to tell them what to do in their revisions because there variations would be too big." She tried to get the students to collaborate, and yet this contradicted her conception of learning as an individual endeavor. In other words, the implementation of process writing is more than adopting a new teaching strategy. It involved more profound issues that posed fundamental challenges to Ching's beliefs about teaching and learning.

9.6.4 Genie: A chance to reexpress themselves

Genie likes to express herself freely. When she writes, she does not like to follow a set of guidelines. When she teaches writing, she emphasizes the importance of creativity and uniqueness. Initially, Genie's understanding of process writing was vague: to provide comments and feedback to students on their writing and to give them an opportunity to revise. The first writing task that she gave them was story writing. The students had no idea how to write a story. Genie reported:

> ... some of them just wrote one paragraph. It was about two hundred words, and just one paragraph. ... They didn't know how to write an introduction, how to develop the ideas, how to use adjectives to enrich their descriptions, to make it [the story] more vivid; they didn't know how to end [the story].

She went over their common problems orally with the whole class. The students were a bit lost because they had never heard of "revision," and the comments given by Genie were too general to be of help. Their revised drafts were no better than the first. Genie sought advice from Marina. Marina went through her writing assignments and advised Genie to give specific comments to individual students instead of just dealing with the common problems with the whole class.

In the second term Genie asked them to write another story. This time following Marina's advice, Genie gave comments to each individual student. In addition, she provided plenty of input. In the prewriting stage, she encouraged them to think of ways of making the story special and arousing the reader's interest. For example, for an advertisement writing task, she gave them sample advertisements and asked them to discuss the persuasive language used. For story writing, she gave them two stories on the same topic, one using chronological development and the other using a flashback. She asked the class to discuss which one they liked more and why. She also took them through how to develop a story, how to end a story, how to build in dialog, and so forth. This resulted in considerable improvement and a substantial difference in length, language, and content between the first and the revised drafts. The improvement that she found was even more noticeable when she compared the students' writing at the beginning and at the end of the school year.

The improvement in students' writing, however, did not involve peer feedback at all. She tried it out once but the students did not respond well to it. The peer comments that they gave were not very helpful, and the feedback from the students was not positive. Consequently, she dropped this component completely, including reading each other's writing. After trying it out for a year, she felt that she had a better understanding of what process writing involves. It is not just giving students a chance to rewrite. The teacher has to help students by giving specific and concrete suggestions for revision. For problems with ideas and organizations, students need to be given a chance to rewrite in order to tackle them.

Genie told me a story about a student who was a very poor writer and how her improvement gave Genie new insights into process writing. She recounted:

> I have a student whose English was very poor, and she wrote a news report about a singer. The first time, the book was full of red marks [from the teacher]: the grammar was wrong; the expression of ideas was poor. I didn't know what she was talking about. I gave her comments, but the revised draft was no better than the first. I gave her a very low mark, about 30-something. She is a good student but her English was very poor, and she was afraid of English. She asked me, "Miss Wan, does that mean I have to rewrite?" I asked if she felt it was very difficult, very time-consuming, and that it might not be that easy for her to do that. However, she said she *wanted* to rewrite the report.... In the revised draft, she didn't just make corrections. She reorganized it and turned it into another piece of writing, and it was really good.... If I hadn't used this process writing approach, and just given her a mark for the first draft, she would get a very low mark, may be 20 or 30 marks [percent]. She would have no chance to improve herself. She would not have a sense of success. If every piece of writing is marked all over by the teacher, and each sentence contains several mistakes, there will not be a lot of improvement even after the mistakes have been corrected. But with process writing, students can reexpress themselves.

The remarkable improvement made by her student left a deep impression on Genie's mind. Her understanding of process writing is no longer just giving students an opportunity to revise their writing. More important, it gives them a "sense of success" that cannot be achieved by product writing. Genie's use of the words *reexpress themselves* is interesting. It suggests that the students do have the ideas. The writing teacher's job is to facilitate the expression of these ideas.

9.7 Summary

In this chapter we have seen how Marina tried to solve the problem of the teaching of writing; a problem that had been bothering her for several years. The challenge that she took on was particularly daunting because of the scale of the implementation, which involved ten teachers and fifteen classes of students. It was also daunting because although she had theoretical knowledge about process writing, she had had no experience of putting it into practice. By taking on the challenge, Marina was "working at the edge of her competence" (Bereiter and Scardamalia, 1993) and in the process of doing so, she developed a new understanding of process writing. In leading her teachers to implement process writing, Marina experienced the "learner's paradox" (Schon, 1987). The theoretical input that she received in the refresher course for panel chairs guided her thinking. She was acutely aware of the importance of not using a top-down approach. She explored how she could give her teachers autonomy and a sense ownership when she monitored the implementation. Instead of *telling* her teachers what they should do, she *demonstrated* how she did it for their reference. Instead of forcing teachers to conduct student evaluations, she made it voluntary. While Marina talked about the implementation in the interviews, she was able to articulate and theorize her new understanding of process writing on the basis of her practical experience. However, she was less able to articulate and theorize her role and how she played out her role in the entire implementation process. As Marina herself is aware, how she could and should play out her role as panel chair is something that she has to come to grips with.

As for the other three ESL teachers, there are interesting differences in the ways that they reconstrued process writing. Genie learned that the teacher has to give more specific guidance in order to help students to rewrite, and she reconceptualized process writing as giving students a sense of success by allowing them to "reexpress." The reconceptualization is still very much at a technical level. Eva's reconstrual of process writing was an interesting continuous process in which new meaning was being assigned and reassigned. Her perception of the roles of the teacher and the students changed. The teacher's role changed from going through a working procedure of marking mechanically to playing an important role in guiding the students. As students analyzed their peers' writing and their own writing, she began to see process writing as not only creating texts but also as learning how to create text from each other. As they made revisions to the drafts, she began to see that revisions could give students a strong sense of ownership of text. As she provided comments on students' writing and as they responded to her comments in their revisions, the teaching of writing took on a new dimension of meaning for her. It became a way of establishing and strengthening her personal relationship with the students. Eva's constant renewal of meaning in the implementation process is congruent with her personal conceptions of teaching and learning and her orientation to theorizing the knowledge that she gained from practice. The struggle that Ching experienced between her conceptions of teaching and learning and those embodied in process writing is interesting. It shows how such conceptions governed the way she made sense of process writing and how she tried to adapt the various elements of process writing so that they became congruent with her conceptions (see Richardson, 1996; Hillocks, 1999; Yung, 2000).

10 Understanding Expertise in Teaching

In this concluding chapter I shall come back to the three questions that guided the case studies of these four ESL teachers: What are the critical differences among expert, experienced, and novice teachers? How does a teacher become an expert teacher? What are the critical factors that shaped the development of expertise?

From the accounts of the four ESL teachers in Chapters 6 to 9, we can see a number of differences between the expert teacher and the novice teacher, many of which have been documented in novice-expert studies. For example, compared to the novice teacher, Genie, the expert teacher, Marina, conducts lessons with much more fluidity and automaticity. She knows the students much better and has a much better rapport with them. She is also more selective in attending to noises and disruptions in the classroom. The question that I wish to address, however, is not what the differences between an expert teacher and a novice teacher are, but rather which of the differences are *critical*; critical in the sense that they are important indicators of expertise and not just experience. I shall argue that the critical differences lie in the way knowledge is developed and held by these teachers. This observation is based on the premise that knowledge is "constituted in the settings of practice" (Lave, 1988, p. 14). In other words, the specific context in which the teacher operates and the ways in which the teacher relates to the context jointly constitute the ways in which the teacher makes sense of his or her work as a teacher. The critical differences between expert and nonexpert teachers, therefore, lie in the different ways in which they relate to their contexts of work, and hence their conceptions and understanding of teaching, which is developed in these contexts (see 10.1).

The second and the third questions will be addressed together because the professional development of these four teachers cannot be discussed separately from the factors that shaped their development, and hence the development of expertise. I shall argue that although there are external factors that affected each teacher's professional development, it is the way they responded to these external factors that shaped their development (see 10.2). To conclude this book, I shall revisit the notion of expertise

10.1 The Nature of Expert Teacher Knowledge

As pointed out in Chapter 4, studies of novice-expert teachers have focused largely on what the expert teachers can do that nonexpert teachers cannot. Many of these studies were heavily influenced by the information-processing model of the mind. The study of the four ESL teachers adopted a different approach and took as the unit of analysis what Lave (1988) refers to as the "whole person in action, acting with the settings of that action" (p. 17). It focuses on the ways in which these teachers relate to their specific contexts of work and make sense of their work as teachers. The findings reported in the previous chapters show that the critical differences among Marina and the three nonexpert teachers, as well as the differences among these three teachers, is not so much what Marina can do that Eva, Ching, and Genie cannot, but rather the way they perceive and understand what they do. For example, Marina has established routines for conducting classroom teaching effectively and efficiently. Some of these routines have been adopted by the other three teachers to a greater or a lesser extent as a result of observing Marina teach, and they often share their teaching ideas and problems. However, there are qualitative differences between their conceptions of teaching and learning and their perceptions of the same or similar routines that each of them used.

Let us take, for example, the routine of asking students to repeat the instructions, which both Marina and Ching use to make sure that students are paying attention. While Marina makes a distinction between times when she demands absolute silence from students and times when she is more permissive, Ching wants absolute silence and attention at all times. Ching would be "easily disturbed emotionally" and "seriously affected" if students were not paying attention or were "messing around with their pens or correction fluids" because this does not accord with her conception of a well managed classroom (see 7.5.3). Marina, on the other hand, wants absolute attention when she is giving instructions for homework and group work. When she is not, she tolerates on-task noise and only disallows off-task noise. Her conception of this routine is to facilitate the achievement of the instructional objective effectively rather than to exert her authority as a teacher. Ching's understanding of this routine is primarily bound up with her conception of a competent teacher, one who is able to keep the students quiet and under control. In other words, the conceptions embedded in similar routines can be very different (see also Yung, 2000). For this reason, the investigation of the conceptions and understanding embedded in teachers' practices is very important in understanding expertise in teaching.

There are three dimensions relating to these four teachers' conceptions and understanding of their work in which critical differences could be identified. The first dimension is how the teachers relate to the act of teaching and the extent to which they integrate or dichotomize the various aspects of teacher knowledge in the teaching act. The second dimension is how they relate to their specific contexts of work, that is, the ways in which their perceptions of their work as a teacher is "situated" in the specific contexts in which they are operating (Leinhardt, 1988; Lave, 1988; Lave and Wenger, 1991), as well as the extent to which they are able to perceive and open up possibilities that do not present themselves as such in their specific contexts of work. Third is the extent to which they are able to theorize the knowledge generated by their personal practical experience as a teacher and to "practicalize" theoretical knowledge.

10.1.1 Integrating aspects of teacher knowledge

In the review of teacher knowledge in Chapter 4, I maintain that teacher knowledge as realized in the act of teaching, referred to by Shulman (1986) as "pedagogical content knowledge," is not a knowledge domain separate from other teacher knowledge domains, but rather is an integrated body of knowledge. In fact, as Calderhead and Miller (1986) and Bennett (1993) point out, the delineation of teacher knowledge as consisting of separate domains is more analytical than real. In actual practice, these knowledge domains are intermeshed (see 4.2.1). In the ensuing section, I shall examine how the four case study teachers relate differently to the teaching act and the extent to which they are able to integrate the various aspects of teacher knowledge.

INSTRUCTIONAL OBJECTIVES AND CLASSROOM MANAGEMENT

In Chapter 7, I proposed that classroom management is inextricably linked to instructional objectives and that a teacher has to manage the classroom in such a way that will best facilitate learning, hence the term *management of learning*. The four case studies show that not all four teachers were able to integrate instructional objectives with classroom management to the same extent. The ways in which these four teachers conducted their first two lessons best illustrate this point. Marina and Eva started their lessons by going into teaching right away and established norms and routines when the teaching situation gave rise naturally and meaningfully to their formulation. They both focussed on achieving the instructional objective of the lesson, which was the use of adjectives to describe people. As far as this aspect is concerned, Marina and Eva are similar. However, while Marina was able to integrate the linguistic objective of the lesson with the communicative need for students to get to know one another at the beginning of the school year, Eva was not quite able to achieve that. The activities that Eva designed served the purpose of *practicing* the use of adjectives to describe personalities but not *using* the adjectives for communicative purposes (see 7.4.1).

Ching and Genie started the lesson by spending a lot of time establishing norms and routines, largely out of context. Their main concern was to make sure that students understand and abide by these rules so that there would not be disciplinary problems later. This is particularly so for Ching who spent the most part of the first two lessons just explaining norms and routines. In other words, both of them were much less able to integrate the establishment of classroom norms and routines with instructional objectives.

The different extent to which these four teachers were able to integrate instructional objectives and classroom management can also be seen from their understanding of group work. For Marina, group work is a means of organizing learning in order to facilitate the achievement of instructional objectives. When she first started teaching, she perceived group work as merely providing more opportunities for students to talk to each other in English. She did not realize that although this could be an objective in itself in ESL lessons, if the language task that students are asked to complete in groups could in fact be done individually, the teacher is not maximizing the benefit of group work. Now she is able to see that in order for students to work collaboratively, the language task for group work should be designed in such a way that students need to work together, to engage in the negotiation of meaning, and to produce output that would be shared with other groups. The sharing of output from different groups opens up opportunities for learning by showing students the different ways the task can be interpreted by different groups. Moreover, the tasks are often designed in such a way that there is an information gap not just *among* the group members but also among the groups themselves, hence creating a communicative need. The small size of the group, four and no bigger than five, facilitates effective collaboration. The actual physical grouping, which is done by simply asking students to turn their chairs around, minimizes the amount of time taken for students to move around and maximizes time for learning. The use of big posters for students to write down their output enables the students to learn from each other and helps Marina to provide corrective feedback for reinforcement of the linguistic objective.

Group work is a regular feature in Eva's as well as Genie's classrooms, and to a lesser extent, Ching's classroom. However, their understanding of "group work" is different. All of them put students into groups. Both Eva and Ching have groups of six whereas Genie has groups as big as seven. All of them use groupings to cultivate a sense of belonging and to get students to participate by group competition. For Eva, this kind of grouping also serves the purpose of facilitating collaborative learning. Like Marina, Eva's group work always culminates in output, and students are asked to share their productions on a big poster. However, Eva is not always able to discriminate between tasks that require collaboration among students and those that can be easily and even better accomplished by students individually, such as sentence transformation. Moreover, while Marina's focus of attention is very much on the achievement of instructional objectives and how group work can help to achieve those objectives, Eva's focus is more on the realization of her personal conceptions of teaching and learning. For example, getting the groups to monitor their own group members' use of English is a means of encouraging students to take responsibility for their own learning (see 7.4.4). Rotating the physical location of the groups to ensure that each group is given equal attention and opportunity to speak and to maintain contact with students at a personal level is a realization of her conception of students as individuals (see 7.4.3). Sometimes her personal conceptions integrated very well with the instructional objectives, but other times they could be at odds with the latter. For example, when engaging in dialog with individual students as a way of maintaining her rapport with them as individuals, the instructional focus of her lesson was lost, and the rest of the class was neglected.

Though Ching organizes the class into groups, she does not engage them in group work very frequently. She is able to make a distinction between grouping and group work, and she is fully aware of the fact that when her students sit in groups but work individually, they are not doing group work. However, she has difficulty integrating collaborative learning with the achievement of instructional objectives because she perceives learning as an individual endeavor (see 9.6.3). Allowing students to conduct group work is perceived as merely catering to the students' preference at the expense of achieving the learning outcome (see 7.5.4).

Unlike Ching, Genie was not aware of the difference between group work and sitting in groups. The purpose of "group work," which is actually *group seating* for Genie, is to enable students to give mutual support and to provide a safe learning environment. The question of whether this kind of grouping would facilitate the achievement of instructional objectives through collaborative learning never crossed her mind. This can be seen from the fact that students sat in groups for all double lessons but not for single lessons. This arrangement was not based on the nature of the language tasks, but rather on the duration of the lesson: group work is not used in single lessons because the amount of time needed to move the desks around would leave little time for teaching. Very often students were doing individual work, such as looking up words in dictionaries and answering the teacher's questions when they were sitting

250   *Understanding Expertise in Teaching*

in groups. When students were asked to work on a task collaboratively, the sheer physical distance between group members sitting around six or seven desks in a noisy classroom made it impossible for them to even hear each other. Consequently, in each group, there were students who did not participate. This was interpreted by Genie as a lack of motivation on the students' part. In other words, Genie's conception of group work is a way of organizing the classroom to achieve purposes which are independent of, and can even be at odds with, the instructional objectives.

ENACTING THE ESL CURRICULUM

Among the four teachers, the knowledge base of Marina is clearly the richest and most elaborate. From her enactment of the ESL curriculum, ranging from a unit to a lesson to a single activity, we can see that she draws on a wide range of teacher knowledge. As pointed out in Chapter 4, teacher knowledge functions as an integrated and coherent whole. However, for analytic purposes, we shall refer to the different aspects of teacher knowledge. The first aspect is her knowledge of linguistics, as evidenced by her critique of the use of reported speech in textbooks (see 8.1.1) and her structuring of language tasks according to their linguistic complexity, as in her in the teaching of the passive voice for example (see 8.3.1). It is also evidenced by the conscious decision that she made, when pressed for time, to focus on the present perfect tense and leave out the adverbs *yet* and *already* because she felt that ensuring that students understood the usage of the present perfect tense was more important (see 8.2.1). The second aspect is her knowledge of teaching in general and communicative language teaching in particular. This can be seen from the guiding principles she formulated for the selection and design of "good" materials and the care that she took in creating information gaps when designing activities so that there is a genuine need for communication. A good example is the design of the task for giving advice. The third aspect is her knowledge of the students. There are plenty of examples. The activities she designed typically showed how she was able to get into her students' minds and anticipate what would interest them, such as the teaching of the bare infinitives and the modals. (See 8.3.1). The fourth aspect is her knowledge of language learning strategies. This is demonstrated in her language awareness raising activities, which include helping students to be aware of structural patterns in grammar instructions as well as to "notice" the language around them (see 7.3.4). The fifth aspect is her knowledge of other curricula, as evidenced in her exploitation of scientific texts for teaching the passive voice (7.3.1). The last aspect is her knowledge of the specific context in which she is operating. This includes her knowledge of the socio-economic status of the students and their living conditions, as can be seen from the vocabulary teaching routine that she developed (see 7.3.2). It also includes her knowledge of the language situation in Hong Kong, as demonstrated in the way she tried to maximize resources for ESL learning by providing a language-rich environment in the classroom and an experiential dimension of ESL learning (see 7.3.4).

Compared to Marina, Ching and Eva's knowledge bases are much less elaborate and less developed, and Genie's is least developed. This is hardly surprising since the development of knowledge is very much related to experience. The critical difference lies, however, in their understanding the act of teaching and hence their ability to integrate different aspects of their knowledge.

Let us consider one aspect of teaching in which critical differences in integration are evident. A major concern for all four teachers is how to make their teaching interesting for students. Marina's students enjoyed her lessons because they were "fun" and "she doesn't just teach." Learning English was described by one of her students as "learning through games" (see 7.3.5). Marina's understanding of teaching is how she could best achieve the instructional objectives from the students' perspective rather than from her own perspective. Therefore, when she selected materials and designed language tasks and activities, she would put herself in the students' shoes and ask what *they* would like to do rather than what *she* would like them to do. This was seen in Chapter 8 when she talked about the teaching of the bare infinitive (see 8.3.1). While Marina is keen to make her teaching fun, she never loses sight of the instructional objective. One is not achieved at the expense of the other.

Eva's lessons were also lively, full of activities, and fun. Like Marina, she sees the fun element of teaching as very important in motivating students to learn. However, in her personal conception of the teaching act, she dichotomizes student interests and the achievement of the instruction objective. Students' interest is her "top priority" and her "concern for students is greater than my [her] concern that students can learn something" (see 8.3.6). In fact, the same dichotomy is found between inculcating moral and social values and achieving instructional objectives. When she can get her students to express their ideals and values in their writing, she considers herself successful irrespective of whether the students have acquired the skills taught (see 6.3.1). Although Eva is fully aware of her priority, she is not always aware of how the instructional objectives are compromised.

In Ching's teaching a similar dichotomy can be found but for different reasons. In her personal conception of teaching, the most important job for a teacher is to "to help students academically," and to "teach" in the sense of being able to present what she has in mind. She is apprehensive about students getting out of control when they play games, and that this will affect their learning outcome. Moreover, fun ideas do not come to her easily. She has difficulty getting into students' minds and anticipating what interests them. She knows that her students find her teaching boring. In response to her students' negative reactions, she is keen to make her teaching interesting and "to inject more fun elements to make my [her] students enjoy the lesson" (See 6.4.1). Therefore, when planning a lesson, her major concern is to find interesting activities for students. As we have seen in her teaching of "comparatives," because of the predominance of this concern, she used an activity, Top of the World, which required the use of "superlatives" because she could not find one for "comparatives." Unlike Eva, however, Ching was fully aware of the discrepancy between the linguistic objective of the lesson and the activity. She made up for the discrepancy by getting students to write comparative sentences using the same adjectives that they used in the activity. In other words, the game was seen as merely a way to "motivate the students and get them involved (in activities)" rather than a meaningful contextualization of the language. Hence, when she moved to teaching the comparatives, she resorted to asking them to write decontexualized sentences (see 8.1.3). Similarly, when she planned the sequence of activities in the teaching of conditionals, students' interests took priority over linguistic complexity, and she started with a linguistically more demanding task. This, as we have seen, caused difficulties for students and adversely affected their learning outcome (see 8.3.7). Again, unlike Eva, Ching was aware of the decision that she was making, and she did struggle over it. She was aware of the first conditional being easier than its metaphorical use in advertisements, although she was not fully aware of the need for her to bridge the gap between the two in linguistic complexity.

Like Ching, Genie is very troubled by the fact that her teaching is monotonous and her students are bored. She has problems coming to grips with what interests her students. Activities that she finds exciting often fall flat in class. Her judgment of whether a lesson is interesting is based on whether students are actively participating. Therefore, when she first got students to sit in groups and found that they interacted with each other to complete tasks, she considered it a "breakthrough." Later on, when she gave them activities from teaching resource books, or activities borrowed from other teachers, she would consider those in which students were actively involved as good activities, regardless of the learning outcome (see 8.3.10). When Genie talked about her teaching, she focused very much on whether the students were responsive and whether they liked the activity. The question of whether the activities achieved the instructional objectives did not figure in her discourse. For example, when she talked about asking the students to draw pictures from a reading comprehension text about birds' nests, she showed me the pictures and was pleased that they were nicely drawn. Her rationale was that "after presenting [the pictures], they are supposed to have understood the main content [of the text]" (see 8.3.12).

To summarize, we can say that Marina perceives students' interests and instructional objectives as an integrated whole in her enactment of the ESL curriculum, and her focus of attention is always on the instructional objectives. In contrast, the other three teachers give students' interests priority over instructional objectives. The underlying reasons are different, however. Eva is neither aware of whether she has achieved the instructional objectives nor does she attach a great deal of importance to it. Ching, on the other hand, is much more aware of what she compromises at the planning stage and tries to retain the instructional objective as best she can while still giving students' interests top priority. Genie does not have a clear idea of how instructional objectives can be achieved and is still trying to understand what it means to make a lesson interesting to students.

The difference between Ching and Eva is due to the powerful influence of their different conceptions of teaching and their disciplinary backgrounds. Eva has no problems catering to students' interests because of her conception of students as individuals and her sensitivity to students' needs. Even when she was conducting lock-step teacher fronted teaching, she would be able to enliven the atmosphere by cracking jokes with them and giving funny examples. However, her lack of knowledge in linguistics made it difficult for her to make sound judgements on whether the linguistic objectives of the activities were achieved. Ching's linguistics background contributed to her awareness of the linguistic objectives that she was achieving. She was not able to integrate the use of games with the instructional objectives because she does not believe it is an effective means of teaching. It only serves as a panacea for *presenting* her knowledge effectively to the students, and therefore even if the games do not achieve the instructional objective, she would not think that it "would be too much of a problem" (see 8.1.3).

10.1.2 Relating to specific contexts and "situated possibilities"

In the previous section I pointed out that the knowledge held by Marina is much richer and more elaborate than that held by the other three teachers. I further pointed out that the critical difference between them is their ability to integrate different aspects of knowledge because of the different ways in which they relate to the teaching act. This is one aspect of teacher knowledge. There is another aspect of teacher knowledge that is *critical* to the distinction between expert and nonexpert teachers. This has to do with the dialectical relation between their knowledge and their specific contexts of work.

Research on teacher knowledge has pointed out the context specific nature of teacher knowledge (see Chapter 4). The knowledge that teachers develop is jointly constituted by their specific contexts of work and their own understanding of and responses to the contexts (Lave and Wenger, 1991; Putnam and Borko, 2000). This kind of knowledge has been referred to as "situated knowledge" (see, for example, Fenstermacher, 1994; Leinhardt, 1988). Freeman (2000, p. 1) refers to it as knowledge that is composed of "local understanding." As pointed out by Benner et al. (1996, p. 352), "being situated" means that one is neither totally determined or constrained by the specific context, nor is one radically free to act in whichever way one wants. Rather, there are "situated possibilities." This means that "there are certain ways of seeing and responding that present themselves to the individual in certain situations, and certain ways of seeing and responding that are not available to that individual" (ibid.). The critical difference between the expert teacher and the nonexpert teachers in this study is the how they interact with their specific contexts of work, of which they are a part, and how they see the possibilities that can be opened up for the effective achievement of instructional objectives.

The contexts of work for the four teachers were largely similar since they were teaching in the same school. However, the ways in which the teachers responded to the context were different. The dialectical relationship between teachers' contexts of work and the way they responded to them entails that their knowledge so constituted is different (see Lave, 1988). Marina was able to see the possibilities for ESL learning in her context of work, and by making use of these possibilities and she shaped a context that was conducive to ESL learning. Let us look at a number of examples. In response to the language situation in Hong Kong and the working-class background of her students, Marina tried to overcome the constraints by creating an "English-rich" environment for them (see 7.3.4). She tried to maximize the classroom for learning English by stipulating that students must use English at all times, and she made use of the class and school bulletin boards for sharing students' work in English. She also encouraged various forms of extracurricular activities that would provide opportunities for students to use English, such as getting students to use English to introduce their work to visitors during the school Open Day. She exploited the easy access to bilingual materials as a learning opportunity by getting the students to find out the English words for things and names of places, and to look for information in English for themselves. The use of realia for teaching is another way of exploiting the special language situation in Hong Kong. All of these strategies serve the purpose of providing opportunities for using English; opportunities of which the students are deprived. In the process of responding to problems that were context specific, Marina gained further understanding of ESL teaching. For example, there is a commonly shared belief among teachers that it is unrealistic to expect average ability students to use English exclusively in the classroom.[1] Marina's insistence that no Cantonese would be tolerated proved that, given appropriate linguistic support, this target is achievable. The knowledge generated by this experience helped her to formulate the language policy for the school where she strongly advocated that no mixed code should be used in content lessons. (See 7.3.4).

Similarly, the vocabulary consolidation routine was developed in response to the fact that students could not get parental support in their school work and that their living environment was not conducive to studying at home. It was also developed in response to her unsuccessful attempts to get students to learn by penalizing them. The effectiveness of the vocabulary consolidation routine helped her to understand further the importance of consolidation in teaching and that teaching is not equivalent to learning (see 8.3.3). The use of old posters, monthly calendars, and photocopy paper package wrappings for presenting language productions in group work is another example of the way Marina responded to her specific working context in which very few resources were available to teachers. By getting students to present their work on big pieces of paper, she gave them a sense of audience when producing their work. Corrective feedback could also be provided effectively and efficiently. As Bereiter and Scardamalia (1993) point out, the nature of expert knowledge is situated not only in the sense that it can be applied to certain specific contexts but also that "it gains strength from those situations" (p. 53).

Some of Marina's classroom practices outlined above were adopted by the other three teachers. However, there were qualitative differences in the way they made sense of these practices. All three teachers required their students to use English in class. Eva and Genie had in place a penalty system for violating the norm. While Eva enforced the penalty system consistently, Genie did not. Ching did not have a penalty system and she did not enforce the requirement. Eva's persistence in getting students to use English resulted in an English-rich classroom, where English was heard and used by students. However, while Marina saw this strategy as part of a number of other strategies to overcome the constraints imposed by the wider linguistic context in Hong Kong on students' opportunities to use English, Eva's understanding of the strategy was confined to the immediate context. Her aim was to get students to practice using the language because they had little chance to do that outside the classroom. Her awareness of the language situation in Hong Kong did not come through strongly. There were also fewer strategies that exploited the specific linguistic situation for English learning purposes. Genie, on

---

1 In the last couple of years, the Hong Kong government stipulated that no mixed code could be used in schools that had declared themselves to be English medium schools.

the other hand, did not enforce the rule persistently because she was still working out how she could deal with the practicalities of making students observe the rules. Her understanding was very much at a technical level. Ching never enforced this rule because she felt that her students had great difficulties switching over from Chinese medium to English medium education. Her main concern, therefore, was that her students understand what she was saying in class. In other words, as far as the medium of communication is concerned, Ching allowed the constraints to dictate her teaching. Consequently, the context of teaching, of which she is a part, is much less language-rich than that of Marina and Eva.

The use of big posters by the other three teachers is another example which shows qualitative differences in their understanding of the practice. Like Marina, Eva asked the students to use big posters for writing down their group work productions. However, she did not use it as regularly as Marina did, nor did she use it consistently for corrective feedback and consolidation. It was seldom used for positive reinforcement. Ching's use of A4 paper instead of big posters when she could not find the latter showed that she understood it as merely a means of getting students to write down their language productions. The small hand writing on the A4 papers made it impossible for the students see the words if Ching were to post them on the board. Consequently, the students had to read their work out to the rest of the class. This is a much less effective way of providing opportunities for peer learning and providing corrective feedback to the whole class. Similarly, Genie used big posters for group work only occasionally, and her inappropriate use of picture drawing to demonstrate text comprehension showed her lack of understanding of the strategy even at the technical level. In other words, the strategy was adopted from Marina with only a partial understanding the functions that it can serve. It did not form part of a number of strategies to maximize resources for learning for the other three teachers.

From the above examples, we can see two common features running through Marina's responses to her context of work. First, instead of being dictated by the contextual constraints, she actively shapes her context of work by transcending these contraints. Second, her responses to her context of work are not discrete and unrelated. Together, they reflect a coherent understanding of the ESL learning situation and her work as an ESL teacher. As Benner et al. (1996) point out, experts are often able to go beyond the immediate situation and see the "big picture" in the sense of being aware of future possibilities and what goes on in the wider context (see p. 154). This awareness of the "big picture" in turn shapes their understanding of and their responses to the immediate context. Marina's awareness of not only the immediate learning context of the students, but also the language situation in Hong Kong, enables her to formulate coherent teaching strategies that are geared to the specific language learning needs of her students. Benner et al. (1996) observe that expert practice is characterized by the ability to "see" and "read" the "salient issues in the situation" without imposing a preconceived set of expectations and to respond to them with increased intuition (p. 142). Marina's expertise lies in her ability to see the salient features of the language situation in Hong Kong and the language learning environment in her school, and her ability to formulate a coherent set of strategies in response to these features.

10.1.3 Theorizing practical knowledge and "practicalizing" theoretical knowledge

In Chapter 2 we have seen that Dreyfus and Dreyfus (1986) characterize experts as being able to make intuitive judgements on the basis of their prior experience in a manner that "defies explanation" (p. 3). Similarly, descriptions of teacher knowledge often emphasize the tacit nature of teacher knowledge. Schon's (1983) theory of professional knowledge, which echoes Ryle's (1949) notion of "knowing how," maintains that professionals' knowing is in the action, and this kind of "knowing-in-action" is tacit; it cannot be articulated. Bereiter and Scardamalia (1993) maintain that what distinguishes experts from nonexperts is "hidden knowledge" (p. 47). Their notion of "hidden knowledge" somewhat resembles Polanyi's (1966) notion of "tacit knowledge," which refers to the unarticulated and even unconscious knowledge that underlies intelligent action. Hidden knowledge, according to Bereiter and Scardamalia, is very much in the heads of experts and not articulated, although it potentially can be.

Dreyfus and Dreyfus (*ibid*.) further observe that expert performance is also nonreflective. According to them, experts engage in reflection or deliberation only when they have time, or when the outcome is critical. For them, detached deliberation is merely "useful" at the highest level of expertise (p. xiv), and it can "enhance the performance of *even* the intuitive expert" (p. 40, my emphasis). In other words, while they recognize that deliberation plays a part in expert performance, it is by no means critical. By contrast, the ability of professionals to reflect and to reframe their understanding of the situation is at the core of Schon's theory of professional knowledge. Similarly, Glaser and Chi (1988) consider experts as having better self-monitoring skills and being more aware than novices of their mistakes and the difficulties that they will come across when solving problems. Along the same line, Eraut (1994) argues that conscious deliberation is at the heart of the work of professionals. He observes that apart from routine cases and well-defined problems that can be handled automatically, there are other cases that are ill-defined problems which require conscious deliberation. He maintains that "it is the ability to cope with difficult, ill-defined problems rather than only routine matters which is often adjudged to be the essence of professional expertise." (Eraut, 1994, p. 152; see 2.2).

The question that I would like to address is: it is true that much of expert teachers' knowledge is developed on the basis of their experience, but how far is it tacit and not capable of being articulated? How far is conscious deliberation a critical feature of expertise, or is it just something that expert teachers engage in only when the situation is unusual or when there is a great risk and responsibility involved, as Dreyfus and Dreyfus (1986, 1996) and Dreyfus (1997) claim? What insights do the case studies of ESL teachers provide in relation to the conflicting views about the differences between experts and nonexperts, and the nature of their knowledge development?

All four ESL teachers entered teaching without any formal professional training. They entered teaching with their own image of what a teacher is and should be like. They also had their own conceptions of teaching and learning that were influenced by their family backgrounds, learning experiences, and life experiences. In Eva's case, her disciplinary background in sociology had a particular strong influence on her. These conceptions acted as the "interpretive lens" through which she perceives and responds to classroom events, students, as well as her context of work (Zeichner, Tabacknick, and Densmore, 1987).

Both Marina and Ching held images of the teacher as a figure of authority. While Marina saw the essential qualities that a teacher should have as being kind and caring, Ching emphasized qualities such as being academically competent, knowledgeable, and "qualified." Marina wanted the students to enjoy learning, whereas Ching wanted to make sure that learning proceeds in an orderly fashion. In the course of Marina's professional development, particularly in her first few years of teaching, she tried to reconcile her image of the teacher as a figure of authority and as a kind and caring person. She also tried to resolve the apparent dichotomy between maintaining discipline in the classroom and making learning enjoyable. She struggled with being herself and putting on a strict front, following the general rule of "don't smile till Christmas" typically passed on to novice teachers (Calderhead, 1984). In terms of maintaining discipline in the classroom, she was highly successful. Her class was the best-behaved class. This was positive reinforcement for her; it showed that being strict and taking an authoritarian stance "worked." For this reason, she remained very strict with her students for the first three or four years. However, as Marina reflected on her experience, she began to question what appeared to be an achievement. She was able to "see" (Lave, 1988, p. 69) that excellent classroom discipline was achieved at the expense of making learning enjoyable. In particular, she was able to reflect on the critical incidents that she described as "regrettable" and she reframed her understanding of the apparent dichotomy between maintaining discipline and helping students to enjoy learning. When articulating her reflections on these incidents, Marina's regret was not that they reflected badly on her as a teacher, but rather that by being more forgiving, she could have "*helped the student* to be mature, to forgive, and to see things from other people's perspective" (my emphasis), and by being unforgiving, she had adversely affected the student's attitude toward learning English. Such reflections changed Marina's understanding of how disciplinary problems should be handled from the perspective of maintaining order in the classroom to how she could best help her students. She began to see the school regulations from the students' perspective and to ask what would help the students rather than what she wanted the students to do. She *reframed* her understanding of what a "well-disciplined classroom" should look like. As we have seen in Chapter 6, the reframing that took place helped her to exercise her judgement on when she needed to be strict and when she could afford to be more lax (see 6.2.1). It helped her see the need to distinguish between on-task noise and off-task noise as well as discriminate between potential disruptive behavior that must be curbed and sheer cheekiness that could be turned into opportunities for learning. The reframing of her understanding of classroom discipline involved a reframing of her role as a teacher. She is no longer a figure of authority whom students hold in awe, but the "agony aunt" to whom students can and will turn when they have personal problems. (See 7.3.2) Marina's own articulation of how she resolved the apparent dichotomy of maintaining classroom discipline and making learning enjoyable became a reference for her future action. I shall refer to this kind of knowledge, which is developed by theorizing practical experience, as "theorized practical knowledge." I would argue that in the development of expert teacher knowledge, conscious deliberation and reflection on experience are central. As Dreyfus and Dreyfus (1986) recognized, detached deliberation enables the expert to avoid "tunnel vision" and experience a change of perspective by focusing on aspects that may seem relatively unimportant on the basis of past experience (p. 38). Detached deliberation is also necessary in order for experts to consider the relevance and adequacy of past experience that seems to underlie intuition. Experts need to question whether what would appear to be the best strategy or move is still relevant in view of the specific situation, and even if it is still relevant, whether it is the best move (see also Dreyfus and Dreyfus, 1996). While Dreyfus and Dreyfus (1986, 1996) argue that there is a place for conscious deliberation, but only when experts have time, I would argue that conscious deliberation is *critical* to the development of expert knowledge.

There is another sense in which Marina's knowledge can be characterized as "theorized practical knowledge." This is the kind of practical knowledge that she developed as a result of her own learning experience. This practical knowledge was made explicit, enriched, and theorized as she was exposed to "formal knowledge" (Bereiter and Scardamalia, 1993, p. 62),[2] in the PCEd program, the refresher course for panel chairs, and the MEd program. There are plenty of examples in the accounts given in the preceding chapters. I will just cite a few for illustration. From her own learning experience in school and in the Geothe Institut, Marina had already acquired a number of skills and strategies for ESL teaching that worked well in her classroom, but she did not know why. For example, she used information gap activities, but she did not know their theoretical rationale or how they were related to communicative language teaching. The theoretical input from the PCEd program helped her make sense of her practices and provided her with a principled way of evaluating and designing teaching activities. As we have seen in Chapter 8, she was able to articulate the principles very clearly. Another example is the strategies that Marina used to raise students' awareness of the English around them and her use of authentic texts. These strategies were based on Marina's own language learning experience and her practical experience of making her teaching materials interesting and relevant to the students. The "formal knowledge" of text analysis to which she was exposed not only helped her to understand the theoretical rationale for using authentic texts for teaching, but also to critique the English that was used in the textbooks. The "formal knowledge" of learner strategies helped her to theorize her own language strategies and how her students learn. The theoretical input on designing and conducting group work enabled her to see group work from a different perspective. Her focus of attention changed from providing an opportunity for students to talk, to getting them to collaborate by assuming specified roles and to produce a linguistic output. As she put her new understanding of group work into practice, she gained a better understanding of the collaborative nature of group work.

Marina's understanding of her role as "an agent of change" is another example. Initially, she saw her role as merely dealing with administrative chores such as taking care of the loop room, checking teachers' marking, and assigning duties. In carrying out this role, she started to implement changes in teaching that involved other teachers. In the course of implementing these changes, Marina began to understand that her position as panel chair enabled her to achieve more than just carrying out administrative chores. Therefore, when she was first introduced to the concept of the panel chair as "an agent of change" during the six-month refresher

---

2 *Formal knowledge* is defined by Bereiter and Scardamalia as "publicly represented" and "negotiable" knowledge (1993, p. 62).

course, it left a strong impression on her mind because she had already been bringing some changes to her panel, such as introducing the teaching of phonetics and specifying the objectives in the scheme of work. Seeing herself as "an agent of change" gave her the impetus to embark on a much larger scale of change, that is, introducing process writing in the junior forms. On the other hand, while Marina identified with the notion of "agent of change," how this role should be played out so that teachers would have autonomy and a sense of ownership was still very much theoretical knowledge to her. The implementation of processing writing was a process where Marina tried to grapple with her role as an "agent of change" through working *with* her teachers and sharing her work with them instead of working *on* them.

The above examples illustrate the interaction between the theorization of practical knowledge through reflection and conscious deliberation, and the transformation of "formal knowledge" into practical knowledge. Such interaction is firmly rooted in practical experience in a specific context of work. Marina's expertise, therefore, lies in her ability to be reflective and to "retain critical control over the more intuitive parts of ... [her] expertise by regular reflection, self-evaluation, and disposition to learn from colleagues." (Eraut, 1994, p. 155). It also lies in her constant pursuit to gain insights into her practical knowledge by seeking theoretical input and to make sense of it in her specific context of work so that it becomes part of personal practical knowledge. As Shulman (1988) argues:

Teachers will become better educators when they can begin to have explicit answers for questions, "How do I know what I know? How do I know the reasons for what I do? Why do I ask my students to perform or think in particular ways?" The capacity to answer such questions not only lies at the heart of what we mean by becoming skilled as a teacher; it also requires a combining of reflections on practical experience and reflection on theoretical understanding (p. 33; see also Freeman, 1991).

It is in the interactive process of theorizing practical experience and practicalizing theoretical understanding that Marina is able to transcend her own "taken-for-granted experiential world as a teacher" and gain what Marton (1994) refers to as "analytic awareness," which is "an explicit and generalizable awareness of the relationship between means and ends in teaching" (p. 39), something that Lortie (1975) maintains is lacking in many teachers.

While Marina was able to reflect on her experiences and to question her own conceptions of teaching and learning, Ching, when she encountered problems, tended to look for explanations that had little to do with her own conceptions of teaching and learning. In her first two years of teaching, her problem of not being able to relate to students was attributed to the students' low ability, her own quiet and "not lively and creative" personality, as well as the language barrier between the teacher and the students created by the language policy of the English panel. The critical incident of finding out that her own class celebrated her colleague's birthday merely gave her the impetus to work harder on her relationship with the students but did not help her to reexamine her image of a teacher. She attributed the successful rapport that her colleagues were able to establish with the students to external factors: for example, their years of teaching experience and the power vested in them, such as their authority as the discipline master. This attribution of problems to outside sources over which they have little control is a strategy that many teachers resort to as a way of coping (see Rosenholtz, 1989). As Grossman (1990) points out, "Learning from experience is neither...automatic nor...effortless" (see also Feiman-Nemser and Buchmann, 1986). How teachers interpret or frame the problems that they come across in teaching is important. If the problem is framed incorrectly, they will look for the wrong solution. Therefore, even when Ching's relationship with the students improved in the third year, she was not clear whether it was because her students were different or whether she herself had changed. In the final analysis, she attributed it to the students being more cooperative or participating more actively in class. Her attribution of the effectiveness of her teaching to external factors is well captured by her analysis of whether her techniques worked: "If it is a cooperative class, it doesn't matter what method it is. I can try it out" (see 6.4.2). Unlike Marina, Ching seldom referred to how her understanding of the students had changed. Even when Ching moved into her sixth year of teaching, she seldom theorized the practical knowledge that she gained as a result of her experience, and she seldom talked about how her conceptions of teaching and learning had changed. The only time she articulated a new understanding of her work as a teacher was at the end of the third year of teaching when she talked about why she liked teaching. However, the new understanding was not revisited in the following two years, probably because she was very preoccupied with her relationship with her senior students and striking a balance between her professional life and family life. Her conceptions of teaching as the teacher being in control and learning as an individual endeavor remained largely unchanged throughout. This is why when she implemented process writing, she went through a struggle because the collaborative and creative nature of process writing fundamentally challenged her conceptions of teaching and learning.

In contrast to Ching, Eva often engaged in theorizing her role as a teacher and her classroom practices. Heavily influenced by her sociology background, she entered teaching with a conception of students as individual human beings. She saw a teacher's mission as helping students learn "how to be a human being," to care for people and things around them, and to develop a set of moral and social values. Helping students acquire academic knowledge was secondary for her. She wanted the students to ask questions and to challenge her authority as a teacher. She formulated her own metaphor of "space" as a way of understanding the autonomy that she had as a teacher, and she explored the space that was available to her to achieve congruence between her job as a teacher and her conception of educational aims. For example, the one-to-one dialog that she developed with her students in the classroom, albeit distracting at times, was her means of developing a personal relationship with the students and treating each student as an individual human being who is worthy of attention. The social, political, and moral content that she put in the teaching materials was her personal way of trying to overcome the "foreignness" of English and to make the teaching and learning of English relevant to her students. She set her own criteria for success in teaching. When her students responded well to her and to the tasks that she gave them, she felt that she had achieved the goals of education that she set for herself.

In the enactment of the ESL curriculum, while Ching followed the textbook and the scheme of work drawn up by the form coordinator closely, Eva asked questions relating to what the objectives meant and whether they were put down in the scheme of work for their own sake. Eva queried the commonly held belief that S1, rather than S2, was the best class for trying out new things. Upon noticing the lack of continuity between the different levels, Eva formulated her own theory of "continuity" in the curriculum by taking S2 and S3 as one complete unit and S4 and S5 as another complete unit. She sought to realize this by looking at the English curriculum in the preceding and following years, and by following the students to S3. She also formulated the principle of integration of skills when planning a unit. Even for simple things like getting students to speak loudly in class, Eva theorized it as a way of making sure that all students can hear what is said because every contribution made by a student is an opportunity for learning. Directing students' answers to another student for evaluation was not just taken as a classroom interaction technique but was theorized as getting students to take responsibility for their own learning. As Eva implemented process writing, she formulated her own theory of process writing. It was given meaning by her as an exploration of the inner thoughts of students, a dual process of creating text and learning how to create text. It was seen as a process in which students exploited the space available to think about their own writing as well as learned how to appreciate their peers' writing. It was also seen as a means of enhancing her relationship with the students as she developed dialogs with them through the questions and comments she made on their writing and the revisions that they made in response. She would make changes to her teaching after long vacations when she had the time to reflect more systematically on her work.

From the above account, we can see that Eva is constantly engaged in formulating her own personal practical theories of teaching and learning. It is "personal" not only in the sense that it is idiosyncratic, but more important, it pertains to her own personal experience. It is, in Clandinin's words, "carved out of and shaped by situations" (1992, p. 125), and it is knowledge that she constructed and reconstructed as she lived out her stories and relived them through reflection. To this extent, we could say that Eva's knowledge is theorized practical knowledge. Eva's theorization is heavily influenced by her social and political participation as an undergraduate as well as her exposure to Marxist ideology. Her lack of disciplinary input in English linguistics and professional input in ESL deprived her of the opportunity to test her own theorization against ESL teaching and learning and linguistic theories and of the opportunity to enrich her own personal practical theories through the dynamic interaction between practical knowledge and theoretical knowledge. Bereiter and Scardamalia (1993) point out that as people try to accomplish tasks and to understand things, they may find that their "informal knowledge" and skill are so insufficient that they may need to draw on "formal knowledge." Repeated occurrence, according to them, will lead to a change in understanding, resulting in knowledge growth. Eva is fully aware of the need for "formal knowledge." She attended refresher courses organized by the government. She also tried to enroll on the PCEd programs at universities. However, because the places were highly competitive, Eva had not been able to get onto any of them. Nevertheless, her own theorization of her practical knowledge helped sustain her enthusiasm and commitment to teaching and look for ways to improve her teaching.

Genie had conflicting images of what she thought teachers were like and what she would like herself to be. She would like to see herself as a friend and a family member of the students; someone who is willing to listen and provide guidance. However, like Marina, she was faced with a dilemma. On the one hand, she was forced to assume the persona of an authoritarian figure in order to maintain classroom discipline. On the other hand, she aspired to live out her own image of a teacher. Genie was at the stage when she was still preoccupied with maintaining classroom discipline and establishing rapport with students. The different measures that she took to manage the classroom for learning were technical and did not involve fundamental changes to her conceptions of teaching and learning. It was not until the beginning of her third year of teaching, when the critical incident occurred with her student, Kenneth, that she reflected on her relationship with her students, and saw disciplinary problem from a different perspective. The capability to engage in this reflection marks the beginning of a stage in Genie's professional development where there is a heightened awareness of the different aspects of her work as a teacher.

The above discussion shows that one of the *critical* differences between expert and nonexpert teachers is the capability of the former to engage in conscious deliberation and reflection. Such engagement involves making explicit the tacit practical knowledge that is gained from experience. This is what I have referred to as the theorization of practical knowledge. It also involves the transformation of "formal knowledge" to personal practical knowledge through the personal interpretation of formal knowledge in the teachers' own specific contexts of work. The deliberation and reflection in which expert teachers engage lead to a heightened analytic awareness of the various aspects of their work as teachers.

10.2 Expertise as a Developmental Process

The biographical accounts of Marina, Eva, Ching, and Genie show that all four teachers were faced with what Schon (1987) refers to as the "paradox of learning," in which teachers are expected to go into teaching and try to do what they do not yet know how to do in order to learn about teaching (p. 93). This is exacerbated by the fact that at the beginning, none of them had professional training. They were overwhelmed by the complex, uncertain, and multifaceted nature of teaching, and they were vulnerable to criticisms and to feelings of failure. Bullough et al. (1992) point out that a beginning teacher is "reminded in various and powerful ways by students, other teachers, and by small private and personal disappointments, of what she cannot do or does not understand." (p. 79). In the case of these four ESL teachers, maintaining discipline and establishing rapport with students loomed large in their perceptions of their competence as teachers. When they were criticized by students as being unfair or inexperienced, or when they felt that they were not as well-liked by students as other teachers, they lost confidence. For Marina and Ching, it was the cause of their self-doubt in their commitment to teaching. As we have seen in their biographies, the transition from one phase to another phase of professional development was caused by a change in their relationship with their students.

For all four teachers the first, and even the second and third years of teaching, which have been referred to as the "exploration" phase of survival and discovery (Huberman, ibid, p. 5), were a period during which they negotiated their roles and self-images as teachers. This is a complicated process which is painful and unsettling (see Bullough et al., 1992; Calderhead and Shorrock, 1997). Huberman observes that positive experience in this phase usually leads to a phase of "stabilization" in which teachers gain confidence in themselves, but negative experience in this phase could lead to self-doubt and reassessment of their commitment to teaching (see 6.1). Relevant to the study of the development of expertise are the following questions: Why was it that Marina was able to move out of the phase of self-doubt and reassessment and progress to the next phase? What kept Marina going after the stabilization phase that prevents her from "getting into a rut" (Bereiter and Scardamalia, 1993, p. 78)? Though both Ching and Eva had the same number of years of teaching experience, why was it that Eva, like Marina, was able to move beyond the phase of self-doubt whereas Ching seemed to move in and out of this phase, even in her fifth and sixth years of teaching?

Bullough et al. (1992) point out that the school context in which the beginning teacher works can either help or hinder the resolution of the learner's paradox. In a context that is unfavorable, such as having little support from colleagues, difficult students, being assigned to teach subjects outside one's area of expertise, playing a role with which a teacher disagrees, and working in isolation, can make life very difficult for the teacher. The four ESL teachers worked in a supportive school context in which they were all able to obtain support from colleagues and the principal, especially in difficult times. Yet, they seemed to respond quite differently to their work as teachers. What are the critical factors that shaped the development of expertise in Marina?

10.2.1 Exploration and experimentation

Huberman (1993b) points out that it is classroom-level experimentation that gives teachers career satisfaction. Improvement in student learning and significant change in students' attitude towards the teacher, towards learning, and towards the school because of their own effort are powerful evidence that they have played their role as teachers effectively. Bullough et al. (1992), in their study of the case histories of six beginning teachers, found that the improvement of specific teaching skills played a crucial role in enabling teachers "to realize in the classroom their images of self as teacher." It was also "an important means for gaining increased control over the teaching situation" (p. 185).

In Marina's case, right from her first year of teaching, she began to explore ways of improving her teaching, to look for more professional input by attending seminars, and to design more interesting activities by reading teaching resources books. The experimentation and exploration in which Marina engaged ranged from small scale, such as the teaching of phonetics and showing students the progress that they had made throughout the school year as a way of motivating them to learn, to large scale, such as implementing process writing. The satisfaction that she gained when she saw her students improving, sustained her enthusiasm for teaching and helped pull her through the phase of self-doubt when she was frustrated and depressed.

Eva's enthusiasm for her work was also very much sustained by her exploration of the "space" that was available to her to try out new things. For example, she wrote her own texts for reading comprehension, and she tried to get her students to respond to reading texts about moral and social values. She gained immense satisfaction when she felt that she was able to achieve her educational aims. Compared to Eva, Ching engaged much less in exploration and experimentation. She stuck closely to the prescribed curriculum and seldom ventured beyond it, largely because of her concern to keep things under control. Genie also engaged in experimentation and exploration to a certain extent, for example, using "group work" and asking students to draw pictures to demonstrate text comprehension. However, she was still at the stage where she was not always able to make sense of why things worked or did not work. Her enthusiasm was sometimes dampened when things that used to work well did not seem to work anymore, as in the case of the use of "group work."

While it is true that in the case of Marina and Eva, experimentation and exploration sustained their enthusiasm in teaching and gave them career satisfaction, I would argue that there is something more to experimentation and exploration than career satisfaction. The experimentation and exploration in which teachers engage are usually conducted to tackle certain problems that they have come across and to open up more possibilities for bringing about effective learning. In the process of doing this, they have to draw on their practical knowledge or the knowledge of their colleagues, and they have to obtain formal knowledge in resources and references on teaching. In the process of interpreting formal knowledge in the context of the specific problem that they have to tackle, or in their specific context of teaching, their practical knowledge is enriched, and they gain further new knowledge that will serve as the basis for future action. This kind of knowledge renewal, or knowledge growth, is vital to the development of expertise. It is in this aspect of knowledge development that Marina is different from Eva. As we have seen in the previous section, Marina's experimentation, such as the implementation of process writing, involved not only trying out ideas from her practical experience, but also the interaction between the formal knowledge that she sought and her own personal practical knowledge.

10.2.2 Problematizing the "unproblematic"

Studies of novice-expert teachers observed that expert teachers, because of their experience, were able to perform much more efficiently than novice teachers. For example, they spend much less time planning lessons because they have a number of well-established routines that they can call upon, and they rely on "what normally works." Similarly, in actual classroom teaching, expert teachers were found to be much more efficient in handling classroom events, more selective, and better able to improvise. Again, it has been argued that this is because they have well-established routines that they can draw upon to attend to a larger number of events. The characteristics of expert teachers have been described as having the ability to perform with "automaticity," "fluidity," and "effortlessness" (see 3.1.5).

As we have seen in Chapter 8, such a characterization does not fully capture Marina's expertise. When planning lessons, Marina spent a great deal of time making detailed preparation, even down to the level of the questions that she would ask, the pictures that she would draw on the board, and the students upon whom she would call. In lesson planning, she would make conscious decisions regarding what questions were more likely to elicit what kinds of responses and how she could make her examples relevant to the students. She would engage in a mental dialog, rehearse the steps, and modify them. Her explanation of why she would spend so much time and make such detailed planning is revealing. She wanted to know the steps by heart so that she would not get lost suddenly. If the lesson did not go smoothly, she would blame herself for being ill prepared or "slow" (see 8.2.1). This is especially the case when she planned for topics that she had not taught before. As pointed out in Chapter 8, this shows that Marina does not treat the task of lesson planning as something which is routinized and "unproblematic." Instead of simply using her established routines, she tries to see how her previous lesson plans can be improved to meet the specific needs of her current cohort of students. As Marina comes across new ideas, she redesigns her plans to try out the ideas. For example, we have seen that when planning the unit on tourism, she redesigned the writing task in order to maximize the benefit of processing writing (see 8.1.1).

Another example is the way Marina "problematized" her apparent success in maintaining classroom discipline and resolved the apparent dichotomy of making learning enjoyable and focusing students' attention on the instructional objectives. Although I discussed this example in the previous section, I would like to dwell on this a bit more here but from a different perspective: a developmental perspective. When Marina first started teaching, maintaining classroom discipline was a problem. At the time, the nature of the problem, as she perceived it, was merely a matter of getting the students to keep quiet in class. She tackled the problem simplistically by being very strict and putting on a stern face, and she was able to maintain excellent discipline because of her students' fear of her. However, the discipline problem, instead of taken as being *eliminated*, was understood by her from a different perspective and at a more sophisticated level. It was seen as a problem of resolving the dichotomy between making learning enjoyable and maintaining discipline, and a problem of distinguishing between on-task and off-task noise. It was a problem that Marina was not even aware of earlier, and she was incapable of even articulating it as a problem.

During the enactment of the ESL curriculum, we can see Marina going through a similar process. Marina started experimenting with teaching materials from various sources early on in her teaching career, and she was constantly expanding her repertoire of teaching strategies and her bank of teaching materials. Expert teachers in the novice-expert literature have been described as having a repertoire of teaching strategies and activities that they could easily draw on when need arises. This is why they were much better able to improvise when teaching. However, this does not seem to apply for Marina. Her explication is illuminating: "I have to select what is *good*. Also, if I have already used a similar activity before, I have to *modify* it so that students will not feel that it is the same activity. I try to give them some *variation*." (My emphases). The clear definition of *good* that she gave for selecting grammar activities showed that while the task of getting materials for teaching was simplistically construed as whether they were interesting by Genie and Ching, it was seen as more complex for Marina. Not only did she have to find interesting materials, she had to find those which satisfied the criteria that she had laid down. And even if they satisfied those criteria, she had to make sure that adaptations were made if similar activities had been used before (see 8.3.1).

To a certain extent, we could see Eva going through a similar process. In her first year of teaching, Eva was preoccupied with handling classroom discipline and getting through her day-to-day teaching. In her second year of teaching, she was able to start asking questions about her work, such as her relationship with the students and about how she could exploit the "space" available to improve her teaching. In her third year of teaching (when she was given the task of coordinating S3), instead of reducing the complexity of the task by simply using materials that were handed down by her predecessor and making minor modifications, she examined the junior curriculum. When she noticed the lack of continuity between the three junior levels, that is, S1 to S3, she tried to ensure continuity by following an S2 class to S3, and later on, an S4 class to S5. She also produced her own materials that integrated the four skills. When she coordinated S2 for the second time in her fourth year of teaching, she found that "it was more hard work." The explanation that she gave is a very good example of the reinvestment of mental resources freed up by experience. She said, "There are certain things that I feel I ought to do, and there is no excuse not to do them because I am already more familiar with the job. I cannot bear not to improve on the overall direction [of the curriculum]" (see 6.3.6). In other words, according to Eva, the experience that she gained in coordinating S2 should enable her to deal with tasks that she did not have the capacity to deal with earlier.

Eva's professional development shows a positive orientation towards problematization. In her first year of teaching, the critical incident where her student complained about her to the form mistress for penalizing the class too harshly was a matter of her rigid interpretation of the school rules. However, instead of simply deleting the black mark from the student's record, she reflected on it and came to the conclusion that "that's not the way to teach." In other words, what could have been treated more simplistically as the interpretation of school rules was problematized by Eva as a more profound issue of how she should relate to her students. In the following year, this was one of the problems that she tackled. As we have seen in Chapter 7, by the beginning of her sixth year of the teaching, Eva had developed an excellent rapport with the students. In her third and fourth year of teaching, she referred to her work as the coordinator of S2 and S3 as providing space for her own professional development. Throughout the course of her professional development, Eva seldom accepted things as they were presented to her. As we have seen in the previous section, she asked questions and tried to find her own answers to these questions. Summing up her own development at the end of her fifth year of teaching, she felt that she had come to grips with making use of resources for teaching and having mastered this, she could start making improvement at the microlevel (see 6.3.6).

Compared to Eva, Ching is less positively orientated towards problematization. An example is her handling of classroom discipline. In her third year of teaching, Ching was able to manage the junior classes successfully by exerting her authority, and by laying down rules and norms, which she consistently reinforced throughout the school year. Unlike Marina and Eva, Ching never problematized the classroom discipline that she achieved. As pointed out in Chapter 7, the problem of noise was taken simplistically as an indication of a disciplinary problem. It was never perceived at a more sophisticated level of whether it is on-task noise indicating enthusiastic involvement or off-task noise indicating disruptive misbehavior (see 7.5.3). This perhaps explains why her image of a teacher did not change over time.

The difference between Ching's and Eva's orientation towards problematization can also be seen from their lesson planning. Eva, similar to Marina, would jot down notes, questions, and illustrations to help students understand some vocabulary items. She would visualize the classroom layout for groupings and put them down. She would also go over the lesson plan the night before as well as before the lesson. However, when Ching was pressed for time, she would "think on her feet" (see 8.2.2). This suggests that Ching relied on the routines that she had developed and "what normally works" when she did not have enough time. While Ching was keen to improve on her teaching and to try out new ideas that she learned from the PCEd program, she emphasized that she did not have time to reflect on what worked and what did not, nor did she have time to seek further input from references and resource books. In the end she relied on her own intuition when preparing materials. When the materials did not work in class, she attributed the cause to students not being well-disciplined or not capable of following instructions (see 6.4.3). In other words, lesson planning did not present itself as a problem to Ching. Similarly, the fact that the materials that she tried out did not work in class was perceived by Ching as a problem external to the materials, and this handicapped her capability to reexamine the problem in a different light.

Bereiter and Scardamalia proposed the notion of "progressive problem solving" (1993, p. 81) and argued that experienced practitioners can deal with problems in two ways. They can reduce the number of problems that they need to solve by using well-developed routines to handle them. Alternatively, they can reformulate the problems at a higher level and reinvest their mental resources that are freed up by experience into solving them, or they can problematize the established routines, so that a higher level of performance can be achieved. According to them, the latter distinguishes the expert from the experienced nonexpert and is *critical* to the development of expertise (see 2.3). They further argue that " ... the effect of progressive problem solving is not only to advance in dealing with the complexities already known to exist but also to expand knowledge in ways that bring more complexities to light" (p. 96).

Bereiter and Scardamalia's notion of "progressive problem solving" suggests that a critical feature of expertise is that experts reinvest their mental resources into solving more and more problems, and that the problems that they solve are more and more complex. By contrast, nonexperts solve fewer and fewer problems as they develop routines to handle them. The findings of the case studies suggest that the critical difference between experts and nonexperts is not that the former solve more and more problems because problems often do not present themselves as such. It is their capability to "see" what appears to be unproblematic as problems that distinguishes them from nonexperts. In Marina's case, for example, she problematized what could even be considered an achievement: her class was the best-behaved class. Similarly, the tasks of lesson planning and the preparation of teaching materials, which should have been "unproblematic" to a teacher who has had eight years of teaching experience, were problematized and tackled with a great effort by her. This contrasts strongly with Ching who did not perceive lesson planning and materials preparation as problematic. In other words, it is the capability of experts to *problematize* the unproblematic, to identify and define problems, rather than to solve *problems that they are presented with* that is the critical distinction between experts and nonexperts.[3]

From the above discussion, we can see how misleading it is to say that "automaticity" and "effortlessness" are the characteristics of expertise. This is not to deny that with experience, expert teachers deal with certain aspects of their teaching automatically and effortlessly. However, this does not distinguish them from experienced nonexperts. It is the problematization of what appears to be unproblematic, and the effort and energy that they put into tackling the problem at a higher level of complexity and sophistication, that distinguish them from nonexpert teachers. In the process of doing so, expert teachers extend their knowledge and capability.

10.2.3 *Responding to and looking for challenges*

Closely associated with the orientation to problematization is the disposition to challenges. This encompasses how one *responds* to challenges with which one is confronted and whether one *seeks* challenges. The relationship between this disposition and the development of expertise is that in the process of responding to and taking on challenges, one has to go beyond one's current level of competence by developing new skills and new knowledge. This is what Bereiter and Scardamalia referred to as "working at the edge of competence" (1993, p. 98). A crucial difference between experts and nonexperts, according to them, is that "Experts . . . tackle problems that increase their expertise, whereas nonexperts tend to tackle problems for which they do not have to extend themselves" (ibid., p.78).

Like all teachers, the four ESL teachers were confronted with challenges of a different nature at different stages of their careers. They responded to them differently, however. One of the biggest challenges that was presented to Marina was taking on the role of a panel chair. We have seen in Chapter 6 that when she was assigned the task, she had no idea of what the job involved. Initially, Marina saw the role as an administrator whose main responsibility was to take care of mundane chores. She found herself having to waste a lot of time dealing with personnel problems that she felt were "very complicated" when she would rather spend the time on teaching. Marina responded to the challenge in ways that helped her to gain a more profound understanding of her role instead of simply carrying out the prescribed duties (see 6.2.6).

---

[3] The term *problematization*, unfortunately, has a negative connotation. It does not give a positive impression of the work that experts engage in. In fact, quite the contrary is the case. The process of being able to identify and define problems, and being able to tackle them, is invigorating and gratifying.

An example is the way she responded to the prescribed responsibility of a panel chair in quality assurance. One mechanism that the school had in place was to conduct classroom observations. Initially she was averse to this practice. She did not see it as an effective means of monitoring quality because such observations might not tell her what her teachers' teaching was really like. Though she was subsequently convinced by the History panel chair that classroom observation was a useful mechanism for finding out what her teachers could achieve, her perception of classroom observation was still very much a monitoring mechanism. When she found that there were lessons that needed improvement, instead of tackling it simplistically by suggesting how her teachers could improve, she invited them to observe her own lessons. She also acted as the mediator by asking them to observe other teachers who were trying out interesting ideas. She believed that teachers knew when their teaching did not go well and that it would be much more useful for them to see alternative ways of teaching. Consequently, a mechanism that was originally intended as a monitoring mechanism was reinterpreted by Marina as an opportunity for learning and collegial support.

Another quality assurance mechanism was checking the marking of homework to make sure that teachers were doing their jobs properly and that there was parity in the marking. Initially, Marina played the role as intended by checking if students' mistakes were spotted by her teachers and if the teachers made any mistakes themselves. Subsequently, however, her focus of attention shifted from the teachers' marking to the students' work. Her discussions with her teachers focused on the problems of students' writing and how to help them rather than the problems with their marking. In both cases the reinterpretation of the quality assurance mechanisms in place in her school involved a fundamental change in her conception of her role as a panel chair from an administrator to a facilitator and a mentor.

Apart from *responding* to challenges in professional ways, Marina also constantly *looked for* challenges, moving from smaller to bigger ones. After Marina had assumed the role for a year, she became familiar with the administrative chores. However, the experience she gained did not result in her sitting back and being more relaxed. Quite the contrary, she reinvested her mental resources into ways of better realizing her role. She went beyond the prescribed duties and tackled more-complex problems that had to do with teaching and learning. She started to experiment with changes in the curriculum that involved other teachers as well, starting with small-scale changes. The implementation of process writing was a big challenge for Marina because she had never tried this out with her own students, let alone leading a team of teachers in doing this. There were few resource materials from which she could draw, though there were many research papers written about it. However, Marina's positive orientation to taking on challenges can be seen from her reactions to the lack of resource materials on process writing: "It is precisely because there aren't many [resource] books on writing that I wanted to work on it." Marina was by no means sure how it would affect student learning outcome. She was prepared to take the risk because of the highly unsatisfactory way writing was taught. The challenge to her was twofold: first, the implementation of process writing in the classroom, and second, its implementation by her panel teachers. She started conceptualizing it by reading up references on process writing when she was on the six-month refresher course and also by consulting teachers from other school on the teachers' network, *TeleNex*. During the implementation, she worked closely with Eva and responded to students' needs by building in learner training at important stages in the writing cycle to help learners to provide as well as to respond to feedback. She was also able to encourage students to focus on content without neglecting the importance of accuracy. In helping her teachers to implement it, Marina explored her role as panel chair by trying not to impose her own ideas on them and giving them a sense of ownership. As she gained a better understanding of what process writing involved, the roles played by peer feedback and teacher feedback, and the kind of scaffolding that should be provided, she was better able to provide guidance for her teachers. At the same time, as she talked to her teachers, she gained a better understanding of what was realistically achievable and the autonomy that should be given teachers to decide on the number of drafts that they required students to produce. After implementing process writing, Marina was able to see it from a different perspective. It was no longer merely a technique to help students write better. Rather, it fundamentally transformed the writing classroom into a context of collaborative learning where the teacher was not the only source of knowledge.

In discussing professional expertise, Eraut points out that "it is the ability to cope with difficult, ill-defined problems rather than only routine matters which is often adjudged to be the essence of professional expertise." (1994, p. 152). Bereiter and Scardamalia (ibid.) suggest that when experts take on novel tasks or tasks that they have chosen to treat in a challenging way, they are able to develop abilities that go beyond their current level of competence. The implementation of process writing by Marina well illustrates her development of expertise as precisely this process.

In terms of responding to and looking for challenges, Eva seems to share some common characteristics with Marina. Like Marina, Eva has a strong urge to improve. For example, in her third year of teaching, she felt that with two years of teaching experience behind her, she could start to work on ways of improving her teaching. She chose to work on an area that she dreaded most – grammar teaching. To improve herself, she observed Marina teach and consulted her frequently. Eva also showed Marina her materials to seek comments and advice. When Eva received negative feedback from her students, she lost confidence in herself. However, this did not deter her from seeking improvement. She took new roles assigned to her very seriously and she referred to them as "promotion." This is an interesting metaphor that captured very well her urge to look for opportunities to extend her capabilities. The best example was her request to be "promoted" to teach S4. The biggest challenge to Eva was her lack of academic training in English linguistics, which was a big handicap for playing out her role as an English teacher. It was the source of her diffidence in herself as teacher. She responded to this challenge by forging a role for herself that she was confident of playing out. She used English teaching as a medium for imparting social and moral values and for helping students to learn "how to be a human being." At the same time, she defied the restrictions imposed on her eligibility to teach senior forms because of her inadequate academic training in English by asking to be "promoted" to S4. The satisfaction that she gained from her successful rapport with the students outweighed the frustration that was generated by not having adequate subject knowledge to teach effectively. This sustained her commitment to teaching (see also Rosenholtz, 1989; Bullough et al., 1992). However, seeking the challenge to be "promoted" to S4 did not seem to help Eva attain a higher level of competence and achievement. Instead, it was a demoralizing experience for her because she had difficulties coping with senior students. This seriously undermined her confidence, as can be seen from her evaluation of herself as being "inadequate in everything" at the end of the fifth year of teaching (see 6.3.5). Taking into the consideration the fact that Eva was "promoted" to be coordinator for S3 just the year before and that she was still struggling with her new role, her "promotion" to teach S4 could well be a challenge that required her to work way beyond the edge of her competence. It was in fact remarkable that given the circumstances, she was still able to take on the coordination of S2 for the second time and work on it harder than before. It did not lead to the reassessment of her commitment to teaching.

Ching faced two biggest challenges in her teaching career, both of which occurred in her fourth year of teaching. The first one was having to reconcile her professional role with her role as a wife, and the second one was being assigned to teach preuniversity classes. The former was something that Marina, Eva, and Genie have not had to face, yet. Ching was presented with the moral dilemma of whether she should give more time to her husband or to her students. Her husband, however, reframed the dilemma for her by saying that she has "many students but only one husband." This reframing is typical of the sex-role that is expected of women teachers in most societies. As Belensky, Clinchy, Goldberger, and Tarule (1986) observed, "Conventional sex-role standards establish a routine for settling self-other conflicts when they occur. Men choose the self and women choose others" (p. 46). This proved to be true for Ching. She responded to the pressure of newly wedded life by trying to refrain from exerting herself and spending a lot of time on lesson preparation and her own professional advancement. When she found that new ideas that she received on the PCEd program did not work in her classroom, she realized that she needed time to reflect on the experience and to improve on the tryout. However, she reduced the complexity of the problem by relying on her intuition instead of trying them out again. Such a compromise did not give Ching peace of mind and conflicts with her husband surfaced after periods of conciliation (see Bullough et al., 1992; Pajak and Blasé, 1989). The solution that she contemplated to resolve the conflict was an epitome of her choice of "other": to work in a primary school where there is only half-day teaching or in an educational organization where she would not have to spend the evening and the holidays marking or preparing for classes. In tackling the problem of relating to senior students, which was another source of great frustration, likewise she reduced the complexity of the problem by attributing the cause of the problem to external factors that were out of her control. Such attribution allowed her to disengage herself from the problem. The psychological balance that Ching had lost was probably one of the reasons why she seemed to be unable to progress beyond the phase of self-doubt and reassessment even after five years of teaching.

The difference, therefore, between Eva and Ching was their disposition to challenges. Eva responded positively to challenges by seeing them as opportunities for her to improve herself. She sought to extend her capabilities by seeking further challenges. By contrast, when Ching was faced with difficult problems, she tried to reduce their complexities and by so doing, minimized her opportunities to further develop her capabilities. Despite Eva's positive disposition to challenges, she was not always able to engage in the kind of learning that typifies the development of expertise when one tackles more difficult problems. By contrast, the challenges that Marina took on and responded to were opportunities for her to "work at the edge of her competence" and consequently, she gained new understandings of her professional roles as well as developed new skills and competence in ESL teaching. This suggests that the critical difference between expert and nonexpert teachers lies not only in whether they are able to reinvest their mental resources to achieve a higher level of performance by taking on challenges, but also in whether they are able to exercise their judgement on their current level of competence and the kinds of challenges that they can take on. The ability to exercise this judgement is very important because of the psychological effect that it is likely to produce. Being able to face challenges and benefit from them has an invigorating effect on self-actualization. This is one of the reasons why Huberman (1993b) found that moving from elementary to secondary teaching or from junior to senior secondary is one of the factors that prevented the onset of self-doubt for many teachers. Similarly, other studies have found that taking on new roles such as becoming a mentor teacher can revitalize teachers' careers (see Fessler and Christensen, 1992; Sprinthall et al., 1996). However, repeated failures when taking on challenges can lead to the same demoralization and self-deprecation that we witnessed in Eva. Bereiter and Scardamalia (ibid.) emphasize the importance of reinvesting mental resources not in disparate activities but in the kind of activity in which experts have been engaged. I would argue that in the process of developing expertise, it is equally important to be able to exercise sound judgement on one's current level of competence and the kinds of challenge that one could and should take on.

10.3 Expertise Revisited

10.3.1 Expert performance and development of expertise

In this book, I have tried to answer the questions: What are the *critical* differences between expert and nonexpert teachers? and What are the crucial factors which would contribute to the development of expertise? In outlining the differences, as illuminated by the case studies of four ESL teachers, I examined the theory of expertise proposed by Dreyfus and Dreyfus (1986, 1996) and argued that though their description of expertise does capture some of the important characteristics of the expert teacher in this study, it does not seem to capture the critical differences between the expert and nonexpert teachers. There seems to be a number of differences between the characterization of expertise by Dreyfus and Dreyfus (*ibid.*) and that put forward in the discussion so far.

While Dreyfus and Dreyfus (1986) strongly emphasize that expertise is nonreflective and that engagement in conscious deliberation and reflection is the exception, I argue that reflection and deliberation are characteristic of expertise, as pointed out by Schon (1983) and Eraut (1994). While they maintain that expert knowledge is tacit and expert performance defies explanation, I argue that the theorization of practical knowledge and the "practicalization" of theoretical knowledge are two sides of the same coin in the development of expert knowledge, and that they are both crucial to the development of expertise. Dreyfus and Dreyfus characterize expertise as effortless and automatic, whereas I characterize expertise as constant engagement in exploration and experimentation, in problematizing the unproblematic, and responding to challenges. I further argue that being able to exercise judgement on whether one can benefit from challenges is crucial to the development of expertise.

Why are there such differences? I would like to suggest that there are two reasons. First, the kinds of expertise that Dreyfus and Dreyfus (1986) tried to elucidate are those that involve skills like driving and chess playing, in which experts can perform with intuition and automaticity. However, not all kinds of expertise involve skills like these. As we have seen in the case of Marina, expertise in teaching involves a great deal of effort in problematizing and accomplishing a teaching task that may be accomplished by intuition and automaticity by the nonexpert teacher. Second, even for the kinds of expertise that Dreyfus ad Dreyfus (1986) elucidated, it seems that they were characterizing *expert performance* rather than expertise. They seem to have confused what happens when experts actually engage in performance and how experts are able to attain such a high level of performance. This can be seen from the fact that on the one hand they emphasize the nonreflective, intuitive, and tacit nature of expertise, and on the other hand they recognize the place of conscious deliberation and theory, though relegating them to secondary importance. For example, they concede that conscious deliberation, which enables experts to see things from a different perspective and to consider the relevance and adequacy of past experiences underlying a current intuition, are "useful" (1986, p. 39). Clearly, when they emphasize the nonreflective and intuitive nature of expertise, they are referring to *expert performance*. However, when they are talking about how conscious deliberation can be useful to experts, they are referring to how experts are able to *develop* or *maintain* their expert performance.

It is interesting, and perhaps revealing, that when Dreyfus and Dreyfus (1986) look at the *development of expertise* rather than expert performance, they concede that theory does have an important part to play. In the context of discussing expertise in nursing, they wrote:

... while practice, without theory, cannot alone produce fully skilled behavior in complex coping domains such as nursing, theory without practice has even less chance of success. In short, theory and practice intertwine in a mutually supportive bootstrapping process as the nursing graduate *develops* his or her *skill*. Only if both are cultivated and appreciated can full expertise be realized (p. 30, my emphases).

Bereiter and Scardamalia (1993) argue that the portrayal of experts as being able to perform effortlessly and automatically is a result of comparing the performance of experts and nonexperts on the same task that is very easy for the former. I would like to argue that most of the disagreements regarding what constitutes expertise arise from the lack of distinction between the nature of the skills involved in different kinds of expertise and the confusion between expert performance and the development of expertise. Once these two distinctions are made, the disagreements will largely disappear because, in the process of attaining and maintaining expert performance in all kinds of skills, experts engage in continuous efforts to improve themselves. Once they lose the characteristics outlined in the development of expertise, they cease to perform at an expert level; they cease to be an expert.

10.3.2 Multiple and distributed expertise

In discussions of expertise, including the discussion in this book, we refer to expert doctors, expert nurses, expert teachers, and so forth. This seems to imply that it is possible for a doctor or a teacher to attain a high level of performance in every aspect related to his or her work. However, this is clearly not the case. A teacher may have developed expert skills in ESL instruction but not in other aspects of her work such as guidance and counseling. In Marina's case, when she took on the role of a panel chair, she had no idea how to lead and manage a subject panel. She also had no idea how to provide leadership in curriculum development. She had to gain competence in performing that role. As Dreyfus and Dreyfus (1986) point out, when experts face new situations and tackle new tasks, they behave like novices. Similarly, in terms of establishing relationship with students, we could say that Eva has attained a certain level of expertise. However, in other aspects, such as handling senior form students, she is still very much a novice and is still going through the trauma of the learner's paradox. Nunan's (1988) interesting study of a well-qualified ESL teacher with thirteen years of teaching experience found that when she was assigned to teach a disparate group of mature learners, she felt lost and she described herself as behaving like a beginning teacher.

Dreyfus and Dreyfus (1996), in the context of discussing expertise in nursing, made the following observation: "Expertise ... does not necessarily apply to a whole skill domain, but to at least some significant part of one. There are, perhaps, no expert nurses but certainly many nurses achieve expertise in the area of their specialization." (p. 36). In other words, it is perhaps more meaningful to talk about expertise in areas of specialization rather than to use general terms like expert doctors and expert teachers because they tend to mask the multiple expertise that is required in professions that are as complex as medicine, and professions that are not only complex but also ill-defined, such as teaching.[4]

Closely related to the notion of "multiple expertise" is the notion that expertise is distributed across individuals. Here, I am drawing on

---

[4] I would like to thank Marlene Scardamalia for pointing this out to me when commenting on the case studies reported in this study.

the notion of "distributed" cognition (Lave, 1988) and the social nature of learning (Lave and Wenger, 1991). The accomplishment of a task at an expert level often requires the pooling together of the expertise of a number of individuals. As Benner et al. (1996) point out, "Expertise is both deliberately and informally pooled. Knowledge is produced not by private individual knowers, but in dialog with others with different vantage points and perspectives" (p. 195). Discussions of expertise have so far focused on how experts strive for excellent performance as though it is an individual endeavor. However, the development of expertise in Marina shows that this is not the case. As I have argued in this chapter, the development of teacher knowledge is jointly constituted by the teachers' specific context of work and their interaction with the context (see 10.1.2). One important aspect of this interaction is the interaction with people in their context of work. As Resnick (1991) points out, this kind of interaction goes beyond providing stimulation and encouragement. The discussions in which teachers engage, or the "discourse communities" in which teachers participate, enable them "to appropriate as their own [the ideas, theories, and concepts provided by the discourse communities] to make sense of experiences" (Putnam and Borko, 2000, p. 5; see also Putnam and Borko, 1997). This is very much evident in Marina's development of expertise. She consulted her principal and her colleagues when she came across problems. She discussed classroom observation as a quality assurance mechanism with the History panel chair. She observed the Chinese History teacher teach when she learned that his teaching was outstanding. She also sought advice from teachers on the teacher network, *TeleNex*, when she was planning the implementation of process writing. The PCEd program, the MEd program, and the refresher course that she attended enabled her to participate in the discourse communities of ESL professionals. The theorization of her practical knowledge and the "practicalization" of her theoretical knowledge illustrate precisely the process that is described by Putnam and Borko cited above.

In this respect Eva is similar to Marina. She consults her colleagues frequently. When she was "promoted" to be the coordinator of S3, she consulted her predecessor with the humility of seeing herself as her apprentice. She looked upon Marina as her mentor and worked very closely with her, trying to pick up teaching ideas and strategies from her as much as she could. She consulted Ching when she had problems with linguistics. The lack of opportunity for Eva to participate in the same range of discourse communities as Marina limited Eva's professional development. By contrast, Ching was much more restrained and much less willing to open herself up when she came across problems. This prevented her from maximizing the opportunities to participate in the professional discourse communities when she was attending the PCEd program. It also minimized her opportunities to benefit from the community of practice in which she could articulate her implicit personal theories, and reexamine and reconceptualize her understanding of her work (see Wood and Bennett, 2000).

The revisitation of the notion of expertise suggests that expertise would be better understood if we make a distinction between expert performance and how experts are able to attain expert performance. In understanding the former, it is important to see expertise as "multiple" because the pooling together of expertise is essential to the achievement of the highest level of performance. In understanding the latter, it is important to see expertise as "distributed" because it is only through constant engagement in professional discourse communities that expert knowledge can be developed and maintained.

10.4 Relevance for Teacher Education

Apart from the theoretical contribution that I hope I have made in understanding the notion of expertise, there are several ways in which the case studies reported in this book may be of relevance to teacher education. First, the rich descriptions of the four ESL teachers, who are in different phases of their professional development, may provide insights for teachers in understanding their own professional development. As Shulman (1986) points out, beginning teachers need such cases of practice to develop their full understanding of their work. In particular, the expert teacher's ways of thinking and ways of learning may serve as a reference for both novice and experienced teachers to think about their work as a teacher and how they learn to teach.

This kind of study is also relevant and necessary in the light of the influence of mentor teachers on student-teachers in the teaching practicum. Mentor teachers are skilled in demonstrating what they can do that novice teachers cannot. However, they are often unable to articulate the basis of their expertise and to justify their actions, hence limiting the profound influence that they could have on student-teachers. Case studies of their peers will help them to raise their awareness of their own actions, and help to make their tacit knowledge explicit.

The critical differences between the expert and the nonexpert teachers identified will help teacher educators, mentor teachers, head teachers, and principals to identify emerging characteristics of expertise early on in young teachers so that they can be supported as well challenged at appropriate phases of their professional development to extend their competence. The notions of "multiple expertise" and "distributed expertise" highlight the importance of fostering a culture of collaboration in which expertise can be pooled, and the importance of encouraging teachers to participate in professional discourse communities so that they can learn from each other.

Teacher development has often been equated with attending more refresher courses or having more hours of training. Such training is often conducted by people who have a limited understanding of how teachers develop expertise in teaching. It is hoped that this book will provide food for thought for those of us who are committed to achieving excellence in teaching.

Appendix 1 Reader's Comment Form on First Draft for the Second Writing Task (Angel's First Draft)

Reader's Name: *Karen*
I think this place is ___*7-11*___

1. What part helped you guess the place?
   Circle the information on the writer's composition that helped you most.
2. Write down what your classmate has written about, e.g. people, shops, etc.

He/she can see/hear	Comments
food	*S*
drink	*+*
bus stop	*+*
Some birds singing	*+*
students	*+*
Some trees	*+*
Old men	*+*

3. In the comment box mark the parts you think are:
   (+) good
   (?) difficult to understand
   (!) too easy
   (S) too short
4. Now, suggest how your classmate can improve his or her writing. Put a √ in the brackets and write your ideas.
   ( ) divide your composition into paragraphs
   (√) give more examples on *food shops*
   (√) you can also write about *details, such as building, shops, see . . .*
   ( ) others: _____

Writer's Notes

1. Did your reader guess your mystery location?
   (√) Yes   ( ) No, because _____
2. Do you think your description was:
   ( ) too easy?   (√) too difficult?
   Why? Because *the details is not enough*

Appendix 2 Learner Training in Making Revisions

A. Here is a composition about a robbery. It is not too good because the ideas are not rich enough and there is no excitement in the story. Read the composition and the comments.

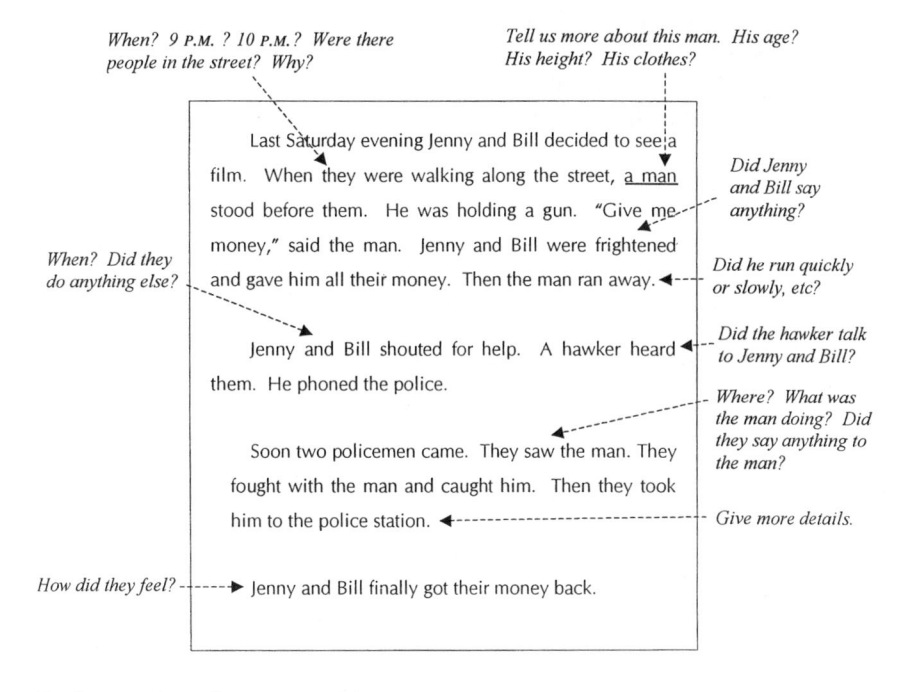

When? 9 P.M. ? 10 P.M.? Were there people in the street? Why?

Tell us more about this man. His age? His height? His clothes?

> Last Saturday evening Jenny and Bill decided to see a film. When they were walking along the street, <u>a man</u> stood before them. He was holding a gun. "Give me money," said the man. Jenny and Bill were frightened and gave him all their money. Then the man ran away.
>
> Jenny and Bill shouted for help. A hawker heard them. He phoned the police.
>
> Soon two policemen came. They saw the man. They fought with the man and caught him. Then they took him to the police station.
>
> Jenny and Bill finally got their money back.

When? Did they do anything else?

Did Jenny and Bill say anything?

Did he run quickly or slowly, etc?

Did the hawker talk to Jenny and Bill?

Where? What was the man doing? Did they say anything to the man?

Give more details.

How did they feel?

B. Improving the composition

We can make the composition better by giving more details and using dialogs. Do the following exercises and find out what can be done.

1. *Giving more details*

   a. "a man stood before them"
      What did the man look [like]? Was he tall or short, fat or thin? Was he strong? How old was he?

285

Now write this sentence again. Think of two adjectives to describe the man, and then describe his age and the clothes he wore.
"a _____ (adj.), _____ (adj) man stood before them. This man was about _____ years old. He was wearing _____."

b. 1. "... a man stood before them."
2. "... a man suddenly jumped out of a dark alley and stood before them."
Which one do you like? Write your reasons down.
I like sentence _____ because _____.

2. Using dialogs

"A hawker heard them. He phoned the police."
What do you think the hawker and Jenny and Bill talked about? Complete the dialog below.
A hawker heard them. " _____?" asked the hawker.
" _____," answered Bill.
" _____," said the Hawker. " _____."

References

Adams, R. (1982). Teacher development: A look at changes in teachers' perceptions across time. *Journal of Teacher Education, 23*(4), 40–43.
Allaei, S. K., & Connor, U. M. (1990). Exploring the dynamics of cross-cultural collaboration in writing classrooms. *The Writing Instructor, 10,* 19–28.
Allwright, R., & Bailey, K. (1991). *Focus on the Language Classroom.* New York: Cambridge University Press.
Anderson, J. (1977). The notion of schemata and the educational enterprise. In R. Anderson, R. Spiro, & W. Montague (Eds.), *Schooling and the Acquisition of Knowledge* (pp. 415–431). Hillsdale NJ: Lawrence Erlbaum.
Anderson, L. M., Evertson, C. M., & Emmer, E. T. (1980). Dimensions in classroom management derived from recent research. *Journal of Curriculum Studies, 12,* 343–56.
Anning, A. (1988). Teachers' theories about children's learning. In J. Calderhead (Ed.), *Teachers' Professional Learning* (pp. 128–145). London: Falmer Press.
Bacon-Shone, J. and Bolton, K. (1998). Charting multilingualism: language censuses and language surveys in Hong Kong. In M. C. Pennington (Ed.), *Language in Hong Kong at Century's End* (pp. 43–90). Hong Kong: Hong Kong University Press.
Ball, D. L. (1991). Research on teaching mathematics: making subject-matter knowledge part of the equation. In J. Brophy (Ed.), *Advances in Research on Teaching* (pp. 1–48.) London: JAI Press.
Ball, D. L., & McDiarmid, G. W. (1990). The subject matter preparation of teachers. In W. R. Houston (Ed.), *Handbook of Research in Education* (pp. 437–449). New York: Macmillan.
Beijaard, D., Verloop, N., & Vermunt, J. D. (2000). Teachers' perceptions of professional identity: an exploratory study from a personal knowledge perspective. *Teaching and Teacher Education,16,* 749–764.
Belensky, J. F., Clinchy, B. M, Goldberger, N. R., & Tarule, J. M. (1986). *Women's Ways of Knowing: The Development of Self, Voice, and Mind.* NY: Basic Books, Inc.
Bell, B., & Gilbert, J. (1994). Teacher development as professional, personal, and social development. *Teaching and Teacher Education, 10*(5), 483–497.
Benner, P. (1984). *From Novice to Expert.* Reading, MA: Addison-Wesley.
Benner, P., Tanner, C. A., & Chesla, C. A. (1996). *Expertise in Nursing Practice: Caring, Clinical Judgment and Ethics.* New York: Springer Publishing Company.

Bennett, N. (1993). Knowledge bases for learning to teach. In N. Bennett & C. Carre (Eds.), *Learning to Teach* (pp. 1–17). London: Routledge.

Bereiter, C., & Scardamalia, M. (1993). *Surpassing Ourselves – An Inquiry into the Nature and Implications of Expertise*. Illinois: Open Court.

Berliner, D. C. (1986). In pursuit of the expert pedagogue. *Educational Researcher, 15*(7), 5–13.

Berliner, D. C. (1992). The nature of expertise in teaching. In F. K. Oser, A. Dick, & J.-L. Patry (Eds.), *Effective and Responsible Teaching: The new synthesis* (pp. 227–248). San Francisco, CA: Jossey-Bass.

Berliner, D. C. (1994). The wonder of exemplary performances. In J. N. Margieri & C. C. Block (Eds.), *Creating Powerful Thinking in Teachers and Students' Diverse Perspectives* (pp. 161–186). Fort Worth, TX: Harcourt Brace College.

Berliner, D. C. (1995). The development of pedagogical expertise. In P. K. Siu & P. T. K. Tam (Eds.), *Quality in Education: Insights from Different Perspectives* (pp. 1–14). Hong Kong: Hong Kong Educational Research Association.

Berliner, D. C., & Carter, K. (1989). Differences in processing classroom information by expert and novice teachers. In J. Lowyck & C. Clark (Eds.), *Teacher Thinking and Professional Action* (pp. 55–74). Louvain: Louvain University Press.

Bloom, B. S. (1954). The thought processes of students in discussion. In S. J. French (Ed.), *Accent on Teaching: Experiments in General Education* (pp. 23–46). New York: Harper Brothers.

Borg, S. (1998). Teachers' Pedagogical Systems and Grammar Teaching: A Qualitative Study. *TESOL Quarterly, 32*(1), 9–37.

Borko, H., & Livingston, C. (1989). Cognition and improvisation: Differences in mathematics instruction by expert and novice teachers. *American Educational Research Journal, 26*(4), 473–498.

Brookhart, S., & Freeman, D. (1992). Characteristics of entering teacher candidates. *Review of Educational Research, 62*, 37–60.

Brophy, J. (1991). Introduction to Volume 2. In J. Brophy (Ed.), *Advances in Research on Teaching* (Vol. 2, pp. ix–xvi). London: JAI Press.

Brophy, J., & Good, T. L. (1986). Teacher behavior and student achievement. In M. C. Wittrock (Ed.), *Handbook of Research on Teaching* (3rd. ed., pp. 328–275). New York: Macmillan.

Brown, S., & McIntyre, D. (1986). How do teachers think about their craft? In M. Ben-Peretz, R. Bromme, & R. Halkes (Eds.), *Advances of Research on Teacher Thinking* (pp. 55–69). Lisse: Swets and Zeitlinger.

Brown, S., & McIntyre, D. (1992). *Making Sense of Teaching*. London: Open University Press.

Buchmann, M. (1984). The priority of knowledge and understanding in teaching. In L. G. Katz & J. D. Raths (Eds.), *Advances in Teacher Education* (Vol. 1, pp. 29–50). Norwood, NJ: Ablex.

Bullough, R. V. (1989). *First Year Teacher: A Case Study*. New York: Teachers College Press.

Bullough, R. V., & Baughman, K. (1993). Continuity and change in teacher development: First year teacher after five years. *Journal of Teacher Education, 44*(2), 86–95.

Bullough, R. V., & Baughman, K. (1995). Changing contexts and expertise in teaching: First year teacher after seven years. *Teaching and Teacher Education, 11*(2), 461–478.

Bullough, R. V., Knowles, J. G., & Crow, N. A. (1992). *Emerging as a Teacher.* London: Routledge.

Burden, P. (1990). Teacher development. In W. R. Houston (Ed.), *Handbook of Research on Teacher Education* (pp. 311–328). New York, Macmillan.

Bygate, M., Tonkyn, A., & Williams, E. (Eds.). (1994). *Grammar and the Language Teacher.* UK: Prenctice Hall.

Calderhead, J. (1984). *Teachers' Classroom Decision-making.* London: Holt, Rinehart and Winston.

Calderhead, J. (1988). The development of knowledge structures in learning to teach. In J. Calderhead (Ed.), *Teachers' Professional Learning* (pp. 51–64). Sussex: Falmer Press.

Calderhead, J. (1993). The contribution of teachers' thinking to professional development. In C. Day, J. Calderhead & P. Denicolo (Eds.), *Research on Teacher Thinking: Understanding Professional Development* (pp. 11–18). London: Falmer Press.

Calderhead, J. (1996). Teachers: Beliefs and knowledge. In D. C. Berliner & R. C. Calfee (Eds.), *Handbook of Educational Psychology* (pp. 709–725). New York: Macmillan.

Calderhead, J., & Miller, E. (1986). *The Integration of Subject Matter Knowledge in Student Teachers' Classroom Practice.* CA: Reed's Limited.

Calderhead, J., & Robson, M. (1991). Images of teaching: Student teachers' early conceptions of classroom practice. *Teaching and Teacher Education, 7*(1), 1–8.

Calderhead, J., & Shorrock, S. (1997). *Understanding Teacher Education.* London: The Falmer Press.

Carlsen, W. S. (1991). Subject matter knowledge and science teaching: A pragmatic perspective. In J. Brophy (Ed.), *Advances in Research on Teaching* (Vol. 2, pp. 115–143). London: JAI Press.

Carter, K. (1990). Teachers' knowledge and learning to teach. In W. R. Houston (Ed.), *Handbook of Research in Education* (pp. 291–310). New York: Macmillan.

Carter, K., Cushing, K., Sabers, D., Stein, P., & Berliner, D. (1988). Expert-novice differences in perceiving and processing visual classroom information. *Journal of Teacher Education, 39*(3), 25–31.

Carter, K., & Doyle, W. (1996). Personal narrative and life history in learning to teach. In J. Sikula, T. Buttery, & E. Guyton (Eds.), *Handbook of Research on Teacher Education* (pp. 120–142). New York: Macmillan.

Carter, K., Sabers, D., Cushing, K., Pinnegar, S., & Berliner, D. (1987). Processing and using information about students: A study of expert, novice, and postulant teachers. *Teaching and Teacher Education, 3,* 147–157.

Chase, W. G., & Simon, H. A. (1973). Perception in chess. *Cognitive Psychology, 4,* 55–81.

Chi, M., Feltovich, P., & Glaser, R. (1981). Categorization and representation of physics problems by experts and novices. *Cognitive Science, 5*(2), 121–152.

Chi, M. T. H., Glaser, R., & Farr, M. (Eds.). (1988). *The Nature of Expertise.* Hillsdale, N.J.: Erlbaum.

Clandinin, D. J. (1986). *Classroom Practice: Teacher Images in Action*. London, Falmer Press.

Clandinin, D. J. (1992). Narrative and story in teacher education. In T. Russell & H. Munby (Eds.), *Teachers and Teaching: From Classroom to Reflection* (pp. 124–137). London: The Falmer Press.

Clandinin, D. J., & Connelly, F. M. (1987). Teachers' personal knowledge: What counts as personal in studies of the personal. *Journal of Curriculum Studies, 19*, 487–500.

Clandinin, D. J., & Connelly, F. M. (1991). Narrative and story in practice and research. In D. Schon (Ed.), *The Reflective Turn: Case Studies in and on Educational Practice* (pp. 258–281). New York: Teachers College Press.

Clark, C. M., & Peterson, P. L. (1986). Teachers' thought processes. In M. C. Wittrock (Ed.), *Handbook of Research on Teaching* (3rd ed., pp. 255–296). New York: Macmillan.

Clark, C. M., & Yinger, R. J. (1979). Teachers' thinking. In P. Peterson & H. J. Walberg (Eds.), *Research on Teaching: Concepts, Findings, and Implications* (pp. 231–263). Berkeley, CA: McCutchan.

Clark, C. M., & Yinger, R. J. (1987). Teacher planning. In J. Calderhead (Ed.), *Exploring Teachers' Thinking* (pp. 84–103). London, Cassell.

Collins Cobuild Grammar of English. (1990). Harper Collins.

Conant, J. (1963). *The Education of American Teachers*. New York: McGraw-Hill.

Connelly, F. M., & Clandinin, D. J. (1985). Personal practical knowledge and the modes of knowledge: Relevance for teaching and learning. In E. Eisner (Ed.), *Learning and Teaching the Ways of Knowing* (Vol. 84th yearbook of the National Society for the Study of Education, Part II., pp. 174–198). Chicago: University of Chicago Press.

Connelly, F. M., & Clandinin, D. J. (1988). *Teachers As Curriculum Planners*. New York: Teachers College Press.

Connelly, F. M., & Clandinin, D. J. (1990). Stories of experience and narrative inquiry. *Educational Researcher, 19*(5), 2–14.

Connelly, F. M., & Clandinin, D. J. (1994). Telling teaching stories. *Teacher Education Quarterly, 21*(1), 145–158.

Connelly, F. M., & Clandinin, D. J. (1995). Teachers' professional knowledge landscapes: Secret, sacred, and cover stories. In F. M. Clandinin & D. J. Connelly (Eds.), *Teachers' Professional Knowledge Landscapes* (pp. 3–15). New York: Teachers College Press.

Copeland, W. D. (1987). Classroom management and student teachers' cognitive abilities: A relationship. *American Educational Research Journal, 24*(2), 219–236.

Copeland, W. D., Birmingham, C., DeMeulle, L., D'Emidio-Caston, M., & Natal, D. (1994). Making meaning in classrooms: An investigation of cognitive processes in aspiring teachers, experienced teachers, and their peers. *American Educational Research Journal, 31*(1), 166–196.

Corno, L. (1981). Cognitive organizing in classrooms. *Curriculum Inquiry, 11*, 359–377.

deGroot, A. D. (1965). *Thought and Choice in Chess*. The Hague: Mouton.

Desforges, C., & McNamara, D. (1979). Theory and practice: Methodological procedures for the objectification of craft knowledge. *British Journal of Teacher Education, 5*(2), 139–152.

Dewey, J. (1902). The child and the curriculum. In J. A. Boydston (Ed.), *John Dewey: The Middle Works, 1899–1924, Volume 2: 1902–1903* (pp. 273–291). Carbondale, IL: South Illinois University Press.

Dewey, J. (1938). *Logic: The Theory of Inquiry*. New York: Henry Holt and Co.

Doyle, W. (1977). Learning the classroom environment: An ecological analysis. *Journal of Teacher Education, 28,* 51–55.

Doyle, W. (1979). Making managerial decisions in classrooms. In D. L. Duke (Ed.), *Classroom Management* (pp. 42–74). Chicago: University of Chicago Press.

Doyle, W. (1986). Classroom organization and management. In M. C. Wittrock (Ed.), *Handbook of Research on Teaching* (3rd. ed., pp. 392–425). New York: Macmillan.

Dreyfus, H. (1972). *What Computers Can't Do: A Critique of Artifical Reason*. New York: Harper & Row.

Dreyfus, H. (1997). Models of expert performance. In C. E. Zsambok & G. Klein (Eds.), *Naturalistic Decision Making* (pp. 17–28). New Jersey, Lawrence Erlbaum.

Dreyfus, H. L., & Dreyfus, S. E. (1980). *A five-stage model of the mental activities involved in directed skill acquisition.* Unpublished report supported by the Air Force Office of Scientific Research (AFSC), USAF, University of California at Berkley.

Dreyfus, H. L., & Dreyfus, S. E. (1986). *Mind Over Machine*. New York: Free Press.

Dreyfus, H. L., & S. E. Dreyfus (1996). The relationship of theory and practice in the acquisition of skill. In P. Benner, C. A. Tanner, & C. A. Chesla (Eds.), *Expertise in Nursing Practice* (pp. 29–48). New York: Springer Publishing Company.

Dunkin, M. J., & Biddle, B. J. (1974). *The Study of Teaching*. New York: Holt, Reinhart and Winston.

Elbaz, F. (1981). The teacher's "practical knowledge:" Report of a case study. *Curriculum Inquiry, 11*(1), 43–71.

Elbaz, F. (1983). *Teacher Thinking: A Study of Practical Knowledge*. London: Croom Helm.

Elbaz, F. (1991). Research on teachers' knowledge: The evolution of a discourse. *Journal of Curriculum Studies, 23,* 1–19.

Ellis, R. (1998). "Teaching and research: Options in grammar teaching." *TESOL Quarterly, 32*(1), 39–60.

Eraut, M. (1994). *Developing Professional Knowledge and Competence*. London: The Falmer Press.

Erickson, G. L., & MacKinnon, A. M. (1991). Seeing classrooms in new ways: On becoming a science teacher. In D. A. Schon (Ed.), *The Reflective Turn* (pp. 15–36). New York: Teachers College Press.

Ericsson, K. A., & Smith, J. (1991). Prospects and limits of the empirical study of expertise: An introduction. In K. A. Ericsson & J. Smith (Eds.), *Towards a General Theory of Expertise: Prospects and Limits* (pp. 1–38). New York: Cambridge University Press.

Field, K. (1979). *Teacher Development: A Study of the Stages in the Development of Teachers*. Brookline, MA: Teacher Center Brookline.

Feiman-Nemser, S. (1983). Learning to teach. In L. Shulman & G. Sykes (Eds.), *Handbook of Teaching and Policy* (pp. 150–70). New York: Longman.

Feiman-Nemser, S., & Buchmann, M. (1986). The first year of teacher preparation: Transition to pedagogical thinking. *Journal of Curriculum Studies,* 18(239–256.).
Feiman-Nemser, S., & Floden, R. E. (1986). Cultures of Teaching. In M. Wittrock (Ed.), *Handbook of Research on Teaching* (3rd ed., pp. 505–526). New York: Macmillan.
Feiman-Nemser, S., & Parker, M. B. (1990). Making subject matter part of the conversation in learning to teach. *Journal of Teacher Education, 41*(3), 32–43.
Fenstermacher, G. D. (1994). The knower and the known: The nature of knowledge in the research on teaching. In L. Darling-Hammond (Ed.), *Review of Research in Education* (pp. 3–56). Washington D. C.: AERA.
Fessler, R., & Christensen, J. (1992). *The Teacher Career Cycle: Understanding and Guiding the Professional Development of Teachers.* Boston: Allyn and Bacon.
Field, K. (1979). *A Study of the Stages in the Development of Teachers.* Brookline, MA: Teacher Center Brookline.
Fogarty, J. L., Wang, M. C., & Creek, R. (1983). A descriptive study of experienced and novice teachers' interactive instructional thoughts and actions. *Journal of Educational Research, 77*(1), 22–32.
Freeman, D. (1991). 'To make the tacit explicit': Teacher education, emerging discourse, and conceptions of teaching. *Teaching and Teacher Education, 7,* 5/6, 439–454.
Freeman, D. (2000). Imported Theories/Local Understandings. Plenary address at the 34th Annual TESOL Convention in Vancouver, March 2000. In *TESOL Matters,* 10.4, (pp. 1, 5).
Freeman, D., & J. C. Richards (Eds.), (1996). *Teacher Learning in Language Teaching.* New York: Cambridge University Press.
Fuller, F. (1969). "Concerns of Teachers: A development perspective." *American Education Research Journal, 6,* 207–26.
Fuller, F., & Brown, O. (1975). Becoming a teacher. In K. Ryan (Ed.), *Teacher Education* (pp. 25–52). Chicago: University of Chicago Press.
Gairns, R., & Redman, S. (1986). *Working with Words: A Guide to Teaching and Learning Vocabulary.* Cambridge: Cambridge University Press.
Glaser, R. (1990). Expertise. In M. W. Eysenk, A. N. Ellis, E. Hunt, & P. Johnson-Laird (Eds.), *The Blackwell Dictionary of Cognitive Psychology* (pp. 139–142). Oxford: Blackwell.
Glaser, R., & Chi, M. T. H. (1988). Overview. In M. T. H. Chi, R. Glaser, & M. Farr (Eds.), *The Nature of Expertise* (pp. xv–xxxvi). Hillsdale, NJ: Erlbaum.
Glazer, N. (1974). Schools of the minor professions. *Minerva* (pp. 346–364).
Goffman, E. (1971). *Relations in Public.* New York: Harper & Row.
Goodlad, J. I., Soder, R., & Sirotnik, K. A. (Eds.). (1990). *The Moral Dimension of Teaching.* San Francisco, CA: Jossey-Bass.
Goodson, I. (1991). Teachers' lives and educational research. In I. F. Goodson, & R. Walker (Eds.), *Biography, Identity and Schooling: Episodes in Educational Research* (pp. 135–152). Dordrecht: Kluwer. London: Falmer Press.
Goodson, I. (1992a). Studying teachers' lives: An emergent field of inquiry. In I. Goodson (Ed.), *Studying Teachers' Lives* (pp. 1–17). London: Routledge.
Goodson, I. (Ed.), (1992b). *Studying Teachers' Lives.* London: Routledge.

Grant, G. E. (1992). "The sources of structural metaphors in teacher knowledge: Three cases." *Teaching and Teacher Education, 8*, 5/6, 433–440.
Grimmett, P. P., MacKinnon, A. M., Erickson, G. I., & Riecken, T. J. (1990). Reflective practice in teacher education. In R. T. Clift, W. R. Houston, & M. C. Pugach (Eds.), *Encouraging Reflective Practice in Education: An Analysis of Issues and Programs* (pp. 20–38). New York, Teachers' College Press.
Grossman, P. (1987). *A Passion for Language: A Case Study of Colleen, a Beginning Teacher*. (Knowledge Growth in a Profession Publication Series). Stanford, CA: Stanford University, School of Education.
Grossman, P. (1990). *The Making of a Teacher*. New York: Teachers College Press.
Grossman, P., & Richert, A. E. (1988). Unacknowledged knowledge growth: A reexamination of the effects of teacher education. *Teaching and Teacher Education, 4*(1), 53–62.
Grossman, P., Wilson, S., & Shulman, L. (1989). Teachers of substance: Subject matter knowledge for teaching. In M. Reynolds (Ed.), *Knowledge Base for the Beginning Teacher* (pp. 23–36). New York: Pergamon.
Gudmundsdottir, S., & Shulman, L. S. (1989). Pedagogical knowledge in social studies. In J. Lowyck & C. M. Clark (Eds.), *Teacher Thinking and Professional Action* (pp. 23–34). Leuven: Leuven University Press.
Harris, J. (1994). *Introducing Writing*. London: Penguin.
Hashweh, M. (1987). Effects of subject matter knowledge in the teaching of biology and physics. *Teaching and Teacher Education, 3*, 109–120.
Hillocks, G. J. (1999). *Ways of Thinking, Ways of Teaching*. New York, Teachers College Press.
Housner, L. D., & Griffey, D. C. (1985). Teacher cognition: Differences in planning and interactive decision-making between experienced and inexperienced teachers. *Research Quarterly for Exercise and Sport, 56*, 45–53.
Huberman, M. (1993a). *The Lives of Teachers*. New York: Teachers College Press.
Huberman, M. (1993b). Steps towards a developmental model of the teaching career. In L. Kremer-Hayon, H. Vonk & R. Fessler (Eds.), *Teacher Professional Development: A Multiple Perspective Approach* (pp. 93–118). Amsterdam: Swets and Zeitlinger.
Jackson, P. W. (1968). *Life in Classrooms*. New York: Holt, Rinehart, and Winston.
James, C., & Garett, P. (Eds.), (1991). *Language Awareness in the Classroom*, London: Longman.
Johnson, K. (1994). The emerging beliefs and instructional practices of preservice English as a second language teachers. *Teaching and Teacher Education, 10*(4), 439–452.
Johnston, S. (1990). "Understanding curriculum decision-making through teacher images." *Journal of Curriculum Studies, 22*(5), 463–471.
Johnston, S. (1992). "Images: A way of understanding the practical knowledge of student teachers." *Teaching and Teacher Education, 8*(2), 123–136.
Kagan, D. (1990). Ways of evaluating teacher cognition: Inferences concerning the Goldilocks priniciple. *Review of Educational Research, 60*(3), 419–469.

Kagan, D. M., & Tippins, D. J. (1992). The evolution of functional lesson plans among twelve elementary and secondary student teachers. *The Elementary School Journal, 92,* 477–489.
Katz, L. G. (1972). Developmental stages of preschool teachers. *Elementary School Journal, 73*(1), 50–54.
Kounin, J. S. (1970). *Discipline and Group Management in Classrooms.* New York: Holt, Rinehart, and Winston.
Krashen, S. (1982). *Principles and Practice in Second Language Acquisition.* Oxford: Pergamon.
Kutz, E., Groden, S., & Zamel, V. (1993). *The Discovery of Competence.* Portsmouth, NH: Boynton/Cook.
Lakoff, G., & Johnson, M. (1980). *Metaphors We Live By.* Chicago: University of Chicago Press.
Lampert, M. (1985). How do teachers manage to teach? Perspectives on problems in practice. *Harvard Educational Review, 55,* 178–184.
Lanier, J. E., & Little, J. W. (1986). Research on teacher education. In M. C. Wittrock (Ed.), *Handbook of Research on Teaching* (pp. 527–569). New York: Macmillan.
Lantz, O., & Kass, H. (1987). Chemistry teachers' functional paradigms. *Science Education, 71,* 117–134.
Lave, J. (1988). *Cognition in Practice.* Cambridge: Cambridge University Press.
Lave, J. (1993). The practice of learning. In Chaiklin, S., & Lave, J. (Eds.) *Understanding practice: Perspectives on activity and context* (pp. 3–32). Cambridge: Cambridge University Press.
Lave, J., Murtaugh, M., & de la Rocha, O. (1984). The dialectic of arithmetic in grocery shopping. In B. Rogoff & J. Lave (Eds.), *Everyday cognition: Its Development in Social Context* (pp. 67–94). Cambridge, MA: Harvard University Press.
Lave, J., & Wenger, E. (1991). *Situated Learning: Legitimate Peripheral Participation.* Cambridge: Cambridge University Press.
Lehrer, K. (1990). *Theory of Knowledge.* Boulder, CO: Westview Press.
Leinhardt, G. (1988). Situated knowledge and expertise in teaching. In J. Calderhead (Ed.), *Teachers' Professional Learning* (pp. 146–168). London: Falmer Press.
Leinhardt, G. (1989). A contrast of novice and expert competence in mathematics lessons. In J. Lowyck & C. M. Clark (Eds.), *Teacher Thinking and Professional Action* (pp. 75–98). Leuven: Leuven University Press.
Leinhardt, G. (1990). Capturing craft knowledge in teaching. *Educational Researcher, 19*(2), 18–25.
Leinhardt, G., & Greeno, J. G. (1986). The cognitive skill of teaching. *Journal of Educational Psychology, 78,* 75–95.
Leinhardt, G., Putnam, R. T., Stein, M. K., & Baxter, J. (1991). Where subject knowledge matters. In J. Brophy (Ed.), *Advances in Research on Teaching, 2* (pp. 87–114). London: JAI Press.
Leinhardt, G., & Smith, D. A. (1985). Expertise in mathematics instruction: Subject matter knowledge. *Journal of Educational Psychology, 77*(3), 247–271.
Leki, I. (1990). Potential problems with peer responding in ESL writing classes. *CATESOL Journal, 3,* 5–17.

Li, J. (1991). Getting students to write stories for children – A project in process writing. *Curriculum Forum, 1*(3), 1–17.

Lightbown, P., & Spada, N. (1990). "Focus-on-form and corrective feedback in communicative language teaching: Effects on second language learning." *Studies in Second Language Acquisition, 12*(4), 429–48.

Lightfoot, S. (1983). The lives of teachers. In L. Shulman & G. Stykes (Eds.), *Handbook of Teaching and Policy* (pp. 241–260). New York: Longman.

Hillocks, G., Jr. (1999). *Ways of Thinking and Ways of Teaching*. New York: Teachers College Press.

Livingston, C., & Borko, H. (1989). Expert-novice differences in teaching: A cognitive analysis and implications for teacher education. *Journal of Teacher Education, 40*(4), 36–42.

Lortie, D. (1975). *Schoolteacher*. Chicago: University of Chicago Press.

Lyons, N. (1990). Dilemmas of knowing: Ethical and epistemological dimesnions of teachers' work and development. *Harvard Educational Review, 60*, 2, 159–80.

Marland, P. W. (1977). *A Study of Teachers' Interactive Thoughts*. Unpublished Ph.D., University of Alberta, Edmonton, Canada.

Marton, F. (1994). On the structure of teachers' awareness. In I. Carlgren, G. Handal, & S. Vaage (Eds.), *Teachers' Minds and Actions: Research on Teachers' Thinking and Practice* (pp. 28–42). London: Falmer Press.

Mcleod, M. A. (1981). *The Identification of Intended Learning Outcomes by Early Childhood Teachers: An Exploratory Study*. Unpublished Ph.D., University of Alberta, Edmonton, Canada.

McCutcheon, G. (1980). How do elementary school teachers plan? The nature of planning and influences on it. *The Elementary School Journal, 81*, 4–23.

McDiarmid, G. W., Ball, D., & Anderson, C. W. (1989). Why staying one chapter ahead doesn't really work: subject specific pedagogy. In M. Reynold (Ed.), *The Knowledge-base for Beginning Teachers* (pp. 193–206). Tarrytown, NY: Pergamon.

McNamara, D. R. (1991). Subject knowledge and its applications: problems and possibilities for teacher educators. *Journal of Teacher Education, 42*(4), 243–249.

Miles, M. B., & Huberman, A. M. (1994). *Qualitative Data Analysis: An Expanded Sourcebook* (2nd ed.). Thousand Oaks, CA: Sage.

Morine, G., & Vallance, E. (1975). *Special Study B: A Study of Teacher and Pupil Perceptions of Classroom Interaction* (Tech. Report No. 75-11-6). San Francisco, CA: Far West Laboratory.

Morine-Dershimer, G. (1979). Planning and classroom reality: An in-depth look. *Educational Research Quarterly, 3*(4), 83–99.

Munby, H., & Russell, T. (1991). Transforming chemistry research into chemistry teaching: The complexities of adopting new frames for experience. In T. Russell & H. Munby (Eds.), *Teachers and Teaching: From Classroom to Reflection* (pp. 90–108). London: The Falmer Press.

Neale, D. C., Pace, A. J., & Case, A. B. (1983, April). *The Influence of Training, Experience, and Organizational Environment on Teachers' Use of the Systematic Planning Model*. Paper presented at the Annual meeting of the American Educational Research Association., Montreal.

Nespor, J. (1987). The role of beliefs in the practice of teaching. *Journal of Curriculum Studies, 19*(4), 317–328.

Newall, A. (1963). The chess machine. In K. M. Sayre & F. J. Crosson (Eds.), *The Modeling of Mind* (pp. 73–89). South Bend, IN: Notre Dame University Press.

Newell, A., Shaw, J. C., & Simon, H. A. (1963). Chess-playing programs and the problem of complexity. In E. A. Feigenbaum & J. Feldman (Eds.), *Computers and Thought* (pp. 39–70). New York: McGraw-Hill.

Newell, A., & Simon, H. A. (1972). *Human Problem Solving*. Englewood Cliffs, NJ: Prentice Hall.

Nias, J. (1984). The definition and maintenance of self in primary schools. *British Journal of Sociology of Education, 5*(3), 267–280.

Noice, T., & Noice, H. (1997). *The Nature of Expertise in Professional Acting: A Cognitive View*. New Jersey: Lawrence Erlbaum.

Nunan, D. (1988). *The Learner-Centred Curriculum*. New York: Cambridge University Press.

Nunan, D. (1992). The teacher as decision-maker. In J. Flowerdew & M. Brock (Eds.), *Perspectives on Second Language Teacher Education* (pp. 135–165). Hong Kong: City University of Hong Kong.

O'Malley, J. M., & Chamot, A. U. (1990). *Learning Strategies in Second Language Acquisition*. Cambridge: Cambridge University Press.

Olson, J. (1992). *Understanding Teaching: Beyond Expertise*. Milton Keynes: Open University Press.

Pajak, E., & Blase, J. J. (1989). The impact of teachers' personal lives on professional role enactment: A qualitative analysis. *American Educational Research Journal, 26*(2), 283–310.

Pajares, M. F. (1992). Teachers' beliefs and educational research: cleaning up a messy construct. *Review of Educational Research, 62*(3), 307–332.

Patton, M. Q. (1990). *Qualitative evaluation and research methods*. (2nd ed.) Newbury Park, CA: Sage.

Peterson, P. L., & Clark, C. M. (1978). Teachers' reports of their cognitive processes during teaching. *American Educational Research Journal, 15*, 555–565.

Peterson, P. L., & Comeaux, M. A. (1987). Teachers' schemata for classroom events: The mental scaffolding of teachers' thinking during classroom instruction. *Teaching and Teacher Education, 3*, 319–331.

Peterson, P. L., Marx, R. W., & Clark, C. M. (1978). Teachers' planning, teacher behavior, and student achievement. *American Educational Research Journal, 15*, 417–432.

Polanyi, M. (1966). *The Tacit Dimension*. Reprinted by Garden City, NJ: Doubleday, 1983.

Powell, R. P. (1992). The influence of prior experiences on pedagogical constructs of traditional and nontraditional preservice teachers. *Teaching and Teacher Education, 6*(3), 225–238.

Prick, L. (1986). *Career Development and Satisfaction Among Secondary School Teachers*. Amsterdam: Vrije Universiteit Amsterdam.

Putnam, R. T., & Borko, H. (1997). Teacher learning: Implications of new views of cognition. In B. J. Biddle, Good, T. L., & Goodson, I. F. (Eds.), *International Handbook of Teachers and Teaching, Vol. II.* (pp. 1223–1296). Netherlands: Kluwer.

Putnam, R. T., & Borko, H. (2000). "What do new views of knowledge and thinking have to say about research on teacher learning?" *Educational Researcher,* 29(1, January–February), 4–16.
Raymond, D., Butt, R., & Townsend, D. (1992). Contexts for teacher development: Insights from teachers' stories. In A. Hargreaves & M. Fullan (Eds.), *Understanding Teacher Development* (pp. 143–161). London: Cassell.
Resnick, L. B. (1991). Shared cognition: Thinking as social practice. In L. B. Resnick, J. M. Levine, & S. D. Teasely (Eds.), *Perspectives on Socially Shared Cognition* (pp. 1–20). Washington, D. C.: American Psychological Association.
Reynolds, A. (1992). What is competent beginning teaching? A review of the literature. *Review of Educational Research,* 62(1), 1–35.
Reynolds, J. A., Haymore, J., Ringstaff, C., & Grossman, P. (1988). Teachers and curriculum materials: Who is driving whom? *Curriculum Perspectives,* 8(1), 22–30.
Richards, J. C., Li, B., & Tang, A. (1995). "A comparison of pedagogical reasoning skills in novice and experienced ESL teachers." *RELC,* 26(2), 1–24.
Richards, J. C., & Lockhart, C. (1994). *Reflective Teaching in Second Language Classrooms.* New York: Cambridge University Press.
Richards, J. C., and Nunan, C. (Eds.). (1990). *Second Language Teacher Education.* Cambridge: Cambridge University Press.
Richardson, V. (1994). The consideration of teachers' beliefs. In V. Richardson (Ed.), *Teacher Change and the Staff Development Process: A Case in Reading Instruction* (pp. 90–108). New York: Teachers College Press.
Richardson, V. (1996). The role of attitudes and beliefs in learning to teach. In J. Sikula, T. J. Buttery, & E. Guyton (Eds.), *Handbook of Research on Teacher Education* (pp. 102–119). New York: Macmillan.
Rosenholtz, S. J. (1989). Workplace conditions that affect teacher quality and commitment: Implications for teacher induction programs. *The Elementary School Journal,* 89(4), 421–39.
Rossman, G. B., & Rallis, S. (1998). *Learning in the Field.* Thousand Oaks, CA: Sage.
Rumelhart, D. E. (1980). The building blocks of cognition. In R. J. Spiro, B. C. Bruce, & W. F. Brewer (Eds.), *Theoretical Issues in Reading Comprehension: Perspectives from Cognitive Psychology, Linguistics, Artificial Intelligence, and Education* (pp. 33–58). Hillsdale, NJ: Lawrence Erlbaum.
Russell, T., & Munby, H. (1991). Reframing: The role of experience in developing teachers' professional knowledge. In D. A. Schon (Ed.), *The Reflective Turn: Case Studies in and on Educational Practice* (pp. 164–187). New York: Teachers' College Press.
Rutherford, W. (1987). *Second Language Grammar: Learning and Teaching.* London: Longman.
Ryle, G. (1949). *The Concept of Mind.* London: Hutchinson.
Sabar, N. (1994). Ethical concerns in teacher-thinking research. In I. Carlgren, G. Handal, & S. Vaage (Eds.), *Teachers' Minds and Actions: Research on Teachers' Thinking and Practice* (pp. 109–124). London: Falmer Press.
Sabers, D. S., Cushing, K. S., & Berliner, D. (1991). Differences among teachers in a task characterized by simultaneity, multidimensionality, and immediacy. *American Educational Research Journal,* 28, 63–88.

Sadro-Brown, D. (1990). 'Experienced teachers' planning practices: A US survey. *Journal of Education for Teaching, 16*, 57–71.

Sardo, D. (1982, October). *Teacher Planning Styles in the Middle School*. Paper presented at the Annual meeting of the American Educational Research Association. Ellenville, NY.

Schein, E. (1973). *Professional Education*. New York: McGraw-Hill.

Schmidt, R. (1994). Deconstructing consciousness in search of useful definitions for applied linguistics. *AILA Review, 11*, 11–26.

Schon, D. A. (1979). Generative metaphor: A perspective on probelm-solving in social policy. In A. Ortony (Ed.), *Metaphor and Thought* (pp. 254–283). New York, Cambridge University Press.

Schon, D. A. (1983). *The Reflective Practitioner*. London: Basic Books.

Schon, D. A. (1987). *Educating the Reflective Practitioner*. San Francisco, CA: Jossey-Bass.

Schram, P., Feiman-Nemser, S., & Ball, D. L. (1989). *Think About Teaching Subtraction with Regrouping: A Comparison of Beginning and Experienced Teachers' Responses to Textbooks* (89–5). E. Lansing, MI: National Center for Research on Teacher Education.

Schutz, A. (1962–73). *Collected Papers Vols. I–III*, The Hague: Martinus Nijhoff, 1962–73.

Schutz, A., & Luckman, T. (1974). *The Structures of the Life-World*. London: Heinemann.

Schwab, J. J. (1964). The structure of disciplines: Meanings and significance. In G. W. Ford & L. Pugno (Eds.), *The Structure of Knowledge and the Curriculum*. Chicago: Rand McNally.

Schwab, J. J. (1969). The Practical: A language for curriculum. *School Review, 78*, 1–23.

Scribner, S. (1984). Studying working intelligence. In B. Rogoff & J. Lave (Eds.), *Everyday Cognition: Its Development in Social Context* (pp. 9–40). Cambridge, MA: Harvard University Press.

Sengupta, S. (1996). *A study of the influences of systematic teaching of revision on L2 learners in a secondary school in Hong Kong*. Unpublished PhD Thesis, Department of Curriculum Studies, University of Hong Kong, pp. 385.

Shavelson, R. J., & Stern, P. (1981). Research on teachers' pedagogical thoughts, judgments, decisions, and behavior. *Review of Educational Research, 51*(4), 455–498.

Shulman, L. (1986). Those who understand knowledge growth in teaching. *Educational Researcher, 15*(2), 4–14.

Shulman, L. (1987). Knowledge and teaching: Foundations of the new reform. *Harvard Educational Review, 57*(1), 1–22.

Shulman, L. (1988). The dangers of dichotomous thinking in education. In P. Grimmet, & G. Erickson (Eds.), *Reflections on Teacher Education* (pp. 31–39). New York, Teachers College Press.

Shulman, L. (1992). Research on teaching: A historical and personal perspective. In F. K. Oser, A. Dick, & J.-L. Patry (Eds.), *Effective and Responsible Teaching* (pp. 14–29). San Francisco CA: Jossey-Bass.

Sikes, P. J., Measor, L., & Woods, P. (1985). *Teacher careers: Crises and continuities*. London: Falmer Press.

Silva, T. (1990). Second language composition instruction: Developments, issues and directions in ESL. In B. Kroll (Ed.), *Second Language Writing: Research Insights for the Classroom* (pp. 11–23). Cambridge: Cambridge University Press.

Simon, H. A., & Chase, W. G. (1973). Skill in chess. *American Scientist, 61,* 394–403.

Sloboda, J. (1991). Musical expertise. In K. A. Ericsson & Smith, J. (Eds.), *Towards a General Theory of Expertise* (pp. 153–171). Cambridge, MA: Cambridge University Press.

Smith, L. M., & Geoffrey, W. (1968). *The Complexities of the Urban Classroom.* New York: Holt, Rinehart and Winston.

Smith, D. C., & Neale, D. C. (1989). The construction of subject matter knowledge in primary science teaching. *Teaching and Teacher Education, 5*(1), 1–20.

Snow, R. E. (1972). *A Model Teacher Training System: An Overview.* (Research and Development Memorandum Ed 066 437). Stanford, California: Stanford Center for Research and Development in Teaching.

Solso, R. L., & Dallop, P. (1995). Prototype formation among professional dancers. *Empirical Studies of the Arts, 13*(1), 3–16.

Spada, N., & P. Lightbown (1993). Instruction and the development of questions in L2 classrooms. *Studies in Second Language Acquisition, 15,* 205–24.

Sprinthall, N. A., Reiman, A. J., & Sprinthall, L. T. (1996). Teacher professional development. In J. Sikula, T. Buttery, & E. Guyton (Eds.), *Handbook of Research on Teacher Education* (pp. 666–703). New York, Macmillan.

Stanley, J. (1992). Coaching student writers to be effective peer evaluators. *Journal of Second Language Writing, 1*(3), 217–233.

Stein, M. K., Baxter, J. A., & Leinhardt, G. (1990). Subject-matter knowledge and elementary instruction: A case from functions and graphing. *American Educational Research Journal, 27*(4), 639–663.

Stenhouse, L. (1975). *An Introduction to Curriculum Research and Development.* London: Heineman.

Swanson, H. L., O'Connor, J. E., & Cooney, J. B. (1990). An information processing analysis of expert and novice teachers' problem solving. *American Educational Research Journal, 27*(3), 533–556.

Synder, J., Bolin, F., & Zumwait, K. (1992). Curriculum implementation. In P. Jackson (Ed.), *Handbook of Research on Curriculum* (pp. 402–435). New York: Macmillan.

Tanaka, Y. (1996). *The comprehension and acquisition of relative clauses by Japanese high school students through formal instruction.* Unpublished doctoral dissertation. Temple University, Japan, Tokyo.

Taylor, P. H. (1970). *How Teachers Plan Their Courses.* London: National Foundation of Educational Research.

Tripp, D. (1994). Teachers' lives, critical incidents, and professional practice. *International Journal of Qualitative Studies in Education, 7*(1), 65–76.

Tsui, A. B. M. (1996). Learning how to teach ESL writing. In D. Freeman, & J. Richards (Eds.), *Teacher Learning in Language Teaching* (pp. 97–120). New York: Cambridge University Press.

Tsui, A. B. M., & Nicholson, S. (1999). Hypermedia database and ESL teacher knowledge enrichment. *Journal of Information Technology for Teacher Education, 8*(2), 215–237.

Tsui, A. B. M., & Bunton, D. (2000). Discourse and attitudes of English teachers in Hong Kong. *World Englishes, 19*(3), 287–304.

Tsui, A. B. M., & Ng, M. (2000). Do secondary L2 writers benefit from peer comments? *Journal of Second Language Writing, 9*(2), 147–170.

Tyler, R. W. (1950). *Basic Principles of Curriculum and Instruction.* Chicago: Chicago University Press.

Van Patten, B., & Oikkenon, S. (1996). Explanation versus structured input in processing instruction. *Studies in Second Language Acquisition, 18,* 495–510.

Veenman, S. (1984). Perceived problems of beginning teachers. *Review of Educational Research, 54*(2), 143–178.

Welker, R. (1991). Expertise and the teacher as expert: Rethinking a questionable metaphor. *American Educational Research Journal, 28,* 19–35.

Westerman, D. A. (1991). Expert and novice teacher decision making. *Journal of Teacher Education, 42*(4), 292–305.

White, R., & Arndt, V. (1991). *Process Writing.* London: Longman.

Willis, J. (1981). *Teaching English through English.* London: Longman.

Wilson, S., & Wineburg, S. (1988). Peering at history through different lenses: The role of disciplinary perspectives in teaching history. *Teachers College Record, 89*(4), 525–539.

Wilson, S. M., Shulman, L. S., & Richert, A. E. (1987). 150 different ways of knowing: Representations of knowledge in teaching. In J. Calderhead (Ed.), *Exploring Teacher Thinking* (pp. 104–124). London: Cassell.

Wineburg, S. S., & Wilson, S. M. (1991). Subject-matter knowledge in the teaching of history. In J. Brophy (Ed.), *Advances in Research on Teaching. Vol. 2* (pp. 305–348). London: JAI Press.

Wodlinger, M. G. (1980). *A Study of Teacher Interactive Decision Making.* Unpublished Ph.D thesis. University of Alberta, Edmonton, Canada.

Wolcott, H. F. (1992). Posturing in qualitative inquiry. In M. D. Le Compte, W. L. Millroy, and J. Preissle (Eds.), *The Handbook of Qualitative Research in Education* (pp. 3–52). New York: Academic Press.

Wood, E., & Bennett, N. (2000). Changing theories, changing practice: Exploring early childhood teachers' professional learning. *Teaching and Teacher Education, 16,* 635–647.

Woods, D. (1996). *Teacher Cognition in Language Teaching.* New York: Cambridge University Press.

Woods, P. (1985). Conversations with teachers: Some aspects of the life history method. *British Educational Research Journal, 2*(1), 13–26.

Yin, R. K. (1994). *Case Study Research: Design and Methods.* Second Edition, Beverly Hills, CA, Sage Publications.

Yinger, R. J. (1979). Routines in teacher planning. *Theory into Practice, 18,* 163–169.

Yinger, R. J. (1980). A study of teacher planning. *The Elementary School Journal, 80,* 107–127.

Yinger, R. (1986). Examining thought in action: A theoretical and methodological critique of research on interactive teaching. *Teaching and Teacher Education, 2*(3): 263–282.

Yung, H. W. B. (2000). *Teachers' beliefs and their teaching of practical work in a school-based assessment scheme*. Unpublished Ph.D. thesis. Department of Curriculum Studies. Hong Kong SAR, The University of Hong Kong, 300 pp.

Zahorik, J. A. (1975). Teachers' planning models. *Educational Leadership, 33*, 134–139.

Zeichner, K. M., Tabachnick, B. R., & Densmore, K. (1987). Individual, institutional and cultural influences on the development of teachers' craft knowledge. In J. Calderhead. (Ed.), *Exploring Teachers' Thinking* (pp. 21–59). London: Cassell.

Zsambok, C. E., & Klein, G. (1997). *Naturalistic Decision Making*. NJ: Lawrence Erlbaum.

Index

Subject Index

administration, and professional development of ESL teachers, 93, 96–9, 103
advanced beginners, and development of expertise, 11
alienation, Marx's theory of, 105
analytical awareness, and theoretical knowledge, 261
analytical thinking, and concept of expertise, 13
anonymity, and ethical issues in case studies, 77–8
apprenticeship, of observation, 62, 86
artificial intelligence, and concept of expertise, 1, 10
assumptions, and beliefs, 61
avoidance strategy, and subject matter knowledge of teachers, 54–5

beliefs, and teacher knowledge, 59–63. *See also* values

Cantonese language, and ESL programs, 68, 74
case studies, of ESL teachers in Hong Kong: and data analysis, 74–5; and data collection, 72–4; and enactment of curriculum, 193–223; and ethical issues, 76–8; and expertise of teachers, 4, 265–77; and lesson planning, 187–93; and linguistic context, 67–8; and management of learning, 139–76; and nature of expert teacher knowledge, 246–65; and planning of curriculum, 177–87; product writing and process writing, 225–43; professional development and life cycle of teaching, 82–134; and school context, 69–70, 102–3; and selection of subjects, 70–2; as units of analysis, 67
challenges, and development of expertise in teachers, 272–7
classroom: instructional objectives and management of, 247–50; interactive phase of teaching and events of, 32–6; and management of learning, 137–9; maximization of for language learning, 150–1, 159–60; and process approach to writing, 237–8
cognitive processes, and stimulated recalls, 72
cognitive psychology, and concept of expertise, 2, 10
competence, and development of expertise, 11

confidence, and professional development of ESL teachers, 118–19
conscious deliberation, and concept of expertise, 13, 14–17
conservatism, and professional development of teachers, 80–1
content knowledge, teacher knowledge as, 50–7
context: dialectical relationship between teacher knowledge and, 64; ESL teachers and linguistic, 67–8; ESL teachers and school, 69–70, 102–3; ESL teachers and relating to specific, 253–7
contingency plans, and lesson planning, 27
continuous process, expertise as, 17–20
coping, and pressure of teaching, 125–6
creativity, and concepts of teaching, 105
culture, management of learning and creation of positive and supportive, 161
curricular knowledge, and concepts of teacher knowledge, 51–2
curriculum: case studies and enactment of, 193–223, 250–3; case studies and planning of, 177–87; pedagogical content knowledge and enactment of, 59

data analysis, and case studies, 74–5
data collection, and case studies, 72–4
decision-making, and interactive phase of teaching, 31
developmental process, expertise in ESL teachers as, 265–77
discipline: and management of learning by ESL teachers, 141–5, 154, 157–8, 166–7, 172; and professional development of ESL teachers, 108, 130–3. *See also* students
discovery phase, of teaching, 79
disengagement phase, in teachers' career cycles, 81
distributed expertise, and multiple expertise, 279–82
diversification phase, of teaching, 80

education, of teachers: and Postgraduate Certificate in Education program (PCEd), 71; relevance of studies of expertise for, 281–2; and teachers' beliefs and classroom practices, 63

303

effective teachers, definition of, 34n4
efficiency: and interactive phase of teaching, 36, 38; in lesson planning, 29
ESL (English as a Second Language), and case studies of teachers in Hong Kong: and enactment of curriculum, 193–223, 250–3; and lesson planning, 187–93; and linguistic context, 67–8; and management of learning, 139–76; and planning of curriculum, 177–87; and professional development, 82–90; and research on expertise in teaching, 3; and research on teacher knowledge, 136–7; and school context, 69–70; and selection of teachers as subjects, 70–2; and teaching of writing, 225–43
ethics, and case studies, 76–8
ethnography, and research on expertise in teaching, 2
evaluation, and process approach to writing, 232–6
experimentation phase, of teaching, 80, 266–7
expertise: case studies and development of, 71–2, 265–77; case studies and nature of knowledge, 246–65; as conscious deliberation and organized knowledge base, 14–17; as continuous process, 17–20; definition of, 1; as intuition and tacit knowledge, 10–14; research on teaching and, 2–3; systematic study and theories of, 9, 20–1; and teacher education, 281–2
expert teachers: identification of, 4–6; and interactive phase of teaching, 30–9; performance and development of expertise, 277–9; and preactive phase of teaching, 23–30; and schemata of knowledge, 39–41. *See also* teachers; teaching
explicit instruction, and grammar teaching, 198, 199, 206, 207, 212, 219
exploration phase, of teaching, 79, 110–11, 266–7
expression, and process writing, 242–3

family, and ESL teachers, 120, 121, 124
flexibility, in lesson planning, 28, 29–30
formal knowledge, and practical knowledge, 260, 261, 264, 265

general pedagogical knowledge, and content knowledge, 58–9
generative knowledge, and concept of situated knowledge, 49
grammar teaching, and enactment of ESL curriculum, 194–201, 204–209, 211–16, 218–21
group work: instructional objectives and classroom management, 248–50; and organization of learning by ESL teachers, 167–8, 173–5; and professional development of ESL teachers, 91; seating arrangements and management for learning, 158–9, 249

Hong Kong. *See* case studies; ESL

images: of teacher and professional development of ESL teachers, 107, 116–17, 123, 126–8, 129, 133; and teacher knowledge, 59–63
immediate decisions, and interactive phase of teaching, 31
implementation, of process approach to writing, 230–2
improvisational skills, and interactive phase of teaching, 36–7, 38
information-processing theory, and expertise studies, 2
interactive phase, of teaching, 30–9
interviews, with teachers and students, 73, 74
Introducing Writing (Harris, 1994), 100
intuition, and expertise, 10–14

knowledge: case studies and nature of expert teachers', 246–65; characterizations of teachers', 65–6; conscious deliberation and organized base of, 14–17; and content knowledge, 50–7; expertise as tacit form of, 10–14; expert teachers and integrated base of, 30; grammar teaching and development of, 200–201, 208–209, 215–16; management for learning and development of, 154–5, 161–3, 168–70, 175–6; reconceptualization of, 57–64; as reflective practice and personal practical, 43–8; research on ESL teachers and, 136–7; schemata of in teaching, 39–41; as situated knowledge, 48–50; and studies of expertise in teaching, 2–3

language, and teacher knowledge, 137. *See also* Cantonese language; ESL; target language
learning: and case studies of management of learning, 139–76; and case studies of professional development of ESL teachers, 85–8; classroom management and management of, 137–9, 247; organization of by ESL teachers, 145–7, 167–8, 173–5; pedagogical content knowledge and management of, 59; process writing and concepts of, 239–41. *See also* teaching
lesson observation, and data collection, 72–3
lesson planning: case studies and ESL curriculum, 187–93; and preactive phase of teaching, 25, 26–8. *See also* planning
life cycle, and careers of teachers, 79–82, 82–135
long-term planning, and lesson plans, 26

Making of a Teacher, The (Grossman), 94
management of learning. *See* learning
mental lesson plans, and lesson planning, 26–8
mentor teachers, and teacher education, 281
metaphors, and teacher knowledge, 59–63
mixed code, and school context in Hong Kong, 82
monitoring, and process approach to writing, 230–2

motivation, and establishment of teacher rapport with students, 151–3
multiple expertise, and distributed expertise, 279–82

narratives, and personal practical knowledge of teachers, 47–8
negative feedback, and grammar instruction, 198, 199
norms: and classroom management, 138; and management of learning by ESL teachers, 165, 173. *See also* routines
novice teachers: and expertise as intuition and tacit knowledge, 10–11; identification of, 4–6; and interactive phase of teaching, 30–9; and preactive phase of teaching, 23–30; and schemata of knowledge, 39–41. *See also* teachers; teaching
NUD*IST (computer program), 75

observation, teachers and apprenticeship of, 62, 86
obtrusiveness, and ethical issues in data collection, 76
ownership, in teaching and professional development of ESL teachers, 109

participation, and management of learning, 160
pedagogical content knowledge: and integration of aspects of teacher knowledge, 247; and reconceptualization of teacher knowledge, 58–9; and theoretical framework for content knowledge, 51–2, 57
performance, and development of expertise, 277–9
personal practical knowledge, and studies of teacher knowledge, 45–8
personal theories, and beliefs, 61
planning: case studies and ESL curriculum, 177–87; preactive phase of teaching and models of, 23–4, 25, 26–8. *See also* lesson planning
postulants, and expertise in teaching, 4
practical knowledge, and theoretical knowledge, 257–65
preactive phase, of teaching, 23–30
problematization, and expertise of teachers, 267–72
problem-solving: concept of progressive, 271–2; and interactive phase of teaching, 37–8
process approach, to teaching of writing in ESL programs, 99–101, 225–43
Process Writing (White & Arndt, 1991), 100
production practice, and grammar instruction, 198, 199, 206, 212, 219
product writing, and process approach to teaching of writing, 225–8
professional development: and case studies of ESL teachers, 82–134; and life cycle of teachers, 79–82
proficiency, and development of expertise, 11
progressive focusing approach, for interviews, 73

quality assurance, and administrative duties of ESL teachers, 97–8, 273

reading, and enactment of ESL curriculum, 209–11, 216–18
reassessment phase, of teaching, 80, 88–9
reciprocity, and ethical issues in case studies, 77
reflection: and professional development of ESL teachers, 94–5, 115; and theory of professional knowledge, 16–17, 43–5
reflective decisions, 31
Reflective Practitioner, The (Schon, 1983), 44
relationships: student-teacher and management of learning by ESL teachers, 151–3; student-teacher and professional development of ESL teachers, 102; teacher-researcher and ethical issues in data collection, 76–7; teacher-teacher and administrative duties of ESL teachers, 98–9
religious organizations, and schools in Hong Kong, 69
renewal phase, of teaching, 80
resources, management of for ESL learning, 147–51
revision, and process approach to writing, 242–3
routines: and classroom management, 138–9; and decision-making, 31–2; and improvisational skills of teachers, 37; and management of learning by ESL teachers, 165, 173. *See also* norms

scheme of work, and planning of ESL curriculum, 177–87
seating arrangements, and group work, 158–9, 249
selectivity: and interactive phase of teaching, 38; and response of expert teachers to classroom events, 34, 35–6
self, and personal practical knowledge of teachers, 62–3
self-doubt, and case studies of professional development of ESL teachers, 88–9, 134
semistructured interviews, with students and teachers, 73, 74
serenity phase, of teaching, 80
short-term planning, and lesson plans, 26
situated knowledge, teacher knowledge as, 48–50
situated possibilities, and specific contexts, 253–7
social awareness, and professional development of ESL teachers, 106
stabilization phase, of teaching, 79–80
stimulated recalls, and data collection, 72
structured input, and grammar instruction, 198, 199, 206, 212, 213, 219
students: complaints from and administrative duties of ESL teachers, 98–9; evaluation and process approach to writing, 232–3; and management of learning by ESL teachers, 151–3; professional development of ESL teachers and relationships with, 102, 105–6,

students (*cont.*)
121–3, 124, 128–9, 129–30. *See also* discipline; learning; relationships
subject matter knowledge: and beliefs and values of teachers, 62; and content knowledge, 50n1, 51–2, 54–7, 58
substantial self, and teacher knowledge, 62
successful teachers, definition of, 34n3

target language, and ESL teaching, 136
teachers: and characterizations of knowledge, 65–6; identification of novice and expert, 4–6; and knowledge as content knowledge, 50–7; knowledge as reflective practice and personal practical knowledge, 43–8; and knowledge as situated knowledge, 48–50; and process approach to writing, 233–7; and professional development, 79–82; and reconceptualization of knowledge, 57–64; relationship with researcher and ethical issues, 76–7; research on ESL and knowledge of, 136–7; studies of expertise and education of, 281–2. *See also* case studies; education; ESL; expert teachers; novice teachers; students; teaching
teaching: concepts of and professional development of ESL teachers, 104–7; interactive phase of, 30–9; preactive phase of, 23–30; process writing and concepts of, 239–41; of reading, 209–11; research on expertise in, 2–3; and schemata of knowledge, 39–41. *See also* case studies; classroom; grammar teaching; learning; teachers; vocabulary teaching
TeleNex (computer network), 71, 95, 103, 274, 280
Technical Rationality model, of professional knowledge, 44
textbooks: and professional development of ESL teachers, 97; and subject matter knowledge, 54–7
theoretical knowledge, and practical knowledge, 257–65
thoughts, and lesson plans, 28
time, maximization of as resource for learning, 149–50. *See also* family

understanding, and professional development of ESL teachers, 89–92
University of Hong Kong, 71. *See also* education, of teachers

values: and professional development of ESL teachers, 106–107, 114, 127; and teachers' personal experiences, 61. *See also* beliefs
video- and audio-recording, and data collection and analysis, 73, 75
vocabulary teaching, and enactment of ESL curriculum, 201–204

writing, process approach to teaching of, 99–101, 225–43
written lesson plans, and lesson planning, 26–8

Author Index

Adams, R., 79
Allaei, S. K., 229
Allwright, R., 193
Anderson, C. W., 58
Anderson, J., 39
Anderson, L. M., 138, 139
Anning, A., 62
Arndt, V., 100

Bacon-Shone, John, 68
Bailey, K., 193
Ball, D. L., 28, 40, 53, 58
Baughman, K., 3
Baxter, J. A., 5, 6, 54
Beijaard, D., 114
Belensky, J. F., 275–6
Bell, B., 62
Benner, P., 9, 12, 254, 256, 257
Bennett, N., 58, 61, 247, 281
Bereiter, C., 2–3, 4, 5, 6, 17–21, 29, 40, 41, 82, 99, 190, 243, 255, 257, 260, 264, 266, 271, 272, 274, 277, 278–9
Berliner, D. C., 2, 4, 5, 25, 28, 33, 34, 38, 41, 176, 193
Biddle, B. J., 53
Birmingham, C., 5
Blasé, Jq. J., 276
Bloom, B. S., 72

Bolton, Kingsley, 68
Borg, S., 63
Borko, H., 25, 26, 27, 36, 37, 39, 40, 64, 188, 193
Brookhart, S., 62
Brophy, J., 3, 31, 37, 40, 51
Brown, O., 79
Brown, S., 25, 27, 190
Buchmann, M., 52, 62, 262
Bullough, R. V., 3, 60, 62, 265, 266, 275, 276
Bunton, D., 68
Burden, P., 79
Butt, R., 62
Bygate, M., 136

Calderhead, J., 23, 24, 26, 27, 28, 31, 58, 60, 61, 62, 63, 72, 134, 138, 139, 145, 173, 178, 187, 190, 247, 258, 265
Carlsen, W. S., 52, 53
Carter, K., 4, 25, 27, 28, 34, 35, 40, 63
Chamot, A. V., 148
Chase, W. G., 15–16
Chesla, C. A., 9
Chi, M., 6, 9, 14–17, 20, 37, 257
Christensen, J., 79, 81, 277
Clandinin, D. J., 7, 47–8, 50, 60, 61, 63, 65, 264

Clark, C. M., 22, 23, 24, 25, 31, 32, 34, 35, 39, 72, 175
Clinchy, B. M., 275–6
Comeaux, M. A., 5, 6, 33, 37, 39
Conant, J., 63
Connelly, F. M., 7, 47–8, 50, 61, 63, 65
Connor, U. M., 229
Cooney, J. B., 5
Copeland, W. D., 5, 30, 35, 72
Corno, L., 34
Creek, R., 28
Crow, N. A., 60, 62
Cushing, K. S., 4, 25, 28

Dallop, P., 9
Demeulle, L., 5
D'Emidio-Caston, M., 5
Densmore, K., 258
Dewey, J., 46, 52
Doyle, W., 23, 30, 31, 34, 36–7, 63, 138, 175
Dreyfus, H. L., 6, 9, 10–14, 15, 16, 20, 29, 45, 257, 258, 259, 277, 278, 279
Dreyfus, S. E., 6, 9, 10–14, 15, 16, 20, 29, 45, 257, 258, 259, 277, 278, 279
Duncan, M. J., 53

Elbaz, F., 3, 7, 45–7, 50, 52, 61, 65, 76, 77, 177
Ellis, R., 136, 198, 200
Emmer, E. T., 138
Eraut, M., 16, 20, 45, 58, 257–8, 261, 274, 277
Erickson, G. I., 64
Ericsson, K. A., 18, 16
Evertson, C. M., 138

Farr, M., 6
Feiman-Nemser, S., 28, 58, 61, 62, 80, 262
Feltovich, P., 9, 37
Fessler, R., 79, 81
Field, K., 79, 80, 81
Floden, R. E., 58, 61
Fogarty, J. L., 28, 32, 35
Freeman, D., 3, 62, 64, 254
Fuller, F., 79, 81

Gairns, R., 204
Garrett, P., 136
Geoffrey, W., 30
Gilbert, J., 62
Glaser, R., 6, 9, 14–17, 20, 37, 257
Goldberger, N. R., 275–6
Good, T. L., 31, 37
Goodlad, J. I., 114
Goodson, I., 62–3
Grant, G. E., 60
Greeno, J. G., 5, 6, 54, 55, 138
Griffey, D. C., 27, 28
Grimmett, P. P., 64
Grossman, Pamela, 3, 51, 52, 54, 55, 57, 58, 59, 62, 63, 94, 193, 262
Gudmunsdottir, S., 54, 56

Harris, J., 100
Hashweh, M., 53

Haymore, J., 54
Hillocks, G. J., 59, 244
Housner, L. D., 27, 28
Huberman, M., 75, 79, 80, 81, 82, 93, 124, 265–6, 277

Jackson, P. W., 22, 30
James, C., 136
Johnson, K., 61
Johnson, M., 60
Johnston, S., 60, 62

Kagan, D. M., 23, 24, 27, 38, 60
Kass, H., 54
Katz, L. G., 80
Klein, G., 9
Knowles, J. G., 60, 62
Kounin, J. S., 23, 30, 138
Krashen, S., 136

Lakoff, G., 60
Lampert, M., 163
Lanier, J. E., 62
Lantz, O., 54
Lave, J., 48–9, 64, 67, 245, 246, 247, 258, 280
Lehrer, K., 61
Leinhardt, G., 3, 4, 5, 6, 7, 16, 28, 49, 50, 54, 55, 56, 138, 155, 197, 247
Leki, I., 229
Li, B., 3
Li, J., 227
Lightbown, P., 198
Lightfoot, S., 80
Little, J. W., 62
Livingston, C., 25, 26, 27, 36, 37, 39, 40, 188, 193
Lortie, D., 62, 86, 261
Luckman, T., 46
Lyons, N., 62

MacKinnon, A. M., 64
Marland, P. W., 32
Marton, F., 261
Marx, R. W., 23
McCutcheon, G., 23, 24, 26, 27, 190
McDiarmid, G. W., 53, 58
McIntyre, D., 25, 27, 190
McNamara, D. R., 58
Measor, L., 80
Miles, M. B., 75
Miller, E., 58, 247
Morine-Dershimer, G., 23, 24, 27, 31, 34
Munby, H., 54, 55

Natal, D., 5
Neale, D. C., 53
Nespor, J., 61
Newall, Allen, 9, 10
Ng, M., 229
Nicholson, S., 9, 136, 137
Noice, H., 9

Noice, T., 9
Nunan, D., 3, 23–4, 35, 36, 279

O'Connor, J. E., 5
Oikkenon, S., 198
Olson, J., 5, 37, 139
O'Malley, J. M., 148

Pajak, E., 276
Pajares, M. F., 61
Parker, M. B., 58
Peterson, P. L., 5, 6, 22, 23, 24, 25, 31, 32, 33, 34, 35, 37, 39, 72, 175
Pinnegar, S., 25
Polanyi, Michael, 7, 43, 44, 65, 257
Powell, R. P., 60
Prick, L., 80
Putnam, R. T., 5, 6, 64

Rallis, S., 75
Raymond, D., 62
Redman, S., 204
Reiman, A. J., 81
Reynolds, A., 35, 176, 193
Reynolds, J. A., 54
Richards, J. C., 3
Richardson, V., 61, 244
Richert, A. E., 50–1, 52, 53, 193
Riecken, T. J., 64
Ringstaff, C., 54
Robson, M., 60, 61, 62
Rosenholtz, S. J., 262, 275
Rossman, G. B., 75
Rumelhart, D. E., 39
Russell, T., 54, 55
Rutherford, W., 136
Ryle, Gilbert, 7, 10, 43, 44, 65, 257

Sabar, N., 74, 76
Sabers, D. S., 4, 25, 28, 32–3, 34, 35, 175, 193
Sadro-Brown, D., 24
Scardamalia, M., 2–3, 4, 5, 6, 17–21, 29, 40, 41, 82, 99, 190, 243, 255, 257, 260, 264, 265, 271, 272, 274, 277, 278–9
Schein, E., 44
Schmidt, R., 136, 198
Schon, D. A., 7, 13, 16, 43–5, 60, 65, 243, 257, 265, 277
Schutz, Alfred, 46
Schwab, J. J., 47, 51
Scribner, S., 49
Sengupta, S., 225
Shavelson, R. J., 31, 32, 35
Shaw, J. C., 9, 10
Shorrock, S., 63, 134, 265
Shulman, L. S., 3, 5, 7, 40, 50–4, 56, 57, 59, 65, 137, 193, 197, 247, 261
Sikes, P. J., 80
Simon, Herbert A., 9, 10, 15–16

Sirotnik, K. A., 114
Sloboda, J., 9
Smith, D. A., 54, 55
Smith, D. C., 53
Smith, K. A., 18, 16
Smith, L. M., 30
Snow, R. E., 31
Soder, R., 114
Solso, R. L., 9
Spada, N., 198
Sprinthall, L. T., 81, 277
Sprinthall, N. A., 81, 277
Stanley, J., 229
Stein, M. K., 5, 6, 54
Stein, P., 28
Stenhouse, L., 76
Stern, P., 31, 32, 35
Swanson, H. L., 5

Tabacknick, B. R., 258
Tanaka, Y., 198
Tang, A., 3
Tanner, C. A., 9
Tarule, J. M., 276
Taylor, P. H., 23
Tippins, D. J., 23, 24, 27, 38
Tonkyn, A., 136
Townsend, D., 62
Tripp, D., 142
Tsui, A. B. M., 68, 136, 137, 227, 229
Tyler, R. W., 23

Vallance, E., 34
Van Patten, B., 198
Veenman, S., 35
Verloop, N., 114
Vermunt, J. D., 114

Wang, M. C., 28
Welker, R., 6
Wenger, E., 48–9, 280
Westerman, D. A., 5, 25, 26, 28, 35, 36, 176, 187
White, R., 100
Williams, E., 136
Wilson, S., 50–1, 52, 53, 54, 56–7, 193
Wineburg, S. S., 54, 55, 56–7
Wodlinger, M. G., 32
Wolcott, H. F., 72
Wood, E., 281
Woods, D., 61, 136, 138, 178, 186
Woods, P., 73, 76, 77, 80

Yin, R. K., 67
Yinger, R. J., 23, 24, 26, 31, 72, 138
Yung, H. W. B., 61, 244, 246

Zahorik, J. A., 23
Zeichner, K. M., 258
Zsambok, C. E., 9